Industrialization and Assimila

Industrialization and Assimilation examines the process of ethnic identity change in a broad historical context. Green explains how and why ethnicity changes across time, showing that, by altering the basis of economic production from land to labour and removing people from the 'idiocy of rural life', industrialization makes societies more ethnically homogenous. More specifically, the author argues that industrialization lowers the relative value of rural land, leading people to identify less with narrow rural identities in favour of broader identities that can aid them in navigating the formal urban economy. Using large-scale datasets that span the globe as well as detailed case studies ranging from mid-twentieth-century Turkey to contemporary Botswana, Somalia and Uganda, as well as evidence from Native Americans in the United States and the Māori in New Zealand, *Industrialization and Assimilation* provides a new framework to understand the origins of modern ethnic identities.

ELLIOTT D. GREEN is Associate Professor of Development Studies in the Department of International Development at the London School of Economics. His research focusses on the origins of ethnic and national identification and the political economy of development, with a regional focus on Sub-Saharan Africa.

Industrialization and Assimilation

Understanding Ethnic Change in the Modern World

ELLIOTT D. GREEN
London School of Economics and Political Science

CAMBRIDGE
UNIVERSITY PRESS

CAMBRIDGE
UNIVERSITY PRESS

Shaftesbury Road, Cambridge CB2 8EA, United Kingdom

One Liberty Plaza, 20th Floor, New York, NY 10006, USA

477 Williamstown Road, Port Melbourne, VIC 3207, Australia

314–321, 3rd Floor, Plot 3, Splendor Forum, Jasola District Centre, New Delhi – 110025, India

103 Penang Road, #05–06/07, Visioncrest Commercial, Singapore 238467

Cambridge University Press is part of Cambridge University Press & Assessment,
a department of the University of Cambridge.

We share the University's mission to contribute to society through the pursuit of
education, learning and research at the highest international levels of excellence.

www.cambridge.org
Information on this title: www.cambridge.org/9781009268363

DOI: 10.1017/9781009268356

© Elliott D. Green 2023

First published 2023

A catalogue record for this publication is available from the British Library.

Library of Congress Cataloging-in-Publication Data

NAMES: Green, Elliott Daniel, author.
TITLE: Industrialization and assimilation : understanding ethnic change in the modern world /
   Elliott D. Green, London School of Economics and Political Science.
DESCRIPTION: New York, NY : Cambridge University Press, 2023. | Includes bibliographical
   references and index.
IDENTIFIERS: LCCN 2022035630 (print) | LCCN 2022035631 (ebook) | ISBN 9781009268363
   (hardback) | ISBN 9781009268370 (paperback) | ISBN 9781009268356 (epub)
SUBJECTS: LCSH: Ethnicity–Cross-cultural studies. | Industrialization–Cross-cultural studies. |
   Assimilation (Sociology)–Cross-cultural studies.
CLASSIFICATION: LCC GN495.6 .G74 2023 (print) | LCC GN495.6 (ebook) |
   DDC 305.8–dc23/eng/20220825
LC record available at https://lccn.loc.gov/2022035630
LC ebook record available at https://lccn.loc.gov/2022035631

ISBN 978-1-009-26836-3 Hardback
ISBN 978-1-009-26837-0 Paperback

For Ashavari and Munia

Who says the Indian race is vanishing?

The Indians will not vanish.

The feathers, pain and moccasin will vanish, but the Indians, – never!

Just as long as there is a drop of human blood in America, the Indians will not vanish.

His spirit is everywhere: the American Indian will not vanish.

He has changed externally but he is not vanished.

He is an industrial and commercial man, competing with the world; he has not vanished.

Wherever you see an Indian upholding the standard of his race, there you see the Indian Man; he has not vanished.

The man part of the Indian is here, there, and everywhere.

The Indian race vanishing? No, never! The race will live on and prosper forever.

—'Changing Is Not Vanishing' (1916), Carlos Montezuma,
aka Wassaja

Contents

Figures

Maps

Tables

Acknowledgements

I have incurred many debts over the many years it has taken me to complete this manuscript. In its preliminary form the argument in Chapter 1 and the empirical analysis of the Soviet *Atlas Narodov Mira* (ANM) data in Chapter 5 were published as an article in the journal *Ethnic and Racial Studies* in 2019 (published by Taylor & Francis Ltd, www.tandfonline.com), and I received helpful comments on that paper from the editor, Martin Bulmer, two anonymous referees as well as Michael Hechter, Atul Kohli, Matthias vom Hau, David Laitin and Maya Tudor. I am grateful as well for their helpful comments to seminar participants at Cornell University (Department of Government), the Graduate Institute of International and Development Studies, LSE (Department of International Development and the Political Science and Political Economy Group), Oxford University (Blavatnik School of Government), Princeton University (Institute for International and Regional Studies), the University of Pennsylvania (Department of Political Science) and the University of Rochester (Department of Political Science), as well as attendees at the Annual Meeting of the American Political Science Association. Taking a sabbatical at Cornell University's Institute of African Development was very beneficial in providing me space and time to consider my argument and evidence, for which I thank Muna Ndulo and Nic van de Walle for their assistance. My current and former colleagues at the LSE have been particularly helpful, including Alice Evans, Sean Fox and Steffen Hertog, and various members of the editorial board of the journal *Nations and Nationalism* have been very helpful in numerous conversations. I would also like to thank Cecilia Lanata-Briones and Ulas Karakoc for research assistance in inputting data from the ANM, and Karina Perez Jvostova, Zhanna Kovaleva, Mélanie Loubet and Alexander Zuev for help with Russian–English translations. Finally, a daylong book workshop on Zoom in January 2021 was incredibly helpful in finalizing the book manuscript, with helpful comments from all participants, namely Cathy Boone, John Breuilly, Jean-Paul

Faguet, Adam Harris, Eric Kaufman, Lauren MacLean, Berkay Ozcan and Ken Shadlen; I would particularly like to thank Cathy Boone for suggesting the book's title.

As regards the case study chapters, I received very helpful comments from seminar participants at the LSE (Turkish Studies Seminar) as well as Lydia Assouad on Chapter 6; seminar participants at Yale University (Center of African Studies, as kindly organized by Kate Baldwin), Edinburgh University (African Politic Research Group, as kindly organized by Sara Rich Dorman), and Cornell University (Institute of African Development) on Chapter 8; and participants at the Annual Meeting of the American Political Science Association and the University of Oxford (Rothermere American Institute, as kindly organized by Pekka Hämäläinen) on Chapter 9. I also greatly benefitted from help from archivists and librarians at Cornell University's Huntington Free Library Native American Collection and the LSE and the British National Archives in London. In Botswana I had a lot of assistance at the Botswanan National Archives, Botswanan Parliamentary library and University of Botswana library, whose collective help in assisting me locate older parliamentary Hansards was particularly useful. (This task interestingly proved to be one of the most difficult bits of fieldwork I have ever conducted in any context!) My fieldwork in Botswana greatly benefitted from a grant from the LSE Department of International Development's Research Committee, as well as conversations with Zibani Maundeni, Christian John Makgala, Gwyneth McClendon, Amy Poteete, Onalenna Selolwane and Jacqueline Solway, among others. I would like to thank Titus Mbuya, the Managing Director of the *Mmegi* newspaper in Botswana, for granting me permission to reproduce Figure 7.2 here. Tony Sole from the Te Puni Kōkiri / Ministry of Māori Development in New Zealand gave me a lot of help with Map 9.1. At Cambridge University Press my thanks go to Robert Dreesen for taking an interest in the manuscript and guiding it through to completion, and to two anonymous referees for their helpful comments.

On a personal level I would like to thank my parents for their ongoing support over many years. As in all else, I save the last and most thanks for Ashavari and Munia, for putting up with my ongoing research demands.

I

Introduction

A number of years ago I had the opportunity to sit down for dinner at a nice restaurant in Kampala, the capital of Uganda, with one of the country's most prominent journalists, Andrew Mwenda, and one of its most prominent academics. Much of the conversation was dominated by Andrew, whose extraordinary knowledge of Ugandan political economy comes across in his magazine *The Independent* as well as his academic writings (cf. Mwenda, 2007; Tangri & Mwenda, 2008; among many others). Amid a discussion of my research interests into ethnic identity and the politics of land in Uganda, Andrew at one point described how a former Army captain had become a minster in President Yoweri Museveni's government, got rich and then bought a large plot of land back in his home region of western Uganda. Puzzled, I asked why he invested his money in this way, as opposed to opening a Swiss bank account, buying foreign property in Dubai or investing abroad in some other way. Andrew's vehement response was simple: 'because this is still an agrarian country, my friend!' According to him, the importance of owning rural land for Ugandan elites trumped their interest in financial security via foreign holdings due to the continued rural nature of the Ugandan economy, and thus explained the preponderance of Ugandan elite investment in local land holdings.

This conversation inspired me to consider the radically different nature of political and economic incentives in rural, agrarian dominated societies like Uganda as compared to urban, industrialized countries that are preponderantly in the Global North. More specifically, I began to consider how the highly fragmented nature of ethnic politics in Uganda, which I had already explored as regards land ownership and internal migration (Green, 2006, 2007), were a consequence of an economy based on agricultural production. The result of roughly a decade of subsequent research is this book, where I argue that industrialization creates incentives for individuals to re-identify ethnically and assimilate from small, more narrowly defined rural tribal identities to larger, more urban-focussed ethnic groups, and that this process is a consequence of the declining economic importance of control over rural land. To understand this process – and the intricacies of my argument – I momentarily take a step back to explain the broader origins of my story by turning again to Africa.

Despite high expectations as countries across Africa became independent of colonial rule in the 1950s and 1960s, the continent soon began to experience widespread problems with state collapse, conflict and underdevelopment in the last three decades of the twentieth century. As such social scientists searched for explanations as to why African states underperformed: particularly influential in this regard was a seminal article by William Easterly and Ross Levine that argued that 'Africa's Growth Tragedy' was a consequence of its high level of ethnic fractionalization (Easterly & Levine, 1997). This paper – which today remains by far the most-cited among all of Easterly's work – has led to a cottage-industry of examining the effects of ethnic fractionalization on various outcomes across the world, including economic growth and unemployment (Churchill & Smyth, 2017; Feldmann, 2012; Gören, 2014; Hjort, 2014; Montalvo & Reynal-Querol, 2005a; Spolaore & Wacziarg, 2009), civil wars (Bleaney & Dimico, 2011; Cederman & Girardin, 2007; Collier & Hoeffler, 2004; Costalli, Moretti, & Pischedda, 2017; Fearon & Laitin, 2003; Haynes, 2016; Hegre & Sambanis, 2006; Manotas-Hidalgo, Pérez-Sebastián & Campo-Bescós, 2021; Miguel, Satyanath, & Sergenti, 2004; Montalvo & Reynal-Querol, 2005b; Walter, 2006; Wegenast & Basedau, 2014), public policy and public goods provision (Alesina, Gennaioli & Lovo, 2019; Beach & Jones, 2017; Churchill, Ocloo & Siawor-Robertson, 2017; Habyarimana, Humphreys & Posner, et al., 2007; Lieberman, 2007; Miguel & Gugerty, 2005), and political party formation (W. R. Clark & Golder, 2006; Harbers, 2010), among other phenomena.

While much of this literature has been useful in understanding underdevelopment in the developing world and in Africa in particular, this body of scholarship largely treats ethnicity as fixed. In one sense, this assumption is non-problematic according to the most basic understanding of ethnicity in the literature, which is that ethnic groups are communities based on the idea that members share some form of common descent (Chandra, 2006; Fearon, 2003; Horowitz, 2000; A. D. Smith, 1991; M. Weber, 1978 [1922]). The question about whether or not members of a given group actually do share common ancestors is largely irrelevant; what matters instead is that a belief in common descent is prevalent enough that it binds people together in a single community. If this belief is common and unchanging, then an assumption that ethnicity is fixed over time is unproblematic.

However, the assumption of fixed ethnic identities has become increasingly problematic due to a shift since the 1960s towards more quantitative methodologies in the field of political economy, which has meant both a greater need for datasets which assign ethnic identities to people as well as the need to assume for game-theoretical purposes the existence of stable ethnic identities which inform players' choices. This conception of ethnicity, where each person has one and only one ethnic identity which is inherited and thus cannot be changed, is known as primordialism. These primordialist assumptions have long been dominant in the political science and economics literature on ethnicity, such that scholars can readily assume that, to take one example, ethnic diversity is an 'exogenously determined social state' (Ordeshook & Shvetsova, 1994, p. 108).[1] To take some examples, a notable amount of recent scholarship uses country-year panel data to examine the effects of ethnicity on a number of outcomes, with different annual measurements for conflict, democracy, GDP, population and price indices over multiple decades (and often up to a half-century), but with fixed measures of ethnic diversity over the same time span (Bleaney & Dimico, 2011; Gören, 2014; Haynes, 2016; Manotas-Hidalgo et al., 2021).[2] In almost all of these studies ethnicity is implicitly assumed to be exogenous to the other variables of interest, with the sole exception of migration,[3] while in the others the authors acknowledge the potential endogeneity of ethnicity but leave its causes and consequences for further investigation.[4]

1.2 THE ARGUMENT

The goal of this book is thus to show that ethnicity is not in any way exogenous to changes in society, and, more specifically, that industrialization causes assimilation. My goal in this section is thus to lay out my argument in detail, which I can do in a series of steps. The first such step is as follows:

1. *People hold multiple concentric ethnic identities, such that they can choose to emphasize one or another of these identities in a given context.*

As noted above, historically scholars have assumed that ethnicity is primordial, such that individuals hold one and only one fixed and unchangeable ethnic identity. This attitude is arguably based on a 'folk' theory of primordial ethnicity held by non-academics (Gil-White, 1999), and goes back

---

[1] Cf. Mauro (1995, p. 692), who similarly writes that 'I assume that the extent to which countries are fractionalized along ethnolinguistic lines is exogenous and unrelated to economic variables.'

[2] See as well Chandra and Wilkinson (2008, p. 534)'s criticism of Przeworski, Alvarez & Cheibub, et al., (2000) along similar lines.

[3] For instance, Miguel and Gugerty (2005, p. 2337) assume that levels of ethnic diversity in western Kenya 'are largely the product of [pre-colonial] historical accident rather than recent migration', thereby foreclosing other explanations for ethnic diversity.

[4] Cf. Cederman and Girardin (2007, p. 176), who note that their use of ethnicity as an exogenous variable in their analysis of civil wars 'does not mean that we believe that identities are primordially given'.

decades or even centuries in the study of ethnicity and identity more broadly, as seen in the writings of the Jewish-American philosopher Horace Kallen, who wrote over a century ago that 'Men may change their clothes, their politics, their wives, their religions, their philosophies, [but] they cannot change their grandfathers. Jews or Poles or Anglo-Saxons, in order to cease being Jews or Poles or Anglo-Saxons, would have to cease to be' (Kallen, 1996 [1915], p. 91).

Recently this assumption has been built into the exercise of quantifying ethnicity in cross-national databases, whereby scholars have assigned people to an ethnic identity without any qualifications about the potential for this identity to vary across time (among others, cf. Alesina, Devleeshauwer & Easterly, et al., [2003]; Fearon [2003]).

However, there is also a long-standing parallel literature identifying this assumption as problematic. Indeed, the idea that people can hold multiple ethnic (or national) identities simultaneously literally goes back centuries: it was perhaps first explicitly expressed by the English historian William of Malmesbury in the twelfth century, who wrote about the existence of Northumbrian, Mercian, East Anglian and Kentish *gentes* (ethnic groups or nations), which were subsumed in the *gens Anglorum* (Bartlett, 2001, p. 43). In early modern Italy it was commonplace for the word 'nation' to refer to both one's region (Piedmont, Sicily, etc.) as well as modern nations like Italy or Germany (Woolf, 2005, p. 299). More recently Max Weber distinguished between three concepts of ethnicity, namely *Völkerschaft* (clan), *Stamm* (tribe) and *Volk* (people), 'each of which is ordinarily used in the sense of an ethnic subdivision of the following one' (M. Weber, 1978 [1922], p. 392). And from the 1960s numerous anthropologists have criticized this singular, fixed conception of ethnicity, instead insisting on multiple identities that co-exist and achieve different levels of salience depending on the context (Gluckman, 1960; Gulliver, 1969).

As such there is now a large literature in which it is widely acknowledged that individuals can have a multitude of identities, many of which can be considered as based on a belief in common descent and thus ethnic in nature.[5] These identities can be held at the same time because they are nested within each other, such that one could conceptualize the smallest group as those with whom one shares a common (mythical) ancestor in a relatively recent generation, with the ancestor increasingly further back in the past as one moves to larger groups.[6] In this context several scholars have previously discussed

---

[5] There is also a literature which has noted a multiplicity of *social* identities available to people, only one of which was ethnic (Eriksen, 1993, p. 30; Okamura, 1981), or concentric versions of the same ethnic identity (Galaty, 1982).

[6] To repeat, nothing I say here should be taken to mean that such ancestors ever existed in the first place, but merely that people *believe* in the existence of common ancestry along these lines. There is, moreover, plenty of evidence that the group of common ancestors a given set of people could share is potentially very wide, considering ever-shifting ethnic descent myths (A. D. Smith, 1998, p. 149).

instances where people choose between two ethnic identities, such that people 'put on the ethnic hat' that best befits a given situation (Gil-White, 1999, p. 807). To take one example from Africa, Posner (2005) argues that Zambians hold both larger linguistic identities (Bemba, Lozi, Tonga, etc.) and smaller tribal identities (Lamba, Lunda, Luvale, etc.), and choose to emphasize one or the other according to which one was more likely to benefit them at a given point of time.

However, there is no reason to stop at only two ethnic identities. In Uganda and many other parts of Africa, for instance, one could be a member of a sub-clan (for instance, the Busito sub-clan within the Nte clan of Buganda), a clan (Nte), a tribe (Buganda), a super-tribe, linguistic or regional group (Bantu-speakers or Southerners, groups which largely overlap) and a race (African). Or, for Native Americans in the United States, one could be a member of the Upper Brulé *thiyóśpaye* (band or sub-clan), Brulé clan, Lakota tribe, Sioux nation and Native American race (J. R. Hanson, 1997, p. 203). Finally, for another example from the USA, a black woman in New York could potentially identity as Trinidadian, West Indian or Black (Chandra & Wilkinson, 2008, p. 521).[7] Figure 1.1 makes this series of groupings graphically clear.

Thus, as Gulliver (1969, p. 21) puts it, 'at any one level the [ethnic] group-ings are, on the one hand, amalgamations of those at a smaller-scale level and, on the other hand, they are constituents of the larger groupings at a wider-scale level'.[8] Rather than thinking in terms of 'hats from the ethnic rack' (Gil-White, 1999, p. 807), a better way to conceptualize these different identities is as different sized Russian (*Matryoshka*) dolls, with individuals possessing multiple identities based on different sized groups.[9] One could also think of a cross-section of these dolls, which would resemble a series of concentric circles representing different social groups. Indeed, this is the model presented by the noted twentieth-century psychologist Gordon Allport in his model of in-groups, moving from the smallest circle, the family, to the nation and eventually all of mankind (Allport, 1954, p. 43). A process of ethnic homogenization would thus consist of shifting one's primary, most salient identity from a smaller doll or circle to a larger one, thereby emphasizing an identity which is shared by more people than the previous identity.

Inasmuch as these identities operate at different levels they do not contradict each other, unlike, say, attempting to be both a Muganda (member of the Buganda tribe) and a Mukiga (from Kigezi in western Uganda), or members

---

[7] For other such examples of multi-level ethnic identities see Moerman (1965, p. 1224), Rousseau (1975, p. 44) and Wimmer (2008, p. 977) using case studies from Thailand, Malaysia and the USA, respectively.

[8] For other similar conceptualizations of ethnicity as a series of nested identities also see G. C. Bentley (1987, p. 35), R. Cohen (1978, p. 387) and Emberling (1997, p. 307).

[9] The analogy is not new; cf. Taras's (1993) description of 'Matryoshka nationalism' in the former Soviet Union.

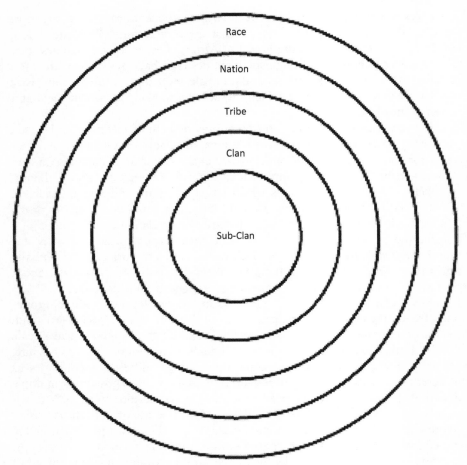

FIGURE I.I. Different ethnic identities as sub-sets of each other

of both the Sioux and the Cherokee nations, or Trinidadian and Jamaican in North America. To quote Allport:

Concentric loyalties need not clash. To be devoted to a large circle does not imply the destruction of one's attachment to a smaller circle. *The loyalties that clash are almost invariably those of identical scope* ... A traitor who serves two nations (one nominally and one actually) is mentally a mess and socially a felon. Few people can acknowledge more than one alma mater, one religion, or one fraternity. On the other hand, a world-federalist can be a devoted family man, an ardent alumnus and a sincere patriot. (Emphases in original; [Allport, 1954, p. 44])[10]

---

[10] It is notable that Allport claims that 'the happy condition [by which] narrow circles can ... be supplemented by larger circles of loyalty ... is not often achieved' (Allport, 1954, p. 46). My argument in this book is that such shifts happen more often than Allport, or others, have thought.

The second stage of my argument is that:

2. *People choose their primary ethnic identity based on the benefits it brings to them.*

To put this in the language of rational-choice scholarship, people choose which of their multiple identities will maximize their utility, or which identity 'serves them best' (Posner, 2005, p. 2). As with the first step this is not a particularly radical assumption, inasmuch as it is the basis for the current scholarship on identity formation in the social sciences labelled as 'instrumentalist'. Here ethnicity is an instrument, or a means to an end, rather than an end in itself, in contrast to the 'primordialist' views noted above; similarly, one can conceive of ethnicity in this sense as 'constructed' rather than fixed, thereby generating a 'constructivist' understanding of ethnicity.[11]

That economic benefits form an important incentive in how one chooses an ethnic identity should be self-evident, since maximizing one's economic utility in general leads to a focus on income by definition. Yet surprisingly this step has remained slightly hidden or obscured in the literature on ethnicity, in part because much of the literature on ethnic change and identity has not come from economics but instead from other disciplines. In particular many instrumentalist scholars have focussed on the political motivations for choosing ethnic identities, such that it is often assumed that 'the sole *raison d'être* of ethnicity and ethnic organization lies in its political functioning' (Eriksen, 1993, p. 55). Thus for Posner (2005), for instance, the focus is on how political institutions (specifically the nature of the party system) alter ethnic identities, while for Laitin (1998) and Posner (2004) the focus instead is on the construction of state borders. Part of the problem is that in none of these cases was the research focus on explaining ethnic change per se, as opposed to demonstrating whether and how certain political phenomena could alter ethnic identities.

Here, however, I focus directly on ethnic change as a research topic, which leads me to focus on the role of income and economics instead of only on politics. More specifically, I ask whether broad trends in economic transformation can explain ethnic change. Ethnic change can be conceptualized qualitatively, as already discussed, but can also be measured quantitatively using measures of the ethno-linguistic fractionalization (ELF) index across time. The ELF index for a given state or area is calculated using the Herfindahl concentration formula, namely by summing the squares of the percentages of all ethnic groups larger than 1 per cent of the population and subtracting this sum from one. Thus an ELF index for a very homogenous country like Haiti, Portugal or South Korea would be a number close to zero, while one with a high amount of ethnic diversity like India, Liberia or Uganda would have a

---

[11] Some authors identify constructivism and instrumentalism as different strands of thought in the study of ethnicity; I prefer to follow Henry Hale (2004) in thinking of them both as a single programme.

score close to one. Similarly, a decreasing ELF index would indicate a process of homogenization, while a rising ELF index would indicate increasing levels of diversity. (I discuss the ELF index in more detail in Chapter 2.)

I now move to my third step, namely that:

3. *The most important factor explaining ethnic change – specifically assimilation – in the modern world is industrialization.*

I argue here that industrialization encourages assimilation as it alters the economic incentives of holding both smaller rural ethnic identity and broader urban ethnic identities. In the first instance industrialization lowers the value of emphasizing rural identities as it lowers the value of rural land relative to other parts of the economy. In the second instance industrialization raises the value of broader industrialized or urban identities which can aid urban residents in getting jobs in the modern economy and/or getting support from other rural–urban migrants in the difficult urban landscape. I specify both of these processes in more detail below.

To understand the effect of industrialization on rural identities it is necessary first to examine the nature of ethnic identity and ethnic diversity in a broad historical context. Recently many economists, ecologists and anthropologists have used quantitative methods to show that latitude is inversely correlated with ethno-linguistic diversity (Ahlerup & Olsson, 2012; Cashdan, 2001; Collard & Foley, 2002; Green, 2013; Sutherland, 2003), such that countries closer to the equator have higher levels of ethnic diversity. Other researchers have similarly found a positive correlation between ethnic diversity and elevation (Cashdan, 2001; Sutherland, 2003; Wimmer, 2015) and differential land endowments (Michalopoulos, 2012).

There are two possible interrelated reasons for these relationships. First, warm tropical environments with predictable climates (as regards the variability of temperature and rainfall) are ideal for becoming self-sufficient in food and thereby create few incentives for inhabitants to migrate or form social ties with people across a large amount of territory (Nettle, 1996). The same logic applies to differential land endowments, which lead human groups to become specialized in growing certain types of crops and thus discourage migration to other areas that are not suitable for the same crops (Michalopoulos, 2012). Second, even if humans had wanted to migrate, mountains, different disease environments and dense tropical rainforests can create physical barriers and disincentives to movement and thereby lead to cultural isolation. In both senses humans are no different from other species, inasmuch as there is also an inverse correlation between latitude and species diversity (Cashdan, 2001). Indeed, the first person to note this relationship was Charles Darwin in his trip to the Galapagos Islands, where he found twenty-five different species of finches which, he hypothesized, had resulted from the effects of being isolated on separate islands.

This quantitative literature on the role of isolation in promoting ethnic diversity has a parallel in qualitative social science as well. From the

Asia-Pacific region there is evidence that poor transport links and rugged terrain have promoted high levels of ethnic or cultural diversity in such contexts as Sarawak (Malaysian Borneo) and Papua New Guinea (Reilly, 2001, p. 174; Rousseau, 1975, p. 34). In pre-colonial Africa 'ethnicities were often founded on the special skills needed to exploit different ecological niches' such that the Fulani of West Africa became associated with cattle-herding while in East Africa the Okiek and Kikuyu became known as hunters and farmers, respectively (Lonsdale, 2012, p. 34). Finally, in South-East Asia Scott (2009, pp. 259–61) has suggested that ethnic groups and their boundaries have formed around particular livelihoods. Indeed, he quotes one European visitor to China from the 1870s who noted that 'the frontiers between different types of soil, between farming and herding, and between Chinese and Mongols coincided exactly' (quoted in Scott [2009, p. 262]). In regions with similar ecologies, however, it is more common to observe 'the homogenizing effects of a common agrarian regime,' as with the Shan of South-East Asia where being Shan became associated with padi planting (Scott, 2009, p. 252). In other words, as with Michalopoulos (2012)'s argument it is 'rugged topography and relative isolation' which leads to ethnic diversity for Scott (2009, p. 265).

Thus in the pre-modern or pre-industrial world isolation encouraged greater ethnic diversity. In such isolated 'folk societies' (Redfield, 1947) it would have made no sense to identify with a foreign ethnic group inasmuch as livelihoods and income within the group depended on other members of that group. In contrast, however, the incentives for ethnic identification change with industrialization as people leave the rural agrarian economy to move to the industrial urban sector, where access to rural land, ethnic-specific agricultural skills and support from one's rural community are all relatively unimportant in making a living. Instead, what is valuable to the new industrial working class is their ability to earn an income through their labour, which can be enhanced by shedding their previous narrow rural identity in favour of a larger identity shared by more people. In other words, as both people and profits move from rural to urban areas, access to labour become more important than land in the acquisition of income and wealth.

Theoretically the first and most forceful such statement identifying the homogenizing incentives of industrialization comes from Karl Marx and Friedrich Engels in their early writings from the 1840s and 1850s. In works such as the *German Ideology* (1846) and the *Communist Manifesto* (1848) Marx and Engels focussed their attention on the division between 'town and country' (Marx & Engels, 1947 [1846], pp. 68–9). More specifically, they claimed that in the countryside individuals are 'united by some bond: family, tribe, the land itself, etc.' and the economy is guided by an exchange between people and the natural environment rather than through other people. The ownership of land is the basis for the economy and thus people remain attached to the land, with 'their mode of production isolating them from one another, instead of bringing them into mutual discourse' (Marx, 1978 [1852], p. 608).

Individual peasants may be said to be members of an ethnic group, class or nation, but without any 'community [or] national bond' they are merely like a 'sack of potatoes' in Marx's memorable phrase.

However, upon entering the scene, the bourgeoisie 'create enormous cities, greatly increase the urban population as compared with the rural, and thus rescue a considerable part of the population from the idiocy of rural life' (Marx & Engels, 1978 [1848], p. 477).[12] Modern industrialization sees a huge shift in the basis of economic production as the basis for the economy and economic growth shifts from land to labour.[13] Here members from previously isolated and separate rural communities come together to work, thereby making manifest for the first time the division between the 'two great classes' of the bourgeoisie and the proletariat. While in rural areas labourers held location-specific capital, in the industrial sector they lose their distinctiveness and become part of a 'floating' army of workers, whereby their exploitation at the hands of the bourgeoisie creates the impetus for class consciousness and subsequent revolution.

Thus, while not claiming explicitly that industrialization promotes assimilation, Marx and Engels were nonetheless clear about the way in which structural transformation created incentives for social homogenization, in two ways. First, the bourgeoisie needed to create a homogenous workforce – or 'privates in the industrial army' (Marx & Engels, 1978 [1848], p. 479) – that it could employ in its factories and shops, a process which I henceforth label the 'top-down' mechanism inasmuch as the process of ethnic homogenization is largely a result of the efforts of the ruling elite. However, Marx is explicit that the process of class formation is a byproduct of modern capitalism rather than a deliberate outcome directed by the bourgeoisie, which has no incentive to create a large, united class opposed to its interests. Instead, there is a second process of homogenization at work whereby members of the proletariat have strong incentives to co-operate through unions and political parties to fight the exploitation of the bourgeoisie. Indeed, Marx and Engels' famous call at the end of the *Communist Manifesto* for workers of the world to unite is essentially based on their belief that, despite their varied backgrounds and cultural/ethnic differences, the advent of the modern industrial economy means that workers' interests now lie together with each other. This second process I label the 'bottom-up' mechanism, since here homogenization is the result of the actions of the non-elite based on what they perceive to be their best interests.

---

[12] Marx saw the parochial and isolated nature of rural life as universal: in his writings on India, for instance, Marx writes of the 'idyllic village-communities' where life is 'undignified, stagnatory, and vegetative' (Marx, 1978 [1853], p. 658).

[13] Marx and Engels clearly distinguish the economic structure of pre-industrial cities from modern industrial cities: in the former case the division of labour was between different guilds while in the latter case it is instead between classes within the same workshop (Marx & Engels, 1978 [1848], p. 474).

Marx and Engels have clearly had a huge amount of influence on theories about the social consequences of industrialization, capitalism and urbanization. Many social scientists who examined these processes in the early and mid-twentieth century came to similar conclusions as Marx in a variety of contexts, including Alessandro Pizzorno in Italy, the Czech-American political scientist Karl Deutsch and his discussion of 'social mobilization', and Louis Wirth in his famous 1938 essay on urbanism (Deutsch, 1953; Pizzorno, 1973 [1962]; Wirth, 1938). In a very different context the South African anthropologist Max Gluckman similarly claimed that rising levels of urbanization and industrialization in Sub-Saharan Africa was transforming social relations on the continent: 'As soon as Africans assemble in towns and engage in industrial work they will begin to form social relationships appropriate to their new situation ... In crisis, common interests arising from industrial and urban association seem steadily to overcome tribal ties and divisions' (Gluckman, 1960, pp. 57, 69).

But perhaps the most important influence of Marx and Engels in this regard was on Ernest Gellner's theory of nationalism, where industrialization is responsible for the rise of modern national identities. While by no means claiming himself as part of a Marxist tradition, Gellner nonetheless similarly drew a sharp divide between the pre-modern rural world and the modern urban world, whereby the former consists of isolated peasant communities leading 'inward-turned lives, tied to the locality by economic need' (Gellner, 2006 [1983], p. 10). Far from there being incentives to homogenize or assimilate, 'no one, or almost no one, has an interest in promoting cultural homogeneity at this social level' (Gellner, 2006 [1983], p. 11), resulting in a society characterized by a high degree of cultural and ethnic diversity.

However, just as for Marx and Engels, industrialization transforms the economic basis of society for Gellner, not necessarily in terms of the means of production but instead in the cultural requirements for obtaining employment. Indeed, employers in the industrial economy require an educated and culturally homogenous workforce – 'like a modern army, only more so' (Gellner, 2006 [1983], p. 27) – which lead them to promote mass education in the former high culture of the state elite in a clear example of a 'top-down' process of assimilation. In particular this emphasis on the role of the intelligentsia in promoting a singular mass culture of industrialization, or 'industrialism' in Gellner's terms, is clearest in his earlier writings on nationalism such as his 1964 book *Thought and Change* (Gellner, 1964).[14]

However, over time Gellner's writings clearly show a move away from a 'top-down' approach towards a 'bottom-up' one. In his later writings Gellner makes it quite clear that the key agent in his theory is 'modern man', whose interest in

---

[14] Gellner (2006 [1983]) does not use the words 'employer' or 'bourgeoisie' here; instead he attributes agency to societies, states and other large 'unspecified globs of humanity', thereby opening him up to David Laitin's criticism that his thesis is 'functionalism gone mad' (Laitin, 1998, pp. 245–6).

employment and participating in modern society lead him (and her!) to assimilate into the new dominant group (Gellner, 1994, pp. 41–3), known as the 'Megalomanians' in Gellner's famous story. This later revision of his theory is much more a 'bottom-up' story of assimilation, whereby ethnic minorities voluntarily assimilate as Megalomanian, and can arguably be distinguished from his earlier 'top-down' story by its emphasis on 'industrialization' rather than 'industrialism' per se.[15]

Before we continue, it is important to note two additional features of the Marxian/Gellnerian framework. First, for both Marx and Gellner industrialization generates incentives for most people not just to identify with a larger ethnic group but specifically with the largest group in society, namely the proletariat and the Megalomanians, respectively.[16] Second, in both cases the process of homogenization is not permanent, inasmuch as it takes place while countries transition to a capitalist, industrialized economy. Thus for Marx the development of class consciousness is one stage in history rather than an ongoing process. For Gellner it is the transition from agrarian society to industrial society which gives rise to nationalism, especially via uneven industrialization. In neither case should we expect homogenization to continue or decline once industrialization is complete. Both of these features then present themselves as additional theories to be tested in this book.

> 4. *The uneven nature of industrialization means that ethnic homogeniza-*
> *tion and assimilation is limited to those groups who have access to urban,*
> *industrial society. Those who are excluded from the transformations*
> *wrought by industrialization will thus continue to hold onto their rural*
> *ethnic identities.*

By bringing formerly disparate people together the process of industrialization counteracts the isolation of the pre-modern countryside and promotes assimilation into a broader ethnic identity. However, this process is uneven, almost by definition, and members of those groups which are left out of the process of industrialization will fail to re-identify accordingly. These consequences of uneven industrialization were first discussed by Karl Deutsch in the 1950s (Deutsch, 1953, pp. 179–80), but were perhaps most clearly described by Gellner in his fictional story about the rise of 'Ruritanian' nationalism. This group of people – who speak related but distinct 'Ruritanian' dialects of the

---

[15] Of course, Gellner is not the only major 'modernist' scholar of nationalism who gave a key role to industrialization in the formation of modern national identities: other key works here include Benedict Anderson's focus on the role of 'print capitalism' and the importance given to urbanization by both Eric Hobswbawm and John Breuilly (B. Anderson, 1991; Breuilly, 1993; Hobsbawm, 1992).

[16] Marx and Engels (1978 [1848], p. 482) clearly identifies the proletariat as the 'immense majority' of society, while for Gellner the Megalomanians is the majority group in Megalomania. Note that, in the case of Marx and Engels the largest group is not the ruling group in society, while for Gellner it is.

Megalomanian language – unite under a common Ruritananian identity in order to better their lot (Gellner, 2006 [1983]). Gellner's theory of this bifurcation of identity between Megalomanians and Ruritanians explicitly relies more on the 'cultural and linguistic' distance of the Ruritanians from the dominant Megalomanian centre (Gellner, 2006 [1983], p. 60), rather than any theory of politics. However, perhaps obscured within his account is also a story of how uneven industrialization is at the root of Ruritanian identity. Specifically, Gellner's story begins with how 'certain other areas of the Empire of Megalomania – but not Ruritania – rapidly industrialized' (Gellner, 2006 [1983], p. 58). It is actually this relative lack of industrialization among the general Ruritanian population, along with the urbanization of a notable but relatively small percentage of the Ruritanian workforce, which led to the creation of Ruritanian nationalism. The role of cultural difference arguably plays a relatively minor part in this story, at least in its ability to predict which groups will assimilate into Megalomania and which will not.

This last part of my story becomes most apparent in the case studies of Turkey in Chapter 5 and Somalia and Uganda in Chapter 6. In the former case the Turkish Ruritanians are the Kurds, whose home area in south-east Turkey remained the least urban and industrialized part of the country. Kurdish intellectuals promoted the formation and maintenance of Kurdish identity in ways which other intellectuals from other ethnic minorities such as the Arabs, Circassians and Laz did not, despite the fact that the cultural difference between the Turkish majority and the Kurds was almost identical to the differences with these other groups;[17] as a result, Kurdish identity and nationalism remains a potent force within Turkey today. In the latter case Chapter 6 examines the two cases of Somalia and Uganda, where most citizens are Ruritanian, rather than Megalomanian, in their continued attachment to their rural tribal or clan identities. The failure to promote industrialization in both countries has led not only to the maintenance of high levels of ethnic diversity but, in the case of Uganda particularly, an ever-increasing level of fractionalization as claims for recognition of new sub-ethnic groups are advanced in the name of gaining and maintaining access to rural land. As in Gellner's story, both countries have seen state failure and attempts at secession, which have been very serious in Somalia, which indicate the lack of an adherence to a common national or super-ethnic identity.

5. *States can play a role in promoting ethnic homogenization by altering incentives associated with industrialization, but not via nation-building or assimilationist policies.*

I focus my primary attention in this book on the role of industrialization in promoting assimilation, but I do not claim that the state plays no role in this

---

[17] Most notably, the Kurds as well as the other three ethnic minorities all speak non-Turkic languages, and all four groups are Muslim-majority like the Turks.

process of ethnic change. The evidence from my case study chapters clearly shows how government policies have altered the nature of industrialization and thus provided incentives for individuals to identify ethnically in different ways. Thus in mid-twentieth century Turkey, for instance, I show that the state both promoted industrialization and provided incentives for individuals to identify as Turkish in order to access jobs in the growing modern, formal economy, which contributed greatly to assimilation among its ethnic minority populations. In the USA and New Zealand, government policies that encouraged rural–urban migration among Native Americans and the Māori, respectively, similarly encouraged the formation and solidification of broader ethnic identities as indigenous people from disparate tribes began interacting in the urban environment.

However, I also provide multiple examples in this book of how government policies either failed to promote assimilation or contributed towards ethnic change in an entirely unanticipated manner. In the first case heavy-handed attempts by the Turkish state to suppress Kurdish insurrections only contributed to the maintenance and increased salience of Kurdish identity up to the present day, and efforts by the US and New Zealand governments to promote assimilation into white society among indigenous populations instead contributed to assimilation into pan-tribal ethnic groups in both cases. Similarly efforts by President Siyad Barre in Somalia to promote a common Somali national identity and curtail clan identities through a number of government policies failed, as did attempts at top-down nation-building in other parts of postcolonial Africa (Bandyopadhyay & Green, 2013).

In the second case I present multiple examples of unanticipated ethnic change that have happened in part due to government efforts. Here, as Karl Deutsch put it using slightly different language, 'no growth of nationalism was foreseen or desired … yet the growth of nationalism was facilitated by the consequences of these acts' (Deutsch, 1953, p. 188). In contrast to Somalia, the Botswanan government has not actively pursued assimilationist or nation-building policies, including maintaining an ethnically biased Upper House of Parliament, yet a lack of such policies did not halt the process of ethnic homogenization. Efforts to keep Botswana a 'nation of farmers', in the words of its first President Seretse Khama (Molosiwa, 2013, p. 242), similarly failed, yet instead the government oversaw a process of industrialization and urbanization that contributed towards nation-building and assimilation into the Batswana majority ethnic group. Perhaps more striking are the examples of the USA and New Zealand, where judicial rulings that granted economic resources to Native American and Māori tribes, respectively, have led to the entirely unintended process of retribalization. Thus legal decisions that granted resources over casino revenues in the US and fishery revenues in New Zealand to individual tribes rather than indigenous peoples as a whole has led to an increase in the salience of tribal identities and an arguable decline in pan-tribal solidarity in both countries.

In the book I do not deny here that states can play a major role in ethnic identity change, but instead claim that this role is (1) often overstated by focussing too much on 'top-down' evidence for ethnic homogenization, and (2) can lead to unanticipated and unintended homogenization as well as increased fractionalization in certain cases. In other words, I attempt here to provide some more context and nuance to our understanding of the relationship between states and ethnic identity. In particular I develop this argument through the use of qualitative evidence in my case studies chapters, which allows me to understand the complex relationship between state policies and ethnic change.

1.3 WHAT THE THEORY DOES *NOT* STATE AND SCOPE CONDITIONS

Thus, to rephrase my argument, industrialization homogenizes populations by raising the relative value of labour over land. According to my theory, industrialization should promote assimilation into the largest group of society, except when individuals are too distinct culturally from the main group, which would lead them to assimilate into another smaller group. This process of assimilation should take place only during the period of industrialization and does not continue once societies have become fully industrialized.

As such it thus makes sense here to note what I am *not* claiming, namely support for either of the two other possible mechanisms that could lead industrialization to promote ethnic homogenization. The first is modernization theory, which can be characterized by the idea that all societies passed through similar stages from tradition to modernity, and that the processes of urbanization, economic growth, democratization and changes in social values all took place together. Modernization theory put a lot of emphasis on how education, literacy, the mass media and greater communication between people brought about shifts towards broader identities. There has long been a suggestion among both scholars like Karl Deutsch and Ernest Gellner as well as policymakers that, where states impose mass education in national languages, assimilation is more likely to take place. One of the main goals of this book, however, will be to show that this 'top-down' model is incorrect, inasmuch as I show using multiple methods across multiple cases that state-imposed literacy and education are not major causes of homogenization independently of industrialization. Indeed, in Chapter 4 I show that measures of mass education and state capacity are not statistically correlated with ethnic homogenization, while rates of literacy are not correlated with assimilation in mid-twentieth century Turkey in Chapter 5. Qualitative evidence from Africa in Chapters 6 and 7 suggest that education and literacy are neither necessary (as in Botswana) nor sufficient (in Somalia) for ethnic homogenization to occur. Finally, I show in Chapters 8 and 9 that there is no relationship between secondary school enrollment and linguistic homogenization among either the Native Americans of the United States or the Māori of New Zealand.

If I am not claiming that it is modernization in general which is driving ethnic identity change, I am also not claiming support for another potential mechanism through which industrialization could alter ethnic identities, namely the 'Minimum Winning Coalition' (MWC) theory. As originally developed by Riker (1962) and applied to the theory of ethnic politics more recently by Chai (2005), Chandra & Boulet (2012), Fearon (1999), Posner (2005) and Van der Veen & Laitin (2012), the MWC states that the goal of a political party or organization is to capture a bare majority (50 percent + 1) of the vote, enough so that it can attain power but small enough that it can re-distribute the maximum amount possible to its supporters. (In contrast, winning 100 per cent of the vote would only yield half the amount of state resources per supporter.) If ethnic or tribal groups are territorially concentrated and roughly coincide with a set of local government divisions, then most of these local governments will have a majority ethnic group whose members can utilize these ethnic identities to take power. In such a scenario there will be no incentive to form broader ethnic identities as any coalition representing a larger ethnic base would therefore have fewer resources per capita available for re-distribution. On the other hand, due to greater levels of ethnic diversity in industrial urban areas, rural–urban migrants from these territorial ethnic groups would not be able to employ their original ethnic identities in forming majority coalitions. It would thus be in their interest to form broader ethnic identities that can capture power in the urban environment, leading to a process of ethnic homogenization.

This thesis is simple and powerful and has found empirical support from Posner (2005) in his study of Zambian politics. Yet there are two problems with the MWC in explaining the examples of ethnic change I examine in this book. First, much of my qualitative evidence suggests that assimilation has taken place in contexts where the relevant actors exhibit no desire to obtain political power and re-distribute resources among their members. Second, using both cross-national data in Chapter 4 and data from mid-twentieth century Turkey in Chapter 5, I do not find empirical support for the prediction that ethnic homogenization should only take place in areas without a pre-existing ethnic majority. In other words, if the minimum winning coalition hypothesis is correct, the fact that every one of Turkey's fifth-seven provinces was recorded as having a majority ethnic group in its 1935 census would suggest that there would be strong incentives for members of these ethnic majorities to *exclude* other citizens from assimilating into these majority groups in urban areas and thereby expanding their size. As such the empirical prediction would be that there should be no relationship between industrialization and homogenization; yet instead the Turkish data shows a robust relationship between urbanization (as a proxy for industrialization) and homogenization.

Finally, before proceeding I need to clarify the scope conditions of my argument in two ways. In the first instance, I do not focus on ethnic change in violent contexts, for two reasons. First, at any given time since 1945 the vast majority of countries in the world have been at peace both externally and internally (Themnér & Wallensteen, 2012), and thus by focussing on non-violent countries my research has greater external validity. Second, there is now a substantial and ever-increasing literature on the role of war and conflict in identity change and formation, specifically on how ethnic/national identity and conflict (and the threat of conflict) can reinforce each other (Darden & Mylonas, 2016; Fearon & Laitin, 2000; Sambanis & Shayo, 2013; Sambanis, Skaperdas & Wohlforth, 2015; Wimmer, 2013), which contrasts starkly with the relative gap in the literature on non-violent identity change, which is something I hope to address here. As such I focus attention here on case studies which do not face the threat of external conflict, and where internal conflict, where it exists, is not associated with ethnic homogenization.

As regards the second scope condition of this book, I do not focus on immigrant or settler societies. The focus here is on how industrialization causes ethnic shift *within* a given population, and not on how outsiders integrate or assimilate into a society. As with the literature on violence and ethnicity, there is a similar vast amount published on how, when and why immigrants assimilate into larger identity groups (whether ethnic, racial or national), in particular in the United States (cf. Alba [2009] and Glazer & Moynihan [1963]), and again there is a relative gap in the literature examining ethnic identity shifts among non-immigrants. As such in this book I largely leave aside considerations of non-native groups in the white settler colonies (Australia, Canada, New Zealand and the United States) as well as discussion of the construction and formation of *mestizo* identities in Latin America, except to note that there is a substantial literature on the homogenizing effects of industrialization and urbanization in both cases (Alvarez, 1966; Blanksten, 1960; Brandfon, 1991; Luebke, 1977; Ostergren, 1991).

1.4 METHODOLOGY AND ORGANIZATION OF THE BOOK

This book employs a mixture of research methods. In Chapters 4, 5 and 7 through 10 I use multi-variate regression analysis to analyse the relationship between industrialization and assimilation, whether in a cross-national context (Chapters 4 and 10) or within individual countries (Chapters 5, 7, 8 and 9). The unit of analysis varies depending on the context: in Chapter 5 I use provincial-level data in Turkey, tribal-level data for Native Americans and Māori in Chapters 8 and 9, respectively, and individual-level data for Botswana in Chapter 7. I also use a variety of descriptive statistics in both tabular and scatterplot form throughout the book, including in some contexts where the number of observations is too small for a meaningful regression analysis.

In contrast, I use historical-qualitative data in Chapters 3 and 5 through 9, which allows me to focus attention on tracing the process by which industri-alization leads to ethnic homogenization. I selected the case studies in these chapters for multiple reasons. In Chapter 5 I focussed attention on Turkey both for data reasons, specifically because it is unique in having provincial-level data on ethnic identity, internal migration and urbanization across multiple censuses during a period of industrialization, and because it forms a 'typical' case of modernization according to multiple sources (Gerring, 2007). In Chapters 6 and 7 I use three relatively comparable African countries as part of a 'most similar' case design, such that they are similar along a variety of key measures (or independent variables) but dissimilar in the outcome of interest (or the dependent variable). More specifically, the cases of Botswana, Somalia and Uganda were all rural, agrarian ex-British colonies upon independence in the 1960s, but have diverged since, such that industrialization has proceeded in Botswana and led to ethnic homogenization, while the lack of industrialization has accompanied continued ethnic fragmentation in both Somalia and Uganda. Finally, I focus on Native Americans in the USA and the Māori in New Zealand in Chapters 8 and 9, respectively, as both cases allow for rare examples of within-case variation as industrialization has proceeded and then been reversed in both cases, at least as regards the relative economic importance attached to tribal land.

In addition to variation in methods across chapters, there is also variation in the degree to which the book is based on primary fieldwork vs a reliance upon secondary sources. Chapters 6 and 7 are both based in part on fieldwork in Uganda and Botswana, respectively, during which I conducted unstructured interviews, examined numerous archives and consulted multiple government and secondary sources not available elsewhere (such as parliamentary transcripts and locally published books and newspapers). My field experience in both cases also helped to clarify my argument, as seen in the opening anecdote to this chapter. Chapter 5 is largely based on primary and secondary material found in the extensive library collections of the London School of Economics and the School of Oriental and African Studies, but also on archival work at the British National Archives in London. Finally, Chapter 6 is based in part on a careful examination of a variety of unpublished and rare material in the Huntington Free Library Native American Collection at Cornell University.

This book is organized as follows. In Chapter 2 I provide an overview of the concepts of ethnicity and industrialization. I first define ethnic groups as descent-based groups and show how vertical ethnic change can take place, both through the consolidation of smaller ethnic groups into larger ones as well as assimilation into a national identity. The chapter also discusses why the book focusses on what I call vertical ethnic change instead of horizontal ethnic change, namely because the former is far more prevalent than the latter. I then provide a similar overview of the concept of industrialization, by focussing on how industrialization has historically involved a shift in the focus of the economy from rural agriculture to urban employment and from land to labour as the predominant factor of production. I justify my use of carbon emissions as my predominant cross-national quantitative measure of industrialization and my use of urbanization as my main proxy for industrialization for regions or communities within countries.

Chapter 3 contains historical support for my argument from the pre-modern and modern worlds. Even though industrialization was very limited in the pre-modern world, I provide evidence that urban, industrial areas allowed for the creation of broader ethno-national identities in the two cases of ancient Greece and Rome. I then discuss theories of the rise of nationalism in the modern world, with close examination of several cases from both Western and Eastern Europe. In particular I examine in more detail how industrialization encouraged assimilation in Germany and the constituent nations of the United Kingdom, before moving on to a discussion of the case of South Africa. In many of these cases I not only show how industrialization led to the growth of broader ethnic identities but how these processes were actively discouraged by the state, most obviously in the case of apartheid South Africa, while in other cases state-promoted assimilation failed.

In Chapter 4 I examine the statistical effect of industrialization on ethnic change. I first take Soviet-era cross-national data measuring ethnic diversity by country in 1961 and 1985 and regress the change in ethnic diversity across these twenty-four years on change in carbon emissions per capita over the same time-period. The results demonstrate a strong negative relationship between ethnic diversity and industrialization, a result which is robust to the inclusion of several control variables and the use of various sub-samples, as well as alternative measures of industrialization such as cement production and urbanization. I also show that carbon emissions are robustly correlated with change in the percentage identifying with the largest ethnic group per state. I then use a new, original dataset consisting of individual country censuses between 1960 and 2020, and show that the same effect holds, both as regards the effect of carbon emissions on ethnic fractionalization as well as robustness checks and multiple alternative measures such as electricity consumption and the share of labour in both agriculture and industry.

In Chapter 5 I examine in more detail my first case study, namely mid-twentieth century Turkey. The presence of high-quality census data from Turkey between 1935 and 1965 allows me to replicate my statistical analysis from the previous chapter at the provincial level to show that urbanization is correlated with increasing levels of people identifying as Turkish; moreover, this relationship is robust to the inclusion of a number of different controls and the use of sub-samples. Qualitative examination of evidence from Turkey suggests that this process was a consequence of economic structural change and incentives provided by the state, such that incentivized assimilation took place in urban Turkey but not in the countryside. Indeed, I show that a lack of industrialization in Kurdistan was responsible for the lack of Turkish identification in the region, despite both violent and non-violent attempts by the Turkish state at assimilating its Kurdish population.

Chapter 6 is the first of two chapters to take a closer look at Sub-Saharan Africa, which is both the world's least-industrialized and ethnically most-diverse continent. Indeed, because the process of industrialization is still very much underway in contemporary Africa, there is ample opportunity to study the effect of industrialization on ethnic diversity using contemporary records. I start in this chapter with an examination of Somalia and Uganda, which are both states which have seen low levels of industrialization and an increase in ethnic fractionalization in recent decades. In Somalia the lack of formal-sector job creation in the 1970s and 1980s contributed both to the collapse of the state along clan lines and a shift by which Somalia has gone from being considered one of the most ethnically homogenous countries in Africa to one of the most diverse. In Uganda a failure to create structural transformation has led to increased competition for land, leading individuals to utilize their often newly formed ethnic identities to claim ownership and title over rural land. I provide evidence from a variety of local land conflicts that revolve around ethnicity, as well as ongoing debates around both the listing of 'indigenous communities' in Uganda's constitution and the creation of new districts.

In Chapter 7 I move onto the case study of Botswana, which, in contrast to Somalia and Uganda, has experienced structural transformation due in large part to its diamond industry. Industrialization in Botswana has led to a sectoral shift out of agriculture as workers have left rural areas to move to cities and join the modern workforce, thereby leading to a decline in the relative value of rural land. I employ both qualitative and quantitative evidence to show that ethnic fractionalization has declined in Botswana since the mid-twentieth century and examine parliamentary debates around ethnic identity. Moreover, I show that this shift has happened not because of but largely despite efforts of the Botswanan state, which has both discouraged rural–urban migration and failed to alleviate institutional ethnic inequalities that persist to the present day. Finally, I consider alternative explanations for ethnic homogenization in Botswana and find them all wanting.

In Chapters 8 and 9 I move from the poorest and least industrial part of the world to some of the world's richest and most industrialized countries, namely the former settler colonies of Australia, Canada, New Zealand and the United States. I focus in particular on the cases of indigenous peoples in the United States and New Zealand, where in both cases we can observe unusual variation over time in the relative importance of land, thereby allowing me a sharper degree of causal identification than with other case studies. I begin in Chapter 8 with the case of Native Americans in the United States and show that urban-ization and the demographic shift out of reservations in the late twentieth century led to widespread re-identification from more narrow tribal identities to a broader Native American identity. Census data from the 1980 US census shows a robust negative correlation at the tribal level between levels of urban-ization and speaking tribal languages at home – but not between high school education and tribal language ability – which adds further evidence that it is not literacy or education that is driving assimilation. However, due to the legalization of Native American casinos from the 1980s, tribal land suddenly became economically valuable and altered the incentives for ethnic homogenization. As expected, I find evidence for an increased salience in tribal identities among Native Americans, which has in some cases led to claims for new tribal land and even new tribal identities.

In Chapter 9 I examine the case of the Māori in New Zealand, which provides me with a second case study of how processes of declining and then increasing values for tribal land has affected ethnic identity. As in the USA, population growth and subsequent urbanization in the mid-twentieth century led to a rise in pan-Māori nationalism, with evidence that native language loss in cities did not halt the rise of *Māoritanga* (Māori-ness). However, judicial rulings that attempted to compensate the Māori for their historical loss of land and livelihoods gave resources to individual *iwi* (tribes) rather than the Māori community as a whole, which has led to a renewed emphasis on *iwi* identity above and beyond a common Māori identity. In particular, I focus on fisheries policies that have allocated money to *iwis* according to their coastline length and show that those *iwi* with longer coastlines have seen higher population growth. I conclude the chapter with a brief examination of indigenous peoples in both Australia and Canada, where I show that industrialization has induced assimilation into pan-tribal identities but a lack of resource allocation to individual tribes has failed to lead to retribalization as it has in the United States and New Zealand.

Finally, in Chapter 10 I close the book by discussing some broader conclusions about the study of ethnicity and ethnic change, while also speculating about future prospects for the relationship between industrialization and assimilation. In the former case I focus on such topics as future quantitative work using data on ethnicity, our normative understanding of individuals who change their ethnic identities, the role of the state in enforcing or promoting ethnic identification and policy implications as regards promoting industrialization. In the latter case I return to my original dataset of country censuses from Chapter 4 to see if the relationship between industrialization and ethnic diversity changes over time. Upon introducing an interaction effect, I find evidence for a declining effect over time, although it appears that the interaction effect is driven by observations from the Americas, a result for which I find evidence in the secondary literature as well.

2

Understanding Ethnicity and Industrialization

2.1 INTRODUCTION

In this chapter my goal is to provide an overview of my two key concepts of ethnicity and industrialization. I begin with the former by providing a definition of ethnicity and examine three hypothetical examples of ethnic change. I then discuss potential problems of horizontal ethnic change and temporary ethnic change. In the second half of the chapter I describe and define industrialization, with a focus on how economies shift out of rural agriculture. I examine carbon emissions as a measure of industrialization and compare it to five other measures of industrialization. I then focus on urbanization as a related phenomenon, such that at the sub-national level urbanization can be taken as a proxy for industrialization. In particular I show how both industrialization and urbanization proceed in a largely monotonic fashion, such that de-industrialization and de-urbanization are rare and usually only temporary.

2.2 ETHNICITY AND ETHNIC CHANGE

Ethnicity is a difficult, almost 'chameleonic' concept to grasp (Connor, 1994, p. 100), in part because it has long been confused with other similar concepts such as race and nationhood. Indeed, as the political scientist Walker Connor has argued, the term was originally used by American sociologists in the mid-twentieth century to refer to minority groups which may have been ethnic in origin but could also be based on race, religion or language (Connor, 1994, p. 101). Here I define ethnicity and ethnic groups in a very simple way, namely those social groups whose identity is based on a belief in shared descent or kinship.

This definition of ethnicity has, however, led to confusion between understandings of race and ethnicity, both in academic circles as well as in everyday circumstances. Historically the two words were used synonymously, as seen in this book's epigraph. In recent UK census questionnaires, respondents have been asked to identify their ethnic group, whose main categories included white, mixed, Asian, black or other, despite the fact that the latter divisions are clearly based on race rather than ethnicity. In contrast, recent census questionnaires in the USA have explicitly asked for the respondent's race; the options include racial categories such as White, Black and American Indian but also arguably ethnic ones such as Chinese, Filipino, Japanese, Korean, Hawaiian and Samoan, among others.

The main reason why race and ethnicity are confused so often is because they are both perceived as identities based in common descent, such that various ethnic groups can together compose a racial group but not vice versa. Indeed, due to the negative association of the concept of race with racism, ethnicity has often been substituted as a synonym for race in official discourse. It is for this reason that many scholars of ethnicity and race do not distinguish the two concepts in their research (cf. Brubaker, 2009; Eriksen, 1993; Horowitz, 2000; Nagel, 1994; and Wallman, 1978). However, for the purposes of this book I use the word race in a very specific way, namely as the broadest type of descent-based identity available to individuals. In other words, to refer back to the discussion on multiple ethnic identities in the previous chapter, race forms the outermost concentric circle or Russian doll in the various types of ethnic identities held by individuals simultaneously.

In the rest of this section I examine ethnic change by graphically illustrating how a hypothetical population can be broken down by ethnic categories. The identity hierarchy is greatly simplified, starting with the nation or national citizenry at the top as it comprises 100 per cent of the population. The next tier is the highest level of sub-national ethnic identity, and so on until I account for all relevant ethnic groupings. I put relevant/salient ethnic identities in light colour and non-relevant ones in dark and list the ELF index for each country-period at the top of each hierarchy. My focus is on the process of assimilation, which I define here as the process by which individuals re-identify from a smaller ethnic group towards a larger one.

2.2.1 Ethnic Change with No Ethnic Majority

I begin with the simplest of my three figures in Figure 2.1, which is representative of states with no clear dominant majority group, as can especially be found in Sub-Saharan Africa.[1] For simplicity's sake I created a country with two

---

[1] (Fearon, 2003, p. 204)'s data shows that 72 per cent of African states have no ethnic majority group.

major ethnic groups, each of which contains 50 per cent of the population and each of which contains two sub-ethnic or clan groups as listed in Figure 2.1. (Ethnic and clan groups as the second and third tiers of the hierarchy could easily be replaced by racial and ethnic groups, respectively, as in apartheid

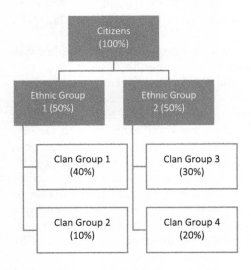

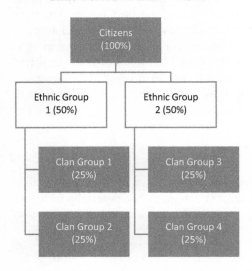

FIGURE 2.1. *ELF and ethnic change, model A (multi-ethnic states)*

South Africa, for instance.) In Time Period 1 the clan groups are the relevant ethnic grouping, which leads to an ELF of 0.700.[2]

In Time Period 2 I consider what would happen if citizens instead drop their clan identity as their most salient identity and instead re-identify along their ethnic identities in tier 2. The ELF thus decreases from 0.700 to 0.500, a sharp drop equivalent from moving from the level of diversity in Pakistan to that of Venezuela in Alesina et al. (2003)'s calculations. Note, however, that members of this country have not necessarily given up their clan identities but have merely shifted their identity to a higher tier. I discuss these types of states in more detail in Chapters 7 and 8, where I focus on the examples of Uganda and Botswana.

2.3.2 Ethnic Change Among Indigenous Groups in Ethnic Majority Countries

In Figures 2.2 and 2.3 I consider countries with ethnic majorities, which comprise over three-quarters of the countries across the world outside Africa (Fearon, 2003, p. 204). I first begin in Figure 2.2 with ethnic majority countries with indigenous groups, with special reference here to the former settler colonies of Australia, Canada, New Zealand and the United States that I examine in more detail in Chapters 8 and 9. Here again there are two main sub-national groups, but this time there is a dominant majority of 90 per cent of the population and a native or aboriginal group of 10 per cent. While the dominant majority identify as a group – as white Americans, for instance, do today even though they have not always done so – the indigenous people are split here between two groups of 5 per cent each in Time Period 1. Thus the relevant ethnic groups in Time Period 1 are the dominant majority and the two native groups which, although at different tiers, nonetheless do not have any overlapping membership and add up to 100 per cent and an ELF of 0.185.

In Time Period 2, however, all members of these two native groups have decided to identify together as a single entity, which means that the relevant ethnic groups are now on the same tier and the country's ELF has dropped from 0.185 to 0.180. This shift is, as in Figure 2.1, vertical, which means that members of aboriginal groups 1 and 2 have not abandoned their previous identity but merely de-emphasized it. Examples of this type of identity change are members of different Native American tribes identifying as Native American, as with other native peoples in Australia, Canada and New Zealand, all of which I examine in more detail in Chapters 8 and 9.

---

[2] The ELF is thus $1 - (0.4^*.0.4 + 0.1^*0.1 + 0.3^*0.3 + 0.2^*0.2)$.

Time Period 1: ELF = 0.185

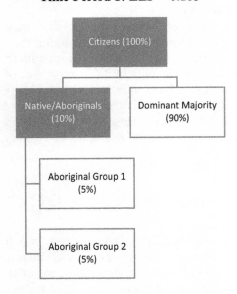

Time Period 2: ELF = 0.180

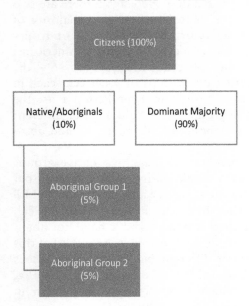

FIGURE 2.2. *ELF and ethnic change, model B (nation-states with indigenous groups)*

2.3.3 Ethnic Change in Ethnic Majority Countries Without Indigenous Groups

Finally, Figure 2.3 presents a model of ethnic majority states without indigenous groups such as most countries in Europe and Asia. Here the picture is more complicated. As before there are two groups in the second tier, one for the nation (70 per cent of the population), and one for ethnic minorities (30 per cent). What is different from Figures 2.1 and 2.2, however, is that there are two nodes coming off the nation instead of only one: the first is the ethnic majority, and the second are the two ethnic minority groups that comprise the ethnic minorities category. The reason for this change is that the existence of a nation

Time Period 1: ELF = 0.460

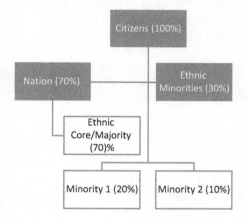

Time Period 2: ELF = 0.335

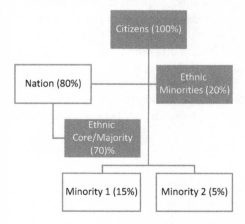

FIGURE 2.3. *ELF and ethnic change, model C (nation-states without indigenous groups)*

captures the creation of a modern national identity that can potentially encompass both the ethnic majority as well as various ethnic minorities. By definition, a majority of the members of this new national group are members of the ethnic majority, and in most cases the names of the new nation will take the name of the majority ethnic group.

This distinction might appear confusing at first, especially to readers from the USA and other settler nation-states, but one only need look at the difference between being English and being British in the UK to see how relevant and important these two concepts are. Indeed, there is clear evidence that many people in England view English as a more narrow ethnic identity and British as a broader national one, such that numerous members of ethnic minorities in England prefer to identify as British rather than English (Condor, Gibson & Abell, 2006; Kumar, 2010; McCrone, 2002).[3] There is of course a historical reason for this division, inasmuch as the English provided an 'ethnic core' or *Staatsvolk* (literally 'people of the state') for the subsequent British nation, as with Castilians in Spain, Amharas in Ethiopia, Persians in Iran, Arabs across large parts of North Africa and the Middle East and Ashkenazi Jews in Israel (cf. Green [2018]).

However, in many countries the name given to the ethnic core/majority and the nation is the same, such that the word 'French' refers to both the ethnic core of France and the French nation. In many cases, such as with the Amhara in Ethiopia (Habtu, 2004, pp. 109–10), there is thus a debate as to whether the ethnic core group is even an ethnic group at all, as opposed to being a nation. Part of the reason behind the confusion between the two concepts of the 'ethnic majority' and the 'nation' is because the English language does not have separate words for both concepts, in contrast to a number of other languages. For instance, the German terms *Reichsdeutsche* (translated as 'Imperial Germans') and *Volksdeutsche* ('ethnic Germans') formerly referred to members of the German nation-state and ethnic Germans, respectively.[4] Similarly the Russian language distinguishes between *россияне* (*rossiyane* or *rossiiane*) and *русские* (*russkiye* or *russkie*), each of which is translated into English as 'Russian' but which refers to the people of Russia and ethnic Russians, respectively (cf. Tolz [1998]). In Turkey, as we shall discuss in more detail in Chapter 5, there is again a clear distinction between *Türkiyeli* ('being from Turkey', or people of Turkey), and *Türk* (ethnic Turks) (Oran, 2014). Nor is this distinction limited to Europe: in Japan the distinction between the ethnic

---

[3] This distinction is in part due to the fact that, unlike the other constituent nations of the UK, England has very little institutional presence and thus has less opportunity to become a civic identity than in Scotland or Wales.

[4] The latter term was coined by none other than Adolf Hitler himself in 1938 (Bergen, 1994, p. 569).

majority, or *minzoku*,[5] and the nation, or *kokumin*, dates back to the 1890s, with a clear understanding of the differences between the two terms by the 1930s (Doak, 1996, pp. 81–5).[6]

To return to my schema, members of ethnic minority groups could potentially re-identify as members of a single ethnic minority group or could re-identify with the nation instead. To take the example I will examine in more detail in Chapter 5, Turkey fits this model well, with ethnic Turks comprising some 80 per cent of the population in the interwar period while ethnic minorities included Kurds, Arabs, Circassians, Greeks and others. In Time Period 1 we can conceive of the country before a common national identity has been forged, such that tier 2 groups are salient and the ELF is 0.460. In Time Period 2, while the two ethnic minority groups maintain their salience, the new national identity has become a salient identity as the ethnic majority members change their identities to a higher tier. Yet not only have all ethnic majority members shifted their identity upwards but so have 10 per cent of the ethnic minority groups (specifically 5 per cent for each group). Thus while many minorities still identify with their group, others have shifted to a sense of national identity instead. Note, however, that the ethnic majority group has not altered in size – instead, what has changed is that ethnic minorities have re-identified with the nation. To stay with the Turkish example, the sharp decline in the percentage of people who identified as Circassians, Pomaks and members of other ethnic minority groups was a result of their decision to re-identify as members of the modern Turkish nation, even while they maintained their original minority identity.

2.3 HORIZONTAL VS VERTICAL ETHNIC CHANGE

The ethnic shifts I have described above are all examples of what might be called 'vertical' ethnic shifts, whereby people move up and down a hierarchy of ethnic identities. As noted in Chapter 1, this shift is not problematic inasmuch

---

[5] This word is the origin for the Chinese word *minzu*, which is normally translated as 'ethnic group'. However, the Chinese language did not borrow the word *kokumin* from Japanese, which has meant that, like English, Korean ('minjok', also from *minzoku*) and Vietnamese ('*dân tộc*'), it has no separate words for 'ethnic group' and 'nation' (C. Keyes, 2002).

[6] Much of the confusion over issues of potential horizontal ethnic change discussed below actually originates in this distinction between ethnic groups and nations which share the same name. To take one example (Chandra, 2008, p. 103) discussed the shifting meaning of Afrikaner group boundaries in twentieth century South Africa, using the word 'Afrikaner' to refer at various points to those of Dutch descent and those of European descent. However, historians such as Giliomee (1989, p. 34) have noted that in the late nineteenth century the term 'Afrikaner' had two meanings: first as an ethnic group consisting of those of Dutch descent, and second as a modern nation consisting of all those of European descent. In the end the term became associated with the ethnic group and the racial term 'Whites' became the preferred nomenclature for those of European descent.

as it does not involve negating any of one's identities but merely involves a shift in emphasis.[7] Because people already have these identities, a 'vertical' shift from one identity to the other is not particularly troublesome or difficult, unlike, say, trying to 'pass' oneself as a member of one race or ethnic group when actually a member of another, or what could be termed a 'horizontal' ethnic shift.[8]

It is worth spending a bit of time here explaining why horizontal ethnic change is so unusual, since the rest of the book focusses entirely on vertical ethnic change. Horizontal ethnic change is rare for two reasons. First, changing one's ethnic identity along horizontal lines can be very difficult. Altering one's name, dress, accent and religion – all of which help to signal descent and kinship – can be legally, socially and/or psychologically difficult (Chandra, 2006, p. 416), which can indeed lead to a 'mental mess' in Allport's language. Indeed, attempting to fit in to one's new identity can be done but, 'like learning a second language in adulthood, the process is exhausting and the results usually far from perfect' (G. C. Bentley, 1987, p. 35). Thus, to take one example, much of the literature on racial passing from Black to White in the USA emphasizes the great difficulties individuals have undertaken in order to successfully pass.[9]

The second difficulty with horizontal ethnic change is that altering one's identity requires being accepted as a member of a new group, which is notoriously difficult. Part of the problem lies in the evidence that most people across different societies are themselves primordialists and thus do not believe that ethnic change is possible in the first place, a phenomenon previously identified as 'everyday primordialism' (Fearon & Laitin, 2000, p. 848) (cf. Gil-White [1999] and Subotic [2010]).[10] Indeed, when the anthropologist Francisco Gil-White (Gil-White, 1999, p. 789) asked a Mixtec Indian from Oaxaca in Mexico on whether one could become Mixtec without Mixtec parents, 'he

---

[7] Chandra (2006, p. 416) calls this process a 'shift in ethnic categories'.

[8] It is for this reason that it is again important to remember that I define ethnic groups here as ultimately based on (belief in) common descent rather than other attributes. For religious groups, for example, horizontal shift is relatively easy and common through conversion and thus may not require any change in language, dress or claims of descent.

[9] See, for instance, the white American journalist John Howard Griffin's (successful) attempt to darken his skin to 'pass' as an African American through the use of drugs and light treatment, as documented in the book *Black Like Me* (Griffin, 2004 [1961]). In Philip Roth's novel *The Human Stain* (and subsequent film) the emphasis is less on the physical difficulties in racial passing and more on the psychology of how passing leads to losing one's personal and family history. Of course, the difficulties involved in racial passing can vary widely within the same group, such that light-skinned African Americans can relatively easily pass as whites but dark-skinned African Americans cannot, with economic consequences for both groups (Caselli & Coleman II, 2013; Nix & Qian, 2015).

[10] Kanovsky (2007) presents evidence that respondents in Ukraine believe that adoption and migration as a child can alter one's ethnic identity; however, he still finds strong evidence for a belief that adults cannot change their ethnic identities and that people can only hold one ethnic identity at a time.

looked at me as though celery stalks had suddenly begun sprouting from my head, and I do believe he feared for my intelligence. "You can only be Mixtec if your parents are Mixtec", he said. "What do you mean?"'

These problems of being accepted as members of a new group occur frequently. For instance, attempts at 'passing' by the Burakumin of Japan, who are physically indistinguishable from other Japanese, often fail due to subtle ethnic markers like their place of origin, speech patterns or lack of kinship relations (Horowitz, 2000, p. 49), while efforts by Indians to pass as members of the Ladino majority group in Guatemala fail unless they sever their social ties by moving to a different part of the country (Van den Berghe, 1968). In India passing is so difficult – since 'in the most crucial circumstances, ethnic credentials are sure to be closely checked through acquaintances, kinsmen and one's natal village' – that one type of traditional entertainer, the *bahurupiya*, specializes in simulating various identities and is paid according to how successful he is at fooling others (Berreman, 1972, p. 577).

Perhaps the most famous historical example of someone attempting horizontal ethnic change comes from sixteenth-century south-west France, when the peasant Arnaud du Tilh attempted to pass himself off as a man named Martin Guerre. The real Martin Guerre had disappeared in 1548, and Du Tilh arrived in his village in 1556, claiming to be Guerre. Remarkably, he was able to fool Guerre's wife and sisters but raised doubts when he attempted to sell part of his family land, a custom which was common among French peasants but not among those like Guerre who came from the Basque region near the Spanish border (Davis, 1983, p. 52). In other words, it was Du Tilh's attempt at passing as a member of another ethnic group, not passing as another individual, that led to the discovery of his fraud.

So far, I have focussed on individual ethnic change rather than inter-generational ethnic change. Indeed, the latter can and does happen far more frequently than the former, inasmuch as children can be brought up to adhere to a different ethnic identity than one or both of their parents due to intermarriage, migration, adoption or other such phenomena. The most important thing to note here, however, is that inter-generational ethnic change is still not horizontal if it involves children adopting an ethnic identity when they have forgotten the memory of their original or previous identity. Indeed, as noted by Rousseau (1975, p. 43) in the case of central Borneo, this is exactly the problem in finding examples of inter-generational ethnic change as 'they are of course not remembered: this is the main point in taking another identity'.

2.4 A BRIEF OVERVIEW OF INDUSTRIALIZATION

In this book I focus on industrialization as a process whereby land is decreasingly important as a site for economic production relative to labour and capital. The most important theory describing this process is arguably W. A. Lewis's (1954) famous two-sector model, which divides the labour supply into two sectors, namely the traditional or subsistence sector, and the industrial or capitalist sector. Lewis posits that the subsistence sector has a surplus of labour such that removal of some of the labour force would not lead to a decline in production, which leads him to call it 'unlimited' in supply. The process of industrialization involves growth in the capitalist sector, thereby drawing in labour at higher wages than are available in the subsistence sector, a process which will continue to the point where wages equalize in the two sectors and there are no longer incentives for labour to shift from one sector to another.

Thus in a broad sense industrialization leads to a shift in the labour supply from agriculture towards the urban industrial sector. The technological innovations that correspond with higher agricultural productivity and the growth of the industrial sector mean that land declines in importance relative to other factors of production, both within the economy as a whole as well as within agriculture more specifically. To put this another way, this shift involves a change from a focus on land-intensive 'Malthusian technology' towards a 'Solow technology' relying upon labour and capital inputs instead (Hansen & Prescott, 2002).

There is a great variety of evidence for Lewis's (1954) model. First, historical records show a decline in land – specifically agricultural land – as a share of wealth from the early modern period to the present. In the UK, for instance, agricultural land as a share of total national wealth declined from 64 per cent in 1688 to 55 per cent in 1798, 18 per cent in 1885 and 4 per cent in 1927 (Deane & Cole, 1969, p. 270). Alongside this process there was a decline in the value of rural land relative to urban land: the ratio of the rental value of farmland and farmhouses to the rental value of housing and shops declined from around 6:1 in the sixteenth and early seventeenth centuries to 2:1 in the 1810s and 1:1 in the 1850s (G. Clark, 2001, pp. 15–16). This decline in the relative value of land as part of the process of industrialization was by no means limited to the UK: in the United States, for example, farmland values as a percentage of GNP declined from 88 per cent in 1870 to 9 per cent in 1990 (Hansen & Prescott, 2002, p. 1209), while agriculture's share of national income declined from 39.5 per cent in 1799 to 12.9 per cent in 1938 (T. W. Schultz, 1951, p. 729). Indeed, one study found a robust negative relationship between the value of rural land and the migration of labour out of agriculture in twentieth-century USA, as would be predicted by Lewis's model (Barkley, 1990).

Another piece of evidence behind Lewis's model is how technological change has led to a decline in the importance of land relative to labour in the economy. More specifically, the shift away from horsepower, which required grazing land, towards labour-intensive outputs like railroads and farm machinery (Hansen & Prescott, 2002, p. 1206), contributed to the replacement of land by labour as a factor of production. The increased importance of other factors of production in spurring agricultural efficiency has thus led directly to the shift out of employment in agriculture in a variety of contexts (Gollin, Parente &

Rogerson, 2002). Thus in England non-agricultural employment overtook agricultural employment in the early eighteenth century (Wrigley, 1985, p. 700), with similar shifts in the Netherlands at the same time and for France and other parts of Western Europe in the nineteenth century (Allen, 2003).

As a result there has a been a long-term decline in the relative size of the labour force in agriculture, which has long been considered a hallmark of industrialization: (Rostow, 1960, p. 71), for instance, discussed how economic 'take-off' was characterized by a drop from around 75 per cent of the labour force in agriculture to 20–40 per cent by the time a country had reached 'maturity'. In the UK this shift has been dramatic: employment in agriculture, fishing and forestry shrank from around 60–80 per cent of total labour in the late seventeenth century to 20–5 per cent in 1850, 8–10 per cent in 1900 and 5 per cent in 1950 (Deane & Cole, 1969, p. 137). In the most advanced economies such as Canada, the Netherlands, Sweden and the UK, employment in agriculture has stabilized at around 1–2 per cent of the workforce in the early twenty-first century.

One possible concern with my argument is that industrialization is not a monotonic process, inasmuch as de-industrialization is a common phenomenon in the developed world. Indeed, the share of manufacturing in GDP generally peaks during the period of industrialization before declining as economic growth becomes more centred around the service sector, and evidence suggests that this peak is actually lower today that it was in the past (Rodrik, 2016). This phenomenon explains why it is common to speak of highly developed countries as 'post-industrial' insofar as their economies are dominated by the service sector, such that services account for more than two-thirds of GDP for almost all countries in North America and Western Europe today.[11]

However, it is important to repeat here that employment in industry is not the same as employment in manufacturing, and that the focus of this book is on the former rather than the latter. World Bank data on employment in industry, which I use in my quantitative analysis in Chapter 4, defines the industrial sector as 'mining and quarrying, manufacturing, construction, and public utilities (electricity, gas, and water)', thereby encompassing a much broader range of professions than solely manufacturing. Moreover, using data on sectoral labour employment is more useful in understanding the nature of employment in society than data on GDP, which only measures value-added, regardless of how many people it takes to produce this value. Thus any phenomenon like conflict or a global recession that causes GDP to fall but does not affect either agricultural or industrial production could cause perverse increases or decreases in value-added as a proportion of GDP, despite a lack

---

[11] Data from the World Bank. The sole exceptions are oil-rich Mexico and Norway, where services account for around 60 per cent of GDP.

of change in employment patterns.[12] As such it is not surprising that, as I show below, a variety of measures of industrialization at the cross-national level are correlated with each other but not with industry as a proportion of GDP.

It would thus be ideal if I could use data on labour force in agriculture and in industry as measures of industrialization in the rest of this book, but, as noted below, continuous cross-national data from the World Bank on both types of employment only exists from 1991 onwards. As such I turn instead to two much better measures of industrialization that I will use throughout this book, namely carbon emissions as a cross-national measure and urbanization as a domestic measure. I discuss each of these measures in turn.

2.5 CARBON EMISSIONS

In my quantitative analysis in Chapter 4 I use a measure of carbon emissions in (logged) metric tons per capita as a proxy for industrialization at the cross-national level. Carbon emissions are a good measure of industrialization for three reasons. First and foremost, carbon emissions are clearly the result of modern industrial economies, mainly via the consumption of coal (comprising roughly 60 per cent of all carbon emissions) but also from other fossil fuels like natural gas (11 per cent), fuel oil (7 per cent) and cement production (7 per cent) (Metz, Davidson & De Conink et al., 2005, p. 81). By sector some 35 per cent of all carbon emissions globally are generated for the purposes of producing electricity and heat, with a large amount of this consumption used for manufacturing items like chemicals, iron/steel, aluminum and paper, among other products. Another 21 per cent of emissions are generated by transportation, with petroleum-based fuels used for cars, trucks, ships and airplanes dominating this sector. Finally, some 19 per cent of emissions are generated by the manufacturing and construction sectors in non-electricity usage, especially via heat and steam generation for producing such things as cement and steel, while 8 per cent of emissions comes from the residential sector (via heating) and 5 per cent of emissions from petroleum refineries (Metz et al., 2005, p. 83). All of these processes are unquestionably essential to the functioning of a modern industrial economy.

Second, thanks to efforts of researchers at the Carbon Dioxide Information Analysis Center in the US, there is high quality annual data on carbon emissions by country dating back to 1960, which itself derives from various UN country questionnaires and national statistical publications. The quality of data on carbon emissions is thus in sharp contrast to other potential measures of industrialization, as discussed further in Chapter 4. Third, carbon emissions

---

[12] Two such examples will suffice here. First, a negative shock to Sierra Leone's GDP as a result of its civil war (1991–2002) led to industry's share of its GDP hitting an all-time high of 38.8 per cent in 1992 before declining after the war ended to 5.2 per cent in 2020. Similarly, the 1973–4 global recession led to all-time highs in industry's share of GDP in countries as varied as Chile, the Netherlands, Somalia, Togo and Venezuela.

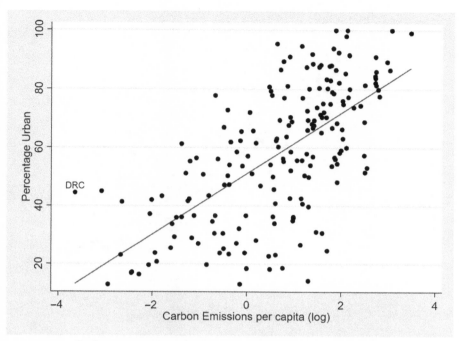

FIGURE 2.4. *Carbon emissions and urbanization in 2018*
(Source: World Bank)

correspond to the non-linear, S-shaped relationship between economic development and industrialization, inasmuch as carbon emissions for pre-industrial societies is low and steady, increases as countries industrialize and then stabilizes as countries increasingly rely upon their service sectors for employment. Indeed, carbon emissions in now-developed countries were flat until the early nineteenth century, then rose rapidly rose until the late twentieth century, and have since largely stabilized at different levels. In metric tons per capita annual emissions in France have remained largely flat at around 6 since the early 1990s, while emissions have stabilized around 9 in Japan since 1990, between 16 and 17 in Canada since 1970, and around 19 in the US since 1980.[13]

Another way to verify the validity of carbon emissions as a measure of industrialization is to compare it to five other variables that capture various elements of industrialization, which I plot here along with the line of best fit and any outliers that arise using the DFBETA post-regression diagnostic test.[14] I start with urbanization, here measured as the percentage of the population living in urban areas;

---

[13] Note that I am not arguing for an inverted-U relationship between economic development and the absolute level of carbon emissions, which is known as the environmental Kuznets curve.

[14] The DFBETA tool calculates the difference in the regression coefficient for a particular variable with and without each individual observation, with the rule of thumb to exclude outliers that yield a DFBETA value greater than |1| (Belsley, Kuh & Welsch, 1980, p. 28).

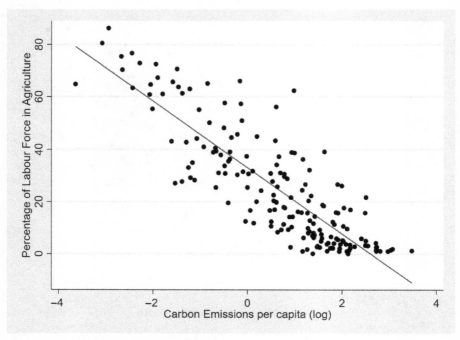

FIGURE 2.5. *Carbon emissions and employment in agriculture in 2018*
(Source: World Bank)

Figure 2.4 shows the data for the log of carbon emissions per capita plotted against urbanization in 2018, which is the latest year for which there exists data for all of the cross-national data I use in this chapter. As can be seen, the relationship is clearly sloping upwards even though the fit is not exact. (This is almost certainly due to the fact that, unlike all the other variables discussed here, each country uses its own definition of urbanization.) The Democratic Republic of Congo (DRC) is the sole outlier, most likely due to the way that its long history of conflict has both driven people to migrate to urban areas and has affected data quality.

I next plot the log of carbon emissions against the percentage of the labour force in agriculture in Figure 2.5, with data also from the World Bank. As noted above, this variable captures the essence of the declining value of land as my operative mechanism, since it measures the degree to which countries become decreasingly reliant upon rural agriculture for their employment. Here the relationship is clearly downward sloping, as expected, with no outliers.

Figure 2.6 plots carbon emissions against the percentage of the labour force in industry, with data from the World Bank. As expected, the relationship is positive, with Qatar the sole outlier due to a high proportion of employment in construction.

In Figure 2.7 I plot carbon emissions against the log of cement production per capita, with data taken from the US Geological Survey. As noted above,

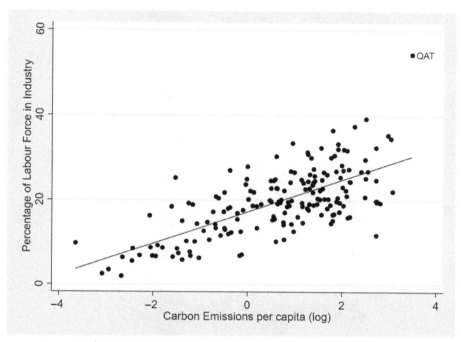

FIGURE 2.6. *Carbon emissions and employment in industry in 2018*
(*Source: World Bank*)

cement production is an important contributor to global carbon emissions and global energy consumption, since it is the main ingredient in concrete, which is the most widely used product in the modern world by weight after water. Unlike other industrial products such as steel and electricity, concrete production is mostly consumed domestically due to relatively high transport costs and wide availability of raw materials (Szabó, Hidalgo & Ciscar et al., 2006), and is thus a relatively good proxy for cement consumption as well.[15] Finally, like carbon emissions, countries at high levels of GDP/capita stabilize their production (Mahasenan, Smith & Humphreys, 2002). As regards Figure 2.7, the sole outlier is Niger, which has only one semi-functional cement factory.

In Figure 2.8 I plot carbon emissions against electricity consumption per capita in kWh (logged), with data from the US Energy Information Administration. As noted above, electricity consumption is a major factor both in carbon emissions as well as an important measure of industrialization in its own right, as seen by its use as a proxy for industrialization in multiple studies

---

[15] We do not have good cross-national data on the consumption of industrial products such as cement and steel.

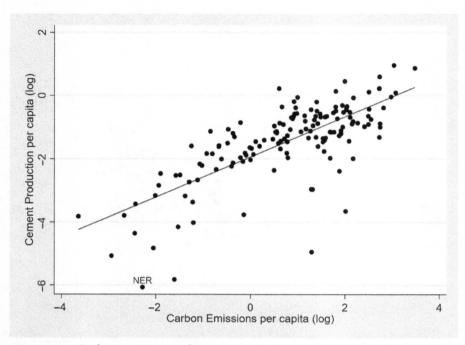

FIGURE 2.7. *Carbon emissions and cement production per capita in 2018*
(Source: US Geological Survey, World Bank)

(Grusky, 1983) and in the importance given its provision by politicians across the developing world (Min, 2015). It is thus not surprising to see a positive and tight fit in Figure 2.8, with the DRC again as the only notable outlier.

The reader may, at this point, wonder about why I have not so far discussed what would appear to be obvious proxy for industrialization, namely GDP per capita itself. The answer should be clear in Figure 2.9, where I plot the relationship between carbon emissions and GDP per capita. There is a clear non-linear relationship between the two variables, such that the GDP per capita has a positive relationship with carbon emissions at low levels of GDP per capita but not at higher levels. This non-linear relationship is clearly driven by the fact that the richest countries in the world have been able to limit and even slightly reduce their carbon emissions. In other words, unlike with the other variables discussed here, GDP per capita does not reach a stable maximum at some given level for advanced economies, and thus does not follow an S-shaped curve.

Finally, to graphically confirm my earlier statement about how it is inappropriate to use sectoral measures of GDP as measures of industrialization, Figure 2.10 plots the relationship between carbon emissions and the share of industry in GDP. While the correlation is positive, it is much weaker than the

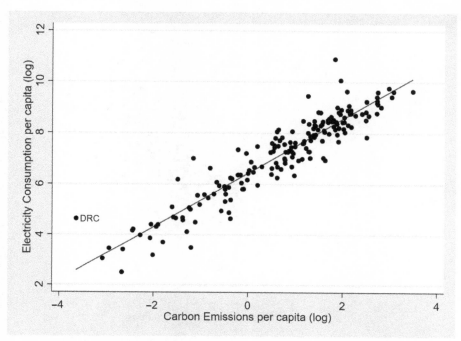

FIGURE 2.8. *Carbon emissions and electricity consumption per capita in 2018 (Source: US Energy Information Administration; World Bank)*

relationship between carbon emissions and the five other measures of industrialization.[16]

2.6 URBANIZATION

The degree to which I can exploit variation in industrialization at the cross-national level is relatively uncontroversial. However, within countries it is more difficult to analyse variation in levels of industrialization due to the degree to which each country's economy is interconnected. Moreover, while carbon emissions are among the best measures of industrialization that we have at the country level, it is very unusual to have data on carbon emissions at the sub-national level except in select developed countries like the USA and UK. Finally, carbon emissions can only be measured based on a geographical unit, which is not useful when discussing ethnic groups within broader populations as I do later in this book.

---

[16] The relationship between the share of industry in GDP and both urbanization and electricity consumption per capita is even weaker than with carbon emissions.

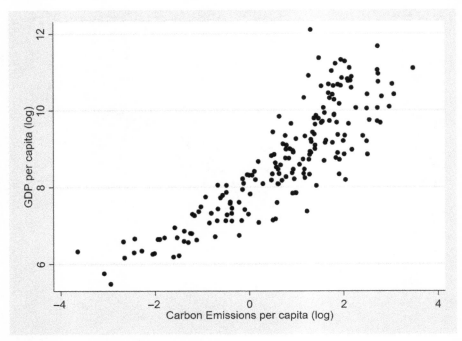

FIGURE 2.9. *Carbon emissions and GDP per capita in 2018*
(Source: World Bank)

Instead, it is easier to operationalize my argument at the sub-national level by examining variation in urbanization instead, which still captures the key mechanism focussing on the relative value of land. Indeed, the main difference between rural and urban areas within countries is the degree to which the former have economies still based on agricultural production and land owner-ship, at least relative to the latter, whose residents are much more likely to work in the industrial or service sectors instead. As such, in the next section I discuss the origins of modern urbanization, before focussing on how urbanization, like carbon emissions, follows an S-shaped curve. Finally, I briefly discuss the sociological literature on urban ethnicity.

To begin with, I am well aware of the problems of conflating industrializa-tion and urbanization, not the least due to the fact that urbanization pre-dates industrialization. There are also examples of industrialization taking place outside cities, such as among the Laz in north-east Turkey, an example I consider in more detail in in Chapter 5. However, for the most part manufac-turing and craft production have long gone hand-in-hand with urbanization, largely due to the specialization that proximity and economies of scale can create in urban environments (Trigger, 1980 [1972], pp. 154–5). Moreover, I would again emphasize here that both industrialization and modern

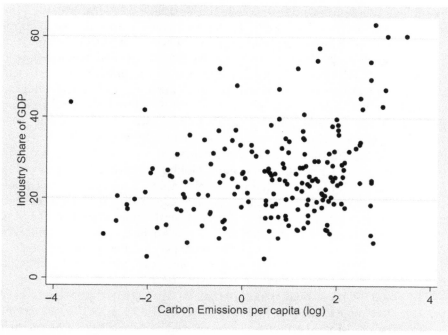

FIGURE 2.10. *Carbon emissions and industry in GDP in 2018*
(Source: World Bank)

urbanization capture the essence of my argument about a shift in the relative economic importance of rural land.

Urbanization, like carbon emissions, was very low throughout most of world history. Indeed, not only were pre-modern towns miniscule compared to today's megacities, they contained few inhabitants who did not rely upon land in some way for their livelihoods. Thus, as Eisenstadt and Shacher (1987, p. 54) note, 'until the Middle Ages, the history of human societies is thus a history of the countryside', inasmuch as it was only during the Middle Ages that a new merchant class developed wealth that was not based on the ownership of land.[17]

Industrialization has allowed for a rapid rise in urbanization in the modern world, both via an increased supply of food for urban workers as well as a demand for urban employment. As regards the former, earlier phases of industrialization led to a large increase in agricultural productivity via such

---

[17] Note Marx's (1964 [1857–8], p. 77) similar claim that 'ancient classical history is the history of cities, but cities based on landownership and agriculture ... Modern (history) is the urbanization of the countryside, not, as among the ancients, the ruralisation of the city.'

technologies such as the modern plough, the Norfolk four-course crop rotation, fertilizers and insecticides, alongside improvements in transportation infrastructure via canals, roads and railways; later phases saw the development of higher yielding seed varieties in the Green Revolution and the widespread availability of herbicides. As regards the demand for urban labour, there is an abundance of evidence that the urban wage premium rose as technological innovation led to a rise in urban productivity, thereby drawing in workers from the countryside (Boustan, Bunten & Hearey, 2013). The rise of the non-agricultural sector in cities – both in terms of manufacturing as well as services – has led workers to migrate from the countryside to cities for employment, thereby driving up levels of urbanization (Gollin, Jedwab & Vollrath, 2016). In many cases these workers migrate simply in anticipation of finding a job rather than the actual existence of one, which can lead to the co-existence of urban unemployment and continued flows of rural–urban migration (Todaro, 1969). Moreover, there is evidence going back to Boserup (1965) and even Adam Smith that the demand for urban residence and the supply of food for urban workers were in many ways symbiotic, such that both caused each other in the case of the UK and other early industrializers.[18]

The result of these dual trends is that modern urbanization levels have increased over time for all countries to a point until they reach a plateau specific to each country. More specifically, countries which have largely stabilized their level of urbanization below 100 per cent include Canada (around 80 per cent since 2000), Sweden (around 84 per cent since 1975), New Zealand (around 86 per cent since 2000) and Australia (around 87 per cent since 1990). While countries may stall along the way – as with the Democratic Republic of Congo, which remained around 30 per cent urban between 1970 and 2000 – actual de-urbanization is a very rare phenomenon in the modern world (Satterthwaite, McGranahan & Tacoli, 2010). In fact, it is so rare that we can claim that a high level of urbanization is as clear a marker of a phenomenon of non-agricultural, industrialized society as we can get.

Before concluding this section, I should comment, albeit briefly, on the large literature on urbanization and ethnicity. For much of the twentieth century urban theorists – many of whom were associated with the Chicago School of Sociology – associated cities and urban spaces not with homogenization and assimilation but instead with fragmentation and segregation, or the opposite of my argument in this book. In particular, scholars of immigrants in the developed world and rural–urban migrants in the developing world drew the conclusion that ethnicity was actually an urban phenomenon, due in part to urban residential segregation and the existence of an urban ethnic division of labour (see Nagel and Olzak, 1982; Olzak, 1983; for an overview of this

---

[18] Cf. Smith's *Wealth of Nations*, specifically Book III, chapter IV: 'How the Commerce of the Towns Contributed to the Improvement of the Country.'

literature). Thus, to quote one such study, there was a general agreement that 'urban areas permit the concentration of large ethnic groupings in segregated communities that persist for generations' (Marcson, 1950, p. 77).

Yet this literature suffered from a notable flaw, namely that it failed to analyse urban ethnicity in a comparative context. More specifically, it viewed ethnicity as a singular and fixed 'modern' type of identity and neglected the existence of rural ethnicity. Rather than observing a process of ethnic homogenization as people substituted larger ethnic identities for smaller ones, the literature instead viewed urban and rural identities as distinct phenomena, contrasting rural 'tribes, villages, bands and isolated communities' with urban, modern ethnic identities (A. Cohen, 1974, p. ix).[19] Among Africanists this confusion arose in part because the word 'tribe' was originally used by Europeans as a political designation for rural pre-colonial polities in Africa. However, by conceptualizing ethnicity in such a narrow way as to exclude tribal or kinship identities, this literature thereby failed to note how industrialization and urbanization were not actually promoting the increased salience of ethnicity but were instead increasing ethnic homogenization as people assimilated from smaller ethnic groups to larger ones. Similarly, the scholarly focus on an ethnic division of labour in cities neglected the rural origins of this division, as discussed in the previous chapter.

Thankfully the focus on cities as barriers to assimilation has become passé within urban sociology since the 1970s, with a turn towards focussing on cities as more complex sites for reshaping identity.[20] One thing that has not changed within the literature on urbanization, however, is an agreement that urbanization is a largely irreversible process by which countries become more urban over time. Thus, if urbanization contributes to assimilation, then assimilation is similarly irreversible. Again, this point should not be misread to mean that people must permanently alter their identities in cities, as the potential exists for the retrieval of smaller ethnic identities by urban–rural migrants, which is exactly what we find in the case of Native Americans and the Māori in Chapters 8 and 9, respectively.

2.7 CONCLUSION

In this chapter I discussed conceptions of both ethnicity and industrialization, as well as the mechanics of how ethnic change happens and how societies industrialize. As regards ethnicity, I focussed on three types of ethnic change depending on the pre-existing ethnic demography of a given state, before noting how the focus of this book will be on what I call 'vertical' ethnic change rather than 'horizontal' ethnic change, inasmuch as the former is far more frequent

---

[19] Also see for instance (Bates, 1974; Horowitz, 2000, pp. 57–64) on this point.
[20] This shift corresponded to the rise of the Los Angeles School of Sociology in the field of urban studies.

than the latter for numerous reasons. I then examined broader theories of industrialization and showed how the transformation to an industrial society involves the shift out agriculture and into industrial employment. As such I discussed the two measures of industrialization that I will use throughout the rest of this book, namely carbon emissions as a cross-national measure of industrialization, and urbanization as a domestic measure, alongside other measures of industrialization such as employment in agriculture (negatively) and industry, cement production and electricity consumption.

Having now set the scene with detailed discussions of ethnicity and industrialization, I now proceed to focus on historical evidence for the relationship between industrialization and assimilation in the next chapter.

3

Industrialization and Assimilation in Historical Perspective

3.1 INTRODUCTION

In this chapter I examine historical qualitative evidence for the influence of industrialization on assimilation, with examples from the ancient world up through the twentieth century. My goal here is to provide evidence that industrialization has promoted ethnic homogenization in a variety of historical contexts and not just in the cases I examine in more detail later in the book. I deliberately focus my attention here largely – but not entirely – on nineteenth- and twentieth-century Europe, because the region provided not only empirical inspiration for both Marx and Gellner but, as the first part of the world to industrialize, Europe also provides a variety of historical cases of industrialization that allow me to test my argument.

To examine this evidence, I divide the rest of this chapter into two. I begin by examining pre-modern evidence in Section 3.2, including an examination of the two case studies of ancient Greece and the Roman Empire. In Section 3.3 I consider the modern period, with a specific focus on examples of industrialization and national identity formation in both Western and Eastern Europe. In particular, I focus on Germany as well as the UK and its constituent nations, where a history of industrialization and urbanization have led scholars to date the emergence of national identities to several different moments in time. I then examine in detail the case of South Africa, where industrialization began in the late nineteenth century but where the white settler elite artificially restricted the assimilative processes that took place elsewhere in the industrial world, eventually leading to a system of apartheid. Finally, in Section 3.4 I conclude.

3.2 PRE-MODERN EVIDENCE ON INDUSTRIALIZATION AND ETHNIC IDENTITY CHANGE

In any analysis of the pre-modern relationship between industrialization and ethnic change it is important to acknowledge three limitations. First and most obviously, low levels of pre-modern industrialization mean that the effects of industrialization on ethnic identity were limited and often only temporary. On the one hand, pre-modern cities certainly contained people that did not depend on access to land for their livelihood, such as priests, bureaucrats and artisans, among others. On the other hand, however, these towns were small and had high mortality rates, which meant that much of the urban population consisted of recent rural–urban migrants. Moreover, since the wealthiest city-dwellers tended to be mostly rural landlords, it is difficult to say that cities were a fundamentally different place than the countryside.

Second, life in pre-modern cities was far more hierarchical and segmented than in the modern period, which meant that the formation of broader identities was artificially restricted. For those who did manage move to urban areas, city governments in medieval Europe restricted citizenship to only certain residents, thereby disrupting the process of broad identity formation that I document in subsequent chapters. Indeed, one estimate is that only around a quarter of all adult urban inhabitants in medieval Europe held citizenship of the town in which they lived, with percentages in the single digits in the Netherlands and Italy (Minns et al., 2019). This restricted access to citizenship was done to limit competition for citizen traders, which is why in major trading ports like Venice urban citizenship was even sub-divided into three types depending on how long claimants could show residence. In other cases, citizenship and even residence were rationed according to location of birth, marriage, occupation, wealth, gender and religion, among other characteristics, which meant that even rural–urban migrants from the surrounding countryside were legally separated from assimilating into urban identities. While guilds sometimes brought together businessmen from different regions with common interests, they were also notorious for excluding people in order to enhance the benefits of membership, such that in cities like Paris and Florence less than 20 per cent of householders belonged to a guild (Ogilvie, 2011, pp. 53–7). All of these restrictions thus clearly limited the potential for ethnic identity change.

Third, my argument in this book revolves around how industrialization induces people to shift their identities from more particular to broader identities, which in turn requires knowing not only people's new identity choices but also their previous identities. Yet while evidence on urban identities can be traced back centuries and even millennia in select cases thanks to the availability of written records, for the most part we do not know which identities rural people chose and whether they changed these identities upon moving to cities for the simple reason that they were illiterate. There is thus a great lacuna in understanding ethnic identity change in the pre-modern world.

Despite these three important limitations, it is still possible to present historical evidence here of a correlation between industrialization and adherence to broader identities, whether along ethnic or national lines. Indeed, as correctly noted by Karl Deutsch, that these processes were rarer in the pre-industrial world – and would often get reversed – did not mean that they were absent altogether (Deutsch, 1953). It is thus perhaps appropriate here to examine the two most notable pre-modern case studies of broader identity formation, namely ancient Greece and ancient Rome, and how industrialization contributed to these processes. In both cases we can observe the rise of an urban, non-agrarian civilization over a period of centuries, which spurred the creation of pan-tribal identities, only to see de-urbanization subsequently leading to the decline and dissolution of these broader identity formations.

Starting with ancient Greece, there is a large literature addressing the question of whether or not a common ethnic or even national identity existed among the ancient Greek peoples, with most recent historians agreeing on a multiplicity of ethnic identities but the absence of an over-arching national identity (Hall, 1997, 2002; Luraghi, 2008; Romeo, 2002). There has been, however, much less of an attempt to examine the degree to which specific urban identities, centred on the city-states, were ethnic in nature and/or were important and salient to ancient Greeks. Sparta provides an important case study in this regard, as its male citizens who underwent its famously intense *agoge* training and education system enjoyed equality under the law while its women were notably liberated relative to other Greek city-states. These men – specifically those who were born as citizens and who could maintain their contributions to regular banquet (*syssitia*) fees – only comprised a minority of Spartan residents inasmuch as they were atop a complex social hierarchy, with free non-citizens (specifically the *mothakes* and *perioikoi*) underneath the citizens but atop the *helots*, who worked as serfs on the Spartans' land. Indeed, Spartan citizens were actually prohibited from practicing agriculture, which was solely the domain of the *helots*, as well as commerce (the domain of the *perioikoi*), thus allowing all males to devote their time to the army. This common non-agricultural experience arguably bonded together Spartan male citizens into a cohesive ethnic community, and even may have allowed for some degree of assimilation of foster sons of non-Spartan origins (*trophimoi*), although the evidence here is admittedly limited (Cawkwell, 1983; P. A. Davies, 2017; Hawkins, 2011).

Ancient Athens, in contrast to Sparta, had much lower levels of vertical hierarchy but arguably less horizontal commonality, inasmuch as not all of its male citizens were not subject to such a rigorous military regime. However, Athens was able to support 200,000 inhabitants more than its carrying capacity would have allowed, which it did through its manufacturing sector and foreign trade. More specifically, its industrial basis consisted of metalworking, leather-work, cosmetics, perfumes, textiles, clothing, footwear, pottery and wood-working, which it was able to exchange profitably with other neighbouring city states (Acton, 2014). The economic success of the Athenian city-state allowed for its numerous famous poets, scientists, mathematicians and philosophers to thrive as they could live entirely urban lives without any attachment to the countryside.

Another distinction between Sparta and Athens was the degree to which the latter allowed foreigners or non-Athenians to settle in the city and integrate into its culture. Assimilation was possible for men of mixed Athenian and foreign descent (*metroxenoi*), and only sporadically for women (Kennedy, 2014). Foreign men could move to Athens and be accepted as full members of the cultural community, with notable examples including such noted scholars as Anaxagoras (from Clazomenae in Asia Minor), Aristotle (from Stagira in Macedonia) and Herodotus (Halicarnassus in Asia Minor). These foreigners, or *metics*, generally could not acquire citizenship (which was bestowed by descent or, rarely, by naturalization) but gradually became up to half of the population of Athens at its height, despite having to pay a special annual tax (the *metoikion*) for the right to live in Athens and being unable to own land, receive special welfare payments and participate in the political life of the city. At least some 30 per cent of *metics* were involved in the manufacturing industry, or a higher proportion than for citizens (Acton, 2014, p. 304); one famous example is Polemarchus, at whose house the first book of Plato's *Republic* takes place and who owned a shield factory in the port city of Piraeus. Scholarly debate continues into the degree to which *metics* were fully able to assimilate into Athenian society, but the fact that Athenian authors such as Plato (in the *Republic*) and Euripides (in his play *Ion*) focussed attention on the complex relationship between *metics* and citizens suggests that some level of cultural and even political assimilation did take place (E. E. Cohen, 2000; Kasimis, 2018; Lape, 2010), at least until the distinction between *metics* and citizens began to erode in the 4th century BC.

In ancient Rome there is evidence of the rise – and fall – of a pan-ethnic common identity over the period of half a millennium. The process of creating a permanent citizenry not reliant upon agriculture for its livelihood should have, according to my theory, generated incentives for citizens to identify with broader communities as the Republic and then Empire became more urban and industrialized, but then later generated incentives to identify more with peripheral, smaller identities as the Empire declined and people returned to the land. And indeed, this is what the historical evidence suggests.

As in ancient Athens, the Roman Republic and later Empire was in part able to maintain large urban populations due to the creation of what some scholars call 'proto-industrial' employment. Many Roman towns, particularly in Gaul, had *fabricae* that employed thousands of people in metalworking and textile production, who in some cases were 'concentrated enough to be regulated like military units and even wore uniforms' (Dark, 2001, p. 25). In many cases towns seem to have been built up around manufacturing, such as the British pottery town of Water Newton (*Durobrivae*) (Dark, 2001, p. 26), although it is still worth noting that what made this style of production fundamentally different from modern industrial production is that the labour force was mostly made up of skilled artisans rather than the unskilled or semi-skilled workers who dominated production in the modern Industrial Revolution (Holleran, 2012, p. 28).

The creation and expansion of the Empire meant bringing even more ethnically varied populations under the control of Rome, which in theory should have prevented or hindered the development of a pan-Roman identity. Yet many Romans clearly conceived of their identity as civic or voluntary, such that it was 'theoretically accessible to all' who adhered to Roman law, in contrast to the more primordialist, descent-based identities ascribed to barbarians (Geary, 2002, p. 50). Roman identity was particularly associated with urban life for writers like Tacitus and Strabo (Lomas, 1998, p. 64), and especially with Rome itself, where rich provincial elites increasingly resided and built large urban villas (Whittacker, 1994, p. 141). Ethnic minorities could assimilate as Romans, with the main requirements a 'willingness to adopt a Roman world view and live in an appropriately Romanized manner' (Lomas, 1996, p. 139). Indeed, pre-Christian rural–urban migrants of non-Roman descent could even rise to become Emperor, as happened in the cases of Macrinus (from Mauretania in modern-day Algeria), Maximinus Thrax (from Moesia in modern-day Bulgaria), Marcus Julius Philippus (from Petrea in modern-day Syria) and Diocletian (from Dalmatia in modern-day Croatia). Other Emperors such as Claudius even celebrated the fact that many of the legendary kings of ancient Rome were of mixed ethnic descent (Gruen, 2013, pp. 2–3): thus, according to the Roman historian Livy in his *History of Rome*, the legendary King of Rome Lucius Tarquinius Priscus was prevented from rising in society in his native Tarquinii due to having a Greek refugee father and thus chose to emigrate to Rome on the advice of his wife. As the late fourth century poet Prudentius puts it, 'a common law makes us equal ... the native city embraces in its unifying walls fellow citizens' (Mathisen, 2009, p. 155).

Nor was the ability to assimilate limited to elites or residents of Rome. On the frontier of the Empire, many Batavians from the modern-day Netherlands re-identified as Romans and/or members of the civic urban community where they resided after receiving citizenship (Derks, 2009). Clear evidence that Romans had nested identities, with tribal/regional identities as sub-sets of a broader Roman identity, can be clearly in the Roman writer Cicero's claim in his *Laws* that:

All municipal [or urban] citizens have two countries – the one, that of their birth, and the other, that of their citizenship ... We justly consider as our country, both the place from where we originated and that in which we have been received. It is necessary, however, that we should attach ourselves by a preference of affection to the latter, which, under the name of the Commonwealth, is the common country of us all ... But still that land which produced us is not much less dear than that which has received us. Therefore I will never disown Arpinum [modern day Arpino, in central Italy] as my country, at the same time acknowledging that Rome is the greater of the two, and that *the other is contained in her*. (Emphasis added; Cicero, 1853, p. 429)

However, in keeping with my theory this process of assimilation was not common among many regional elites outside Rome who relied upon rural land ownership for their livelihoods and thus 'remained fiercely attached to the regions in which they owned their estates' (Geary, 2002, p. 67). Indeed, Roman law clearly distinguished between *provincialis* (provincials) and the *populus Romanus* (Roman people), with the former noted by identifying with their province (Mathisen, 2009, pp. 149–50). The power of urban, non-agrarian assimilation thus often failed to reach the provinces, where attachment to local land remained the primary salient identity for both elites and non-elites alike.

As the power of Rome gradually subsided and the population of Rome fell relative to other parts of the Empire, many Imperial citizens outside Rome re-adjusted their identities towards local identities that were better suited to their day-to-day lives (Derks, 2009; Geary, 2002, p. 59). Indeed, 'when the imperial political superstructure began to fall apart in the fifth century, people were forced to choose loyalties from among the new smaller communities within which they found themselves' (Amory, 1994, p. 5), such that Romans re-identified as barbarians rather than the other way around. This shift became increasingly the case to the point where, by the eighth century, the now dominant Lombards had assimilated Romans into their own identity within central Italy (Geary, 2002, p. 126). The circle had thus become complete, with the collapse of the Empire heralding the collapse of pan-Roman identities and the advent of more narrow, rural identities in large parts of southern Europe.

3.3 THE MODERN WORLD, WITH CASE STUDIES FROM EUROPE AND SOUTH AFRICA

Skipping forward by more than a millennium, the Industrial Revolution famously began in England in the eighteenth century, with technological innovation leading to more mechanization and the onset of rural–urban migration. The rest of Western Europe followed soon thereafter, as did the United States, Canada, Japan, Australia and New Zealand. The rise of industrialization in the modern world coincided with many other factors, including urbanization, democratization, the modern bureaucratic state and the demographic transition, but also the onset of the age of mass nationalism. As such, there has arguably been at times too much of a concern in the literature on nationalism on trying to understand the 'top-down' formation of nationalist ideologies and state policies rather than on understanding the 'bottom-up' rise of national identities and processes of ethnic homogenization, whether or not they were the result of elite or state influence.[1]

In this section my goal will be to sketch out how the increased salience of broader ethnic/national identities came about as a consequence of the

---

[1] To name just a few examples of this 'top-down' approach to understanding nationalism, see (Alesina, Reich & Riboni, 2020; Cinnirella & Schueler, 2018; Kedourie, 1960).

Gellnerian/Marxist processes identified in Chapter 1. I will focus largely on Western Europe, as that is where industrialization proceeded most rapidly in the nineteenth century, with special attention to Germany and especially the UK. However, I also discuss Eastern Europe and finish with the case of South Africa, historically the most industrialized country in Africa, where white settlers deliberately tried to interrupt or halt the processes of broader ethnic identity formation that governments elsewhere were eager to encourage.

3.3.1 European Case Studies

In Europe there is a great deal of evidence from the literature on nationalism that shows how industrialization has promoted assimilation. One of the most famous examples of this phenomenon is France, which has long been seen as having a strong sense of national identity. However, despite efforts by both the *Ancien Régime* and revolutionary state to promote a common sense of identity through the education system (Bell, 2001), most of France remained rural and remarkably linguistically and culturally diverse in the early nineteenth century. The key change that created a more unified country was industrialization: as the historian Eugen Weber famously argued, peasants became Frenchmen (and Frenchwomen) only in the late nineteenth century through the related processes of urbanization, industrialization and education and the resultant 'spread of urban values' (E. J. Weber, 1976, p. 22). More specifically, the Industrial Revolution led many peasants to migrate to urban areas, which they helped to homogenize by 'shattering the hold of local speech and lore in the urban centers' (E. J. Weber, 1976, p. 290). Thus, for instance, the new cotton industry in the Vosges region of eastern France 'all but wiped out the local dialect when country people moved into small industrial centers where French or an unfamiliar dialect obtained' (E. J. Weber, 1976, p. 78). Of course this process was not completely uniform, and thus areas that remained relatively agricultural and rural, such as the Flemish-speaking Westhoek region on the Belgian border, remained culturally distinct until later (Baycroft, 2004). But what makes France relatively unique in this regard is that Westhoek was the exception rather than the rule as France's industries were relatively evenly dispersed geographically: textiles were produced in Lyon, the North and Alsace; coal and iron in Auvergne, Lorraine and the North; canning and shipbuilding in Nantes and, more recently, aeronautics in Toulouse. Indeed, even rural areas famous for their distinctive agricultural products developed full-scale industries in the late nineteenth century, with the growth of the champagne industry, for instance, leading to the incorporation of its workers into a wider French national identity (Guy, 2003). The result was that assimilation took place not just in Paris but in multiple urban sites across the country, thereby dampening the development of any competing ethnic or national identities (Gourevitch, 1979, pp. 312–13).

France's more unified experience with industrialization and nationalism can be contrasted with several other European examples where uneven industrialization had important consequences on the development of modern national identities. One clear example is the rise of nationalism in the Spanish Basque country, which was historically organized according to largely 'autonomous' farmsteads that had few social or economic links between them (Heiberg, 1975, p. 191). While poverty drove many to emigrate to France and the USA in the early nineteenth century, a rise in iron ore production and steel manufacturing from the 1860s onwards led to in-migration and urbanization in Bilbao and other cities. This increase in economic activity led to the rise of a new Basque urban middle class, whose leading members began to promote a common sense of Basque identity and lobby the Spanish state for a separate status based on the unity of the Basque people.[2] The reason that industrialization led to an increase in Basque rather than Spanish national identity was because local rural–urban migrants moving to work in the new industrial economy headed to Bilbao rather than Madrid, which instead 'remained the political-administrative capital of an agrarian plateau' (Gourevitch, 1979, p. 311). Indeed, it is not accidental that the two most industrialized peripheral parts of Spain at the time, namely the Basque country and Catalonia, were the ones that developed the strongest support for separate national identities, whereas other less industrialized areas like Galicia or Valencia failed to develop any such strong sentiment (Payne, 1971, p. 42).

Another Western European case which saw uneven industrialization contribute to an uneven development of national identity was Belgium, where the nineteenth century saw the French-speaking southern region of Wallonia increasingly dominated by coal mining and steel industries in the *sillon industriel* (industrial furrow) that drew in workers from around the country, including from the northern Flemish-speaking Flanders region (Erk, 2005, p. 555). This rapid industrial revolution and the assimilation of these North-to-South internal migrants into the dominant Francophone culture led to what one set of authors calls the 'peak' of Belgian national identity between 1900 and 1925 (Degn, Hansen & Magnussen et al., 2004, p. 138). However, the late twentieth century saw a similarly rapid shift by which Wallonia increasingly de-industrialized while Flanders simultaneously drew upon light industries to become wealthier than Wallonia, a shift which was not, however, accompanied by a reversed South-to-North migration as the new industries were smaller in scale and could draw labour from nearby towns. This sudden change in economic position meant that there was no longer a common industrial hub where Belgians from different language communities came together, and thereby contributed to the rise of Flemish separatist nationalism.

In nineteenth-century Italy industrialization in the north was accompanied by a continued agrarian stagnation in the south. The result was some degree of

---

[2] In contrast, Basque nationalism initially 'encountered apathy in the rural areas' (Da Silva, 1975, p. 231).

South–North migration which was, however, overshadowed by huge amounts of emigration from southern Italy abroad, especially to North and South America. The continued relative lack of industrial, urban spaces for northern and southern Italians to interact with each other into the twentieth and twenty-first centuries led to the rise of the *Lega Nord* political party, which today claims a separate Padanian identity for northern Italy that has no historical precedent but which has nonetheless consistently won elections in northern Italy since the 1990s (Giordano, 2000). As with Belgium and Spain, it has been the richer, more industrialized North which has developed its own sense of regional or national identity. In contrast, however, the more agrarian South – whose residents continue to complain about being treated as backward or lazy by northern Italians (Johnson & Coleman, 2012) – has yet to develop a regional identity of its own, which is consistent with my theory.[3]

Like Western Europe, Eastern Europe also saw significant industrialization in the nineteenth and early twentieth centuries, albeit starting later and from a lower level, which transformed ethnic identities in the region.[4] For instance Bohemia (in what is now western Czechia) became the most industrialized region in the Austro-Hungarian Empire in the nineteenth century in large part due to its coal reserves and machine manufacturing industry in Prague. As elsewhere 'industrialization and urbanization drew displaced peasants into cities, fostered the growth of middle classes and eroded differences among people from different regions and speakers of different dialects' (Roshwald, 2001, pp. 15–16). The result was the birth of Czech nationalism in Bohemia, which was complicated by the presence of a sizeable German-speaking minority opposed to an independent Czech nation-state. Indeed, the fact that industrialization in Bohemia and elsewhere led to the growth of national identities rather than the consolidation of cross-ethnic class identities famously led the Austrian politicians Karl Renner and Otto Bauer to develop their Austro-Marxist theory of extraterritorial autonomy, where they argued that citizens should become recognized members of non-territorial national groups, thereby helping to de-politicize ethnicity and encourage class formation. This theory, while vigorously opposed by Bolshevik leaders in Russia and never

[3] Italy's 2018 legislative elections saw a very strong North–South divide, whereby centre-right and centre-left parties (including the *Lega Nord*) won in the North while the populist Five-Star Movement won in the South. Despite the fact that the leader of the Five Star Movement is from southern Italy, neither he nor the party claims to represent southern Italy.

[4] The different trajectories of nationalism in Western and Eastern Europe was famously simplified into a civic/ethnic divide by Kohn (1945), whereby in the former case national identities were built around civic bonds of citizenship while in the latter they were built around ethnic descent. This distinction can, to the degree which it accurately describes the two regions, in part be attributed to the historical lack of civic, urban spaces across much of Eastern Europe on which common civic bonds could be built. To take one example, what few nineteenth-century cities existed in what is now Belarus were inhabited not by Belarusians but by Jews, Poles and Lithuanians (Danskikh, 2008).

implemented in full, was nonetheless a rare and valiant attempt to marry industrialization, nationalism and Marxism into a unified framework.

Further east in Russia, industrialization and urbanization brought large number of people into St Petersburg, which became the eighth most populous city in the world by 1914. Of its 2.2 million inhabitants, over two-thirds were not born in the city and were largely of peasant extraction. Many of these migrants had been, in Trotsky's phrase, 'snatched from the plough and hurled into the factory furnace', and increasingly worked in large enterprises far from their rural homelands. The social effects of this structural change in cities like St Petersburg included a major disruption to Russia's age-old system of social estates in which citizens were grouped for tax purposes, and which persisted past the abolition of serfdom in 1861 up until the Russian Revolution (S. A. Smith, 2017, pp. 38–41), particularly as regards the distinction in cities between peasants and urban dwellers. The result, as Lilian Riga puts it, was the growth of 'new ethnic or interethnic identities based on occupation, profession, craft or culture' (Riga, 2012, p. 26), whose continued formation was radically interrupted by the 1917 Revolution and subsequent civil war.

In Ukraine, then on the western edge of the Russian Empire, coal mining began in the 1890s after the Welshman John Hughes founded a steel mill in the town which would be later named after him (Yuzovka, now Donetsk) in the Donets Coal Basin (or Donbas region), while further west the area around Kryvyi Rih became the Russian centre for iron production by 1900. This region increasingly drew in internal migrants from the Empire, including some local Ukrainian migrants but mostly Russian peasants from further afield. Those Ukrainians who migrated to the factories increasingly identified as Russian rather than the other way around (A. Miller, 2015, pp. 358–62), with Ukraine's first-ever census in 1926 showing a clear, positive correlation between levels of industrialization and Russian-language use among Ukrainians (Krawchenko, 1980, pp. 340–1). In contrast, in other areas of Ukraine peasants largely remained on the land and avoided industrial jobs, thereby halting any large-scale assimilation into Russian identity as happened in the Donbas. The result was a cultural split within Ukraine that led Donbas residents to refuse to join a Ukrainian Soviet Republic after the 1917 Revolution until they were told to do so by Moscow (Pirie, 1997, pp. 48–51), alongside evidence that inhabitants of Donetsk continued to identify with their multi-ethnic Donbas homeland rather than with Ukraine even before war broke out in the region in 2014 (Zimmer, 2007). The ongoing conflict in Ukraine between a pro-Russian East and a pro-EU West is thus in part a consequence of a history of uneven industrialization.

A final case from Eastern Europe is Romania, which, like other countries in the region, retained a largely agricultural economy up until World War II. Like other communist regimes in the post-war era, it focussed on promoting industrial growth as a part of a Cold War strategy to match Western Europe; however, Gheorghe Gheorghiu-Dej's government was unusually obsessed with industrialization as part of its break with Moscow, which wanted Romania to continue to produce agricultural products. As such, Romania's industrial production increased more than five-fold between 1953 and 1968, or more than any other country in Europe during that time span (Chirot, 1978, p. 471). As part of this policy the government not only focussed attention on rapid housing construction in major cities like Bucharest but also deliberately encouraged the creation of industrial employment in more rural areas in order to avoid uneven industrialization (Chirot, 1978, p. 475). The result of this profound shift was to encourage large numbers of peasants to work in the urban industrial economy and thereby re-orientate their sense of solidarity away from their rural brethren and instead towards the Romanian nation (Petrescu, 2009, p. 532). The downfall of the communist regime led to a re-balancing of the economy away from industry, leading both to net urban–rural migration and increased social tensions, such that former mining areas like the Jiu valley 'have very diverse communities initially united by the danger of working underground but strongly divided today' (Constantinescu, Dascălu & Sucală, 2017, p. 119).

I now turn to the more detailed case study of post-unification Germany, which had two major industrial sites in the Ruhr Valley in the west and Silesia in the east. To start with the former, the valley north of the Ruhr River and east of the Rhine became the centre of Germany's heavy industry from the 1830s onwards, first with coal and then later focussing on iron and steel. In particular, the advent of steam engines in the early nineteenth century allowed workers to mine much deeper for coal than they had been able to before, which created a huge demand for workers from across Prussia and, after 1871, Germany. Many migrants who came from neighbouring regions, or *Nahwanderer*, took up more middle-class positions, while those from further afield, the *Fernwanderer*, were more likely to take lower-class jobs (Tampke, 1978, p. 5). One such group that migrated to the region were some 400,000 Poles from Germany's more agricultural eastern territories, who were recruited by agents looking for cheap unskilled and semi-skilled labourers. So many Polish-speakers migrated west that by the beginning of the twentieth century some 30 per cent of workers in the Ruhr were from the Polish-majority provinces of eastern Germany. For the most part these migrants began to integrate themselves into local life: as the son of one Polish migrant later wrote, 'there was no antagonism between [Germans and Poles]. Their work united them.' Indeed, Poles and German Catholics found common interests, such as at the Fifth Festival of Catholic Associations in Dortmund in 1885 when they came together for speeches and discussion and ended their meeting with salutes to both the Kaiser and the Pope. As the German historian Volker Berghahn notes, the Ruhr area was thus marked by both 'feelings of solidarity' and 'political cooperation' between Germans and Poles, who were keen on integrating themselves into their new home (Berghahn, 1999, pp. 21–6).

However, both mine owners and the German government tried to halt the integration of Polish migrant workers. In the former case employers deliberately encouraged residential segregation in order to prevent class solidarity. In the latter and arguably more consequential case Otto von Bismarck's new German government targeted the migrants as part of the state's *Kulturkampf* (cultural struggle) against the Catholic Church and against the opposition Catholic Centre Party. This policy was also driven by Bismarck's anti-Polish sentiments, derived in part from concerns about the potential for secession or armed conflict in Germany's Polish-majority eastern regions. The result was increasingly draconian regulation on the use of the Polish language, leading up to making it outright illegal to speak any language but German in the *Reichsvereingesetz* (Imperial Association Law) of 1908, as well as the increasing prominence of radical German nationalists who denied the possibility of Polish integration and assimilation and sought to remove Poles outright from German territory. The inevitable result was a backlash among the Polish migrants, whose cultural associations became increasingly politicized and whose rates of inter-ethnic marriage with Germans began to decline. Thus, 'by the time of the outbreak of World War I prospects of a further radicalization of German official policies and attitudes had replaced all hopes for the integration and long-term voluntary assimilation of a sizeable ethnic group into German society' (Berghahn, 1999, p. 28).

These tensions between Germans and Poles in the Ruhr were, however, significantly reduced after World War I with the creation of a Polish nation-state and the Weimar Republic, which re-introduced laws protecting minority languages. While some Ruhr Poles chose to migrate to the new Polish state or west to France or the USA, the large number who chose to stay in Germany saw more opportunities for integration and assimilation, including running for and winning office in local elections up until 1933 (Murphy, 1983, p. 3). There is thus evidence of Ruhr Poles 'Germanizing' their names in the 1920s and 1930s, while football players of Polish descent not only became prominent members of the famous local FC Schalke 04 team but also joined the German national team (Blecking, 2015, pp. 288–9), at least up until Hitler took power in 1933 and revived the anti-Polish sentiment of the Reich.

A different situation arose in Germany's other major industrial belt of Silesia, which is now part of Poland but which was previously mostly part of the German Empire prior to World War I (with a small part controlled by Austro-Hungary). Starting from the early nineteenth century the region saw the development of a large-scale coal and steel conurbation that was densely linked by railways, and consequently drew in many local migrants who spoke a diverse group of German and Polish dialects, but not large numbers of migrants from other parts of Germany. However, those Germans who did emigrate to the region largely did so to take high-paid administrative positions, which led to an initial three-fold division of labour along ethnic lines in the greater region between German bureaucrats, Silesian labourers and Polish farmers (Wódz & Wódz, 2006, pp. 83–5).

The mixing of populations that happened in the industrial areas of Silesia over decades led to an increasingly coherent form of Silesian identity alongside a new Silesian German-Polish creole – which 'predominated among workers in factories and mines' (Kamusella, 2005, p. 450) – and a separatist movement that wanted to establish a Silesian nation-state in opposition to both Germany and Poland. However, the partition of Silesia after World War I saw both German and Polish state officials suppressing any sense of common identity in the region – which the Germans saw as too Polish, and the Poles as too German – and this suppression continued after the territory was unified, first under Nazi rule and then as part of Poland after World War II. The staying power of the Silesian ethnic identity, forged through industrialization despite nearly a century of assimilative nation-building policies of one kind or another, can be seen in the fact that over 170,000 people identified as Silesian in the 2002 Polish census, making it the largest ethnic minority in the country (Kamusella, 2004).

The second major European case study I wish to examine here is England (and the UK), which many writers on the topic of nationalism have identified as the first nation in the modern world, although they differ radically on the timing of when the English nation came to be. I briefly revisit this debate with a focus on the role of urbanization, industrialization and non-agricultural employment in the creation of an English national identity. I then compare the English experience with that of Scotland, Wales and Northern Ireland, where industrialization similarly played a major role in the formation of modern national identities.

Beginning with medieval England, there is plenty of evidence of pre-modern urbanization and industrialization, such that, by the end of the eleventh century, a significant percentage of English residents 'no longer lived in isolated farmsteads or in hamlets, but in villages and market towns' (Gillingham, 1992, p. 400). In contrast to the much more rural Celtic peripheral areas of Britain, England had a functioning money economy open to all: as one observer from the 1180s put it, 'no one keen on making money need die poor here' (Gillingham, 1992, p. 401). Indeed, it is this proto-industrialization of England which allowed its government to mass-manufacture ammunition and thus expand its reach over Ireland and Wales while defeating the Scots in battle in the late Middle Ages (Gillingham, 1992, p. 402). It is thus not a coincidence, then, that a variety of historians find evidence for a self-conscious English national identity in this period, with a sense of common, distinctive ethnic identity present among at least a substantial minority of the population (Foot, 1996; Gillingham, 1992; Turville-Petre, 1996). The incipient levels of urbanization and industrialization in England were thus able to dissipate regional identities as well as integrate those of foreign descent such as the Danes and Normans.

Moving on to the sixteenth century, England continued to have a relatively high level of urbanization and non-agricultural employment compared to other parts of the British Isles and Europe more generally due to the enclosures, a shift to larger farms and harsher poor laws, a trend that continued through the seventeenth, eighteenth and nineteenth centuries (O'Brien, 1996). Trade with the New World led both to the rise of a class of people reliant upon trade and seafaring for their livelihoods as well as new amounts of wealth concentrated in cities. These 'push and pull' factors led to large amounts of migration to London from all around England, particularly from the Midlands in central England. One such migrant was the playwright William Shakespeare, along with many of his fellow poets and actors such as Michael Drayton, Fulke Greville, John Heminges and Richard Tarlton; other English migrants to London in the sixteenth and seventeenth centuries also included major cultural figures like the historians John Foxe (from Lincolnshire) and Thomas Fuller (Northamptonshire), bookseller John Playford (East Anglia) and the poets Edward Dyer (Somerset) and John Dryden (Northamptonshire).

As such, the sociologist Liah Greenfeld, like Kohn (1945) before her, identifies the genesis of English national identity in the Tudor Reformation period of the sixteenth century. Basing her argument partially on the end of English claims to France after the Hundred-Years War as well as the birth of an English national church under Henry VIII, she also explicitly ties much of the birth of the English nation to a new period of 'unprecedented mobility' that drew in a growing middle class, due in part to the demise of the clergy after Henry VIII split from Rome (Greenfeld, 1992, p. 47). This rising urban elite was both diverse in terms of its origins and increasingly educated at university, where intermixing also occurred.[5] While some have disputed the degree to which this middle class was actually new or just larger than before (Kumar, 2003), it is still clear that much if not most of those who conceived of themselves as English in this period drew their incomes in cities and not from agricultural rent.

Lastly, we turn to the onset of the Industrial Revolution in the eighteenth century, when the Kingdom of Great Britain (as it became in 1707) saw rising incomes via rural–urban migration and the creation of a new non-agrarian workforce. This period saw a sharp rise in the number of urban residents, with England reaching twice the Western European average level of urbanization by the late eighteenth century (Wrigley, 1985, p. 707). This period also marked the greater integration of Scotland and Wales into an actual British economy for the first time, as well as the ever-increasing might of the British Empire, both of which created spaces within Britain and abroad, respectively, where British citizens found commonalities with each other beyond the confines of their rural identities.

---

[5] There is a separate literature on the role of Europe's urban universities in promoting broader ethnic and national identification which I do not have the space to cover here; cf. Kibre (1948).

As such, the historian Linda Colley turns towards the eighteenth century as the definitive century for the formation of a British, not English, identity. While Colley's argument is primarily about the role of Protestantism and wars against the French in the formation of the British nation, she nonetheless acknowledges the way that urbanization and industrialization promoted an attachment to the idea of Britain, such that 'men and women living in or near towns ... seem always to have been among the busiest and most reliable of patriots' (L. Colley, 1992, p. 369). As with Greenfeld, Colley also places special emphasis on London's role in bringing people together from all across Britain: not only did it house a much larger proportion of the state's population than Paris or Madrid, it also brought together the commercial and political elite in one location (L. Colley, 1992, p. 64).

Inasmuch as urbanization was not, however, evenly spread throughout Britain, we should not expect to see a uniform attachment to this new British identity, and indeed Colley suggests that a lack of urbanization in eighteenth-century Wales was in part responsible for its citizens' ethnic distinctiveness and lack of interest in joining the British army (L. Colley, 1992, pp. 295–6). Indeed, the formation of Scottish and Welsh national identities also deserve some attention in this context. As for the former, historically Scotland was even more ethnically diverse than England, with its strong Lowland/Highland divide that overlapped with strong linguistic, religious and cultural divisions, not to mention a history of distinct clan identities within the Highlands (Carter, 1974). Even after Scotland was subsumed into the Kingdom of Great Britain, with its Parliament dissolved after 1707, it still maintained national institutions such as the Kirk and its own legal and university system, all of which allowed for Scots of various backgrounds to interact in non-agrarian settings and plausibly led to some form of national identity before the Industrial Revolution (Withers, 2001). But there is substantial evidence that Scotland's various communities really began to be subsumed into a broader Scottish identity in the eighteenth and nineteenth centuries as various forces – including the Empire but also processes such as the Highland Clearances and agricultural modernization that contributed to industrialization and urbanization – incentivized individuals in Scotland to identify in broader terms, both as Scottish and British (Davidson, 2000). Rural–urban migration to cities such as Dundee, Edinburgh and particularly Glasgow – or the 'second city of the Empire' as it was known in the nineteenth century – led to a decline in Gaelic-language use from around 25 per cent of the Scottish population in the early eighteenth century to 6–7 per cent in the late nineteenth century (Withers, 1998). At the same time, uneven economic growth within the UK, whereby England maintained higher levels of income per capita throughout the process of industrialization, meant that Scotland – and the broader Celtic periphery – functioned as an 'internal colony' to put it in the language of Hechter (1975). This Gellnerian emphasis on the consequences of uneven industrialization on the development of Scottish nationalism in particular is also echoed in Tom Nairn's *The Break-Up of Britain,* which is even more explicitly based on a dependency theory model of industrial cores and peripheries as an explanation for the rise of nationalism in Scotland and the world more generally (Nairn, 1977).

We now turn to Wales, whose independent institutions, unlike in Scotland, were abolished far before the advent of industrialization and nationalism in the sixteenth century. Wales was for centuries largely considered a backwater of England and never given equal billing as one of the constituent nations of the UK alongside Ireland, England and Scotland, as still seen today in its lack of representation of the British Royal Standard or flag of the Sovereign.[6] However, the growth in employment in Wales's coalfields and slate quarries in the nineteenth century 'brought about something like the birth of a self-conscious Welsh nation out of a traditional Welsh peasantry' (Hobsbawm, 1999, p. 279). Thus, as one Welsh historian put it, 'if there was one outstanding cradle of the Welsh national revival, it can be found ... amid the blast furnaces and winding-shafts of the working-class metropolis of Merthyr Tydfil' (K. O. Morgan, 1971, p. 156). Yet at the same time industrialization also brought about the spread of English in Wales, as it also did in Scotland, thereby aiding the simultaneous growth in identification with a broader British identity.

Finally, we turn to Northern Ireland, where Belfast became a world-famous industrial centre for both shipbuilding and linen manufacturing in the nineteenth century, such that its population doubled between 1841 and 1871 and doubled again between 1871 and 1901 (when it overtook Dublin in population). This rapid urban growth drew both Protestants and Catholics into contiguous areas of Belfast, which, according to two authors, 'provided the basis for violent conflict ever since' (Hayes & McAllister, 2001, p. 902). At first glance the Northern Irish experience would appear to provide counter-evidence for my argument, inasmuch as we would expect industrialization to produce broader identity formation rather than sectarian conflict. Yet a more nuanced reading of industrialization in Northern Ireland suggests both that industrialization did indeed yield some degree of broader identity formation via the Belfast Trades Council and various pan-sectarian strikes organized by trade unionists like James Larkin (Moore, 1972, p. 27), and also that sectarian differences were an example of what Gellner (2006 [1983], p. 64) called 'entropy-resistant traits' that could not be broken down by industrialization. Indeed, even Marxist scholars of the Troubles in Northern Ireland have recognized the degree to which the 'false consciousness' of sectarian differences 'was to a degree turned into "true consciousness" of real interests', in part due to state opportunities provided to Protestants in Northern Ireland that reinforced

---

[6] The current Royal Standard, which originated in Queen Victoria's time, has quadrants representing Ireland, England and Scotland; when flown in Scotland the Scottish quadrant is represented twice, while when flown anywhere else, the English quadrant is represented twice.

sectarian identities (Moore, 1972, p. 29).[7] Having said all of this, the timing of the Troubles in the context of the economic history of Northern Ireland is noteworthy: de-industrialization after World War II, which saw the sharp decline in both linen production and shipbuilding and the rise of unemployment, arguably contributed to the rise of sectarian violence in the 1960s (Rolston, 1980, p. 74), while the economic growth of the 1990s helped bring the conflict to an end (as did a decline in religiosity). The Northern Ireland experience thus provides some evidence both for the role of industrialization in preventing sectarian violence but also for the importance in understanding the role of religion as an 'entropy-resistant trait' in halting broader identity formation.

In conclusion, the result of this centuries-long process of the formation of multiple, nested British identities was the emergence and maintenance of English, Scottish and Welsh ethnic identities and a British national identity which only partially subsumed the former, while sectarianism complicated identity formation in Northern Ireland. This strange hybrid existence – as exemplified by the existence of English, Northern Irish, Scottish and Welsh football teams, but a British (and Irish) Davis Cup and Olympics team – is in many ways a consequence of the fact that industrialization in the British Isles both preceded and was coterminous to the creation of the UK and the formation of a British national identity. The continued conflicts over British vs English/Irish/Scottish/Welsh nationalism – manifested most recently in the debates over Brexit – are thus a legacy of centuries of identity formation, industrialization and political change.

3.3.2 The South African Case Study

I examine multiple African case studies later in the book, but here it is important to briefly touch upon the one major case of industrialization in Africa prior to decolonization, which is South Africa. What makes South Africa distinct from my European examples was that the political and economic elite was not only from a different ethnic group as the rural–urban migrants working in industrial areas (as in Bohemia and the Ruhr valley), but that they were from a completely different racial group, with the former largely comprised of the descendants of Dutch, French and British settlers while the latter consisted of members of native African ethnic groups. Moreover, unlike in Europe, this white South African elite was vastly outnumbered by the South African black community. Cognizant of the 'entropy resistant' nature of racial barriers which foreclosed significant assimilation between racial groups as well as their demographic inferiority, the white South African elite thus grew very concerned

---

[7] Note the similarities in the way the Catholic–Protestant divide halted larger identity formation in Northern Ireland to the way the Catholic–Protestant divide inhibited similar processes in the aforementioned case of Germany's Ruhr valley.

about the way industrialization encouraged broader identity formation among black South Africans and adopted increasingly harsh measures to disrupt this process.

The history of industrialization in South Africa began with the discovery of diamonds and, most importantly, gold in the late nineteenth century, which led to a massive rise in the demand for cheap indigenous labour and the migration of more than 50,000 black Africans per year to the mines in the early 1870s. Mining drew in huge amounts of external capital as well as continued European settlement and generated high levels of economic growth over the next century. The expanding economy led members of the white elite to consolidate their various settler states into the Union of South Africa in 1910.

However, the geology of South Africa's mineral sites meant that production costs were high, and efforts by the white elite who owned the mines to get enough Africans to continue to come and work on them on low wages were not very successful as many Africans still preferred to labour on their own farms and on their own terms. The resultant high rates of desertion and concomitant high pay in order to keep workers on site thus led to the local *Diamond News* calling black labour both 'the most expensive in the world' and 'the most unmanageable' in 1872 (Meredith, 2007, p. 43). After trying and failing to fill this demand through enticing Chinese and Indian immigrants, the white settler minority increasingly oppressed the indigenous African majority by expropriating their rural farmland and imposing new taxes which had to be paid in cash, in order to compel local men to work for cheap in the mines.

Yet, while successful at generating the necessary labour force on the mines, the effect of this forced migration was, as elsewhere, an increase in inter-ethnic solidarity among 'detribalized' Africans that had the potential to threaten white minority rule (Van den Berghe, 1967, pp. 49–50). Thus there was a serious concern among officials in the British War Office in the 1900s that a breakdown in chiefly authority as a result of emigration to the mines would mean a 'general fusion of the hitherto antagonistic tribes' and thus result in a great threat to white settlers (Harries, 1989, p. 98). Similarly, the South African Native Recruiting Corporation of the Chamber of Mines expressed a concern during a strike in 1920 that 'the different tribes will become more and more in sympathy with one another, with a growing disregard of loyalty to their respective tribal chiefs and a fusion of common interests under the guidance of the educated classes of natives' (Harries, 1989, p. 99).

The result was various efforts by the white elite to disrupt broader identity formation among black South Africans. Thus the mine owners not only gave the African workers fixed-term contracts (from a few months up to a maximum of two years), after which they had to return back to their rural homelands, but also stopped men from bringing their wives and children with them as a means to discourage permanent urban settlement. Miners were housed in hostels which were designed like prisons, inasmuch as they were largely closed to the outside world. Mine managers deliberately recruited workers from different areas in order to create an ethnically diverse workforce, with the miners governed by their own ethnically specific *induna* (middle manager) and housed along ethnically segregated lines in order to prevent worker solidarity (Crush, 1994, p. 311). Any attempts by African workers to form unions were suppressed, such as the crushing of the African Mineworkers Union after a strike in 1946. Finally, in 1948 white voters elected the pro-segregation National Party to power, which began to formalize the system of apartheid that instituted the use of pass laws and promoted African residence in separate rural tribal Bantustans. Apartheid legislation in particular focussed on preventing Africans from living in cities, which included a law that removed South African citizenship from blacks (in place of citizenship of one of the ten Bantustans, whose political independence was only recognized by South Africa), while other laws declared that Africans could only live in urban areas if they had formal employment, could not run a business in a city without a special permit and always had to carry their identity documents with them. At the high point of apartheid in the 1960s and 1970s the government forcibly resettled at least two million Africans, including both Africans removed from inner cities to far-distant townships and a large number of 'surplus' or 'idle blacks' taken from cities back to their tribal homelands (Turok, 2012, p. 9).

All of these measures were moderately successful in preventing inter-ethnic solidarity in opposition to the apartheid regime, at least initially. However, Africans continued to migrate to cities both because of the poor living conditions in the Bantustans (which had low quality land and no industries to speak of) and due to the demand for labour in the non-mining industrial and service sectors. Coupled with a growing black population and a relative decline in the demand for labour which saw a rapid increase in unemployment, the result was large African populations in major cities that grew increasingly militant. Attempts to replicate the ethnically segregated nature of the Bantustans and mining hostels in the townships though a system of indirect rule failed, leading to military rule by the apartheid state (Ashforth, 1997, p. 115). In response to demands from the African labourers the government legalized trade unions in 1979, which led to the establishment of the National Union of Mineworkers (NUM) in 1982 under the leadership of future President of South Africa Cyril Ramaphosa. The NUM was instrumental in helping to defuse the ethnic tensions that arose within the segregated mining hostels and in breaking the power of the ethnic *induna* through the creation of elected committees in the mines, thereby contributing towards greater inter-ethnic solidarity (Bezuidenhout & Buhlungu, 2010, pp. 247–9). The townships that housed so many of the African urbanites became the centre of the anti-apartheid struggle by the 1980s and were increasingly run by community-organized Civic Associations which were organized across ethnic lines. The efforts of the white minority to prevent inter-ethnic solidarity and identity formation among black South Africans thus ultimately failed with the election of the ANC to power in the 1994 elections under the leadership of Nelson Mandela.

3.4 CONCLUSION

In this chapter I have examined evidence from both pre-modern and modern eras to show that the homogenizing effects of industrialization and urbanization are widespread. A variety of case studies from ancient Greece and Rome to various countries in Europe and South Africa illuminated how the creation of a class of people who rely upon labour rather than access to land for their livelihoods allowed new broader identities to form in a variety of contexts. In contrast, however, uneven industrialization – as in the cases of Belgium, Italy, Spain and Ukraine – has led to the uneven development of broader national identities, which has in turn contributed to the creation of regional and independence movements.

I have two points to make here before concluding this chapter. First, as noted above my focus on Europe was determined by its historical importance to both Marx and Gellner, as well as other theorists of nationalism and ethnicity, as well as its longer history of industrialization and urbanization than other parts of the world. This choice should not be taken as a sign that there exists strong counter-evidence to my argument from other parts of the world. To take one region not examined elsewhere in this book, there is evidence from multiple countries across the Asia-Pacific region for the role of industrialization in promoting ethnic homogenization and assimilation in the twentieth century. For instance, in Malaysia rural–urban migration has led to the consolidation of regional and national identities (Bruner, 1961; Chai, 1996), while in South Korea industrialization has promoted the formation of broader identity formation among workers who formerly had 'no sense of collective identity beyond family or kinship circles' (Koo, 2001, p. 11). Rural villagers' ethnic identification in mid-twentieth century north-east Thailand was based on 'local differences and emphases', in contrast to migrants to Bangkok from the same region who increasingly held 'wider ethnic orientations' (Keyes, 1966, p. 364). In Taiwan large-scale urbanization among indigenous peoples has led to broader forms of aboriginal identification very much along the lines in the USA and New Zealand that I discuss later in the book (Huang & Liu, 2016). Finally, in Papua New Guinea migrants to urban areas have abandoned their local tribal identities in favour of regional identities or even a 'highland' vs 'coastal' dichotomy (Levine, 1999, p. 170).

Second, one common feature about the processes of ethnic homogenization described above is that they took place in many instances despite state efforts, not because of them. Many of my examples provided evidence of governments trying to prevent the formation of broader ethnic identities outside the control of the state inasmuch as they posed a threat to political order, such as in the case of Polish and German workers in the Ruhr Valley of Imperial Germany. But the most obvious example here is the case of South Africa, whose white minority elite worked hard to prevent not only inter-racial integration but even inter-ethnic solidarity among its black majority.

In contrast, there exist numerous cases of modern states which attempted to promote assimilation among their citizens but failed, including efforts by Imperial Germany and Russia, Revolutionary France and Franco's Spain to ban the use of minority languages. Nor are these cases of failed nation-building limited to Europe: activist governments in Africa whose nation-building policies failed spectacularly include the Democratic Republic of Congo under the leadership of Mobutu Sese Seko, whose efforts to 'Africanize' his name, the name of the country and the names of major cities while also abolishing federalism, nationalizing land ownership, outlawing ethnic associations and promoting new national dresses and dances all failed to halt the descent into Africa's bloodiest-ever civil war in the late 1990s. Similarly, in Ethiopia, Emperor Haile Selassie's efforts in promoting both religious and linguistic homogenization in addition to creating a national service scheme for university students led not to assimilation but instead to the fall of the monarchy, civil war, famine, the secession of Eritrea and the creation of an ethnic federal system in the 1990s (Bandyopadhyay & Green, 2013). In later chapters I shall describe in more detail similar failed attempts at promoting a common identity among Native Americans and in twentieth-century Turkey, all of which suggest the limited ability of states to control identity formation in unfavourable circumstances.

4

Cross-National Evidence

4.1 INTRODUCTION

The evidence presented in the previous chapter suggests that industrialization historically played a major role in making societies more ethnically homogenous via the creation of non-agricultural employment and the declining relative value of land. In this chapter I test this argument by using two separate cross-national datasets that cover 168 countries and the period 1960–2018 between them. I use carbon emissions per capita as my main measure of industrialization (with alternative measures) and show that industrialization is robustly correlated with both ethnic fractionalization (negatively) and the proportion of the population identifying with the largest ethnic group in each country (positively).

There are several ways to go about examining the quantitative relationship between industrialization and ethnic diversity. The simplest way would be to regress a measure of ethnic diversity on some measure of industrialization in a cross-sectional database in order to see if there is a correlation between lower levels of diversity and higher levels of industrialization. However, there are two problems with examining a cross-sectional relationship between industrialization and ethnic diversity. First, a cross-sectional correlation does nothing to identify the causal relationship between the variables. In particular it could be that industrialization causes lower diversity, or lower diversity causes industrialization, or that both variables are the result of a third unknown variable, such as economic growth and/or increasing state capacity. Inasmuch as the goal of this book is to show that industrialization causes homogenization, this type of analysis is not particularly helpful.

A second such problem is that countries measure ethnicity in different ways. One issue is particularly important here, namely the fact that in some countries the largest ethnic group is the ethnic majority or *Staatsvolk*, as discussed in

Chapter 2. In such countries being French or Japanese has two meanings, one at a narrower ethnic level and one as a broader national identity, and censuses do not distinguish between these two meanings. In other parts of the world like Sub-Saharan Africa or settler societies such as the USA and Australia, however, the largest ethnic group is not a *Staatsvolk*, such that being a member of the largest group is not the same thing as being a member of the national community. The result is that in countries like Germany or Vietnam one can claim on a census to be ethnically German or Vietnamese, while in Kenya or Canada, for example, there are no census options allowing one to identify as ethnically Kenyan or Canadian, which means that comparing ethnic diversity across these two sets of countries is problematic. As such I control here for country-specific factors, either by using a long-difference regression, where I regress change over two points in time in levels of ethnic diversity on change in industrialization in a cross-sectional dataset,[1] or by including country fixed effects with panel data. In both cases the result is that I am only measuring change across time within each country.

In the rest of the chapter I examine the quantitative relationship between industrialization and ethnic diversity, first in my use of Soviet ethnographic data from 1961 and 1985, and the second from a new, original database of individual country censuses from 1960 to 2018. In each case I describe the data and focus on the robustness of my results.

4.2 INDUSTRIALIZATION AND ETHNIC CHANGE, 1961–1985, WITH SOVIET DATA

One of the more important sources for researchers into the history of ethnic diversity across countries is the country-level ELF scores for 1961 and 1985 from the two editions of the Soviet *Atlas Narodov Mira* (henceforth ANM), both of which were authored or co-authored by the Russian ethnographer Solomon Bruk (Bruk, 1986; Bruk & Apenchenko, 1964). The data for the two Atlases were themselves based on individual country censuses, UN data, Soviet ethnographic journals and other sources, and each edition lists the total population for each country before listing individual ethnic groups and their sizes, often in a large amount of detail. For instance, the 1985 dataset lists 148 ethnic groups for Indonesia ranging in population from 74 million Javanese and 20.5 million Sundanese to 5,000 Wodani, 4,000 Manusela and 3,000 Ambelau, among others. In other cases the Atlas lists the population of

---

[1] This is the same rationale for using long-difference regressions in examining the effect of life expectancy on economic growth (Acemoglu & Johnson, 2007), military expenditure on trade (Acemoglu & Yared, 2010), trade on economic growth (Feyrer, 2009) and GDP/capita on happiness (Stevenson & Wolfers, 2008). It is notable that all of these papers are from economics; the practice of using long-difference regressions in other social science disciplines seems to be quite rare.

very small ethnic groups, such as the Alacalufe of Argentina and Chile, whose populations in 1985 were estimated at 100 and 200 people, respectively. However, in a small number of very homogenous countries such as Haiti, Japan and Poland, the ANM only lists one ethnic group per country, with the rest of the population listed as 'other'; I address this issue in more detail below. (See Appendix Table A.3 for a list of all countries included in the dataset.)

The dataset – which was originally collated by Roeder (2001) but which I independently confirmed from the original sources[2] – is ideal for my purposes for several reasons. First, unlike in a previously well-used dataset from C. L. Taylor and Hudson (1972), the Soviet data treats groups like Hutus and Tutsis in Rwanda and Burundi and African Americans and European Americans in the USA as separate groups despite the fact that they speak the same language. Thus it can record ethnic assimilation from smaller to larger groups, and can also account for assimilation from ethnic minorities into ethno-national identities in such states as France, Russia and China. Second, it has long been the only extant dataset that measures changes in ethnicity over time across the whole world.[3] Third and finally, it covers a large enough amount of time to uncover substantial amounts of ethnic change.

The dataset is, however, slightly problematic for two reasons. First, several countries are missing from the dataset. The Soviet data does not include, for instance, ELF scores for small countries or territories like Monaco, Kiribati, Montserrat and Western Sahara. More importantly, the dataset excludes countries whose borders changed during the period in question, namely Bangladesh/ Pakistan and Vietnam; in other cases of countries which subsequently united (like Germany and Yemen) or split up (Czechoslovakia, the USSR and Yugoslavia) the Soviet data exists but is unusable due to the absence of measures of carbon emissions and/or international migration data.

Second, the ANM dataset is potentially problematic due to its reliance upon census data, inasmuch as it is possible that it is not really capturing ethnic identity but rather identities imposed or at least circumscribed by state officials (B. Anderson, 1991; Kertzer & Arel, 2002; Nagel, 1994). While this would be a serious problem if one was only examining a cross-sectional relationship, the use of long-difference regressions mean that such census inaccuracies would cancel out as long as they are consistent across the two Atlases. To ensure consistency I examined whether groups listed for one country in one Atlas were listed in the other; for cases where the listings are not consistent I either

---

[2] I departed from Roeder's (2001) data in several cases to better reflect change in ethnic identities, as detailed in Appendix A.5 below.

[3] This is in contrast to Wimmer, Cederman & Min (2009), who collect country-level data on change in ethnic fractionalization across time but only for politically relevant ethnic groups, and Alesina et al. (2003) and Fearon (2003), who do not attempt to provide a snapshot of ELF data for a single year. Campos & Kuzeyev (2007) compile data on ethnic change between 1989 and 2002, but only for twenty-six post-communist countries.

corrected the data or deleted the countries from the analysis, as detailed in Appendix Table A.5. I also examined sub-sets of countries which exclude potentially problematic cases as identified in the literature, as explained below. One such group would be former British colonies, which arguably have a legacy of greater fractionalization than other former colonies due to a colonial interest in preventing ethnic homogenization (A. L. Robinson, 2014); another includes African and European countries, which have lower rates of ethnic enumeration on censuses than other parts of the world (Morning, 2008).

I use change in the log of metric tons of carbon dioxide (CO_2) emissions per capita as my primary measure of industrialization for the reasons noted in Chapter 2.[4] While the data quality for carbon emissions is high, for smaller countries there is the concern that measurement errors in population size could bias my results, leading me to drop micro-states which had a population of less than 50,000 in 1961 such as Bermuda and Greenland from my analysis.

4.2.1 Data Analysis

My empirical analysis uses change in ELF between 1961 and 1985 as the primary dependent variable, with change in log of carbon emissions per capita between 1961 and 1985 as the primary independent variable. I also add one control variable to all regressions, namely change in the percentage of immigrants between 1960 and 1985.[5] Such an exercise allows me to test the primordial assumption that ethnicity will only change due to the entry and exit of people from the population group in question, namely via international migration. (Inasmuch as variance decreases with population size the migration data suffers from heteroscedasticity, leading me to employ robust standard errors.)

As I use two different regression models in this chapter, for clarity's sake the long-difference model can be expressed as

$$\Delta ELF_i = \zeta + \gamma_1 \Delta CE_i + \gamma_2 \Delta M_i + \varepsilon_i$$

where for country i ΔELF_i is change in ELF between 1961 and 1985, ΔCE_i is change in carbon emissions and ΔM_i is change in the percentage of migrants, and ε_i is a normally distributed error term.

Of course, when using a relatively small number of observations it is important to check for outliers which may be driving any results. Therefore I used the DFBETA outlier detector tool and found three clear outliers, namely Kuwait, Qatar and the United Arab Emirates.[6] In all three cases local labour shortages

---

[4] As with some other variables here I take the average value between 1960 and 1962 to account for missing values.

[5] The change in the beginning date is due to the fact that, like other demographic data from the UN, this variable is measured in five-year increments.

[6] Kuwait, Qatar and the UAE all had DFBETA values of |1.3| or greater for either change in carbon emissions or change in migrant stock, with no other observation above |0.6|.

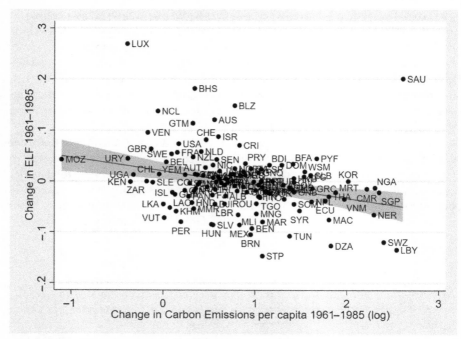

FIGURE 4.1. Change in ELF and carbon emissions, ANM data

led governments to recruit large numbers of workers from other parts of the Middle East and South Asia to work in their oilfields, which saw immigrants becoming the majority of the population between 1960 and 1975. Moreover, population data in these countries is notoriously questionable, as noted in an earlier attempt to collect cross-national ELF data by Fearon (2003, p. 219). As a result I exclude all three countries from my analysis here. (For descriptive statistics and more complete definitions of the variables see Panel A of Appendix Table A.1 and Appendix Table A.4, respectively.)[7]

Figure 4.1 depicts a graph of the relationship between change in ELF (on the y-axis) and change in carbon emissions (on the x-axis) between 1961 and 1985 with 95 per cent confidence intervals. To take two countries on the graph as examples of the relationship between carbon emissions and ethnic homogenization, in Algeria carbon emissions increase from 0.53 tons per capita in 1961 to 3.24 in 1985, while the proportion of the population identified by Soviet researchers as Algerian Arab rose from 73.8 per cent to 82.1 per cent and those belonging to Berber minorities declined (leading the ELF to drop from 0.426 to

---

[7] It is immediately clear from Figure 4.1 that, despite passing the DFBETA test, Saudi Arabia is far away from the trend line. If it is excluded then the coefficient on the carbon emissions is considerably larger.

0.299). Similarly, in Romania carbon emissions per capita increased from 3.01 tons to 8.55 tons while the proportion identified as ethnically Romanian rose from 86.0 per cent to 88.4 per cent and those identified as Hungarian and other ethnic minorities declined (leading to a fall in the ELF from 0.252 to 0.208).

My initial set of results is presented in Table 4.1. In column #1 I regress change in ELF on change in carbon emissions while controlling for change in international migration. In column #2 I control for initial levels of ELF, carbon emissions and immigrants as a proportion of the population to account for the possibility that the relationship between change in ELF and carbon emissions is spurious due to the effects of initial levels on subsequent change for all three variables.[8]

In columns #3–8 I add six additional variables in six separate specifications due to missing data and potential problems of multi-collinearity that result from including too many explanatory variables in one specification.[9] In column #3 I control for change in GDP per capita from 1961 to 1985, with data from the World Bank. In this case it is possible that it is not actually industrialization that is driving ethnic homogenization but instead an increase in wealth, which may come from sources other than industrial production. (Obvious examples here would include natural-resource-rich countries which can experience economic growth which crowds out industrialization, a phenomenon known as 'Dutch disease' which I discuss in Chapter 7.)

I next turn to the potential effects of political change, in particular democratization. There is a long-standing literature in political science dating back to Lipset (1959) that suggests a causal effect of modernization and industrialization on democratization, which could have an independent effect on assimilation. In particular it is plausible that, as countries democratize, ethnic minorities will suffer less discrimination and ethnic conflict will decline (Wimmer, 2015), leading eventually to nation-building and ethnic homogenization. As such in column #4 I use the Varieties of Democracy polyarchy measure to control for change in democracy over the period.

I next test the argument from both Marx and Gellner, as well as from Malešević (2013) and Wimmer (2015), that ethnic homogenization is driven by the ruling elite via state policies. There are two ways to operationalize the effects of states on ethnic identity change. The first draws explicitly on Gellner's emphasis on schooling as a means to homogenize populations. In particular it is

---

[8] Acemoglu and Johnson's (2007) long-difference model showing a correlation between change in life expectancy and change in GDP per capita between 1940 and 1980 drew criticism from Bloom, Canning & Fink (2014) on this exact point. More specifically, Bloom et al. (2014) show that the negative and statistically significant relationship between change in life expectancy and change in GDP per capita becomes positive and statistically significant upon controlling for initial levels of life expectancy and GDP per capita.

[9] The problem of missing data is particularly egregious in the case of African states that only became independent in the early 1960s and are thus often missing data on such measures as taxation as a percentage of GDP and infant mortality.

TABLE 4.1. Industrialization and ethnic change

Dependent Variable	ELF	ELF	ELF	ELF	ELF	ELF	ELF	ELF	Largest Ethnic Group
Additional Controls	None	ELF, CO_2, Migrants in 1961	Δ GDP per capita (logged)	Δ V-Dem Polyarchy Index	Δ Mean Years of Schooling	Δ Taxation as a % of GDP	Δ Infant Mortality (logged)	Δ Newspaper Circulation per capita	None
	(1)	(2)	(3)	(4)	(5)	(6)	(7)	(8)	(9)
Δ CO_2 emissions per capita, 1960–85 (log)	-0.031*** (0.008)	-0.029*** (0.008)	-0.032*** (0.008)	-0.027*** (0.010)	-0.033*** (0.010)	-0.037*** (0.009)	-0.034*** (0.008)	-0.033*** (0.011)	0.023*** (0.006)
Δ Immigrants as % of Population, 1960–85	0.478** (0.209)	0.547*** (0.205)	0.336 (0.269)	0.441* (0.230)	0.481** (0.242)	0.417 (0.356)	0.308** (0.156)	0.563* (0.292)	-0.270** (0.119)
Controls		0.003 (0.017)	0.013 (0.009)	0.026 (0.021)	-0.004 (0.005)	0.101 (0.122)	-0.006 (0.010)	-0.002 (0.011)	
		0.005 (0.003)							
		0.144 (0.095)							
Constant	0.024*** (0.009)	0.014 (0.011)	0.022** (0.009)	0.017** (0.009)	0.033** (0.013)	0.025** (0.013)	0.015 (0.011)	0.025** (0.010)	-0.021*** (0.007)
N	131	131	95	118	110	85	88	91	131
R^2	0.224	0.301	0.236	0.204	0.252	0.280	0.233	0.251	0.132

* $p \leq 0.1$, ** $p \leq 0.05$, *** $p \leq 0.01$ (two-tailed test); robust standard errors in parentheses. The three controls listed in column #2 are for initial levels of ELF, CO_2 emissions per capita (log) and immigrants as a percentage of the population.

possible that declining levels of ELF are a consequence of increased fluency in state languages and/or education policies promoting assimilation among ethnic minorities. Thus in column #5 I use data from Barro and Lee (2010) to control for change in the mean number of years of school attended, which is calculated for the majority of countries in my sample.[10]

Another way to operationalize the effect of state policies on ethnic identity is to consider the role of state capacity, whereby stronger states are able to enforce or incentivize ethnic homogenization while weaker states are unable to do so (Wimmer, 2015). In particular this emphasis not just on the existence of a modern state, but the potential variation in its power over its citizens is most obvious in Tilly (1994) but also Benedict Anderson's (1991) description of 'official nationalism'. The classic measure of state capacity is taxation, inasmuch as tax collection involves an efficient bureaucracy that is able to extract taxes from a large number of citizens (Thies, 2009; Tilly, 1994). Thus in column #6 I control for change in taxation as a percentage of GDP, with data from the Cross National Time Series Data Archive (CNTSDA). (The results are the same if I instead compute change in tax revenues collected per capita.) Another measure of state capacity is infant mortality, which has been shown before to be robustly positively correlated with state failure (King & Zeng, 2001). Infant mortality is also an excellent measure of the quality of public goods provision, inasmuch as it is an unambiguously undesirable phenomenon which all states have the incentive to reduce as low as possible, and because its measurement is not particularly controversial relative to other measures of public goods provision (Abouharb & Kimball, 2007). Moreover, there is evidence that reductions in infant mortality come about through an increase in the quality and quantity of public goods provision rather than merely through higher levels of income (Kudamatsu, 2012). As such in column #7 I control for change in the log of infant mortality rates, as taken from UN demographic data.[11]

In column #8 I control for Anderson's (1991) argument that the creation of modern nations is the result of print capitalism, specifically how readers of newspapers and books come to conceptualize and 'imagine' their membership in the national community and a world of nations, using data on change in newspaper circulation per capita from the CNTSDA. (Controlling for change in book production per capita yields a smaller sample with almost identical results to those in column #8.) Finally, in column #9 I change the dependent variable to change in the size of the largest ethnic group, which is the most obvious mechanism that could be driving the decline in ELF across countries. More specifically, it could be that the largest ethnic group in each country is

---

[10] Data on school enrolment data and literacy from the CNTSDA exists for a smaller number of countries and yields similar results.

[11] Other measures of state capacity such as road density or doctors per capita yield the same results with a smaller number of observations.

growing in size as members of ethnic minorities increasingly identify with it over time, a process which corresponds to the Marxian/Gellnerian framework discussed above.

As seen in Table 4.1, the results are quite striking: the coefficient for change in carbon emissions is always statistically significant at the 1 per cent level for both change in ELF and change in the size of the largest ethnic group, despite notably reduced sample sizes in columns #3–8, while the coefficient on the migration variable is statistically significant in only half of these regressions. Indeed, despite very different sample sizes the coefficient on the carbon emissions does not vary widely around its mean of –0.03 in columns #1–8. (When regressing change in the largest ethnic group the coefficient is similarly robust when adding the same controls.) Using this average coefficient, an increase in one standard deviation of log of carbon emissions in metric tons per capita would lead to a 0.02 decline in ELF over the period in question or an average increase of 1.8 per cent in the percentage of people identifying with the largest ethnic group per country.

While these numbers appear small, a 0.02 decrease in ELF is equivalent to a population split evenly between two ethnic groups moving to one split 60 per cent in favour of the larger group and 40 per cent for the smaller one. Moreover, there is considerable heterogeneity in change in ELF within the dataset: for instance, countries like Libya and Oman were able to erase 33 per cent of the difference in ELF between them and Ireland over this short twenty-four-year period. Indeed, it is important to remember that the aforementioned recent theories of the origins of ethnic diversity from Ahlerup and Olsson (2012) and Michalopoulos (2012) propose mechanisms that work over hundreds, thousands and even tens of thousands of years, so any notable amount of change in ELF over a quarter of a century is an impressive feat.

To test for robustness I examine a variety of different-sized samples in Table A.2 in the Appendix. I use sub-samples excluding Africa, excluding all but African countries, and excluding the Americas, Asia and Europe. I exclude former British colonies to account for the possibility of lingering post-colonial effects of colonial policies on ethnic identities, as noted above. I then exclude all countries where the ANM only lists one ethnic group to account for the possibility that data on minority ethnic groups in such countries may be poor. Finally, I excluded states with populations under 500,000 in 1961 to allow for the possibility that measurement error might be greater among countries with small populations. In none of these regressions do the results differ from those reported in Table 4.1.[12]

---

[12] For additional robustness checks not reported here I also excluded former French colonies, states with large (>10 million) populations in 1961 and states with a history of civil war during the period to account for the possibility that violence may have altered identities in these countries. Finally, I included continent fixed effects as control variables. In none of these cases do my results change.

TABLE 4.2. *Industrialization and ethnic change, with alternative measures of industrialization*

	Dependent variable: change in % ELF, 1961–85	
	(1)	(2)
Δ in Cement production per capita, 1961–85 (log)	−0.013*** (0.005)	
Δ in Urbanization, 1960–85		−0.159** (0.067)
Constant	0.011 (0.007)	0.015** (0.009)
N	109	145
R²	0.209	0.131

* $p \leq 0.1$, ** $p \leq 0.05$, *** $p \leq 0.01$ (two-tailed test); robust standard errors in parentheses. Immigrants as a percentage of the population is included as a control variable in all regressions but is not shown here.

A further step is to employ alternative measures of industrialization, which is useful not only as a robustness test but also to provide evidence for the operative mechanism, namely the declining value of land. I employ two such alternatives here, namely cement production and urbanization, both of which I discussed already in Chapter 2. My first alternative measure of industrialization is cement production, with data from the CNTSDA in the form of cement production in metric tons per capita. However, I have to take the log of each observation in order to normalize the data, which means that I must assign an arbitrarily low value to a good number of countries which have zero values for 1961 and some positive value for 1985. Moreover, there are several countries with zero values for both years, as well as many (such as Angola, Cyprus, Hungary and Vietnam) for which there is missing data. The second alternative measure is urbanization, or the increase in the percentage of people living in urban areas, with data from the UN Population Division. I am unfortunately unable to use other data such labour employment in agriculture or industry due to a lack of observations.

With these caveats about data quality, I list the results in Table 4.2: in both cases the coefficients have the right sign and are statistically significant at accepted levels.

4.3 CENSUS DATA ON ETHNIC FRACTIONALIZATION

As noted above, the ANM data is largely based on census data, along with other sources. An alternative to using the ANM is thus to use census data directly, where it exists, which allows me to use much more up-to-date data on ethnicity than the ANM. Much of this data is available from the United

Nations, with data from 1995 available from the Demographic Statistics Database for all Population and Housing datasets that have been reported to the UN Statistics Division (UNSD), while it was possible to collect earlier data from various annual UN Demographic Yearbooks. In many cases the data was available but not listed by UNSD, such as for Bosnia and Herzegovina, Cuba and the United States and thus I collected the census data directly from the relevant country censuses. As can be seen in Appendix Table A.1, the result is a dataset spanning the years 1960 and 2018 with a mean year of 1996; it is spread across six continents, with data from both large states (China, India and the United States) and small states (Bermuda, New Caledonia and Saint Kitts and Nevis).

As noted already, census data has to be handled very carefully inasmuch as the collection of data on ethnic groups can be very political and controversial, such that many countries no longer collect data on ethnic identity. Indeed, in countries as varied as France, Germany, (post-genocide) Rwanda, Spain and Tanzania there has an explicit attempt to reduce the salience of ethnicity by not including ethnicity on censuses (Morning, 2008, p. 243), not to mention the case of Turkey which we examine in the next chapter. It is thus not surprising that this dataset is missing data from a majority (twenty out of thirty-six) of countries in the OECD (Organization for Economic Co-operation and Development), and all countries from the Middle East and North African region other than Iran. However, as listed in Appendix Table A.3, it contains data from forty countries not included in the ANM data, such as the majority of post-Soviet and post-Yugoslav successor states alongside post-colonial states like Botswana, Malaysia, Namibia, Saint Lucia, Suriname and Zambia which were not yet independent when the first ANM was published.

Of course, the addition or deletion of ethnic categories from censuses can have a major effect on ethnic identification, which means that I have had to drop a number of country-years and entire countries from the dataset. Thus I included the 2004 and 2012 censuses from Suriname but excluded its earlier 1964 or 1972 censuses as the latter failed to include a 'mixed' category that was included in later censuses; similarly I only use the US censuses from 1960 to 1990 as from 2000 there was a new option to identify with more than one race. Finally, I dropped country censuses where the proportion of people grouped as 'other' was irregular.[13] When adding data for carbon emissions and immigrant stock, which are available only between 1960 and 2018, I am thus left with a main dataset of ninety-two countries, or 70 per cent of the size of the ANM data.

The last caveat to make about the census data is that, unlike with the ANM dataset, there are wide differences across countries in the nature of the data, both in terms of the number of observations per country (two in many cases to

---

[13] For instance, the proportion of residents of Côte d'Ivoire marked as 'other' rose from less than 1 per cent in its 1975 census to 28.1 per cent in 1988 and back down to 1.1 per cent in 1998, which led me to drop the 1988 census from my analysis.

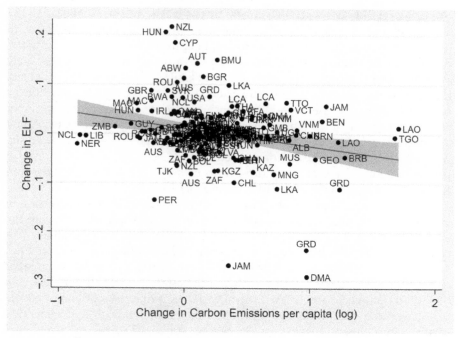

FIGURE 4.2 Change in ELF and carbon emissions, census data

seven for New Caledonia), the start date (1960 in many cases to 2011 in Iran and 2006 in Ireland) and the gaps between years (five years in a number of cases to forty years in Ghana). Due to this heterogeneity I cannot use the long-difference model I used with the ANM dataset and instead regress contemporaneous measures of ELF on measures of industrialization while controlling for country fixed effects as a means to measure change over time in ethnic fractionalization within countries (rather than across them). I also include a linear time trend and weight the results by country to account for the different number of observations per country, while clustering the standard errors at the country level.[14] Formally, the specification is

$$ELF_{it} = \zeta + c_i + \lambda t + \gamma_1 CE_{it} + \gamma_2 M_{it} + \varepsilon_{it}$$

where c_i is the country fixed effect, t is the time trend and, for country i at time t, ELF_{it} is the measure of ELF, CE_{it} is the measure of carbon emissions and M_{it} is the percentage of migrants, while ε_{it} is an error term distributed normally.

Panel B of Appendix Table A.1 gives the descriptive statistics for the census dataset; it is interesting to note that the mean, minimum and maximum

---

[14] The results are robust to the inclusion of a quadratic time trend, decade-fixed effects or a cubic spline with three knots.

country-level ELF scores are all comparable to the ANM data. Figure 4.2 shows a scatterplot of change in log of carbon emissions against change in ELF with 95 per cent confidence intervals after dropping the two outliers of Brunei and the Seychelles, demonstrating a clear downward-sloping relationship. Here again two cases exemplify the relationship: in Chile carbon emissions per capita increased from 2.34 to 3.52 tons between its 1992 and 2002 censuses, while the proportion identifying as 'non-indigenous' rose from 90.0 per cent to 95.4 per cent over the same time span. Similarly, in Georgia carbon emissions per capita increased from 0.85 tons to 2.42 between its 2002 and 2014 censuses, during which the proportion who identified as ethnically Georgian increased from 83.8 per cent to 86.8 per cent while those who identified as Armenian, Azeri and Russian all declined (as did the ELF from 0.291 to 0.240).

I list the results from this analysis in Table 4.3. In the baseline regression in column #1, the coefficient on the carbon emissions variable is negative while the immigrant stock variable is positive and both are statistically significant at conventional levels. I then add controls for five of the additional variables from Table 4.1 in columns #2–6, with the data too sparse to use for newspaper circulation per capita; the results are again consistent with Table 4.1. The only major difference here among the control variables is that the schooling variable is negative and statistically significant in column #4, yet with a considerably smaller sample than in Table 4.1. Finally, in column #7 I use the size of the largest ethnic group as the dependent variable, where the coefficient on carbon emissions switches sign and retains statistical significance at $p = 0.053$.

As before I am interested in using alternative measures of industrialization as a robustness check and I can again use cement production and urbanization as I did in Table 4.2. Annual data on urbanization is available from the World Bank; with cement production, however, I had to use CNTSDA data up to 1998 and thereafter data from the US Geological Survey in its annual Minerals Yearbook Surveys from 1994 to the present. However, due to the number of more recent observations in the census database I can add the three additional alternative measures of industrialization discussed in Chapter 2, namely electricity consumption per capita and the proportion of labour employed in agriculture and industry. The data is sparser for these three alternative measures, with data on electricity consumption only available since 1980 while the data on sectoral employment is only available from 1977 to 1981 and from 1991.[15]

Given these caveats, I present the results in Table 4.4. The coefficients for all five measures of industrialization have the right sign and are statistically significant at the 5 per cent level, except for electricity consumption (which is statistically significant at the $p = 0.055$ level). Particularly striking is the tight fit between sectoral employment and ethnic change given in columns #4 and #5,

---

[15] The earlier data is drawn from individual World Development Reports while the latter data is drawn from World Bank Development Indicators. The results are nearly identical if only the latter is used.

TABLE 4.3. *Industrialization and ethnic change with census data*

Dependent Variable	ELF	ELF	ELF	ELF	ELF	ELF	Largest Ethnic Group
Additional Controls	None	GDP per capita (logged)	V-Dem Polyarchy Index	Mean Years of Schooling	Tax as a % of GDP	Infant Mortality	None
	(1)	(2)	(3)	(4)	(5)	(6)	(7)
CO_2 emissions per capita (log)	-0.031**	-0.021**	-0.024**	-0.023**	-0.038**	-0.030**	0.023*
	(0.013)	(0.010)	(0.011)	(0.010)	(0.016)	(0.013)	(0.012)
Immigrants as % of population	0.811***	0.844***	0.747***	0.739***	0.877*	0.785***	-0.544***
	(0.247)	(0.258)	(0.274)	(0.228)	(0.455)	(0.232)	(0.163)
Control		0.012*	-0.056	-0.015**	-0.065	0.011	
		(0.007)	(0.033)	(0.007)	(0.162)	(0.019)	
Constant	0.382***	0.304***	0.413***	0.451***	0.371***	0.334***	0.704***
	(0.026)	(0.048)	(0.029)	(0.039)	(0.047)	(0.075)	(0.018)
Country fixed effects	yes	yes	yes	yes	yes	yes	yes
Time trend	yes	yes	yes	yes	yes	yes	yes
Countries	92	92	75	70	58	90	92
N	263	256	209	203	144	256	263
R^2 (within)	0.149	0.181	0.142	0.168	0.175	0.143	0.124

* $p \leq 0.1$, ** $p \leq 0.05$, *** $p \leq 0.01$ (two-tailed test); robust standard errors in parentheses. The data is weighted by country.

TABLE 4.4. *Industrialization and ethnic change using census data, with alternative measures of industrialization*

	Dependent variable: ELF				
	(1)	(2)	(3)	(4)	(5)
Cement production per capita (log)	−0.011** (0.005)				
Urbanization (%)		−0.214** (0.107)			
Electricity consumption per capita (log)			−0.018* (0.010)		
Agricultural employment (as a % of total)				0.206*** (0.067)	
Industrial employment (as a % of total)					−0.373*** (0.094)
Constant	0.334*** (0.041)	0.490*** (0.046)	0.441*** (0.062)	0.242*** (0.051)	0.440*** (0.039)
Country fixed effects	yes	yes	yes	yes	yes
Time trend	yes	yes	yes	yes	yes
Countries	75	100	83	81	81
N	183	286	213	189	189
R² (within)	0.147	0.076	0.173	0.230	0.286

* $p \leq 0.1$, ** $p \leq 0.05$, *** $p \leq 0.01$ (two-tailed test); robust standard errors clustered at the country level in parentheses. Immigrants as a percentage of the population is included as a control variable in all regressions but is not shown here. The data is weighted by country.

despite its relatively small coverage. I present a scatterplot for change in both labour and industrial employment in Figures 4.3 and 4.4 (after dropping the sole outlier of Macao in the latter case).

4.4 CONCLUSION

In this chapter I examined the cross-national relationship between industrialization and ethnic change, using two different datasets. I first used data from two Soviet ethnographic atlases to examine the relationship between change in carbon emissions per capita and ethnic identity between 1961 and 1985, first by examining change in ethno-linguistic fractionalization and then the percentage identifying with the largest ethnic group. I found that both relationships were robust to the addition of numerous control variables and the exclusion of

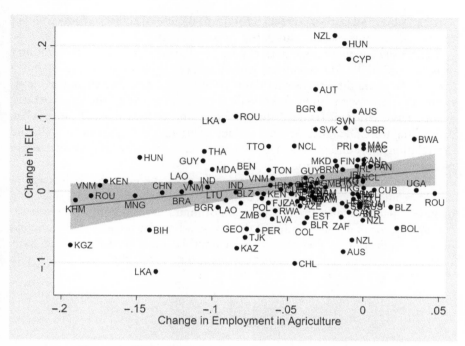

FIGURE 4.3. Change in ELF and change in employment in agriculture, census data

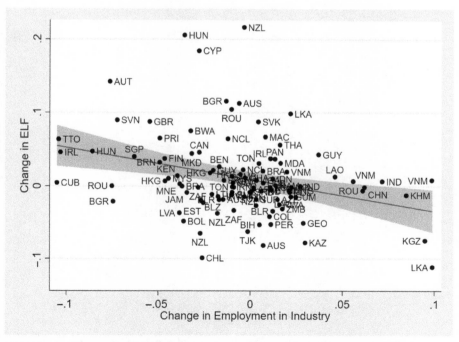

FIGURE 4.4. Change in ELF and change in employment in industry, census data

various sub-samples; they were also robust to the use of cement production per capita and urbanization as alternative measures of industrialization.

I then used a new, original dataset based on data directly taken from country censuses on ethnic identification, with a smaller number of countries but a longer time scale than the Soviet data. Here too, carbon emissions was negatively correlated with ethnic fractionalization and the size of the largest ethnic group. The coefficient retained the right sign and statistical significance when controlling for GDP per capita, democracy, schooling and taxation as well, and the relationship continued to hold when using a wide variety of alternative measures of industrialization.

The evidence in this chapter thus strongly suggests a role for industrialization in promoting ethnic homogenization, but not for the role of state schooling or state capacity as measured by taxation or infant mortality. It is thus consistent with an argument that individuals choose a broader identity in the context of industrialization, rather than have it imposed on them by a strong state. I continue to examine this argument in more detail with the case of Turkey in the next chapter.

5

Industrialization and Assimilation in Mid-twentieth-Century Turkey

5.1 INTRODUCTION

In the previous chapter I showed how industrialization is correlated with assimilation at the cross-national level. Ideally one should also be able to observe a statistical relationship between industrialization and ethnic change at the sub-national level as well, with administrative units instead of countries as the level of observation and censuses as data sources. Yet attempting to demonstrate this relationship for a given country is difficult for multiple reasons. First, as industrialization is a temporary process, I cannot use data from countries that have already industrialized. Second, as in the previous chapter it is necessary to control for internal migration – usually measured by the proportion of individuals born in a given administrative unit – and such data would need to be collected across multiple censuses. Third, when such data is collected it is usually only measured at the highest governmental unit – that is, a province – but in only a few countries are there enough provinces to make any statistical exercise meaningful, thereby eliminating most countries in the world which have a small number of provinces.[1] Third, tracking changes over time in ethnic diversity requires the existence of two or more censuses that disaggregate ethnic diversity by province and measure ethnicity in comparable ways across these censuses. Finally, the censuses need to contain provincial-level data on some measure of industrialization, most likely urbanization levels, as well as demographic and/or economic control variables.

These requirements eliminate the vast majority of possible case studies from analysis here. First, it is very rare to find provincial ethnicity data recorded

---

[1] Only nine countries currently have more than forty provinces. When using two-way fixed effects and clustering at the level of analysis, as I do below, Angrist and Pischke (2009, p. 319) recommend a minimum number of forty-two clusters to avoid statistical bias.

across two censuses: in Latin America, for instance, Mexico is the only country
to have such data in two censuses (but is unusable here due to very high pre-
existing levels of urbanization). Second, even among those countries with a
sufficient number of provinces like the Philippines (eighty regions since 2006),
ethnicity data is often collected at an even higher regional level (for which there
are no local governments). Finally, boundary changes between censuses mean
that many provinces are not comparable across time, especially when provinces
are consolidated or new provinces are created out of parts of more than one
older province.

The only country which I found that can satisfy all of these requirements is
Turkey, which recorded census data on ethnicity by province for all censuses up
until 1965. While the 1927 census was Turkey's first after the fall of the
Ottoman Empire, it failed to record data on urbanization. The 1935 census
was the first to record provincial data on urbanization and ethnic diversity, and
was also the first in a series of quinquennial (every five years) censuses that
lasted through 1990, after which the census became decennial. (I also make use
of quinquennial censuses in New Zealand in Chapter 9.) Due to the rise of
Kurdish nationalism in the late 1960s, census officials stopped publishing data
on ethnic identity after the 1965 census; questions on ethnicity remained on the
census through 1990 but the data, if it was collected, was never published or
made available to researchers (Dundar, 2014, p. 398).[2] Using data on the
number of each provinces' inhabitants who were born in that province, I can
calculate the percentage of inhabitants who were internal migrants for each
census.[3] For these and other censuses the Turkish government collected data
over the course of one day, usually in October, during which all residents were
told to stay at home and thousands of people were employed as enumerators.[4]

One objection to the use of census data is that individuals might have an
incentive to identify as members of the majority ethnic group in order to access
public services, thereby leading to unreliable results. However, in the case of
Turkey there is evidence that authorities actually disapproved of the declaration
by some Jews that they would identify as Turkish on the 1927 census, respond-
ing that 'our aim is only to collect statistical information' (Dundar, 2014,
p. 390), while in the case of the Kurds there is evidence that the state used
census data to determine subsequent assimilation policies, rather than forcing
Kurds to declare themselves as Turkish (Dundar, 2014, p. 391). While some
scholars have claimed that Turkish social statistics during this period were

---

[2] This suppression of census data on ethnicity coincided with a general push within Turkey to stop
collecting ethnographic data on ethnic, linguistic and religious minorities from around 1970
(Andrews, 1989, pp. 43–4).

[3] I am not the first researcher to take advantage of mid-twentieth-century Turkey's high quality
census data; cf. Farooq and Tuncer (1974).

[4] Personal communication with Professor Taner Oc, who was an enumerator for the 1965 census;
27 November 2013.

generally high quality (Munro, 1974, p. 642), another more recent scholar has suggested that data on ethnic minorities after 1950 may have been inaccurately recorded in some cases (Mutlu, 1996, pp. 519–21), and thus I use a number of robustness tests, as described below.

Beyond the issue of data quality, mid-twentieth-century Turkey is an ideal case study of industrialization and ethnic change for several reasons. First, it has a large population and thus minor fluctuations in census data – as for instance with small countries as discussed in the previous chapter – would not have affected what was the nineteenth-most populous country in the world in 1950. Second, mid-twentieth-century Turkey was at the time considered a paradigmatic example of modernization (Szyliowicz, 1966; Ward & Rustow, 1964), such that it was one of Lerner's (1958) primary case studies in his famous study of modernization in the Middle East. Kemal Atatürk, President of Turkey from 1923 to 1938, launched a wholescale project of political, social and economic reform upon taking office, ranging from enshrining secularism and democracy to promoting land reform and industrialization. In particular, many of his reforms revolved around promoting a common sense of Turkishness, which I address in more detail below. Third and finally, we can observe widespread variation in industrialization and urbanization rates across Turkey in this period. Indeed, despite Lerner's (1958, p. 118) claim that urbanization was limited to western Turkey, the second- and fourth-highest absolute increases in urbanization levels between 1935 and 1965 occurred in the southern and eastern provinces of Adana (18.2 per cent) and Gaziantep (17.2 per cent), respectively. On the other hand, some provinces such as Gümüsane and Muğla saw urbanization levels increase by less than 2 per cent over the period, while in one province (Nidi, in Central Anatolia) the level of urbanization actually dropped from 19.7 per cent to 19.3 per cent over the period in question.

The quantitative results from this exercise, as presented below, confirm my argument that industrialization, as measured by urbanization levels, is robustly correlated with ethnic homogenization in mid-twentieth-century Turkey. Moreover, I also present qualitative evidence that the Turkish government incentivized assimilation in urban areas by requiring individuals who wished to enter the modern urban economy to identify as Turkish. In contrast, however, the more isolated Kurdish areas of south-east Turkey saw little assimilation due to low levels of industrialization, which thereby failed to generate incentives for individuals to switch their identity from Kurdish to Turkish. Indeed, the variation in both Turkish government policies towards its ethnic minorities as well as the degree to which members of these groups actually assimilated into Turkish society over this time period adds to previous evidence about how governments can aid or speed up the process of ethnic homogenization by promoting industrialization, as well as how more heavy-handed or violent policies can instead trigger processes of resistance to homogenization and outright secessionist movements. In other words, here again the evidence supports a very nuanced understanding of the role of the state in forming modern ethnic and national identities.

In the rest of the chapter I first introduce the Turkish case study before examining qualitative and then quantitative evidence for my argument.

5.2 BACKGROUND ON TURKEY

Modern Turkey was born out of the ashes of the Ottoman Empire, which was on the losing side in World War I. Despite the fact that Turkey lost large amounts of former Ottoman territory in the treaties which concluded the war, it retained the whole of Anatolia as well as part of Thrace across the Sea of Marmara, and thus the new Turkish government came to power in a country that was far from homogenous. Indeed, as seen in Table 5.1, Turkey had a dozen ethnic minorities which constituted at least 1 per cent of the population in at least one of its provinces in 1935. This number in turn represents only a fraction of the proverbial 'seventy-two and a half' ethnic groups that supposedly live in Turkey (with the half representing the Gypsies/Roma; Andrews, 1989, p. 47), although many of these groups are actually sub-ethnic groups of the Turks such as the Yörük or Tahtacı. For a map of Turkish provinces and cities in 1935, see Map 5.1.

The most prominent of Turkey's ethnic minority groups are the Kurds, who are concentrated in south-eastern Turkey and formed a majority of the population in six provinces and 9.2 per cent of the total population of Turkey in 1935. As a sizeable minority concentrated close to Turkey's international borders with Iraq and Iran (with their own Kurdish populations on their side of the border), the Kurds attracted a great deal of political and military attention from the Turkish government over this and subsequent periods, as we shall see in more detail below. Inasmuch as the Kurds speak a variety of different dialects and are split between Sunni and Shia/Alevi Islam, they are clearly reminiscent of Scott's (2009) claims about the fractured ethnic identities of the mountain peoples of south-east Asia discussed in Chapter 1.[5] Indeed, one main reason why Atatürk and his successors gave so much attention given to assimilating Kurds was due to long-standing beliefs that the Kurds were actually just 'mountain Turks' and not a separate ethnic group. Thus, according to the

---

[5] This is not the only interesting parallel between Scott's (2009) descriptions of the upland peoples of South-East Asia and the Kurds. In his 1936 report on Turkish Kurdistan, Abeddin Osman, Inspector-General of the Eastern region at the time, wrote of two kinds of Kurds: one 'about whom it is not known how and when they first appeared as Kurds, and another group who were Turks, but became assimilated to Kurds in various circumstances'. One of these circumstances included an Ottoman-era law that exempted Kurds from military service and thereby incentivized 'many Turks to describe themselves as Kurds' (Gökay, 1997a, p. 160). Scott (2009, p. 326) similarly describes the ethnogenesis of the upland peoples of south-east Asia as former valley-dwelling people who had run away to the hills in part as a way to escape the demands of the state and assimilated into hill societies.

TABLE 5.1. *Ethnic minorities in Turkey, 1935–1965, total percentages and number of provinces with more than 1% of the population (out of 54)*

Ethnic group	1935 %	1935 # of provinces	1945 %	1945 # of provinces	1955 %	1955 # of provinces	1965 %	1965 # of provinces
ELF	0.252		0.213		0.188		0.183	
% Turkish	86.02		88.33		89.85		90.12	
Kurdish	9.16	23	7.86	21	6.98	22	7.07	19
Arabic	0.95	7	1.32	6	1.25	6	1.16	6
Greek	0.67	3	0.47	2	0.33	2	0.15	2
Circassian	0.43	11	0.35	4	0.33	4	0.19	3
Laz	0.39	2	0.25	3	0.13	2	0.08	1
Armenian	0.36	1	0.30	1	0.23	1	0.11	1
Georgian	0.35	6	0.21	3	0.22	5	0.11	1
Jewish	0.26	2	0.27	3	0.14	1	0.12	0
Pomak	0.20	4	0.07	3	0.07	2	0.07	3
Bosnian	0.15	1	0.07	1	0.05	0	0.06	0
Albanian	0.14	0	0.08	0	0.05	0	0.04	0
Tatar	0.09	1	0.05	1	*		*	
Abkhazian	0.06	1	0.05	1	0.06	1	0.01	0

* Tatars were no longer listed as a separate ethnic minority from 1950

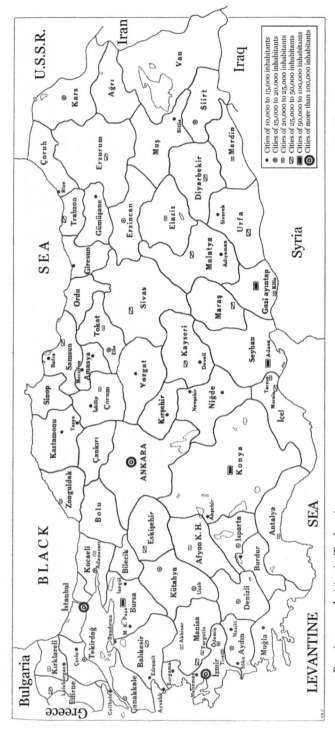

MAP 5.1. Provinces and cities in Turkey in 1935

Turkish General Nuri Bey speaking in 1930, 'the racial differences between the Kurds and the Turkmans, Circassians and Armenians [are] very doubtful', and Kurds 'derive very largely from Seljuk Turks, who preceded the Ottoman invasion' (Gökay, 1997a, p. 160).

Other minority ethnic groups in Turkey can be divided in two, namely Muslim and non-Muslim groups. To begin with the former, Turkey's Muslim minorities can in turn be divided between indigenous groups such as the Arabs, Laz and Pomaks, who live at the southern, north-eastern and north-western edges of the Turkish state respectively, and the descendants of modern immigrant groups like the Abkhazians, Bosnians, Circassians and Tatars who settled mostly in western Turkey. None of these ethnic minorities constituted more than 20 per cent of the population in any one province in any of the mid-twentieth-century censuses, with the sole exception being the Arabs who constituted 37.4 per cent of Hatay province when it joined Turkey in 1939.

Turkey's non-Muslim minority groups include Armenians, Greeks, Laz and Jews, all of whom have suffered various forms of discrimination under numerous Ottoman and/or Turkish governments, most obviously with the genocide of the Armenians during World War I. By the 1930s the vast majority of Armenians who survived the genocide had emigrated, leaving only a small minority in Istanbul, with a similar history of out-migration and settlement in Istanbul for Jews and Greeks, most of whom had been forcibly deported to Greece in the 1920s. The only non-Muslim minority which largely avoided out-migration and migration to Istanbul were the Georgians, who were scattered throughout Turkey with a plurality located in the north-eastern province of Çoruh.

As in other pre-modern rural contexts, Turkish ethnic minorities have long been defined through their distinctive occupations and geography. Many Turks have historically called the Kurds 'mountain people' due to their residence in the rocky eastern Anatolian plateau (Heper, 2007, p. 163), while the old Turkish proverb claims that 'a Laz who has not seen the sea is called a Kurd' due to the location of the Laz homeland on the shores of the Black Sea (Benninghaus, 1989, p. 500). So too do the Kurds have an old saying (Hotham, 1972, p. 180):

> Kurds who have seen the sea are Lazes
> Kurds who ride a horse are Circassians
> Kurds who are stupid are Turks

Similarly, ethnic physical stereotypes are historically common in Turkey, with the Kurds seen as 'swarthy' and with 'aquiline noses' while the Laz have 'light hair and blue or green eyes' (Andrews, 1989, p. 30); the Circassian word for a Turk is *Tlepagh*, which also translates as 'short, plump, fat and dwarf' (Kaya, 2005, p. 139). These stereotypes only confirm the fact that ethnic differences continue to exist among the Turkish citizenry, despite the efforts of various Turkish governments to downgrade the country's level of ethnic diversity.

5.3 QUALITATIVE EVIDENCE FOR ETHNIC HOMOGENIZATION
IN MID-TWENTIETH-CENTURY TURKEY

The evidence presented in Chapter 4 was consistent with the hypothesis that
industrialization promoted ethnic homogenization via a bottom-up rather than
a top-down process, such that government capacity and schooling had little
importance relative to the role of individual incentives to assimilate. Here the
data from Turkey adds to this evidence, especially if we examine the various
attempts of the Turkish government to forcibly assimilate some of its ethnic
minorities. However, the evidence here does suggest that the Turkish government played an important role in encouraging assimilation by incentivizing
identification as Turkish in urban areas as industrialization spread throughout
most of the country.

5.3.1 The State of Turkey in the 1920s and 1930s

As a result of World War I, the breakup of the Ottoman Empire and the
migration of non-Turkish minorities, Turkey saw its overall population decline
between 1914 and its first post-war census in 1927 alongside sharp declines in
urban populations in Istanbul (down by 39 per cent) and other large cities like
Izmir and Edirne (Findley, 2010, p. 277). Moreover, Greek soldiers retreating
at the end of the Greco-Turkish war in 1922 deliberately destroyed infrastructure and housing in western Anatolia, while the Armenian genocide left eastern
Anatolia severely depopulated (Kalaycıoğlu, 2005, pp. 61–2). Thereafter there
remained some debate, at least until the mid-1930s, as to whether Turkey's
economy should be more agricultural or industrial, such that 'peasantists'
wanted to promote economic development in the countryside; while this group
gradually lost power in Ankara, as late as the early 1940s the General Secretary
of the ruling Republican People's Party (CHP) was Memduh Esendal, who was
known within Turkey as the 'enemy of industry and industrialized civilization'
(Karaömerlioğlu, 1998, p. 85). As such, the government moved to prevent
rural–urban migration as much as possible: not only did it aid rural farmers
by introducing heavy grain subsidies in 1932 such that, by the late 1940s,
domestic wheat prices were twice as high as the world price, it also tried to keep
rural taxes very low in an effort to win over non-urban voters (R. D. Robinson,
1963, pp. 128–9).

The result was that, while Atatürk made huge efforts to modernize Turkey
socially, economically and politically in the 1920s and 1930s, by the onset of
World War II it was very far from being an industrial, urban, modern country,
with agricultural production still the dominant sector of the economy and
people very much tied to the land by economic necessity. To quote a confidential Foreign Office memorandum from William Edmonds, a British Embassy
official who visited Kahramanmaraş in south-central Turkey in 1930, the
countryside remains 'sullen and aloof from modernising tendencies. The local

landowners are very powerful. The peasants are little better than serfs. Little seems to have been done in the way of breaking up big estates.' Further to the east in Diyarbakır, Williams noted that the roads were 'execrable' and 'industry is dead', in part due to the 'inaccessibility' of the region (Gökay, 1997a, pp. 28, 30, 34). Another British official visited to Afyon province in western Turkey in 1937 only to note that it was 'extraordinarily remote', such that 'the remoter villages are almost completely cut off from the outside world … It would appear that these districts have been little affected by the ideas of the new Turkey' (Gökay, 1997b, p. 219).

Turkey's quasi-feudal rural relations, which could perhaps more be appropriately described as a system of sharecropping, were apparent to local scholars as well. Writing in the early 1920s, the Turkish sociologist Ziya Gökalp wrote that in southern Turkey 'peasants are not unlike the medieval European serfs. They cannot move to another town without the permission of the lord of the village. These lords are entitled to use any of the properties of the villagers at their will.' In Diyarbakır province in particular, 'the life, property and honour of the people are in the hands of the chiefs', such that 'medieval feudal institutions are still alive in a country with a constitutional regime' (Berkes, 1959, pp. 140–1). Indeed, the Turkish word for landlord, *ağa*, can be broadly translated as a man who 'exercises great local power and authority over the peasantry' (Ahmad, 1977, p. 143).

Atatürk died in 1938 and was succeeded by İsmet İnönü, who continued as president until 1950. After World War II Turkey began to see relatively rapid rates of industrialization and urbanization, as seen in Figure 5.1. More specifically, due to increased agrarian mechanization as a result of the Marshall Plan,[6] good rainfall and mild amount of land redistribution towards peasant smallholders, Turkey saw a substantial amount of rural economic growth after World War II, with agricultural production doubling between 1947 and 1953 (Findley, 2010, p. 325). However, far from directly aiding landless peasants, as Adnan Menderes' government had planned, these developments only increased rural unemployment, such that rural residents were able to take advantage of the new road networks to emigrate to urban areas (Kalaycıoğlu, 2005, p. 79). Indeed, of the 1.8 million hectares that were re-distributed towards peasants between 1945 and 1962, only 8,600 came from private landlords, with the rest from the state, thereby actually reducing the ability of peasants to use such lands for grazing as they had done so in the past (Ahmad, 1993, pp. 115–16). Moreover, as one local observer noted, in south-central Anatolia industrialized agriculture meant that those with small plots of land who could not afford the use of a tractor could no longer make a living from farming, thereby increasing rural–urban migration (Ahmad, 1977, p. 135). As such, urban squatter

---

[6] Thanks in part to American aid the number of tractors in Turkey increased from some 1,700 in 1948 to 42,000 in 1960 (Findley, 2010, p. 325).

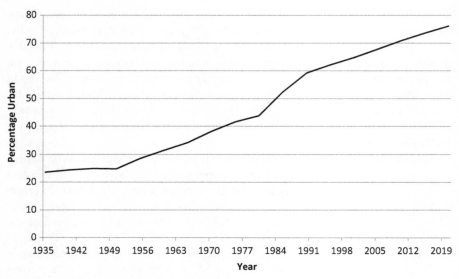

FIGURE 5.1. Urbanization in Turkey, 1935–2020
(*Source:* Mustafa Kemal & Naci, 2009, p. 5; United Nations, 2019)

settlements, or *gecekondus*, grew quickly such that by the mid-1960s a majority of inhabitants in the Anatolian cities of Ankara and Erzincan and 45 per cent of inhabitants in Istanbul lived in slum housing (White, 2010, p. 432). Indeed, the Turkish government was increasingly concerned about urbanization inasmuch as its 'leaders feared the possibly politically disruptive influence of an industrial proletariat which had cut all ties with the land and had broken away from the protective stability and security of village life' (R. D. Robinson, 1963, p. 117).

5.3.2 Government Efforts at Enforcing Assimilation

Atatürk and other members of his CHP government drew a sharp contrast between the pluralist, multi-cultural nature of the Ottoman Empire, and the modern Turkish nation-state, whose citizens were to be Turkish and only Turkish. This focus on national homogeneity was paramount for the new state: for instance, Atatürk's interior minister Şükrü Kaya noted that 'the biggest responsibility of a government is to assimilate all who live within its boundaries into its own community ... While many people did not assimilate [in the past], the Ottomans suffered from that' (Aslan, 2011, p. 79). Of course, discussion of Turkish national identity necessarily meant a focus on defining what it meant to be Turkish. On the one hand, the 1924 Constitution explicitly stated that 'the People of Turkey, regardless of religion or race, are Turks as regards citizenship' (Çağaptay, 2004, p. 87), suggesting that being a Turkish citizen did not require assimilation into the Turkish ethnic group. Yet on the other hand Atatürk strongly associated being a member of the Turkish nation with speaking Turkish: at a history congress in Istanbul in 1932, he claimed that:

One of the significant characteristics of the nation is language. One, who regards himself as a member of the Turkish nation, should first of all and in every case, speak Turkish. If, someone, who does not speak Turkish, claims membership to Turkish culture and community, it would not be right to believe in this. (Quoted in Çağaptay, 2004, p. 89)

As such Atatürk and his successors focussed on promoting assimilation among Turkey's numerous ethnic minorities, primarily the Kurds but also Arabs, Circassianss, Laz and Pomaks, among others. Laws encouraging assimilation were numerous: for instance, since surnames were still a rarity in Turkey at the time, the 1934 Law on Surnames gave every family two years in which to choose a surname, which had to be taken 'from the Turkish language' (G. Lewis, 1974, p. 123).[7] Various additional assimilation policies proposed by the government for multi-ethnic eastern Turkey included encouraging ethnic intermarriages between Turkish-speaking civil servants and ethnic minority women, prohibiting the use of ethnic minority languages in public, ensuring that soldiers from the east spent their military service in other regions and mandating that only non-native civil servants were posted to the east.

Government efforts at assimilating Kurds were especially strong, largely due to their aforementioned demographic dominance in border regions near Iran and Iraq. In 1925 thousands of Kurds rose up in a rebellion led by Sheikh Said against the Turkish government, which managed to suppress the revolt after a few months. In response the government established a special department known as the Eastern Region Reform Commission (ERRC), which proposed two major recommendations. First, it encouraged the creation of inspectorate-generals that would govern over rebellious provinces under the control of an inspector-general who reported directly to Ankara and whose authority prevailed over both civilian and military personnel. The first such inspectorate-general was created across six eastern provinces in 1928, followed by second one in Thrace from 1934 and a third and fourth in eastern Turkey in 1935 and 1936, respectively. The goal of the inspectorate-generals was to explicitly encourage Turkification, which in the east included prohibiting the use of the Kurdish language, improving transportation links in the region, stationing Kurdish army recruits outside the region and teaching Turkish to women (Yeğen, 2009, p. 601).

The second proposal of the ERRC was an ambitious plan to turn the Kurdish majority of the eastern region into a minority, both by re-settling some 500,000 Turkish-speaking immigrants from the Balkans to south-eastern Turkey over the next ten years, and forcibly re-settling Kurds who had been

---

[7] Thus names could not include several suffixes such as '-yan, -of, -ef, -vic, -is, -dis, -pulos, -aki, -zade, -mahdumu, -veled, and -bin' which indicated foreign origins (Bayar, 2011, p. 124).

involved in the rebellion in western Anatolia. In response the Turkish government passed the Law of Settlement of 1934, granting it the power to evacuate residents of all non-Turkish majority regions if it so wanted. This law divided the country in three areas: the first was zones consisting entirely of 'populations who share the Turkish culture'; zone two was areas to which ethnic minorities 'who are to adopt the Turkish culture' are to moved, and zone three was the areas to be evacuated, which were closed to new settlement. The law stated that 'The Ministry of the Interior is entitled to ... re-settle nomads who do not share the Turkish culture [a euphemism for Kurds], by spreading them around to Turkish towns and villages' (Çağaptay, 2002, pp. 72–3); in all cases they were always to remain a minority in their new homes so as to make them 'Turkish in language, tradition and desire' (Üngör, 2008, p. 30). This law was then followed by additional recommendations encouraging intermarriage between Turks and Kurds, especially Turkish male civil servants and female Kurds, as well as the establishment of boarding schools in the region (Yeğen, 2009, p. 602).

As an additional measure to promote assimilation among Turkey's ethnic minorities, Atatürk's government established Turkish People's Houses (*Halkevi*) across Turkey in the 1930s and 1940s, reaching a total of 478 in 1950. Built on the older Ottoman institutions of the *Turk Ocakları* (Turkish Hearths) and with the support of the aforementioned peasantists opposed to urbanization and industrialization, the People's Houses were designed both to promote modern/Western cultural norms among the Turkish population and to promote assimilation in non-Turkish areas, and as such they offered language courses and registered children in Turkish-language boarding schools (Lamprou, 2015, pp. 70–1). While the People's Houses were mostly located in cities and towns, the government also created People's Rooms (*Halkodaları*) in rural areas from 1939 onwards, reaching a total of 4,322 by 1950.

The result of these various policies, as noted by a 1943 government report, was far from a success. While exact numbers are not available, nowhere close to half a million Turks were evacuated from zone three, and only 25,381 Kurds, or less than 2 per cent of the total population of Turkish Kurds, were compulsorily re-settled in western areas by 1943. The re-settlement policy was thus abandoned in the mid-1940s, in part due to a decline in rebel military capacity among the Kurds but also due to the introduction of multi-party elections in 1946, which led to a more relaxed attitude towards assimilation. Indeed, after a law was passed in 1947 allowing re-settled Kurds to return home, 22,516 (or 88.7 per cent) of those displaced moved back to their hometowns (Yeğen, 2009, p. 604), while the inspectorate-generals were all abolished under the new Democrat Party regime in 1952.

Nor is it clear that other assimilation policies were very successful either. The People's Houses and People's Rooms became overly associated with the CHP, inasmuch as the Houses' property was actually owned by the CHP and only CHP members could become House or Room directors; as such in 1951 the newly elected Democrat Party government chose to close them both down. In any case, neither the Houses nor the Rooms ever reached even their initial intended target, which was 500 for the former and 10,000 for the latter (Karpat, 1963, pp. 61, 63); moreover, the fact that Turkish villages tended to have small populations and were spread out from each other, meant that the Houses and Rooms only impacted a fraction of Turkey's total rural population (Karaömerlioğlu, 1998, p. 71). At the local level, not only were the Houses and Rooms viewed as tools of the ruling party but their leaders were seen as uninterested in the views and opinions of local people, instead relying on the ideology of 'for the people, despite the people' (Karaömerlioğlu, 1998, pp. 83–4). In some areas the Houses were popular, but only because they were used as coffeehouses and places for playing cards and even praying (Aslan, 2011, pp. 89–90). Finally, attempts by the Houses and Rooms to attract local women were a particular failure in the conservative Kurdish areas of eastern Turkey, where officials had to recruit the spouses of local state officials instead (Aslan, 2011, p. 80).

As regards attempts at indoctrinating Turkish nationalism and assimilation via the education system, there is evidence that disproportionately more money was spent on school buildings than on books and teacher-training, and villagers saw the schools and its teachers as being imposed on them (R. D. Robinson, 1965, p. 6). In Kurdistan, the area which needed the most attention as regards nation-building, there were often neither enough teachers nor enough buildings, and those teachers that were there were often insulting and intolerant towards their Kurdish students (Aslan, 2011, p. 86). Similarly, efforts to convince Kurdish girls to attend Turkish-language boarding schools faltered: in one case in Elâzığ province in the 1940s, a government official tried and failed to persuade villagers to send their daughters to the boarding school, only to be confronted by claims that Ankara's real agenda was to take their girls by force and marry them off to Turkish men. After warning the locals of the army's power and history of suppressing rebellions in the area, the worker woke the next morning to find 'an empty village, as all the villagers had gone to work in the fields before she woke up. She left without recruiting any girls for the school' (Aslan, 2011, pp. 75–6).

5.3.3 Incentives for Assimilation in Industrial/Urban Turkey

Arguably one of the reasons why the Turkish government abandoned its violent attempts at re-settling the Kurds in the 1940s was due to the fact that increasing levels of industrialization had begun to draw in Kurdish labour to cities in western Turkey, effectively accomplishing the same task but in a much less violent and more voluntary manner. Far from increasing ethnic diversity in the most rapidly urbanizing parts of Turkey, rural–urban migrants wishing to enter the modern economy instead encountered strong incentives to assimilate (Andrews, 1989, pp. 38–9). The Law of Government Employees (*Memurin*

Kanunu) from 1926, for instance, noted that 'one had to be a Turk to be a government employee' and the Press Law of 1931 only allowed Turks to own and manage journals and magazines (Özdoğan, 2010, pp. 51–2). Other laws mandated that only Turks could practice as lawyers, pharmacists, sea captains and medical doctors, while the ruling CHP mandated in 1931 that only those citizens 'who speak Turkish and who accept Turkish culture ... may join the party' (Bayar, 2011, p. 119).

We can also see increasing linkages between members of urban society during this period at the same time as ethnic minority backgrounds became less important in day-to-day life. Thus 'as ethnic differentiation decreased, people [in Istanbul] were often categorized more according to socio-economic status than ethnicity' (Grabolle-Çeliker, 2013, pp. 252–3). More recently, for young rural–urban migrants from the Kurdish-dominated Van province in eastern Turkey interviewed by one scholar in the 1990s and 2000s, 'the pursuit of educational and other goals was more urgent than being or speaking Kurdish' (Grabolle-Çeliker, 2013, p. 253). Indeed, it is not at all surprising that Kurds who have moved to western cities support Kurdish political parties far less than their rural brethren and today vote along socio-economic rather than ethnic lines (Grigoriadis, 2006, p. 451).

The same incentives applied to other minorities like Circassians, who, in the tens of thousands, 'moved to the cities, and, during a short period of time, were completely dissolved among the Turks. Their isolation from their traditional ethnic environment, pressure of the Turkish urban culture, cosmopolitan values of modern industrial communities, interethnic marriages, and other factors have expedited their rapid Turkification' (Chochiev, 2007, p. 223).

By creating numerous incentives to identifying as Turkish, Atatürk and his successors were clearly focussed on creating a modern homogenous nation-state out of the ruins of the multi-ethnic Ottoman Empire. Thus the large expansion in the non-agricultural economy, which saw its share of employment increase from 15 per cent in 1950 to 37 per cent in 1970 and 51 per cent in 1985 (Bulutay, 1995), greatly increased the incentives for ethnic minorities to identify as Turkish. Moreover, industrialization in Turkey was relatively spread out throughout the whole country. It is true that private-sector investment was concentrated in Istanbul and north-west Anatolia due to good communications infrastructure and a well-educated workforce. However, the government responded to this imbalance by deliberately locating factories in other parts of the country. Thus, for example, in the first Five Year Plan of 1935, the government created notable industrial factories in central Anatolia (textile mills in Kayseri and Konya and a cement plant at Sivas), the western Black Sea region (an iron and steel plant at Karabük), the Mediterranean region (a brimstone factory in Isparta), the Aegean region (a textile mill in Aydın), Eastern Anatolia (a textile mill at Malatya) and South-Eastern Anatolia (a cement factory in Diyarbakır province) (Arnold, 2012, p. 367). The placement of these factories was done primarily to prevent greater migration to Ankara, Izmir and Istanbul, especially among easterners, as well as due to the location of natural resource inputs (Arnold, 2012, p. 368).

5.3.4 Explaining Non-assimilation in Kurdistan

We would not expect this process of ethnic assimilation in Turkey to be even, as the gains from assimilation would have been much higher in cities than in the countryside. Indeed, one common theme running through analyses of mid-twentieth-century Turkey is the large degree to which development and modernization were almost completely restricted to urban areas, with rural parts of the state increasingly left behind (Gellner, 1994; R. D. Robinson, 1963; Szyliowicz, 1966). Thus assimilation efforts were more successful in rapidly urbanizing provinces like Adana and Kocaeli than in the less urbanized and more isolated Kurdish-dominated provinces of Mardin, Muş and Van. According to one account, Kurds in these provinces were 'cut off from the rest of the country by their remote location in the mountainous southeastern regions, divided along tribal lines, and economically dependent on local landed elites, [and thus] remained largely unaffected by the new regime's policies of assimilation and modernization' (Ergil, 2000, p. 125). Far from being a new problem, the autonomy of the Kurdish areas dated back centuries via Ottoman policies of indirect rule, such that local chieftains had ultimate power over everything except tax collection and foreign policy.

The Turkish government's approach to governing its Kurdish provinces was twofold. One was to impose a violent military occupation on the province of Tunceli, which was seen as the most rebellious territory in all of Turkey. Local inhabitants had a history of rebellion against Ottoman authority, due both to their distinct Zaza Kurdish dialect and minority Alevi Islamic beliefs, which had led to centuries of persecution at the hands of Turkey's Sunni Muslim majority. In 1935 Atatürk's government passed the co-called 'Tunceli Law', which turned the district of Dersim (from the Zaza 'silver gate') into a new military-run province named Tunceli (from the Turkish 'iron fist') and imposed a new inspectorate-general on the new province and surrounding region the following year. Unlike the other inspectorate-generals, this inspectorate was led not by a civilian but by a military officer, whose goal was to 'tame' Tunceli (Çağaptay, 2006, p. 48). In response to military rule a rebellion broke out in 1937, which was violently suppressed by both ground troops and aerial bombardment over the following months. Estimates of the number of people killed vary from 10,000 to 70,000, with an ongoing scholarly debate as to whether or not to call the actions a genocide or simply an ethnocide (Ayata and Hakyemez, 2013, p. 135). While the rebellion was successfully halted by the end of 1938 the Tunceli law was not repealed in 1946; the high levels of violence meted out on the residents of Tunceli has left it as the least-densely populated province in Turkey even today. The extremity of the Turkish government's response to the rebellion can be seen in the official apology issued in 2011 by then Prime

Minister Recep Tayyip Erdoğan, who noted at the time that 'Dersim is the most tragic event in our recent history' (Ayata and Hakyemez, 2013, p. 131).

A second approach of the Turkish state in Kurdistan was non-violent but totally aloof from local society, where 'state institutions seemed suspended balloon-like over rural localities' to use Boone's (2003, p. 32) apt words. To take one example, the percentage of residents in Mardin province (in south-eastern Anatolia, bordering Syria and Iraq to the south) identifying as Turkish in the census only rose from 6.9 per cent in 1935 to 8.9 per cent in 1965. Some insight can be gained from the memoirs of the Kurdish writer Musa Anter, who grew up in the province in the 1920s and 1930s:

> There was no one either in the village or in the area who knew a word of Turkish. As the tax collectors were local, it was easy to communicate with them. But the arrival of the gendarmes was a calamity. We could not understand what they wanted: whether it was chickens, eggs, lambs, money or firewood for their barracks. As the villagers did not know what was wanted of them, they were beaten and insulted. We were ready to give everything the gendarmes asked for. Such was the custom, and we believed that this was what government was about. (Quoted in Mango, 1994, p. 977)[8]

Moreover, there is no indication that this situation changed in the intervening decades. Indeed, in January 1960 the British embassy in Ankara recorded the details of a month-long visit of a British traveller to Hakkâri province, which then bordered Mardin and Siirt provinces to the west, Iraq to the south, Iran to the east and Van province to the north. The confidential letter sent to the Foreign Office back in London deserves quoting at length, in part because of its rich description of Kurdistan at the end of my period of enquiry here and in part because it has never before been published:

> Except for one or two centres in the *vilayet* [province], notably Hakkâri town itself and Yüksekova, there is virtually no Turkish administration there at all. Traditional Kurdish life thus goes on very much as it has for hundreds or thousands of years. The Turkish authorities make no attempt to levy taxes on the Kurds who live outside the main settlements. Their sole activity consists of occasional forays into Kurdish villages or camps to secure young men for the army. The Kurds in these settlements always have advance knowledge of when the press gangs are coming and the young men who do not wish to be called up take to the mountains for a few days until the soldiers have left ...
>
> We enquired whether this state of nature was agreeable to the Kurds. Our interlocutor said that on the whole he thought it was ... The Kurds' principal complaint about absence of Government was that the area was infested with bears, which came down from the mountains every night to raid the vines ... On the whole, however, the tribesmen have few regrets about their way of life ...

---

[8] See a similar statement from Szyliowicz (1966, p. 275), who notes that villagers in the area were totally isolated from the Turkish state 'except for occasional visits from the gendarmerie and the tax collector, whom they feared and hated'.

In the primitive society in the remoter regions of Hakkâri, where each valley is divided from its neighbour by a mountain range generally rising some 10,000 ft, and where walking is the only means of transport, there seemed no indications whatever of any political consciousness ... The Hakkâri Kurds are so isolated, or uninterested, that they do not even possess wireless [radio] sets.[9]

Thus in Kurdish areas the chieftains continued to control land rather than the central government (Heper, 2007, p. 112), due to weak efforts from Ankara at land reform in the 1940s and an aborted attempt to forcibly relocate fifty-five of the biggest Kurdish landlords to western Turkey by Cemal Gürsel's military government after 1960, which saw the landlords quickly return back home, 'more powerful than ever' (Hotham, 1972, p. 181).

Of course, it could be that the primary cause behind the lack of assimilation in Turkish Kurdistan was less to do with delayed industrialization than the absence of the Turkish government, inasmuch as it was unable to impose a sense of being Turkish on isolated Kurdish citizens. Indeed, when it was not suppressing rebellions there is evidence that the Turkish state was quite weak in eastern Turkey: many administrative and military positions went unfilled as officials did not want to work in the region, and those who did failed to learn Kurdish and therefore could not communicate with the locals (Aslan, 2011, p. 85). However, what is clear from the above evidence is not only the absence of the Turkish government in the region but also how completely self-sufficient the region's Kurds were, with no particular desires from the central government (except protection from bears!). Indeed, the lack of interest in learning Turkish among Kurds documented by administrators of People's Houses made sense, given the fact that 'economic payoffs, which typically constitute the main incentive for assimilation, were slim for Kurdish speakers' (Aslan, 2011, p. 82). With so few reasons to identify as Turkish it is thus no surprise that assimilation was poor to non-existent in the Kurdish region.

Moreover, the policy of keeping the region underdeveloped was in part a deliberate strategy on the part of the CHP government to prevent the rise of Kurdish nationalism: for instance, Fevzi Çakmak, who was Chief of the Turkish General Staff from 1921 to 1944, claimed that 'economic development and wealth would accelerate the level of consciousness and thus lead to development of nationalism among the Kurds' (Kiliç, 1998, p. 6). While there is some justifiable controversy about the degree to which this policy was deliberate (Heper, 2007, pp. 5, 141), there is no doubt that the region continued to remain underdeveloped through the end of the twentieth century. In any case, it

---

[9] National Archives, London, FO 371/153093: Confidential letter from the Chancery of the British Embassy in Ankara to the Eastern Department, Foreign Office, London; 4 January 1960. One British official wrote on the cover page of the letter on 18 January 1960 that 'this suggests that, in the remoter areas of E[astern] Turkey at last, the Kurds are being left very much to themselves. This is wise of the Turkish government, though it is no more than realistic in view of the terrain and the primitive nature of the tribes.'

is clear that the economic isolation that was a result of underdevelopment in Kurdistan prevented Kurds in Kurdistan from assimilating into Turkish society as Kurds in western Turkey had done.

5.4 QUANTITATIVE EVIDENCE

So far qualitative evidence suggests that the Turkish government was able to encourage assimilation in urban areas, not necessarily through coercive means but through incentivizing identification as Turkish as a means to partake in the modern economy. In contrast, however, the lack of industrial transformation in Kurdish areas meant that locals did not assimilate or identify as Turks. This relationship between urbanization and homogenization should be apparent through the use of a panel dataset, specifically by regressing a measure of ethnicity on the percentage urban at the level of the province while controlling for province and year fixed effects. While quinquennial censuses took place between 1935 and 1965, the 1940 census failed to record information on ethnicity due to the constraints of World War II, and thus I chose to use the 1935, 1945, 1955 and 1965 censuses in my dataset to construct a balanced sample.

There is considerable variance across the dataset in the percentage identifying as Turkish, with many province-observations close to 100 per cent while in other cases it is under 10 per cent. For instance, the percentage identifying as Turkish was under 20 per cent of the population for most observations for Hakkâri, Mardin and Siirt provinces, due to large numbers identifying as Kurdish in all three cases. Indeed, many eastern provinces in 1935 were so strongly Kurdish in composition that they had a low ELF index, and thus an increase in the proportion identifying as Turkish would lead to an increase, not a decrease in ELF. As such I drop the use of ELF as my main dependent variable here and instead focus solely on explaining variation in the proportion identifying as Turkish.

The number of provinces in Turkey increased over this time span from fifty-seven to sixty-seven. In most cases new provinces were simply created out of one older one, but in two cases the new provinces were created from two older provinces. To resolve this issue I have chosen to maximize the number of observations per province, which led me to drop the 1935 observations for those provinces split between 1935 and 1945 and drop the 1965 observations for provinces split after 1955.[10] The province of Hatay joined Turkey in 1939 and thus only joins the dataset from 1945. Finally, I drop Turkey's two most urban provinces from my analysis, namely Ankara and Istanbul, as they

---

[10] For provinces split or created between 1945 and 1955 I chose to keep the earlier 1935 and 1945 data so as to yield at least fifty observations per census year. (Keeping the later data yields more observations overall but only forty-seven observations in 1935; the results are robust to the use of this alternative dataset, as well as to weighting the data by province.)

saw unusually high levels of urban growth during the period that make them incomparable to processes of urbanization elsewhere.[11]

It is important to note that this period saw large amounts of internal migration and emigration: anti-Semitic riots in Thrace in 1934 led many Jews to migrate to Istanbul or Palestine, a special tax on non-Muslims and converts in 1942 led the government to send those who could not afford to pay to work camps in eastern Turkey while others fled the country, and many Greeks, Jews and other non-Muslims left the country in the wake of anti-Muslim riots in 1955 (Kuyucu, 2005, pp. 370–1; Toktas, 2005, pp. 404–8). However, the censuses list the number of citizens per province who were born in that province, thereby allowing me to track the non-native population growth as a means to control for migration as I did at the cross-national level in the previous chapter.[12]

In addition to controlling for internal migration, I also add a dummy variable capturing whether or not a province was under the rule of an inspectorate-general in a given year, under the assumption that in such settings individuals may have felt coerced into identifying as Turkish in the census. I also introduce two other measures of state capacity as controls. In particular Lerner's (1958) focus on urbanization as a means for modernization suggested that it was important only inasmuch as it promoted literacy, and there is a danger here that the same problem could occur here. Indeed, Atatürk introduced the use of the Latin alphabet in 1928 which, along with the implementation of co-education across all education levels in 1927 heralded in an era of sharp increases in literacy, with primary school enrollment going from 343,498 in 1924 to 1.5 million by 1950 (Findley, 2010, p. 283). In the villages the state created Village Institutes (*Köy Enstitüleri*) from 1940 onwards for the purposes of training the local youth to become rural teachers. The expectation was that the institutes would not only teach skills but also 'promote nationalism and Kemalism and Turkify the peasants' (Findley, 2010, p. 284). Additionally it is possible that urbanization is merely a proxy for increased desire for literacy in Turkish, such that those who migrated to the cities were also those interested in becoming educated and assimilating into Turkish society (Saran, 1974, p. 354). In order to examine the effect of education or literacy I add a control provincial literacy levels.[13]

A second alternative explanation for ethnic homogenization could come from the Turkish government's effort to decrease the isolation of certain provinces by building roads and railways to connect them with the rest of the

---

[11] As with the previous chapter, these two outliers can be confirmed using the DFBETA outlier detection test.

[12] The results do not change if I exclude from my analysis east-central Anatolia or the Aegean/ Mediterranean coastal region, which saw significant internal out-migration and immigration during the period, respectively (Munro, 1974).

[13] Turkish censuses across this period did not have a standard definition of literacy (R. D. Robinson, 1963, p. 124); as such I use Ahn's (2011) adjusted data.

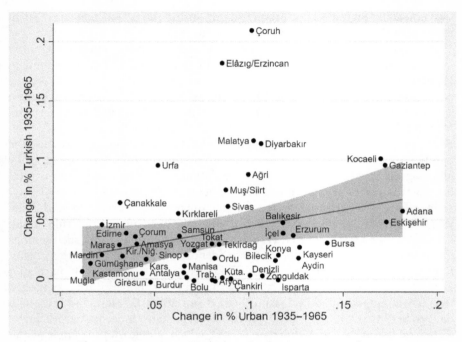

FIGURE 5.2. Change in percentage Turkish and urbanization in Turkey, 1935–1965

country. Indeed, in a 1930 speech inaugurating the new railway connecting Sivas with Ankara and western Turkey, the then Prime Minister İsmet İnönü noted that:

The Turkish nation alone has the right to claim ethnic and racial rights in this country. No other element has this right. The day when this railway reaches the frontier all hesitation will disappear, all intrigue will be without effect in the face of this fact which will then be established in absolute fashion. (Vanly, 1971, p. 32)

As a result the Turkish government focussed a great deal of energy in expanding the road network, such that the total length of highways in the country increased spectacularly from 12,000km in 1947 to 29,000 km in 1955 and 40,000 km in 1960 (Gürel, 2011, p. 203). In order to capture the effect of improvements in transportation I used Government of Turkey data on the number of kilometres of roads per province from 1939, 1945, 1956 and 1963 to estimate data for the census years.[14]

Figure 5.2 depicts the relationship between changes in percentage Turkish and urbanization between 1935 and 1965 with 95 per cent confidence

[14] Prior to 1939 Turkish statistics only listed data on new roads built or old roads repaired, while after 1963 road density is only listed by region (totalling sixteen) rather than by province.

TABLE 5.2. *Descriptive statistics for Turkey data*

	N	Mean	St. Dev.	Minimum	Maximum
% Turkish	222	0.846	0.251	0.056	1.000
% urban	222	0.218	0.090	0.060	0.503
% non-native to province	221	0.107	0.090	0.016	0.475
Length of roads (in kilometres)	224	690.218	330.323	168.444	2055.857
% literate	221	0.375	0.138	0.059	0.695
% under inspectorate-general rule	224	0.129	0.336	0	1

Note: The data does not include Ankara or Istanbul provinces or Tunceli province in 1945, for reasons explained in the text.

intervals; it only includes the fifty-one provinces for which I have comparable data in both years (and uses the names of the provinces in 1935). The figure shows a clear positive relationship between the two variables but contains two notable outliers, namely Çoruh (later split into Artvin and Rize in the 1940s) and the combined provinces of Elâzığ and Erzincan, both of which saw larger proportional increases in their Turkish population than would be predicted by their rates of urbanization. I return to the former case below as it is less of an outlier than it appears; the latter case, which I take as one unit as the provinces of Bingöl and Tunceli were created out of parts of Elâzığ and Erzincan in the 1940s, can be explained by the aforementioned violent response to the 1937–8 Dersim rebellion which killed large numbers of residents. (Inasmuch as the Tunceli Law that placed the province under military rule lasted until 1946, I drop earlier Tunceli observations from my analysis below.) The descriptive statistics are listed in Table 5.2.

I begin my analysis in Table 5.3 with column #1, which controls for the proportion of non-natives in each province alongside the inspectorate-general variable. In column #2 I add in the two measures of state capacity, namely literacy and road coverage. In column #3 I drop the fifteen provinces that were at least 20 per cent Kurdish in 1935 to account for any particularities that resulted from Turkish efforts to assimilate its Kurdish citizens, as described above, while in column #4 I drop all instances of provinces ruled by Inspectorate-Generals.

As expected, the coefficient on the urbanization variable is negative and statistically significant across all four specifications; using the average coefficient size from columns #1 and #2 means that an increase of one standard deviation in the urbanization variable is equivalent to an increase in the percentage Turkish by 0.024, or 10 per cent of the standard deviation. Interestingly, neither of the two state capacity measures are statistically significant in column #2, which indicates the lack of effect state efforts at

TABLE 5.3. *Urbanization and ethnic change in Turkey, 1935–1965*

Provinces	Dependent variable: percentage Turkish			
	all	all	>20% Kurd in 1935	Not under IG rule
	(1)	(2)	(3)	(4)
Urbanization (%)	0.257***	0.287***	0.165**	0.282***
	(0.086)	(0.090)	(0.076)	(0.092)
Non-native to province (%)	−0.055	−0.066	−0.053*	−0.059
	(0.051)	(0.053)	(0.027)	(0.067)
Under inspectorate-general rule	−0.022**	−0.021*	−0.010	
	(0.011)	(0.011)	(0.007)	
Road coverage, km (log)		−0.001		
		(0.007)		
% literate		−0.056		
		(0.032)		
Constant	0.789***	0.818***	0.924***	0.808***
	(0.016)	(0.045)	(0.015)	(0.019)
Province fixed effects	yes	yes	yes	yes
Year fixed effects	yes	yes	yes	yes
Provinces	61	61	45	61
N	221	220	168	192
R^2 (within)	0.311	0.322	0.468	0.270

* $p \leq 0.1$, ** $p \leq 0.05$, *** $p \leq 0.01$ (two-tailed test); robust standard errors clustered at the province are in parentheses. All data is from Government of Turkey except data on literacy, which is from Ahn (2011, p. 212).

modernization had on Turkish identification. Similarly surprising is the negative and statistically significant coefficient on the inspectorate-general dummy variable in columns #1 and #2, which could be interpreted as a result of reverse causality but also as a mark of how unsuccessful the CHP government was at forcibly suppressing Kurdish identity in eastern Turkey in comparison to the lighter touch under the subsequent Democrat Party leadership. Indeed, these results are consistent with the claim that the CHP 'regime's ham-fisted methods' were indeed counterproductive in that they managed only to 'alienate non-Turkish ethnic groups and stimulate the inception of nationalist movements by their elites' (Üngör, 2008, p. 31). The coefficient on the urbanization variable retains its statistical significance but drops in magnitude in the results without provinces with sizeable Kurdish populations in column #3, most likely because of a reduced sample size, while the size and fit of the urbanization variable improve in the results without provinces under the rule of inspectorates-general in column #4. These robustness tests show that the effect of urbanization was not limited to particular areas of the country or due to any potential problems in counting Kurdish citizens.[15]

As noted above, there is one notable unexplained outlier from Figure 5.2, namely Çoruh province in north-eastern Turkey on the border with Georgia. Here the population identifying as Turkish shifted from 73.8 per cent in 1935 to 77.8 per cent in 1950 and 94.8 per cent in 1965 despite seeing low rates of urbanization over the same time period.[16] The largest ethnic minority in 1935 by far was the Laz or Lazi, a minority group split between Turkey and south-west Georgia who speak a Kartvelian (South Caucasian) language and practice Sunni Islam in Turkey (and Eastern Orthodox Christianity in Georgia). Within Turkey the Laz have long been known for their distinctive crops, settlement patterns and accent when speaking Turkish, which developed over centuries of isolation from the Anatolian interior due to the Pontic mountain chain (Meeker, 1971). The sharp drop in residents who identified as Laz between 1950 and 1965 coincided with the development of a major tea industry in the region that employed some 60,000 people, which brought modernization to the region in the form of tea-processing factories, jobs in construction, commerce and public administration and the provision of health and educational services. (It also turned Turkey into the fifth-largest tea producer in the world.) Traditional, ethnic-specific crops such as corn, hazelnut and red cabbage saw a decline in production over the same time period, as did the older form of collective agriculture (*İmece*) which was typical for the Laz (Yücel, 2016, p. 79). The result of these economic changes, according to Hann and Béller-Hann (1998, p. 245), was that residents of the region began to 'associate themselves with the rapidly developing western parts of Turkey, and certain not with the economically backward regions of eastern Anatolia', leading one British official visiting the region in 1954 to exclaim that the Laz 'can now be considered to have been assimilated' (Gökay, 2008, p. 221). In other words, in Çoruh the tea industry took the place of urbanization in encouraging the Laz to re-identify as Turkish as they entered the modern economy.

5.5 CONCLUSION

In this chapter I shifted my attention from the cross-national level to the sub-national level in mid-twentieth-century Turkey, where I used both qualitative

---

[15] Mutlu (1996, pp. 524–5) claims that the 1965 census was flawed in under-counting Kurdish citizens and presents adjusted data on Kurdish identification by province (but does not do so for earlier censuses). To account for his claims I re-ran all four specifications after adjusting the data on percentage Turkish (by assuming that any changes between the raw and adjusted data solely affected the percentage Turkish rather than any other ethnic identities) and dropped the 1965 census entirely from my analysis. In neither case are my results notably different.

[16] Ethnic change in the province was not driven by change in the percentage of non-natives, which increased only from 2.4 per cent to 4.1 per cent over the thirty-year period.

and quantitative evidence to show that industrialization promoted ethnic homogenization, and that this relationship is robust to the use of sub-samples and
various control variables. Moreover, as with the previous chapter the
evidence suggests that other potential variables that have previously been
hypothesized to promote homogeneity are not correlated with decreasing ethnic
diversity. For instance, there is no evidence that literacy has any effect on
decreasing diversity, which matches the evidence presented by Lange (2012)
on how education actually contributes to inter-ethnic violence rather than
reducing it.

These results are not by themselves surprising. Indeed, none other than
Ernest Gellner himself noted how Kemalist nation-building attempts in
twentieth-century Turkey had only affected the elites, with the masses only
affected later through 'urban growth and migration to the towns' (Gellner,
1994, p. 83). Moreover, there is no evidence that the trends identified in this
chapter reversed after 1965. Just as assimilation among the Kurds was slow
between 1935 and 1965, such that the decline in the percentage who identified
as Kurdish was less than one-quarter of the initial proportion in 1935, so too
has assimilation among rural Kurds proceeded slowly in the past half-century.
Using Demographic and Health Surveys from the 1990s, Gündüz-Hoşgör and
Smits (2002) found a statistically significant correlation between urbanization
and intermarriage among both Turks and Kurds, with residence in large cities
positively correlated with intermarriage and rural residence negatively correlated when including controls for age, gender, education and region. The rural/
urban differences among Kurds are particularly strong, with mixed marriages
accounting for 22.0 per cent of all marriages in large cities but only 4.5 per cent
in the countryside (Gündüz-Hoşgör & Smits, 2002, p. 427).

In contrast to the Kurds, there is continuing evidence for a lack of salience
for Laz identity, with Laz cultural leaders claiming that 'the Laz people identify
themselves primarily as Turks and secondarily as Laz' (Sarigil, 2009, p. 6)
alongside evidence of linguistic assimilation due to the fact that identifying as
Turkish has become to be 'seen as being modern, cultured, and urban' (Serdar,
2019, p. 346). Even the opening of the state border with Georgia in 1988,
which allowed for much greater communication between Laz on both sides of
the border, ironically led to greater, not lesser, identification as Turks among
the residents of north-eastern Turkey (Hann, 1997, pp. 149–50). Indeed, one
recent scholar of Laz assimilation has explicitly argued that the process of
Turkish language acquisition was very much driven by a Gellnerian logic of
'inextricably linked economic and symbolic rewards' (Serdar, 2019, p. 345).

The Turkish case thus provides robust sub-national evidence for my theory
that industrialization provides incentives for people to adhere to larger ethnic
identities, and that the state can play a role in aiding this process by providing
incentives to joining the modern, industrial economy. It is, however, possible
that Turkey is exceptional in this regard, in part due to its unusual legacy of
being the successor state to a multi-ethnic empire. It is also possible that the

dynamics of industrialization in the mid-twentieth century (especially in a period of high economic growth after World War II) were particularly suited to ethnic homogenization, and thus have less relevance to the contemporary world. In response to these concerns I turn to evidence from Africa in the next two chapters, both to bring the story more up to date but also to examine three additional case studies in more detail.

6

Cases of Non-industrialization in Africa

Somalia and Uganda

6.1 INTRODUCTION

I now move my analysis to Africa, which remains the least urbanized and industrialized of all continents. Indeed, in his critique of Gellner's theory of nationalism, Laitin (1998, p. 245) claims that Gellner's theory of nationalism cannot explain the rise of nationalism in Africa inasmuch as Africa has not experienced industrialization. On the one hand, Laitin is correct that most of Africa has yet to see the kind of industrialization we saw in the case of Turkey in the previous chapter, with mechanized agriculture, the rise of a strong manufacturing sector and large-scale urbanization. Yet, on the other hand, there is nonetheless long-standing evidence on the role of rural–urban migration and non-agricultural employment in promoting ethnic homogenization in the continent, such that urbanization in the mid-twentieth-century 'loosened kinship ties, accelerated social communication between "detribalized" ethnic groups, and, in general, contributed to "national" integration' in the words of the noted political scientist James Coleman (J. S. Coleman, 1954, p. 411). Indeed, as I review below, there is evidence from multiple contexts that Africans have often assimilated into larger ethnic groups to find security and prestige in the difficult urban environment, especially in the immediate post-independence period. However, as economic collapse and stagnation began to become more and more common across the continent from the 1970s, these processes of integration and assimilation stalled, leaving many Africans instead to retreat or at least maintain their rural tribal identities in order to access land in the countryside.

In this and the next chapter I examine three contrasting countries' experience with industrialization and ethnic diversity. More specifically, in this chapter I examine the two 'negative' cases of Somalia and Uganda, which have seen industrial stagnation alongside increasing ethnic fractionalization, before

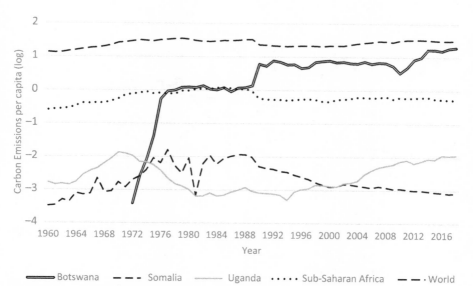

FIGURE 6.1. Carbon emissions in Botswana, Somalia and Uganda, 1960–2018 (*Source:* World Bank)

contrasting them with the 'positive' case of Botswana in the next chapter as a prototypical case of industrialization contributing to ethnic homogenization. I have chosen these three cases for several reasons. Most notably, all three countries emerged from colonialism in the 1960s with very low levels of industrialization and a high reliance upon agricultural employment. Indeed, Botswana and Uganda were among the ten least-urbanized countries in the world in 1950, at 2.7 per cent and 2.8 per cent urban respectively, with Somalia only marginally higher at 12.7 per cent. Similarly, all three countries had very low levels of carbon emissions in the early 1970s (when the data begins for Botswana), at 0.14 metric ton per capita or lower, or less than one-sixth of the Sub-Saharan African average at the time.

However, as Figures 6.1 and 6.2 make clear, Botswana rapidly industrialized and urbanized through the next few decades to reach and surpass the Sub-Saharan African average levels of carbon emissions per capita and urbanization. Indeed, its annual increase in percentage urban was the highest in the world at 4.7 per cent per year between 1950 and 2020.[1] Thus by 2018 its emissions were 3.64 tons per capita, or higher than the average for Latin America and the Caribbean (2.64), while by 2020 it had an urbanization level

---

[1] This high level is not an artefact of the choice of beginning or end dates; with an annual urbanization rate of 6.0 per cent Botswana also had the highest rate in the world between 1960 and 2010 and the only rate above 5 per cent.

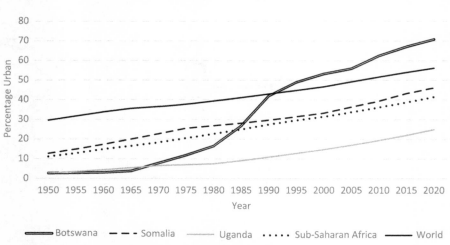

FIGURE 6.2. Urbanization in Botswana, Somalia and Uganda, 1950–2020
(*Source:* United Nations, 2019)

of 70.9 per cent, or roughly the same as Ukraine (70.5 per cent) and Italy (71.0 per cent). In contrast, both Somalia and Uganda failed to keep pace with the Sub-Saharan African average on carbon emissions and only experienced a steady but slow increase in their levels of urbanization over the same period.

The consequence of these differential experiences with industrialization has, I argue here, been a notable contrast in the nature of ethnic identity across these three countries. While Botswana has developed a strong sense of national identity that has de-emphasized ethnic diversity, both Somalia and Uganda in turn have seen numerous political upheavals and civil wars fought along ethnic lines. More specifically, in Somalia clan identities have become arguably more important to ordinary citizens than their common ethnic Somali identity, despite very substantial top-down nation-building efforts under President Siyad Barre. In Uganda the continued lack of industrialization has led to increased levels of ethnic fractionalization and highly ethnicized politics that has focussed on the control over land and the creation of new districts.

In the rest of this chapter I begin by providing an overview of the historical relationship between industrialization and ethnic homogenization across Africa, with a focus on the 1950s and 1960s. I then introduce the Somali and Ugandan case studies, where in each case I show how industrialization has stalled, leading to a subsequent rise in ethnic fractionalization and the higher salience of ethnic identities due to struggles over land ownership. In the case of Somalia the collapse of the formal economy led to an increased focus on clan membership instead of on the overarching Somali ethno-national identity promoted by the Somali government, while in Uganda the failure to create enough urban formal employment has led to ethnic claims to land, an ongoing debate about the state recognition of Uganda's indigenous ethnic communities and ethnic claims over the creation of new districts.

6.2 INDUSTRIALIZATION AND ETHNIC CHANGE IN MODERN AFRICA

In sharp contrast to a more primordial understanding of African ethnicity among scholars today, in an earlier era there was a substantial academic focus on the dynamics of ethnic assimilation in late colonial and post-colonial Africa. This process was originally titled 'super-tribalism' back in the 1950s by Jean Rouch (1956, pp. 163–4), in the sense of the creation of 'super-tribal' identities that encompassed multiple ethnic groups or tribes. Due in part to the coincidence of the dominance of modernization theory with the dual processes of political independence and economic growth in Africa, anthropologists and political scientists paid a great deal of attention to the integrative effects of urbanization during this period (Bates, 1974, pp. 467–8; Epstein, 1967; Gluckman, 1960; Kasfir, 1979, pp. 370–1; Wallerstein, 1960, p. 133).

One of the reasons this process drew so much attention is that there were often multiple types of ethnic homogenization taking place at the same time. Indeed, we can break down the types of people undergoing a process of ethnic change within the African context into three groups: immigrants, internal migrants who created new ethnic groups and internal migrants who assimilated into older ethnic groups. In the first case, which was the basis for Rouch's (1956) neologism, there is evidence from countries such as Côte d'Ivoire, Ghana and Uganda on how foreign immigrants appeared to replace an emphasis on their ethnic identities with a new broader pan-ethnic identity, particularly in urban areas (Edel, 1965; Skinner, 1963). Such a process is not dissimilar from the American immigrant experience of assimilation but, as Walker Connor has correctly pointed out, this experience is not generalizable to the vast number of non-immigrants around the world who do not voluntarily cross international borders (Connor, 1994).

The second group prone to assimilation were internal migrants from smaller groups who created new, larger groups upon leaving the countryside. The Ibo of Nigeria, Jola of Senegal, Duala of Cameroon, Luyia and Mijikenda of Kenya and Bangala of the DRC are all classic examples of previously different ethnic groups amalgamating into larger ethnic identities as urban migrants found commonalties among each other and transferred these new identities back to their rural brethren as well (Eckert, 1999; Nugent, 2008; Southall, 1970; Willis, 1993; M. C. Young, 1976). For instance, in a very detailed study Harries (1989) discusses the origins of the Tsonga ethnic group in early twentieth-century South Africa. Here both British colonial interests in providing rural ethnic chiefdoms for African labourers, as well as Swiss missionaries intent on reducing the dialects among the peoples in their area of interest into a single written language, were instrumental in the consolidation of a new Tsonga identity. However, it is also clear that the structural break of migration and urbanization played a major role in the formation of a Tsonga identity, as migrants acquired fluency in the Tsonga lingua franca on the mines or neighbouring schools and began to see the differences between themselves and other South Africans. These migrants developed an incipient ethnic consciousness as a 'means of survival in an unfamiliar and competitive world and they spread their ideas and experiences into rural areas where people had little concept of the existence of a Tsonga or Shangaan "people"' (Harries, 1989, pp. 102–3).[2]

In a similar story, Ranger (1989) discusses the creation of a large Manyika ethnic identity in eastern Rhodesia (now Zimbabwe) out of smaller groups of people who identified as subjects of particular chiefs. He gives due importance to the influence of Protestant and Catholic missionaries but also to the role of rural–urban migration, whereby migrants to towns in Rhodesia and South Africa banded together and obtained jobs as domestic servants or waiters by building upon previous migrants' good reputation in those two professions. Thus 'there was little point in maintaining a distinct Makoni or Ungwe identity in the towns, and little possibility of doing so' inasmuch as other Africans identified the migrants as such (Ranger, 1989, p. 141). However, in the 1930s a second process of ethnic consolidation commenced in Rhodesia, with Manyika and other groups starting to self-identify as Shona, again in part due both to a linguistic homogenization movement that created 'standard Shona' and the homogenizing process of urbanization, such that by the 1950s Shona had become a powerful source of ethnic identity (Ranger, 1989, p. 143).

Third and finally, there are multiple examples of rural–urban migrants assimilating into already pre-existing ethnic groups. In the town of Guider in northern Cameroon, for example, rural–urban migrants assimilated into Fulbe identity such that 'to be urbanized means to be Fulbeized' (E. Schultz, 1984). The same logic applies to urban migrants who assimilated into already-existing groups such as northern Nigerian migrants who began to identify as Hausa in the southern city of Ibadan (A. Cohen, 1969). In these and other cases rural–urban migrants aligned and identified with dominant ethnic groups as a means to access public goods, particularly in non-democracies (Green, 2021).

Much of these processes of ethnic assimilation continued into the 1960s due to favourable economic and political conditions across the continent. However, the 1970s saw the advent of increasingly drastic and serious state crises that afflicted post-colonial African governments, leading to economic collapse and violent civil war in many cases. The decline in the growth of the urban formal sector alongside stagnation in industrial growth led many Africans to cling to ethnic identities as a way to maintain access to rural land, either as a form of

---

[2] The creation of a Tsonga Bantustan in apartheid South Africa – first named the Matshangana Territorial Authority and then later Gazankulu – was thus a consequence rather than a cause of this new Tsonga identity.

security or as a place where they could work the land when employment in the cities dried up. The examples below of Somalia and Uganda make this link between industrialization and the increased salience of ethnicity clear.

6.3 UNDERDEVELOPMENT AND ETHNIC FRACTIONALIZATION IN SOMALIA

I now turn to the chapter's first case study, namely Somalia. (See Map 6.1 for a map of Somalia by region.) Somalia is in many ways so similar to Botswana that it is now quite common to compare the two in discussions of post-colonial African development.[3] First and most obviously, the vast majority of both countries' citizens adhere to the same religion and speak highly related but distinct dialects of the same language. Much of what linguistic variation exists in Somalia is, as in Botswana, a result of a pre-colonial split among various states or sultanates, with each led by a clan or tribe comprised of a core group which could claim to trace its ancestry back to the founding of the group but open to assimilation of non-clan members (Besteman, 1996, p. 583). Indeed, as in Botswana, clans in Somalia could 'adopt' foreigners, who would then become Somali, albeit as clients within the clan lineage (Webersik, 2004, p. 523). In both Botswana and Somalia sharp ethnic distinctions have long been drawn along economic lines, such that the *Jareer* or Bantu minority in Somalia were not considered true Somalis as they farmed while the rest of the Somali population herded cattle, while San hunter-gatherers were and still are considered distinct from the rest of the Botswanan population due to their livelihoods.

Economically and geographically the two countries are similar in that the vast majority of land is semi-arid and thus not arable; as a result the dominant rural economic activity is herding livestock for the purposes of export (predominantly camels, goats and sheep in Somalia and cattle in Botswana), alongside agriculture.[4] Finally, just as Botswana has the institution of the *kgotla* (public meeting), at which any adult man can speak, so too does Somalia have a long tradition of egalitarian political participation such that 'in most judicial and political assemblies any adult male of a clan has the right to speak at any time' (Laitin, 1976, p. 451). This relative cultural homogeneity led both countries to emerge from colonial rule with some degree of political uniformity, leading them both to adopt a presidential system elected not by the citizenry but rather by the National Assembly. However, their high levels of poverty as a result of their traditional herding livelihoods made them among the two highest

---

[3] For other notable comparisons between Botswana and Somalia see Acemoglu, Johnson & Robinson (2003), Abdi Ismail Samatar (1997) and Wimmer (2018).

[4] As I show below, the focus on cattle herding in Botswana has resulted in a very detailed and lengthy vocabulary around cattle; similarly, Somali has a large number of specialized terms related to camels, of which Somalia has more than any other country in the world (Banti, 2000).

MAP 6.1. Map of Somalia by region

recipients of foreign aid per capita in post-colonial Africa and led a large number of citizens to seek incomes abroad, leading to large receipts of remittances from emigrants (in South Africa in the case of Botswana, and the Gulf countries for Somalia) (Laitin, 1976, p. 452).

Yet despite these numerous similarities, ethnic identification in the two countries diverged notably in the last couple of decades of the twentieth century. Indeed, while, as I show in the next chapter, Botswana presents a case

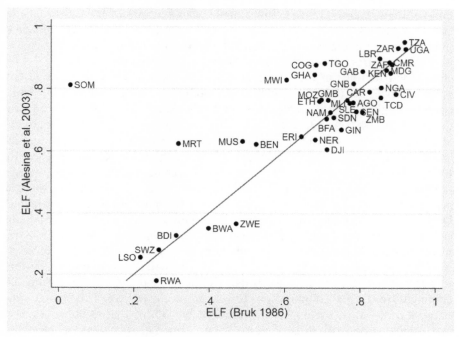

FIGURE 6.3. Ethno-linguistic fractionalization in Africa according to Alesina et al. (2003) and Bruk (1986)

of post-colonial assimilation, Somalia presents a diametrically opposite case of increasing ethnic diversity. Somalia was formerly considered one of the most ethnically and religiously homogenous countries in Africa, with a population almost entirely comprised of Somali-speaking Muslims. Data from the Soviet *Atlas Narodov Mira* yields an ELF score of 0.077 in 1961 (Bruk & Apenchenko, 1964), the lowest in Sub-Saharan Africa and comparable to Denmark (0.049) and Sweden (0.083); in 1985 it had an ELF score of 0.032 (Bruk, 1986), comparable to Iceland (0.033) and Ireland (0.029). In both cases it was ranked within the top twenty least fractionalized countries in the world. Yet by 2003 both Alesina et al. (2003) and Fearon (2003) recorded an ELF score of 0.812, putting it among the top twenty *most* fractionalized countries in the world, as can be seen in Figure 6.3 when we compare African countries' ELF scores from the early 1980s according to Bruk (1986) and after the turn of the millennium twenty years later (Alesina et al., 2003).

What had happened to explain this sudden shift in Somalia? A strict primordial line would suggest that changing levels of fractionalization would most likely come about via a shift in the ethnic composition of the population due to migration. It is true that, for a moment in the late 1970s, there was a massive influx of immigrants into Somalia at a ratio of sixty per 1,000 residents, or third-highest in the world after Western Sahara and the UAE, but most of these migrants were fellow Somalis who fled eastern Ethiopia after the Somali army invaded in 1977. Thus by 1980 some one-quarter of Somalia's population was comprised of migrants. However, the Ethio-Somali War ended in 1978 and from the early 1980s Somalia saw negative net migration as citizens left for jobs in the Gulf States (as discussed in Chapter 4) while the onset of civil war in 1988 saw Ethiopian refugees return to Ethiopia, while continued fighting plus drought led even more Somalis to abandon the country in the early 1990s (Gundel, 2003). The civil war and chaos affected southern Somalia in particular, which is where members of the Bantu minority group largely lived. Thus a disproportionate number of refugees in Kenya were Somali Bantus, who comprised 7.9 per cent of the Somali population across three refugee camps in Kenya in 1994 (Declich, 2000, p. 27), in contrast to the 2.2 per cent to 6 per cent of the total population of Somalia estimated by Alesina, Devleeshauwer & Easterly et al. (2003), I. M. Lewis (2002, p. 7) and Menkhaus (2003). In other words, if anything, migration flows since the 1980s should have served to make Somalia more ethnically homogenous rather than more diverse.

What instead happened in Somalia was that Somalia's salient ethnic division was re-calculated at a lower level, namely the clan, thereby turning Somalia overnight from largely homogenous to very ethnically diverse. This change was a result not of the whim of researchers but instead a response to the real fragmentation of ethnic identity within Somalia, such that people who formerly claimed to speak the same language more recently began to consciously differentiate themselves as belonging to different groups (Laitin & Posner, 2001). Thus over the course of the 1990s Somalis increasingly recognized their clan diversity and challenged the idea of a Somali nation, thereby helping to 'unmask' Somali nationalism, as one anthropologist put it (Besteman, 1996, p. 587).

What explains this rapid shift in ethnic salience? One potential explanation is that the Somali government failed to promote any nation-building policies. Yet here the argument is inadequate. Siyad Barre, who was President from 1969 to 1991, continuously tried to de-emphasize the public salience and importance of clan/ethnic identities, most notably by barring the previously common greeting question of 'what is your clan?', with offenders sent to jail (Laitin, 1976, p. 456), while also creating new provinces after independence that cut across clan lines and repeating the slogan 'Tribalism Divides – Socialism Unites.' In a well-attended ceremony in November 1971 in a Mogadishu sports stadium Barre even attempted to symbolically 'bury' clannism, marking the occasion by ritually cremating an effigy of each clan and declaring it to be 'Somali National Clanism Funeral Day' (Omolesky, 2017). Barre also de-emphasized the importance of clan ties by decreeing that social events were to be held henceforth in government-owned orientation centres, rather than in leading clan families' houses, while also replacing the use of blood compensation (*diya*) given by one clan to another in cases of murder with the use of a formal system of justice (Balthasar, 2012, p. 108).

In perhaps his most important nation-building policy, Barre's government promoted the adoption of the Roman alphabet as the national script for the Somali language in 1972 after long-standing debates about how to write Somali, while also declaring it the sole official language and initiating a huge mass literacy campaign in the mid-1970s that helped to united Somalis linguistically (I. M. Lewis, 2002, p. 216). As part of this drive, the government opened the Somali National Library in 1976, created a Somali Language Commission in order to produce new primary school textbooks, commissioned poets to write poems praising the new orthography and subsidized the publication of new books in Somali (Caney, 1982, p. 33). The exact numbers are unclear, but it is clear that, because of this drive, at least half of the adult population became literate during the 1970s (Balthasar, 2012, p. 110). Moreover, Barre's regime also focussed on the architecture of nation-building by erecting multiple large national monuments in Mogadishu commemorating men and women who had fought for independence like Mohammed Abdullah Hassan and Hawa Taako, as well as a new cultural centre in 1985 to house the National Museum, National Theatre and National Library.

One of the biggest criticisms of Barre's nation-building efforts was that government policies favoured his Marehan sub-clan (of the Darod clan), as well as the Ogaden (Barre's maternal clan) and the Dhulbahante (Barre's son-in-law's clan), known together locally as MOD (I. M. Lewis, 2002, p. 245). However, there is counter-evidence that the composition of his cabinets (later Supreme Revolutionary Councils) provided at least some representation for the country's major clans (I. M. Lewis, 2002, p. 221). Moreover, even if Barre was ethnically biased in his cabinet appointments or spending on public goods, this would have not been in any way unusual for post-colonial African governments, including and even especially in neighbouring Kenya (Burgess, Jedwab & Miguel et al., 2015; Kramon & Posner, 2016), none of whom saw such a shift in ethnic identification or the collapse into anarchy of post-Barre Somalia.[5] Finally, accusing Barre's clan bias as being responsible for the increased salience of clans from the 1980s is plausibly to mistake symptom for cause, much in the same way that outsiders blame African underdevelopment on corruption without a full understanding on the deeper reasons why African governments rely upon co-ethnics for support. (It is especially difficult to focus on Barre's clan bias as causal when there is evidence that it dated back to when he was merely an army general in the mid-1960s, or far before the collapse of the Somali state; Ingiriis, 2016, p. 171.)

---

[5] It is of course difficult or even impossible to accurately compare the degree of ethnic favouritism in Barre's Somalia to other African countries given a lack of adequate pre-1991 survey or night-time luminosity data, which are the two main data sources used to measure ethnic favouritism in the political economy literature. What is clear, however, is that there are serious questions about the degree to which ethnic favouritism has been over-attributed to post-colonial regimes in Africa as regards education and public employment policies (Simson & Green, 2020).

Alternatively, it is plausible that a lack of state capacity to provide public goods, as argued by Wimmer (2018), prevented citizens from adhering to a broader Somali identity. Yet there is plenty of evidence that the Somali state could and did provide for its people, most notably in the drought of 1974 which led to the loss of one-quarter of all domestic animals. Just as with the Botswanan government's successful attempts to avert a famine a decade later, the Somali government was able to mobilize large number of students and other locals to provide relief to upwards of one-third of the country's population (I. M. Lewis, 2002, pp. 217–18). Moreover, the aforementioned literacy campaign coincided with a five-fold increase in school enrollment from 1970 to the late 1980s, alongside a 5.5-fold increase in the number of teachers and a rise in the central government's annual budgetary allocation to education from 6.8 per cent in 1969 to 11.3 per cent in 1977 (Warsame, 2001, p. 351). At the tertiary level the Somali National University was created in 1969 in Mogadishu but expanded in size in the 1970s, while its former teaching college in Lafoole in neighbouring Shabeellaha Hoose region was re-made as a stand-alone university in 1973. Finally, Barre's government decided in 1971 to guarantee public service employment to all secondary school graduates (International Labour Organization, 1989, p. 27). In summarizing Barre's achievements in his first decade in office, David Laitin (1979, p. 114) was not alone in his praise:

> Barre has done much for the Somali nation. He has united the people sufficiently for them to agree on the Latin script for the Somali language, now the official medium of communication, and this decision has had a monumental impact on the creation of a literate and aware population. Also, he has responded to the drought which threatened the economic basis of Somali society with forthright courage ... Development programs have given the Somalis a spirit of confidence and purpose which has induced both civil servants and ordinary citizens to work hard for common goals.

Yet despite these numerous achievements clan identity became the major ethnic cleavage in Somalia in the subsequent decade due to the onset of violence and then civil war; as one scholar put it, 'in an increasingly insecure environment, clan affiliation gained added importance' (Webersik, 2004, p. 528). The idea that individuals would 'retreat' to their ethnic identities in the face of state collapse seems plausible, yet the question remains as to why clan identities were more important than other potential cleavages within Somali society. Indeed, there is strong evidence of a major racial cleavage between Somalis and the Bantus of southern Somalia, many of whom were descendent from slaves from further south in East Africa and were thus not considered 'true' Somalis despite their collective decision to assimilate into Somali culture and adopt clan identities (Webersik, 2004, p. 524). Moreover, clan identities were and are inherently unstable due to a history of exogamous marriages which led individuals to not only have relatives across numerous geographically dispersed clans but also allowed people to adopt identities of other lineages (Bradbury, 2008, p. 13).

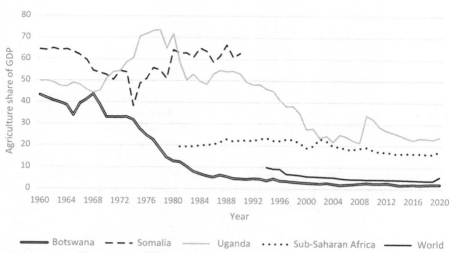

FIGURE 6.4. Agriculture as a share of GDP in Botswana, Somalia and Uganda, 1960–2020
(*Source:* World Bank)

Instead, the reason why clan identity became so important in Somalia was arguably the failure to create any significant amount of non-agricultural, urban formal-sector employment in the decades after independence, thereby halting the process of identifying as a member of a larger Somali ethnic group. As Figure 6.4 shows, while agriculture's contribution to GDP started out higher in Somalia (64 per cent) than Botswana (43 per cent) in 1960, both countries followed similar downward-sloping trends through the 1960s and early 1970s (with the 1974 drought in Somalia explaining the sudden decline in that year).[6] However, thereafter the trends diverge, such that agriculture continued to decline to under 10 per cent of GDP in Botswana in the 1980s but actually increased in Somalia to levels above that in the 1960s before the data line disappears in the early 1990s due to state collapse.

The contrast between the droughts in Somalia in the 1970s and in Botswana in the 1980s is particularly important. While, as we shall see in the next chapter, there was a huge amount of rural–urban migration in the latter case, in the former case there was no mass migration to the cities; instead, the government attempted to re-settle poor pastoralists as farmers in southern Somalia across six settlement schemes, with three devoted to agriculture livelihoods and three to fishing. While initially successful, the re-settled population slowly bled away due in part to poor planning of the schemes and the

---

[6] I use data on agriculture's share of GDP despite the limitations noted in Chapter 2 about such measures, as data on sectoral employment by industry does not go back futher than 1990.

infrastructure surrounding their livelihoods (Hitchcock & Hussein, 1987, p. 34). Instead, many farmers and fishermen eventually returned home to herding cattle, which flourished as an industry in the 1980s in contrast to other sectors in the economy (I. M. Lewis, 2002, p. 258).[7]

As elsewhere, much of the increased salience over clan identity in Somalia revolved around the control over land. Interestingly, prior to independence pastoral land was open to all Somalis but cultivable land was held under specific clans. Thus locals had control over valuable land and would allow 'strangers' to come and graze only with permission and if they were en route elsewhere (Shepherd, 1989, p. 55). Yet, as happened in Botswana (and other parts of Africa), Barre transferred all communal land rights to the central government in 1975 (M. Roth, 1988). This policy was done in part to remove power over land-management from the clans and to hand it over to central government; the result, ironically, was to increase inter-clan struggles over central government control. To take the example of the inter-riverine area of southern Somalia, one researcher found evidence that 'foreign' villagers identified as members of the Hubeer sub-clan of the Rahanweyn clan as a means to access property (Helander, 1996). Indeed, in the 1980s development funds poured into Somalia in anticipation of a new World-Bank funded dam on the Jubba River in Gedo region, which led to an even greater focus on controlling access to irrigation and the 'relatively durable asset of land' (Besteman, 1996, p. 585).

The continued economic importance attached to land was a direct consequence of the Barre regime's disastrous handling of the economy. Indeed, while the plaudits issued by Laitin (1979) above on Barre's nation-building projects were echoed by multiple other scholars at the time, the same scholars also noted how terrible the country's economic prospects were (Ahmed I. Samatar, 1987, pp. 872–3). In particular the government failed to invest in rural economic productivity that would have allowed labour to be released into the urban and industrial sectors. In a passage reminiscent of the lack of reach of the Turkish state in Kurdistan from the previous chapter, one anthropologist noted at the time that 'the state has not extended its control much farther into the pastoral rangelands: in recent discussions in Mogadishu [in 1979], high government officials conceded that an occasional veterinarian's visit was all that most nomads ever see' (Aronson, 1980, p. 19). This neglect was a consequence of the government's collusion with traders rather than nomadic producers, who then struggled to compete in the Saudi market against Sudan and other exporters (Aronson, 1980, p. 21); this situation became even worse when Saudi Arabia banned livestock imports from Somalia in 1984 for health reasons. Similar inefficiencies characterized the agricultural sector, where farmers lacked

---

[7] The failures of these settlement schemes should not be taken as a sign that the state had a uniquely low level of capacity, given the notable failures of settlement and villagization schemes elsewhere in Africa and the developing world (Scott, 1998).

access to inputs, technical assistance, services and irrigation, as well as the neglected fishing sector (Ahmed I. Samatar, 1987, pp. 878–9).

The result of this lack of rural investment led to poor export earnings, which hampered the ability of the government to import the crucial raw materials necessary for Somalia's infant industries. Industry's contribution to GDP thus reached a peak of only 3.8 per cent in 1978 before it declined to 1.6 per cent by 1984 (World Bank, 1987, p. vi). Calculated according to the parallel market rate this mean that industrial production was worth US$0.8 per capita at the time, or one of the lowest levels in the world (World Bank, 1987, p. 2). Ongoing problems with a lack of inputs into the economy – linked in part to the disruption of oil supplies after the onset of the Iran–Iraq war in 1981, as well as the lack of a national electricity grid – were partially responsible for low levels of utilization of industrial capacity. To take one example, the Jowhar sugar refinery in Shabeellaha Dhexe region, which was the oldest operating industrial establishment in the country since it was set up by Italian investors under colonial rule, operated at only 5 per cent capacity in the 1980s and often shut for months at a time (A. L. Gray, Jr., 1989, p. 126). The same held for various industrial products as a whole: sugar, milk, pasta and flour, textiles and canned fruit and vegetables all reached their peak production levels in the late 1970s before declining (Ahmed I. Samatar, 1985, p. 37). The result was that manufacturing exports as a proportion of all exports peaked at around 20 per cent in the early 1970s before falling close to zero by the end of the decade, in contrast to live animal exports, which increased from around 50 per cent to 90 per cent of all exports over the same time period (Laitin & Samatar, 1984, p. 69).

At the same time high levels of inflation caused public sector wages to drop in value to less than 3 per cent by 1989 compared to their value in the early 1970s (Mubarak, 1997, p. 2028), leading many public sector workers to moonlight in the informal economy. While public service employment continued to grow through 1983, in part compensating for a decline in private sector employment over the same period, that year saw the suspension of the aforementioned guaranteed employment scheme for secondary school graduates and a subsequent stagnation in public sector employment as the government's fiscal crisis started to spiral out of control (International Labour Organization, 1989, p. 27). As regards the private sector, informality subsumed the formal sector due to a growth in smuggling and a black market for foreign exchange and other goods and services (Mubarak, 1997, p. 2028). The result was a stagnation in the private sector employment between 1978 and 1986 in absolute terms and an actual decline in relative terms due to population growth (International Labour Organization, 1989, p. 28), leading to a worsening problem with urban unemployment and a significant problem of 'brain drain' as educated Somalis fled abroad, especially to the Gulf (UNDP, 2001, p. 82). Thus by the mid-1980s the informal sector had become the largest employer of labour in the economy, including in such sectors as health, education and finance (Mubarak, 1997, p. 2029).

As such, urban dwellers had to rely upon access to rural land and clan networks for support. 'The informalization of the economy, therefore, reinforced the importance of [clan] kinship in commercial networks as the medium of political discourse and as a social safety-net' (UNDP, 2001, p. 142), which in turn led to a decline in importance for other social identities. In particular educational qualifications and any form of cross-clan associations were no longer important in finding employment (UNDP, 2001, p. 143). The resultant association among ordinary Somalis between clan membership and the country's economic collapse can be seen in the fact that opposition movements like the Somali National Movement – whose leaders later founded the independent state of Somaliland in 1991 – blamed the state of the economy on the government's 'dynastic and clan-based structure' in their public pronouncements (Bakonyi, 2015, p. 250).

The one added element that was the real straw that broke the camel's back of the Somali state – and one factor that makes Somalia almost unique among post-colonial African states – was its participation in a proper inter-state war, namely President Barre's invasion of the Ogaden region of Ethiopia in 1977 and subsequent defeat the next year. The invasion led to an increase in the salience of clan identity in multiple ways. First, it cost Barre politically as his support within the army began to crumble, and he increasingly relied upon his own kin for support. Second, the aforementioned huge number of Ethiopian Somali refugees who temporarily settled in northern Somalia received both land titles and arms from Barre in anticipation of an Ethiopian invasion, thereby leading to increased resentment among the local Isaaq population (Balthasar, 2012, p. 128). Finally, the influx of arms into the country that was a result of the war led to a rapid decline in the state's Weberian monopoly of violence despite Barre's increased spending on the military. In other words, as Besteman so aptly puts it: 'Coming of age in a heavily militarized environment characterized by widespread economic decline, many youths recognized that their best chances for economic improvement lay with attaching themselves to a warring faction in the hopes that the patronage system would eventually benefit them. Kinship ties provided the primary means of seeking patronage' (1996, p. 591). It is therefore not surprising that the military factions that arose to overthrow Barre in 1991 were based on clan identities, with the Ogaden-based Somalia Patriotic Movement, Isaaq-based Somali National Movement and Hawiye-based United Somali Congress. These and other factions physically destroyed much of the Barre government's efforts at nation-building in Mogadishu, including the National Museum, National Library and multiple national monuments; the complete failure of Barre's project can be seen in the way librarians and other officials trying to protect national treasures were accused by militiamen of being 'faqash', or filth, which also became a code-name for members of the president's Darod clan (Nur, 2017, p. 12). The result has been three decades of near-anarchy in southern Somalia, with a series of unstable governments controlling little more than Mogadishu and 'elected' by delegates representing a small fraction of the electorate, while in the north the government of Somaliland declared independence and has continued to function as a state despite a complete lack of international recognition.

Indeed, if anyone needed further evidence for the persistent importance of clan identity in Somalia, it can be found in the composition of the National Constituent Assembly, whose task it was to debate a new constitution for Somalia in 2012 and which was comprised of thirty elders drawn from each of the four major clans (Darod, Dir, Hawiye and Rahanweyn) with another fifteen from a coalition of minority groups. This '4.5' power-sharing formula was then implemented in the country's new lower house of parliament, the House of the People, with sixty-one seats to each major clan and thirty-one to minority groups. As Omolesky (2017) pointedly points out, Barre's attempt to bury clannism ignored the Somali tradition of death as a beginning rather than an end, such that his nation-building efforts have ironically led to an increase in salience of the clans rather than their decline.

Thus, to summarize, clans became more important than ethnicity in Somalia due to the need to control state resources. Without a functioning private-sector capitalist economy, individuals instead focussed on controlling the state, including access to foreign aid and ownership of fertile agricultural land in southern Somalia. As such, instead of using their Somali identity to access employment in the modern, urban sector, contemporary Somalis have had more of an incentive to identify with their clans as means to obtain jobs and livelihoods, especially after the collapse of the state in the 1990s. The continued salience of clan identity thus meant that all of President Barre's aforementioned efforts at nation-building were ultimately worthless inasmuch as they became associated with his clan rather than the Somali nation, which explains the destruction of so many Somali national institutions in the wake of state collapse in the 1990s.

6.4 AGRARIAN ETHNIC IDENTITY IN UGANDA

I next turn to the experience of Uganda, which, like Somalia, has seen both low levels of industrialization and increasing ethnic fractionalization in the post-colonial era. (See Map 6.2 for a map of Uganda by district.)[8] As noted above, Uganda has seen very low rates of industrialization since independence, for several reasons. Unlike Botswana Uganda does not export natural resources – at least not at the present – and thus has not seen the sectoral shift out of agriculture that occurred in Botswana. As indicated in Figure 6.4, while agriculture as a percentage of GDP dropped precipitously in Botswana from 43.4 per cent in 1960 to 2.1 per cent in 2020, in Uganda the drop was far less severe,

---

[8] As in Turkey, Uganda's districts are named after their principal town. The map is from the early 2000s when Uganda had fifty-six districts; later maps with more districts are too detailed to reproduce here.

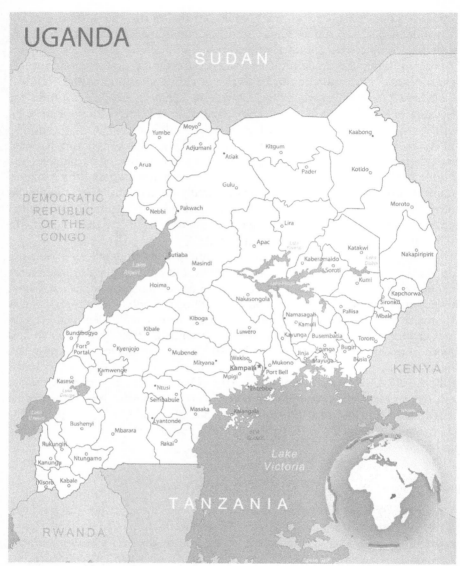

MAP 6.2. Map of Uganda by district

from 49.9 per cent to 23.9 per cent over the same time span; in fact, the shift out of agriculture in Uganda has stagnated since the early 2000s, even as other African states and the world economy as a whole has continued to see sectoral change. (This stagnation is largely due to the recovery of the coffee sector and the recent rise of floriculture, as well as the higher domestic demand for food due to population growth.) Indeed, Uganda has never had any serious problems with drought except in its under-populated north-east region and has thus not seen the same pressures to leave rural areas as in Botswana. Thus the political conflicts of the 1970s and 1980s under Presidents Idi Amin and Milton Obote led to a revival in agriculture as a percentage of GDP as the rest of the economy collapsed; they also led to substantial reverse migration from the two largest cities of Jinja and Kampala as people who lost jobs as a result of the economic collapse fled to the countryside to obtain enough food (Bigsten & Kayizzi-Mugerwa, 1992, p. 1425; Jamal & Weeks, 1993, p. 68).[9] The result is that Uganda has continued to urbanize, especially after President Museveni took power in 1986 and brought peace to most of the country, but at such a slow rate that it has even failed to keep pace with the sluggish Sub-Saharan African average, as seen in Figure 6.2.

Uganda's problems in promoting industrialization can be seen in part in Figure 6.1, with rising carbon emissions from 1960 to 1970 but a subsequent decline through to the early 1980s, followed by stagnation until the mid-1990s and a slow subsequent rise, albeit far below the Sub-Saharan African average. The decline in the 1970s is most obviously attributable to both the exile of the Asian population in 1972, whose large industrial interests were nationalized by Idi Amin but were subsequently mismanaged, as well as the dictatorial and haphazard rule of Amin, both of which led to a sharp decline in industrial output. The halt of the decline in the early 1980s corresponds both with the beginning of the repatriation of stolen property to the Asian community as well as the end of Amin's rule in 1979 and the return of elections in 1980. The growth in carbon emissions since the 1990s has arguably been driven by the rise of the service sector from less than 25 per cent of the economy in 1980 to 50 per cent by 2008, which was in part due to liberalization and privatization efforts under President Museveni since the late 1980s that resulted in a doubling of income per capita over a twenty-year period and a decline in levels of poverty. This trend, however, has been driven by relatively less labour-intensive sectors such as tourism and telecommunications, which has not led to significantly higher levels of employment outside agriculture. Thus, according to one recent analysis, 'economic liberalism has triggered rapid growth with no fundamental socio-economic transformation' (Obwona, Shinyekwa & Kiiza et al., 2014, p. 9).[10]

One of the major impediments to structural transformation in Uganda has, until recently, been its stubbornly high fertility rate and subsequently high dependency ratio and rate of population growth. The addition of around

---

[9] The historically Asian-dominated city of Jinja in particular saw an absolute drop in its population directly as a result of Amin's decision to exile Ugandan Asians in 1972; it has long since lost the status of the country's second-largest city to Gulu in northern Uganda, which has grown in size largely due to the LRA (Lord's Resistance Army) civil war.

[10] In a sense, then, Uganda has more recently followed the exact opposite pattern of Somalia in the 1970s, with a focus on 'hands off' neoliberal reforms rather than 'hands on' nationalization; yet in both cases there has been a lack of structural transformation of the economy.

400,000 new entrants into the labour market each year has led many workers to work in agriculture in rural areas due to low job prospects in urban areas and the continued growth in the amount of arable land in the countryside (Hausmann, Cunningham & Matovu et al., 2014, p. 5). The result is that Uganda maintains one of the lowest unemployment rates in the world (at 1.6 per cent in 2019, according to the latest World Bank figures) but also has one of the lowest levels of agricultural productivity in the world as labourers do not enter the formal job market but instead work on small plots without any economies of scale (Hausmann et al., 2014, p. 7).

The consequence of low levels of industrialization in Uganda has been to increase the relative importance of control over land. Inasmuch as land in Uganda has historically been linked to ethnicity, as elsewhere in Africa, ethnicity has not only remained political salient in Uganda but continues to be discussed in a highly primordial fashion. More specifically, the indirect rule system of government instituted by European colonial officials across their African colonies allocated access to local land along ethnic lines, such that members of locally dominant ethnic groups – known in various contexts as indigines, *originaires* or *autochthones* – could hold land under customary tenure while those were not indigenous to the area – or settlers, *non-originaires* and *allochthones* – could not, except under special circumstances. This system, which served to save European administrators money in their never-ending and largely unsuccessful quest to turn a profit in their African territories, meant that Africans in rural areas were largely treated as subjects of their local ethnic or tribal chiefs, while those (few) who lived in cities led the lives of state citizens, in Mamdani's (1996) memorable language. In Uganda not only did access to land depend on one's ethnic identity, but the nature of the land tenure system varied across the country, with customary ownership common across the poorer parts of the north and east and a freehold system in the centre and west, which in the case of the Buganda kingdom (centred around the capital city of Kampala) was styled *mailo* land (after the word 'mile') according to the 1900 Agreement legalizing British oversight of the Buganda kingdom.

Post-colonial efforts to reform this system by removing the power of local chiefs over land focussed in many African countries on nationalizing land tenure as part of their governments' interest in building up new cross-ethnic national identities. In Uganda these efforts took the form of the Land Reform Decree (LRD) of 1975 under President Amin, whereby all privately owned land was declared henceforth to be owned by the state and allocated to tenants as leasehold property. However, in practice the effect of the LRD was minimal, inasmuch as it did not lead to any widespread reallocation of land rights; as such ethnically demarcated access to land continued in a *de facto* if not *de jure* fashion. In 1993 President Museveni allowed for the restoration of the four southern kingdoms of Buganda, Bunyoro, Busoga and Toro, but only as cultural institutions and thus did not allow them to recapture rights over public land that they held in the 1960s. The 1995 constitution officially abolished the

1975 LRD, and the subsequent Land Act of 1998 under President Museveni similarly failed to change patterns of land tenure in any real way, although it possibly helped to secure greater freedom from eviction for many tenants across the country (Green, 2006).

The result is that laws over land tenure in contemporary Uganda look something like a palimpsest, with multiple sets of land reforms passed one on top of the other, none of which have been fully implemented (and none fully ignored either). The effect of a lack of any major changes in the nature of land ownership from the early colonial period to the present has been to maintain a strong ethnic link between land and ethnic identity, despite the fact that land is not officially allocated to ethnic communities and has not been for over half a century. To understand how ethnicity continues to structure land rights in Uganda, I turn to three examples. First, I examine the ethnicization of land conflicts in central Uganda, specifically in the kingdoms of Buganda and Bunyoro. Second, I describe national debates around the codification of indigeneity in the country's constitution, in which primordial understandings of ethnicity dominate. Third and finally, I detail the history of district creation under President Museveni's rule and the way in which it has become politicized along ethnic lines.

6.4.1 Land Rights and Ethnicity in Central Uganda

As noted above, multiple systems of land rights exist across Uganda, such that customary tenure is common across the northern and eastern halves of the country with freehold tenure more common in the centre and west. If we are to find evidence of a de-linking of ethnicity and access to land anywhere in Uganda, we should expect to find it in the central and western regions, where land has long become commodified due to its higher value (which in turn is related to its central location close to the capital city of Kampala) and non-indigenes have thus long had the opportunity to purchase it. Indeed, in colonial-era Buganda local landlords were happy to rent their land to non-Baganda migrants from other parts of Uganda, as well immigrants from Rwanda and Burundi, in part because the non-Baganda were easier to exploit (Green, 2006, p. 374). The effect of this arrangement, however, was to encourage large-scale xenophobia towards non-Baganda settlers, such that the number of non-Baganda who accessed such land remained small and, among those who did, many assimilated and re-identified as Baganda (Richards, 1954).

While, as noted, the 1998 Land Act failed to significantly alter the identity of the landlord class, it shifted control over public land from the centralized Uganda Land Commission in Kampala to individual Land Boards at the level of the district (the highest level of local government in Uganda). The result of the Act has been that control over the district government, and thus control over public land, has become a major site for political struggle in contemporary Uganda. One such case comes from Buliisa district in western Uganda, which borders Lake Albert to the west and was historically part of the Bunyoro kingdom. While formerly part of Masindi district, most of whose residents were ethnically Banyoro, the district was carved out in 2006 with members of the local Bagungu ethnic group as the new ethnic majority. Upon its creation access to land in the district was already limited due to the presence of Uganda's largest wildlife park, Murchison Falls National Park, which, along with other protected areas, constitutes 80 per cent of the total land area in the district (Muhereza, 2015, p. 7). After ethnically Banyarwanda *Balaalo* (herdsmen or pastoralists) increasingly migrated to the district from 2003 onwards to graze their herds of cattle due to high population densities in south-west Uganda, violent clashes over land erupted in 2007, drawing anti-riot police and national attention (Green, 2008a, p. 445). The subsequent exploitation of oil resources on the shores of Lake Albert has led to even more political struggles about who controls land in Buliisa, with the *Omukama* (king) of Bunyoro kingdom demanding a 12.5 per cent share of oil resources in his kingdom, including in Buliisa as it was part of the colonial (and pre-colonial) territory of Bunyoro. However, the response from Bagungu leaders of Buliisa district has been to try to 'secede' from the Bunyoro kingdom under the new name of *Obukama bwa Bugungu* (kingdom of Bugungu) under the grounds that they are ethnically different from the Banyoro, a move which has been resisted strongly by the Bunyoro kingdom leadership (Monitor, 2013).

The migration of Ugandans from its more densely populated south-western region to other parts of the country has not, however, been limited to Buliisa district. Members of the Bakiga ethnic group from the Kigezi region near the border with Rwanda have long migrated to other less densely settled parts of western Uganda, which in many cases has led to conflict over land ownership. For instance, in Hoima district (also part of Bunyoro kingdom) hundreds of Bakiga migrants were evicted from their land in 2002, out of whom 160 later camped outside the Uganda parliament building in protest at their treatment before being re-settled temporarily at a sports stadium in Kampala. When the government then attempted to permanently re-settle these Bakiga in Kiboga district in the western part of the Buganda kingdom, violent protests in Kiboga among local Baganda due to concerns about the potential for Bakiga political dominance in the area led to the decision to re-locate the Bakiga to an undisclosed location in Mubende district further south (Green, 2007, p. 727).

Perhaps the most important example, however, of how ethnicized land rights continue to be in Uganda comes from the district of Kibale in central-west Uganda. What is today Kibale district was previously the two counties of Buyaga and Bugangaizi, a core part of the pre-colonial kingdom of Bunyoro. Upon their arrival in the country, however, the British granted the territory to the neighbouring kingdom of Buganda as part of their subjugation of Bunyoro in the early 1890s. This loss, along with other territorial transfers at the onset of colonial rule, led to continued resentment in Bunyoro against the British over the life of the Ugandan Protectorate. As Buyaga and Bugangaizi counties were largely populated by Banyoro – unlike the other areas granted to Buganda – their inhabitants also continued to oppose Bugandan rule over the course of colonial rule; this resistance was institutionalized in 1921 with the establishment of a local pressure group named the Mubende Banyoro Committee (MBC).[11] Nonetheless, despite repeated protests and petitions from both the *Omukamas* (kings) of Bunyoro and the native Banyoro of Buyaga and Bugangaizi, the British refused to reverse their earlier decision.[12]

Much of the anger of the Banyoro revolved around the fact that the British had introduced freehold landholding in Uganda in 1900 and had thereby granted Baganda landlords much of the best land in Buyaga and Bugangaizi.[13] Despite the fact that the Banyoro were eventually granted a referendum in 1964 on whether they wanted to remain part of Buganda or re-join Bunyoro, the issue of land ownership never arose. Thus, despite an overwhelming vote to secede from Buganda in the referendum, the Baganda landlords continued to own land in the area, although due to the ongoing resentment about Bugandan overrule, they dared not bother come and collect any rent on their property.[14]

While over the next forty years Buyaga and Bugangaizi saw little change in their land-holding structure, the area did see a large amount of in-migration from other parts of Uganda, especially of ethnic Bakiga from south-west Uganda from the 1970s onwards. While there was initially little tension between the native Banyoro and immigrant Bakiga, a second influx of Bakiga in the early 1990s began to raise tensions between the two groups due to the rising local political influence of the Bakiga settlers. The settlers' political strength first became apparent when they elected Robert Kakooza, a Mukiga, as MP for Buyaga county in 1996; Kakooza was, however, replaced by Ignatius Musisira, a Munyoro, in the subsequent 2001 election.

By this time Kibale district had been formed out of Hoima district in accordance with President Museveni's long-term plan to decentralize power to local Resistance Council (RC) governments, including the aforementioned decentralization of control over public land, while also increasing the number of districts in Uganda.[15] Local conflict was thus sparked off by the election of Fred Ruremera, a Mukiga, as district chairman over the incumbent Munyoro Sebastian Ssekitolekko in early 2002. The MBC, which had been resurrected in response to Ruremera's campaign the previous year, launched a campaign of

---

[11] Buyaga and Bugangaizi were part of Mubende district, one of four sub-divisions of colonial Buganda.

[12] This so-called 'lost counties' issue is covered in more detail in Green (2008b).

[13] The *Kabaka* (King) and his administrators in the Buganda kingdom were allowed to choose the best land as their freehold property after signing the Agreement, leaving the other 48 per cent of land in the region to become Crown land.

[14] Interview with Kibale District Chairman George Namyaka, Kibale, Uganda; 9 August 2005.

[15] The RCs were renamed Local Councils in Uganda's 1996 Constitution.

violence that included hate speech on its local KKCR radio station. Violence inevitably broke out after the election, with several Bakiga murdered – and two children beheaded – by Banyoro extremists and many more being threatened with expulsion from the district, leading to the deployment of anti-riot police. President Museveni responded with his first-ever – and so far only – use of clause 202 of the 1995 Constitution of Uganda, which allowed him to take over the rule of a district in exceptional circumstances, thereby negating Ruremera's election. Indeed, rather than reprimand the MBC or other extremists, Museveni replaced Ruremera with George Namyaka, a native Munyoro, to calm the situation.

All of these cases of ethnicized land conflict in Uganda are thus a consequence of the continued association of land rights with ethnic identity, despite the admirable efforts of the government to de-ethnicize land rights by granting them to elected local governments rather than kingdom governments, at least in the southern half of the country. Indeed, this shift drew praise from the Ugandan academic Mahmood Mamdani, who had chaired the government-appointed 1987 Commission of Inquiry into the Local Government System that recommended the decentralization of government to locally elected councils. In the 1990s Mamdani claimed that the Museveni government's 'shift in the basis of rights from an exclusive and localized ([ethnic] descent) principle to an inclusive and generalizable (labor) one was of enormous significance' (Mamdani, 1996, p. 208), such that it stood as a lesson for the rest of Africa in how to break the power of ethnicity over the countryside. However, in hindsight it now appears that Mamdani's praise was premature, since the decentralization and democratization of control over land in Uganda has failed to de-ethnicize the countryside and may have even generated more conflict than it solved.

6.4.2 Debates over Indigeneity in Uganda

Another way to examine the degree to which ethnicity in Uganda remains not only highly salient but understood as rural in origin, with an explicit link to control over land, is the way it has been codified in Uganda law. Indeed, in its laborious process of writing the 1995 constitution, the Ugandan Constituent Assembly decided to list the fifty-six 'indigenous communities' of Uganda in the constitution's Third Schedule or Appendix, with indigeneity defined as being a resident community in Uganda on 1 February 1926, which was the last time the borders of Uganda had been altered. The consequence of being listed in the schedule is being listed as an ethnic category in subsequent national censuses and allowing members of such groups to identify as such without worrying about being exiled or losing citizenship (as indeed happened to members of the Asian community in 1972 under Idi Amin's presidency).

The number of indigenous groups listed has remained a hot political issue in Ugandan politics to the present day. Indeed, the original draft constitution in

1993 only included forty-eight groups, which was two fewer than were listed in the 1959 colonial census, which led to controversy in the Constituent Assembly debating Uganda's constitution and the subsequent inclusion of an additional eight groups. The Uganda government then constituted a Constitutional Review Commission (CRC) in 2003, or only eight years after the constitution was promulgated, in part to deal with claims that not all indigenous communities had been listed. After a recommendation by the CRC that 'detailed inquiries should be made in the claims of some communities that they existed as indigenous communities but were not listed in the schedule of indigenous communities' (Government of Uganda, 2003, p. 159), in 2005 the parliament introduced a bill amending the constitution by adding nine additional ethnic groups to the schedule. In the debate over the bill, MPs tellingly adopted a very primordial understanding of ethnicity, focussing on such issues as language, homeland and customs. Thus, for instance, Ugandan Asians of Indian descent were not included on the original or amended list of indigenous communities, despite being present in Uganda in 1926, for the simple reason that MPs considered them a nationality rather than an ethnic community. In defining what it meant to be an indigenous ethnic group and why Asians should not be listed, the Makerere University academic and then Minister for Local Government Tarsis Kabwegyere (Igara County West) asked in parliament, 'What is their totem, what is their ancestral origin and what is the name of their ancestor?'[16] Those arguing for the inclusion of certain groups noted their history above all else: for instance, Simon Wananzofu (Bulambuli) claimed in support of one group that 'I want to confirm to this House that the Shana tribe is a community in Bulambuli County, Sironko District [in eastern Uganda]. They have stayed in Sironko for more than 100 years and they are a Bantu-speaking people . . . They are more than 12,000 Bantu people and are Ugandans like you and I.'[17] In the end the parliament supported the amendment, leading to the expansion of the list of indigenous communities to sixty-five in total.

Far from the inclusion of new groups in 2005 putting this matter to rest, the issue of who is and is not included in the list of indigenous communities has continued to simmer. Indeed, the members of the Benet group, who largely reside in Kapchorwa District in eastern Uganda, subsequently complained that they deserved to be listed in the schedule (Monitor, 2008). In 2012 the exact wording of the schedule came up for debate in parliament again, when Fred Omach (Jonam County) claimed that:

The Jonam people are a tribe of their own and not a clan among the Acholi people. They are recognised in the Constitution of the Republic of Uganda as tribe No. 43 and,

---

[16] Parliament of Uganda Hansard, 15 August 2005. Available at <www.parliament.go.ug/docu ments/5086/hansards-2005-august>

[17] Parliament of Uganda Hansard, 20 July 2005. Available at <www.parliament.go.ug/documents/ 5085/hansards-2005-july>

therefore, it is not acceptable for any person or group of persons to refer to them as a clan. I would like to lay this particular page 212 of the Constitution of the Republic of Uganda, in which it is clearly an ethnic group of its own.[18]

Finally, members of the Maragoli community, who are descended from ethnically Luhya Kenyan immigrants who settled in western Uganda as early as the late nineteenth century, have continued to argue for their recognition in the constitution, going so far as to present their case before parliament in 2015. Despite being denied their claim, Maragoli leaders have continued to press for their inclusion, in large part due to their desire to secure claim to land which was allocated to members of the group in the 1950s by the Omukama of Bunyoro (Manby, 2018, p. 69), with one MP (Jack Lutanywa, Kibanda South) petitioning the Uganda parliament in 2020 to introduce a new amendment to the constitution recognizing the Maragoli (Independent, 2020).

6.4.3 Ethnicity and District Creation in Uganda

One of President Museveni's most successful political strategies since he took office in 1986 has been to create new districts, which have burgeoned in number from thirty-three when he first took office to fifty-six in 2000, eighty in 2006, 112 in 2010 and 135 in 2020. This process, which has been described by the local neologism 'districtization', has generated a new source of local patronage for Museveni due to the creation of new jobs in both public administration and the private sector (especially in construction, due to a mandate that district capitals should be constructed as close as possible to the centroid of any new district). Indeed, despite the scorn poured on this exercise by both donors and members of the educated elite in Kampala, as well as evidence that district creation does not lead to greater access to public goods, voters in newly created districts have nonetheless responded by voting at higher levels for Museveni and his political party across multiple elections since the 1990s (Green, 2010b).

One major reason why many Ugandans have demanded new districts is due to the desire to transform what were ethnic minorities in the old district into majorities in a new district, along the lines of the Bangungu in Buliisa district mentioned above. On the one hand, the government has not explicitly linked ethnicity to district creation. Both President Museveni and the aforementioned Commission of Inquiry into the Local Government System have rejected attempts at creating ethnically homogenous districts in cases where minority groups did not face discrimination within their district, with the Commission of Inquiry also rejecting the creation of Busia district in eastern Uganda as it 'has the potential of undermining the trend towards Tororo [district] becoming a successful ethnic "melting pot"' (Government of Uganda, 1987, p. 130).

---

[18] Parliament of Uganda Hansard, 23 February 2012. Available at <www.parliament.go.ug/docu ments/1073/hansards-2012-february>

On the other hand, district creation has nonetheless been driven by a *de facto*, if not *de jure*, balkanization of rural politics in Uganda due to in large part to the power over land granted to district governments. Indeed, while the listing of 'indigenous communities' in the Third Schedule of the constitution has not ostensibly been the basis for new district creation, ethnic groups do appear to have a greater claim to their own district once they are recognized in the constitution. It is thus no coincidence that the previous item on the parliamentary agenda prior to the creation of new districts on 20 July 2005, was the aforementioned proposal to add nine additional ethnic groups to the Third Schedule, leading to one MP complaining to the parliament, 'let us not start creating tribes like we are going to create districts'.[19]

We have already seen how district creation along ethnic lines led to conflict over land in the case of Buliisa in central-west Uganda. I now provide two additional cases which demonstrate how the process of 'districtization' has both become wrapped up with ethnic-based access to land and demonstrates how ethnic identity continues to be understood in a primordial fashion in Uganda. The first such case comes from the division of Kabarole district in western Uganda into three districts in 2000. (Kabarole is the only district in Uganda not named after its capital, namely Fort Portal, which owes its name to a nineteenth-century British colonialist.) While Kabarole was and is seen as the core territory of the Toro Kingdom and thus home to the Batoro ethnic group, it has also been home to various indigenous minority communities such as the Bakiga, Banyankole and Batagwenda. By the late 1990s members of these minority communities, all three of whom are listed as indigenous in the constitution, felt confident enough to petition Museveni for the creation of two new districts, Kyenjojo and Kamwenge, along ethnic lines. As Batoro would no longer be dominant numerically in these two new districts, kingdom supporters were worried that Kyenjojo and Kamwenge would 'secede' from the kingdom; moreover, with control over land now vested in District Land Boards, Batoro would no longer oversee land allocation in the new districts. Thus, as reported by Ugandan journalist (and Kabarole native) Andrew Mwenda at the time, 'people are even arming themselves for a possible war' in the region (Mwenda & Mugisa, 1999), leading to intense talks between various military and security leaders from Kampala and local leaders. In the end President Museveni relented and explicitly went back on his previous commitment against the creation of new districts along ethnic lines and allowed the creation of the new districts.

A second example comes from ethnically Japadhola-dominated Tororo district in eastern Uganda, where a number of minority Iteso residents in Tororo county started to petition the government for their own district in 1998. A Commission of Inquiry appointed by the central government in

---

[19] Parliament of Uganda Hansard, 20 July 2005. Available at <www.parliament.go.ug/documents/5085/hansards-2005-july>

2005 agreed to create the proposed Mukuju district but failed to assign the current district capital, whose residents are split between the Japadhola and Iteso, to the new district. The rift led to ethnic divisions in the February 2006 parliamentary race, with many local Iteso supporting the Ugandan Asian candidate Sanjay Tana against the incumbent MP for Tororo Municipality, Yeri Ofwono. After winning the election, Tana escaped a petrol-bomb attack at his residence in April 2006, while in August soldiers from the Ugandan Peoples Defense Forces (UPDF, the Ugandan army) forcibly broke up a meeting of Tororo county councillors on the behest of the district chairman. In October 2006 the UPDF was again deployed in town after rumours that local Iteso extremists were planning on burning down the district headquarters.

The government has continued to delay the creation of the new district despite sporadic outbreaks of violence, such as in 2017 when one man was killed in protests during which Jopadhola activists claimed that Iteso were 'trying to grab their land' (NTV Uganda, 2017). Afterwards the government sent a ten-member team to London in 2019 to establish the 'historical' boundaries between the two areas by examining colonial maps (The Independent, 2019). This attempt drew a response from a group of Jopadhola elders, who claimed in a report that they were the 'aboriginal' people of Tororo and that the creation of a new district based on Iteso 'ethnic expansionism' would be 'tantamount to conquering and humiliating the Jopadhola' (Padhola Elders' Forum, 2019). Indeed, part of this debate has even consisted of establishing the origin of the name of the district as a means of claiming who is autochthonous to the area and thus its rightful ruler: Jopadhola activists claim that the word 'Tororo' originates in the Dhopadhola phrase 'season of mist' while Iteso activists claim it derives from the Ateso phrase 'where to pass' (Papa, 2014).

6.5 CONCLUSION

In both Somalia and Uganda we can observe how a lack of structural transformation out of rural agriculture and into the formal, urban, industrial sector, has led to increasing levels of ethnic fractionalization along clan lines in Somalia and tribal lines in Uganda. In both cases this lack of assimilation has contributed to various amounts of ethnic conflict, namely state collapse and anarchy in Somalia and continued conflict over land in Uganda. While both countries continue to urbanize, albeit at relatively slow rates, the lack of any continued focus on creating non-agrarian livelihoods means that this trend is unlikely to alter any time soon.

The experience of both countries in this regard is instructive in understanding the origins of ethnic conflict in contemporary Africa. For instance, there is now a substantial amount of evidence around the negative effects of codifying ethnicity in law on ethnic conflict and violence (Brubaker, 1996; Lieberman & Singh, 2012, 2017), such that the codification of ethnicity can lead to an increased salience of ethnic divisions and a breakdown in inter-ethnic relations. Both Somalia and Uganda have indeed codified ethnic divisions, via the membership of its House of the People and the listing of 'indigenous communities' in its constitution, respectively. However, as the evidence above suggests, for both countries the codification of ethnicity was a consequence of the failure to generate supra-ethnic or more homogenized forms of identity, rather than a cause. Indeed, in Somalia the House of the People was created to smooth clan tensions and help end a state of anarchy. In the Ugandan case there has been no shortage of people demanding the government cease officially listing of tribes. To take two out of many examples, in the main opposition newspaper one commentator noted in 2014 that 'this tribalisation of Uganda citizenship might serve political ends but in the long run, it may break this country. We, therefore, need to get the courage to detribalise the Constitution by scrapping the list, thus taking away the basis of those who want to use tribes to further their personal interests' (Bichachi, 2014).

Similarly, during the parliamentary debate in 2005 one MP, Ephraim Kamuntu (Sheema County South), made an effort to dismiss the whole debate as a topic not fit to be discussed in parliament:

We should have a Department of Anthropology. That is the only one, which could give authentic information about identification of these tribes ... Why don't we get rid of these tribal identifications and be identified as Ugandans? We would have solved a whole thing by a stroke of a pen? What are we keeping here? Even for purposes of ownership, claiming land, this constantly raises problems of wrong people being identified differently. Being Ugandan we should be sufficient and we should rule out this.[20]

Yet these voices have been relatively few compared to those who not only want to keep listing communities in the constitution but want to have their tribe listed as well. The most recent example of this phenomenon has been the members of the Indian community, who, as noted above, are not listed on the grounds that they are not 'indigenous' to Uganda. Attempts to recognize the Indian community led President Museveni in a 2019 speech to agree in principle to have 'another tribe called Wahindi [the Swahili word for Indians] in our constitution', which could lead him to offer land to the Indian community as members of an indigenous tribe (Kwesiga, 2019). Here, as in Somalia and other African contexts, there thus appears to be no end in sight to the continued politicization of clan or tribal identities so long as the basis for the economy remains agrarian and rural.

---

[20] Parliament of Uganda Hansard, 15 August 2005. Available at <www.parliament.go.ug/docu ments/5086/hansards-2005-august>

7

'Cattle without Legs'

Structural Transformation in Botswana

7.1 INTRODUCTION

In the previous chapter I examined the two cases of Somalia and Uganda as countries where a failure to shift the economy out of the rural agricultural sector has led to a lack of ethnic homogenization and increased levels of ethnic fractionalization. Here I examine another African country which has experienced a very different trajectory, namely Botswana. (See Map 7.1 for a map of Botswana by district.) In contrast to Somalia and Uganda, Botswana is well known for its exceptional political stability and economic development in Sub-Saharan Africa. It has not only avoided the conflict of nearby countries like Angola and Zimbabwe but had the highest level of GDP growth per capita in the world between 1965 and 1995, or higher than East Asian Tigers like South Korea and Singapore over the same time period (Acemoglu, Johnson & Robinson, 2003, p. 82). Unlike in other African countries such as Côte d'Ivoire and Kenya which have experiences periods of high economic growth, Botswanan development has not been followed by political strife; instead, Botswana's last four presidents have all resigned from office peacefully, most recently in 2008, when the outgoing President Festus Mogae received the Ibrahim Prize for Achievement in African Leadership, and again in 2018 when Ian Khama handed power over to Mokgweetsi Masisi.

Botswanan political development has been paralleled by its structural transformation from one based on agrarian rural production to an urban-centred industrial economy, as seen in its rapid urbanization, decline in the share of GDP devoted to agriculture and rise in carbon emissions. This immense change, along with the government's decision to place diamond revenues in the hands of the central government, has contributed to assimilation into the Batswana ethnic group as citizens no longer place high value on their tribal or ethnic minority identities. Botswana thus not only provides a prime example of

MAP 7.1. Map of Botswana by district

political stability and economic development in the African context, but also shows clearly how industrial transformation can lead to ethnic homogenization in a continent known for its high levels of ethnic fractionalization.

In the rest of this chapter I first examine the nature of structural transformation in Botswana, before providing an overview of Botswana's ethnic structure. I show that, far from encouraging assimilation, institutional dominance by the major Batswana tribes in the upper house of parliament, the House of Chiefs, has actually led to ethnic strife and the appointment of a government commission in 2000 that examined ethnic inequality in the country and how to resolve it. I then present both quantitative and qualitative evidence on how the shift out of agriculture – and the lack of tribal control over diamond revenues –

has generated incentives for Botswanans to identify in much broader ethnic terms. In the former case I show a consistent decline in Botwana's level of ethnic fractionalization since independence and then use recent Afrobarometer survey data to show that there is a robust negative relationship between agricultural employment and non-ethnic identification. In the latter case I examine both the ethnographic literature as well as parliamentary debates around the House of Chiefs and ethnic inequality in general; in contrast to evidence from Uganda in the previous chapter, I show here how industrialization has encouraged a constructivist understanding of ethnicity which has helped to ease ethnic tensions.

7.2 THE PROCESS OF INDUSTRIALIZATION IN BOTSWANA

As shown in Figures 6.1, 6.2 and 6.4 in the previous chapter, Botswana's political and economic success has accompanied rapid structural transformation and industrialization. Indeed, it is easy to forget just how rural and underdeveloped Botswana was before it achieved political independence in 1966. As noted in the previous chapter, Botswana is similar to Somalia in the historical basis of its economy on cattle herding, such that in the 1970s it had the highest ratio of cattle to humans of any country in the world (Government of Botswana, 1979, p. 12). The historic importance of cattle for Batswana is reflected in the vocabulary of the Setswana language, which has a remarkably large number of words to describe specific colour patterns of cattle, such as -*gweba* ('red and white spotted', for male cattle only), -*phatshwana* ('black and white patches', female cattle), -*tilodi* ('black and white spotted', male cattle), -*tlhaba* ('dark brown on muzzle', male cattle) and -*ramagana* ('mottled red/brown and white', female cattle) (I. R. L. Davies, Macdermid & Corbett et al., 1992).[1]

In the colonial period Botswanans were restricted to agricultural employment, with modern commercial activities limited to Europeans and Indians (Mogalakwe, 1997, p. 27). As regards settlement patterns within the tribal reserves, Botswana had long had large villages where residents settled for part of the year, leading some scholars to call them 'urban villages' or 'agrotowns' (Gwebu, 2006b, p. 425). However, the actual urban nature of these villages is questionable considering the short amount of time Botswanans actually spent in them. A clear indication of just how infrequently they were occupied can be seen in colonial attempts at whooping cough and diphtheria inoculation in 1956, which had to be given three times with one month between each vaccination. The colonial government knew that its best chance to catch people in the

---

[1] In fieldwork conducted in south-eastern Botswana in the early 1990s among monolingual rural adults, I. R. L. Davies et al. (1992) found that male respondents were far more likely to list these cattle-specific colour terms than women when asked to list all colour terms that they knew, which is consistent with the traditional gendered division of labour in Botswana.

villages was during the rainy season from September through December. However, when the innoculation team arrived for their third and final visit in December 1956 at the Bakwena Reserve:

they found that in response to tribal custom, on the appearance of certain weather conditions, the Chief had ordered the seasonal migration to the agricultural lands. The village was practically vacant. The schools were closed for the holidays. There was nothing which could be done about it. The evacuation had occurred earlier than was usually the case. With the evacuation of Molepolole [village] every Bakwena district village similarly was vacated. All the children of the vital 0–5 years age group, and many of other age groups, were scattered with their families miles apart in the hundreds of square miles of almost trackless lands in the Reserve, there to stay probably until August or September, 1957... The cattle and agricultural lands are any distance up to 40 or 50 miles from the central villages and the huts on these farming lands are widely scattered, one or two at each group. Almost all of them are inaccessible by wheeled traffic.[2]

From this basis Botswana has seen rapid rates of urbanization and industrialization since the 1960s, for multiple reasons. First, Botswana was the only colony in Africa whose administrative capital was outside its territory, specifically in the South African town of Mafikeng. Thus the establishment of Gaborone as the new capital in 1965 meant not only an influx of staff but also construction workers, which still employed some 23 per cent of the city's residents in the early 1980s (Silitshena, 1984, p. 117). Second, the threshold definition of urban areas was altered in the 1980s from 15,000 to 5,000 people, which explains in part the way the level of urbanization jumped from 26.7 per cent in 1985 to 41.9 per cent in 1990.[3] Third, Botswana experienced its worst-ever recorded drought from 1981 through 1985, which contributed to rural–urban migration and the abandonment of agriculture.

However, the most important cause for structural transformation in Botswana has been the growth of its diamond industry. Inasmuch as Botswana's diamonds are found in volcanic pipes known as Kimberlite pipes (named after the town of Kimberley in South Africa), they require capital-intensive equipment and are easily fenced and controlled, unlike the alluvial diamonds found along riverbeds that are more common in countries such as Angola and Sierra Leone.[4] Thus, upon the discovery of diamonds in Orapa, Central District, soon after independence, the Botswanan government set up

[2] Botswana National Archives, S. 558/8, Report on Whooping Cough/Diphtheria Immunization Campaign, 1957, pp. 4, 7.

[3] If anything, the re-definition merely brought Botswana's urbanization rate to a more accurate level than it had been before, inasmuch as the new policy re-defined urban areas along the lines then used by the United Nations. Indeed, previously scholars such as Silitshena (1984) had complained that the country's urbanization rate was artificially low due to the fact that some fifteen towns with 5,000 or more residents were classified as villages rather than urban areas.

[4] Not surprisingly, there is now a substantial literature discussing how kimberlite diamond deposits are conducive for industrialization while alluvial diamonds help to generate civil wars by funding rebels (Olsson, 2006).

the De Beers Botswana Mining Company (DBBMC) as a joint partnership with De Beers. After originally only owning 15 per cent of the company, the government increased its ownership stake to 50 per cent in the early 1970s, after which diamond production quickly took off and became the country's largest export. Debswana, as the DBBMC has been known since 1992, has become the country's second largest employer after the government and is the largest producer of diamonds in the world by value. More recently De Beers – which is 15 per cent owned by the Botswanan government and gets around 70 per cent of its global supply of diamonds from Botswana – shifted its Sightholder sales of rough diamonds in 2013 from London to Gaborone, thereby generating even more local revenue and employment within the industry.

Evidence from the literature on natural resources suggests that exporting minerals like diamonds can lead to a shift out of agriculture in a process known as Dutch disease, whereby exports lead to an appreciation in the value of a country's currency, which in turn makes other exports –including agricultural products – more expensive. In Botswana the government has somewhat avoided Dutch disease by keeping its currency, the pula, tied to the South African rand and thus preventing it from becoming over-valued. However, Botswana has still suffered from the problem of a declining agricultural sector as people have migrated to cities to take advantage of jobs created by diamond exports and industrialization more broadly. Efforts by the government to counter urbanization go back decades, with President Seretse Khama noting in parliament in 1978 that 'in order to slow down urban migration our commitment to the development of rural Botswana remains a major priority',[5] while also stating that 'Botswana must remain a nation of farmers' (Molosiwa, 2013, p. 242). Yet practical measures such as providing food and cash payments to non-urban households during the drought of the 1980s failed to halt rural–urban migration,[6] and more recent efforts by the government to hand out seeds to farmers in order to encourage them to continue to work in agriculture have instead led many recipients to sell the seeds instead of using them.[7]

The consequence of Botswana's rapid industrialization and urbanization can be seen in Figure 7.1, which tracks milk, fruit and vegetable imports as a proportion of total domestic supply from 1961 to 2013, using data from the FAO (Food and Agriculture Organization).[8] What is particularly striking is the coincidence between the onset of diamond production in 1972 and the first tons of imported milk the next year. In all three cases imports begin to rise rapidly in the 1970s before peaking around 2000, which coincides with the stabilization

---

[5] Parliament of Botswana Hansard #63, 20 November 1978, p. 2.
[6] Interview with Professor Onalenna Selolwane, Gaborone; 28 June 2012.
[7] Interview with Professor Christian John Makgala, Gaborone; 9 July 2012.
[8] The FAO data altered its data collection techniques after 2013 and thus that is the last year for which there exists comparable data reaching back to the 1960s.

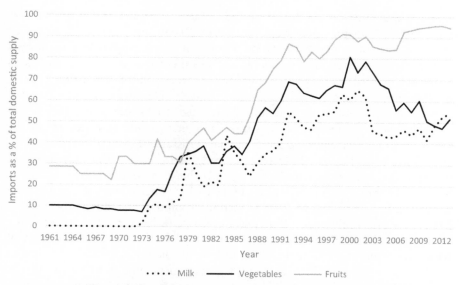

FIGURE 7.1. Food imports (as a percentage of total domestic supply) in Botswana, 1961–2013
(*Source:* FAO; United Nations)

of carbon emissions rates (in Figure 6.1 of the previous chapter) and agriculture's share of GDP (in Figure 6.4).

As a result of this rapid structural transformation, access to tribal land has become decreasingly important to Botswanans working in the modern urban sector who want to earn cash, which is also known as *dikgomo tse di senang maoto* ('cattle without legs') in the Babirwa dialect (Molosiwa, 2013, p. 265). Formal-sector employment has been driven in part by the Botswanan government, such that there was an annual growth in government consumption of 12.5 per cent between 1980 and 1989, or the largest in the world during that time period (World Bank, 1991, p. 219). During the rapid urbanization of the 1970s and 1980s this expansion meant that roughly half of the population of Gaborone was employed by the national or local government, with another 23 per cent taken by the construction industry (Silitshena, 1984, p. 117). Another major factor in the increase in urban formal sector employment in the 1980s included the South African apartheid government's attempt to reduce foreign migration as a means to curb unemployment and unrest among black South Africans in the late 1970s and 1980s, which led annual labour migration to South African mines to peak in 1976 at 40,390 per annum, after which it dropped down to 19,648 in 1986 and to under 2,000 by 2002 (Gwebu, 2006a, p. 121). This reduction of job opportunities in South Africa meant that when the drought of the 1980s hit rural Botswanan households poorer citizens chose to migrate to cities within Botswana rather than across the border for work as they had done in previous droughts (Currey, 1987, pp. 74–5). The result of these sectoral shifts was that the total number of people employed in the formal sector in 1972 was 48,000, compared to 35,000 citizens working abroad (with roughly one-third of Botswana's male labour force in South Africa alone), while by 1989 it was 182,200 and 17,900, respectively (Harvey, 1992, pp. 350–1).

Formal-sector job growth continued through the 1990s and 2000s, especially in the manufacturing, education and finance/business sectors; in the former case such schemes as the Financial Assistance Policy allowed the government to subsidize new industries. Indeed, the rapid growth of the diamond industry has meant that manufacturing and other parts of the modern economy have not kept pace as a proportion of GDP, which appears to indicate a lack of diversification; however, when examined in absolute terms, these other sectors have grown healthily over a long period of time (I. Taylor, 2012, pp. 474–5). High rates of formal-sector unemployment and income inequality – both of which are common to southern Africa in general – have not led to social conflict or reverse urban–rural migration as government initiatives such as the *Ipelegeng/ Namola Leuba* public works programme provide enough support to maintain a decent lifestyle (Siphambe, 2007). Indeed, it may sound odd to champion a high unemployment rate in Botswana, which, at 18.2 per cent in 2019 was one of the highest in the world and much higher than the very low rate in Uganda discussed in the previous chapter. Yet the rate is a sign of people actively looking for work in the formal sector, as opposed to relying upon informal or rural agricultural employment (as in Somalia and Uganda).[9] While in other contexts a high urban unemployment rate may induce urban–rural migration (such as in Zambia in the 1980s and 1990s), the process of urbanization in Botswana appears to have become permanent inasmuch as Botswanans increasingly retire in urban settings rather than in the countryside (Griffiths, 2019, p. 34). Thus, by the early 1990s two scholars of Setswana could claim that 'Gaborone is no longer just a place of work to be deserted on weekends and holidays when sojourners visit their relatives in the villages and elsewhere. The city has come to be viewed as a place of permanent residence; and to visit relatives in the villages is gradually becoming infrequent' (Jansen & Tsonope, 1991, p. 105).

A sign of the formalization of the labour market in Botswana can be seen in the growth of the country's largest public service union, the Manual Worker's Union (MWU). Drawing from mostly low-paid, un-educated workers, the union is largely comprised of women who work for the central government, local governments and parastatals. While its membership comes from across the country and different indigenous groups, it has arguably been able to

---

[9] As such it is not surprising to find evidence that the size of the informal economy as a percentage of GNP in Botswana is among the smallest in Africa (Schneider, 2002).

articulate a form of national identity across ethnic and regional divisions, according to a magisterial study of the MWU by Pnina Webner (P. Werbner, 2014, p. 4). In particular the MWU was able to sponsor a major strike in 2011 for increased wages, which constituted the first legal strike in the country's history and which brought together 93,000 workers across five public sector unions in a powerful show of national unity.

Before concluding this section, it is useful to consider additional qualitative evidence of structural transformation in Botswana. One such example is change in the use of the Setswana language, where there has been a sharp loss of familiarity with the cattle-specific colour terms mentioned above alongside the creation of new Setswana words like *modiredi* ('employee', first attested in 1984), *mohumagatsana* ('unmarried woman', 1984) and *ikgasolola* ('to make an impatient gesture and drive away', 1985). Moreover, new loan words from English or Afrikaans that were first attested after 1966 included those for 'bank', 'cement', 'company', 'cooperative', 'engine', 'firm', 'insurance', 'lawyer', 'mall', 'office', 'percent' and 'tractor', among many others (Jansen & Tsonope, 1991, p. 122; Laws, Davies, Corbett & Jerrett et al., 1995). In contrast to the Somali example from the previous chapter, the evidence suggests that these terms were created by ordinary Botswanans rather than via active government involvement in language policy, inasmuch as primary school teachers have complained about the lack of many agreed-upon scientific and mathematical terms in Setswana (Nfila, 2002).

Another piece of evidence for the broader societal effects of structural transformation comes from Botswana's currency and postage stamps, which have been the site of study for scholars of ethnicity and nationalism in other African contexts (Fuller, 2008; Hammett, 2012). As previously noted, the national currency is the pula, or 'rain', which was chosen upon independence first as the one-word national motto and then in 1976 was selected as the country's currency via public consultation to replace the use of the South African rand; the choice of name indicates the degree to which rain was historically important to farmers and herders in Botswana's arid environment. (The blue colour of rainwater also comprises most of the Botswanan national flag.) The first banknotes issued in Botswana in the late 1970s and early 1980s had the president's image on the obverse while the reverse included images of cows (the 1-pula note), women threshing grain and weaving baskets (2 pula) and gemsbok antelope (5 pula); by the time of the 2009 issue, however, the new notes showed images of mining equipment (the 20-pula note) and diamond sorting and an open-pit diamond mine (50 pula). In contrast, Uganda's shilling banknotes have continued to employ pictures of its flora and fauna as well as grain silos and people picking cotton; the last shilling banknotes issued in Somalia in the early 1990s as well as more recent banknotes from Somaliland similarly contain images of animals, banana trees and people picking cotton, herding cattle and weaving baskets.

As regards postage stamps, among the first issues after independence included an image of the country's largest abattoir in Lobatse, a variety of Christmas stamps with rural village scenes and several series with traditional handicrafts, grain storage containers and milk containers. Yet by the 1990s BotswanaPost issued a series of stamps celebrating the country's first National Road Safety Day (with images of 'children on the road', 'careless overtaking' and, inevitably, 'cattle on the road')[10] alongside depictions of the national railway, Radio Botswana, aircraft, and, in 2010, a series on energy sources with individual stamps for coal, solar power voltaic panels and compact fluorescent lights.[11] In contrast Somalia's postage stamps in the 1970s and 1980s featured such themes as the centenary of Lenin's birth, the introduction of the new Somali script and men in a variety of military uniforms before the postal service was suspended in 1991, while Uganda's postal authorities have long continued to focus on serving international stamp collectors with series about British royals, various American presidents and the flora and fauna of Uganda.

7.3 ETHNICITY IN BOTSWANA: AN OVERVIEW

Before examining the process of assimilation in Botswana, it is important to discuss the nature of ethnic divisions within the country. Botswana's ethnic structure is unusual by African standards as it, unlike most countries on the continent (but like Somalia), has a *Staatsvolk* (ethnic core) in the form of the majority Batswana ethnic group (69 per cent of the population in 1961 according to Bruk & Apenchenko [1964]) which is comprised of a number of sub-clans or tribes (*merafe* [Batswana tribes]). (Here it is important to distinguish the Batswana ethnic group – with members known as *Batswana tota* [real or genuine Batswana] – from Botswanan citizens [simply *Batswana*], due both to the presence of ethnic minorities in Botswana and the presence of Batswana across the border in South Africa.) Among the country's ethnic minorities include related Bantu groups like the Babirwa, Batswapong, Bahurutshe Bakhurutshe and Bapedi, and unrelated groups such as the Herero, Yeyi and, most importantly, the Kalanga (12 per cent of the population in 1961), as well as the hunter-gatherer San or Basarwa grouping (9 per cent, which itself is made up of seventeen ethnic groups). A government attempt to enumerate all ethnic groups in Botswana in 2000 listed thirty-six Bantu groups and fifteen San groups for a total of fifty-one indigenous ethnicities (Government of Botswana, 2000, pp. 145–6), or almost the same number as those listed in the 1995 Ugandan constitution.

Upon independence these Batswana tribes and minorities were comparable in their distinctiveness to ethnic groups elsewhere in Africa, such that

---

[10] <www.stanleylisica.com/viewimage.html?mv_arg=1820048700>
[11] <www.stanleylisica.com/viewimage.html?mv_arg=1820090600>

individuals would have been able to identify themselves and others as members of distinct groups. Indeed, Batswana tribes were historically distinguished from each other not only according to their home area but also by their dialect of Setswana and the totem (*sereto* or *seano*) of their chief and paternal kin, which indicated a common origin. Traditionally people would refrain from eating, killing or even touching their totem animal, and would greet or address each other not by name but by the name of their totem (Schapera, 1938, p. 6).

Ethnic minorities, on the other hand, had a history of specializing in livelihoods reminiscent of the discussion of pre-industrial societies in Chapters 1 and 5; thus the Herero commonly worked with livestock, the Hambukushu and Yeyi in crop production, fishing and basket weaving, and the San in hunting, gathering and crafts (Poteete, 2013, p. 187). In the case of the Babirwa, their name derives directly from their original livelihood as sheep-herders, from the Setswana word for black sheep ('pirwa') (Molosiwa, 2013, p. 10). An example of how older, pre-industrial shifts in livelihood patterns can lead to ethnic change in the Botswanan context can be found in the case of the Bateti, who historically spoke a Basarwa language but acquired land in the nineteenth century and became farmers around the Boteti River in what is now the Bangwato-dominated Central District. Thus, in order to distinguish themselves from other Basarwa who remained hunter-gatherers, many Bateti began to take offence to being called Basarwa and even invented Bangwato lineages as part of their process of assimilation as Batswana (Cashdan, 1986, p. 312).

Under British colonial rule the country was divided up among the eight most prominent Batswana tribes, namely the Bangwato, Bangwaketse, Bakgatla, Balete, Batlokwa, Batawana, Barolong and Bakwena, even though there were many parts of the country where the titular tribe comprised a minority of the population. Nonetheless individuals could only access land through the chief of each Tribal Reserve, which created an incentive to identify with the chief's tribe for the purposes of land administration. This system of indirect rule was essentially the same as it was elsewhere in colonial Africa where tribal administrative boundaries failed to match the demographic distribution of ethnic groups. The political weight of these individual tribes can be seen in the decision of British administrators to deliberately situate the country's new capital on land formerly owned by the British South Africa Company, as it was a neutral site relatively close to the population centres of six of the eight major tribes, despite not being anywhere close to the geographic midpoint of the country.[12] Indeed, it is precisely because Gaborone was historically ethnically neutral that urban conflicts over land, of which there are many (Onoma,

[12] Interview with Professor Onalenna Selolwane, Gaborone; 28 June 2012. In this sense the placement of the capital in Gaborone was less like the centrally located placements of the capitals of Tanzania (Dodoma) and Brazil (Brasilia) and more like the decisions to find a politically neutral location for the capitals of Nigeria (Abuja) and the United States (Washington, DC) (Bandyopadhyay & Green, 2013, p. 109).

2009), have not become ethnicized in the way they have been in neighbouring Tlokweng (as described below).

Ethnicized access to rural land was not altered upon independence, whereupon the government maintained colonial laws that only allowed fellow 'tribesmen' to acquire land in each tribe's designated area. In 1968 the government passed the Tribal Land Act, which took powers over land away from chiefs and granted them to new District Land Boards, where the chiefs nonetheless continued to hold *ex officio* positions (Ng'ong'ola, 1997). Only in 1993 did the national government officially allow all citizens to access tribal land in an amendment to the Tribal Land Act, but tribal inequalities in the local allocation of land continued to persist, in part because tribal chiefs still maintained *ex officio* membership in local district councils (R. Werbner, 2002, p. 677).

At the national level the upper house of parliament, the House of Chiefs (*Ntlo ya Dikgosi*), institutionalizes ethnic dominance by granting automatic seats to traditional chiefs from the eight principal Batswana tribes but none to the smaller Batswana tribes, Kalanga, San or other minorities, which in some cases have larger populations than some of the principal tribes. In contrast to other ex-colonies which eliminated the *de jure* power of chiefs after independence, Botswana remains one of only three countries in Africa to have an upper chamber representing traditional leaders, alongside the almost entirely ethnically homogenous countries of Lesotho and Somaliland. While the House of Chiefs only has advisory powers without any ability to initiate or block legislation, it is nonetheless important enough that it has drawn a large amount of controversy within Botswana for the way it systematically discriminates against ethnic minorities. Both in response to public pressure as well as concerns from the ruling Botswana Democratic Party (BDP) leadership that failing to address the issue could endanger political stability, the government launched a commission in 2000 under the leadership of former Minister Patrick Balopi into reforming sections 77–9 of the constitution that governed the composition of the House of Chiefs. This exercise led to vociferous debates in parliament, in the national media and across the country before the commission resolved to add more members to the House of Chiefs while still maintaining the permanent status of the eight principal tribes. In the end the Balopi Commission report noted clearly that 'Botswana must address problems relating to tribalism, and to perceived discrimination against the so called minority ethnic and language groups' (Government of Botswana, 2000, p. 89). The divisive nature of both the constitution and the commission was summarized in a political cartoon in the main national newspaper *Mmegi/The Reporter* – here reproduced as Figure 7.2 – whereby a patient named 'Botswana' suffering from a huge boil (marked as sections 77–9 of the constitution) exclaimed '*Ijoo! Tlhe Rra O Tla Mpolaya!*' ('Oh! You are Killing Me!') as Patrick Balopi attempted to pierce the boil.

The underlying ethnic tensions that were brought to the surface by the Balopi Commission shows the degree to which the Botswanan government has not been proactive in promoting nation-building. Indeed, while some have

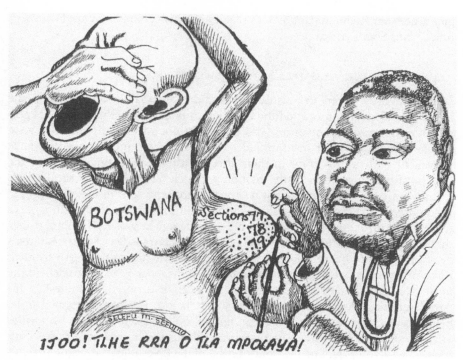

FIGURE 7.2. Political cartoon in *Mmegi/The Reporter*, 29 September 2000 ('Oh! You are killing me!')

claimed that the government has suppressed minority rights by imposing the use of Setswana in schools (Nyati-Ramahobo, 2009; Solway, 2004), Setswana is only used as the language of instruction for the first year of primary school, followed by English thereafter, which is in part a consequence of the lack of scientific terminology in Setswana noted above. The result is that there is relatively little literature or media published in Setswana, which contrasts quite starkly with the Somali example from the previous chapter. As regards other types of nation-building policies, neither Botswana's second-largest city of Francistown (named after an English explorer) nor any other cities have been re-named with more African names since independence, in contrast to numerous other African countries; similarly there have been no efforts at introducing any mandatory or national service requirements that have been common in countries such as Angola, Ethiopia, Ghana, Nigeria and Zambia and have been shown to have a positive effect on national integration (Bandyopadhyay & Green, 2013; Schroyens, 2019). Finally, Gaborone remained unusually bereft of national statues or monuments for decades after independence, at least until the Three Dikgosi Monument was erected in Gaborone in 2006 that commemorated the three tribal chiefs (*Dikgosi*) who convinced British officials to guarantee that Bechuanaland would remain a British colony and not be incorporated into South Africa.

7.4 EXPLAINING ASSIMILATION IN BOTSWANA

In other words, given the institutionalization of tribal inequalities and the relatively paltry attempts at nation-building in Botswana we would not expect to see evidence of assimilation, and especially not so before land laws were changed in 1993.[13] Yet institutional barriers to ethnic homogenization have proven to be less important in their effects on ethnic identification than the structural transformation of the economy, which has meant that rural ethnic identities are no longer important to Botswanans who seek to make a living in urban areas. Perhaps the biggest policy decision that enabled this shift to take place – and prevented Botswana from experiencing the violent 'resource curse' that has plagued so many post-colonial African states – was Seretse Khama's decision to centralize mineral rights at the level of the national government rather than the tribal level, even though his Bangwato tribe stood to benefit the most from tribal control over the country's initial diamond revenues. In his party's election manifesto in 1965, the year before Botswana attained independence, Khama wrote that 'leaving mineral rights vested in tribal authorities and private companies must necessarily result in uneven growth of the country's economy... It will be the policy of the BDP Government to negotiate with all parties concerning the takeover of the country's mineral rights by the Central Government' (Gapa, 2017, p. 12). Khama's momentous decision was self-interested in a far-sighted way, in that vesting diamond revenues at the tribal level would benefit him in the short term but not necessarily the long term, since Botswana's diamond deposits had yet to be mapped properly at that time – and indeed the country's (and the world's) richest diamond mine turned out to be the Jwaneng mine in the Bangwaketse-dominated Southern District. While perhaps angering his fellow Bangwato – at least temporarily – Khama was thus able to avoid the consequences of uneven access to mineral resources that had already led the DRC into conflict after independence along the classic Gellnerian lines spelled out earlier in the book.

The consequence of Khama's decision was to make tribal identities economically irrelevant, which meant that rural–urban migrants would be free to experience the social change wrought by industrialization in their new city dwellings. Thus already in the early 1990s one study noted that 'people who have moved from the rural areas to the towns are experiencing a very rapid shift of social position ... The persons who move permanently out of the villages and settle in places like Gaborone find themselves in an environment

---

[13] Lieberman and Singh (2012) disagree on this point, classifying the level of ethnic institutionalization in Botswana as 'weak/none'. However, they do not discuss Botswana's land laws and only mention the House of Chiefs briefly.

where no social relations are given beforehand' (Jansen & Tsonope, 1991, p. 89). This shift out of rural areas led to the decline in the power of the *kgosi* (chief) over marriage and family law, not to mention the allocation of land, which itself has contributed to much less deferential and more liberal attitudes towards *dikgosi* in daily settings (Holm & Botlhale, 2008, p. 83).[14] Indeed, in 2002 Mosadi Seboko became the first-ever female chief of a major tribe in Botswanan history when she took over as *kgosi* of the Balete people, and then made history again when she became the first female chairperson of the House of Chiefs in 2003.[15]

The idea that a major shift in ethnic identification took place in late twentieth-century Botswana, such that clan identity played a decreasing role in peoples' daily lives, is echoed across multiple ethnographic accounts. For instance, the noted Swedish linguist Tore Janson and his Botswana co-author Joseph Tsonope described a 'shift of allegiance' among Batswana away from identification with the *merafe* towards identification with the nation in the early 1990s (Jansen & Tsonope, 1991, p. 89). The Botswanan sociologist Onalenna Selolwane has also noted how younger generations of minority communities have mainly begun adopting 'the dominant ethnic Tswana identity' as their own (Selolwane, 2004, p. 6). Similarly, the American anthropologist Jacqueline Solway, who has worked in the Kalahari Desert region of western Botswana, wrote that:

urban spaces have proved to be locations where minority status is less debilitating; where the publicly declared stance of ethnic neutrality is most legitimate; and urban life has provided an enabling context for minorities to join and partially 'assimilate' to national life. Thus the urban experience has contributed to the creation of a unifying national identity on the part of Botswana's citizens. (Solway, 2004, p. 132).

Finally, in her ethnographic fieldwork in Botswana's Central District in the 1980s and 1990s, the Israeli anthropologist Pnina Motzafi-Haller documented strong evidence of shifting ethnic identities during a period of rapid socio-economic change. In particular she saw how Basarwa or San identities had changed a generation after independence, such that individuals would assimilate from Basarwa into Batswana, while others who lost status could become Basarwa if they stayed too long in the 'bush'. Indeed, emphasizing the way the country had changed, one of her informants told her that 'the things of the remote past are not the way things are today', while one village headman told

---

[14] To take one example, in 1999 so many people attended a visit by the then reigning Miss Universe and Botswanan national Mpule Kwelagobe to a community meeting chaired by the local *kgosi* that many had to stand. However, according to Batswanan tradition subjects cannot stand when a *kgosi* is speaking, and thus the *kgosi* ordered attendees to sit down; instead of complying, however, many locals simply left the meeting (Holm & Botlhale, 2008, p. 83).

[15] Marking this shift away from traditional norms, when Seboko was installed as *kgosi* she received not the traditional gift of cattle but instead a Toyota 4 × 4 pick-up truck alongside a computer, vacuum cleaner and washing machine (Matemba, 2003, p. 63).

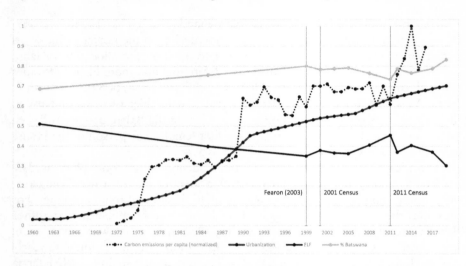

Note: Ethnicity data to the left of Fearon (2003) is from the Soviet ANM (1961 and 1985); data to the right is either from the Afrobarometer or the Botswanan Census (2001 and 2011)

FIGURE 7.3. Industrialization and ethnic fractionalization in Botswana, 1960–2019
(*Source:* Afrobarometer; Bruk, 1986; Bruk & Apenchenko, 1964; Fearon, 2003; World Bank)

her 'there are no Basarwa, no Babirwa, no Bangwato. We are all Batswana' (Motzafi-Haller, 2002, pp. 180, 182). Concluding her study – and summarizing the changeable nature of ethnic identity in Botswana in general – she argued that 'the constitution of the ethnic category here, as it is in many other places, is a product of social distinctions drawn in specific settings and not an essentialized, pre-given category' (Motzafi-Haller, 2002, p. 183).

Survey and census data suggests that Botswana has indeed seen a decline in ethno-linguistic fractionalization in Botswana over the past sixty years, as indicated in Figure 7.3. For a baseline we turn to the Soviet ANM data from Chapter 4, which records a sharp decline in ELF in Botswana between 1961 and 1985 from 0.51 to 0.40, due largely to an increase in the percentage which identified as Batswana from 68.6 per cent to 75.5 per cent. Next, the data collected by Fearon (2003), which was drawn from a variety of sources from the late 1990s, yields an ELF score of 0.35 and a Batswana percentage of 80.0 per cent, followed by the Kalanga at 8 per cent and the Basarwa at 3 per cent.[16] I then use data from the 2001 and 2011 Botswanan censuses, which collected data on first-language usage; the former was the first census ever to record language use, while the latter showed a tripling in the proportion

---

[16] The Fearon (2003) data on Botswana corresponds exactly with the data listed in Scarritt and Mozaffar (1999), which itself is drawn from a variety of sources including Abdi Ismail Samatar (1997) and Solway (1994). As such I list the date of the data as 1999, not 2003.

speaking Ndebele and Shona from 2001 to 2011 due to the sudden influx of migrants from Zimbabwe. Finally, I then include data on home-language usage from the Afrobarometer survey rounds 2 (2003) through 8 (2019), which I use rather than ethnic identification as it corresponds to the same categories used in the Soviet data and Botswanan censuses. I then compare the ELF and proportion Batswana- (or Setswana-speaking) to the same data from the previous chapter on carbon emissions per capita (here normalized as a proportion of its maximum value) and urbanization.

As Figure 7.3 indicates, Botswana has become less ethnically diverse while the proportion that is Batswana or Setswana-speaking has grown over time, and these changes have occurred at the same time as the country has industrialized and urbanized. It is also important to note how the four sources concord with one another – especially as regards the consequence of Zimbabwean immigration, which peaked around 2010 – thereby demonstrating further confidence in the validity of the data used.

I now turn to Afrobarometer data on ethnic and national identification, which allows me to assess the individual determinants of identity choice. The Afrobarometer question on 'what is your ethnic community, cultural group or tribe?' in Botswana has been asked in every survey since round 3 (2005) at the level of the tribe (*merafe*) rather than the ethnic group; while the surveys do not include a 'Motswana' option per se, they, like all Afrobarometer surveys, do include the option of answering that the respondent identifies as a '[national] only', or 'doesn't think of [your]self in these terms'. In Botswanan this question is worded as being 'Motswana only', which thus has allowed Batswana respondents to identify ethnically rather than tribally. The subsequent question in the Afrobarometer asks respondents who did give an ethnic identity to assess whether they identify more strongly with their ethnic group than the nation, equally, or more with the nation than their ethnicity. While the latter question has drawn a fair amount of attention in the study of African nationalism (Depetris-Chauvin, Durante & Campante, 2020; Green, 2018; A. L. Robinson, 2014), there is as yet no detailed analysis of variation in refusing to identify with an ethnic group in the former question.

What is striking in the Botswanan data is the high number of individuals who identify as 'Motswana only', which came to 5.1 per cent of respondents in round 7 (2017), or higher than any other of the thirty-one countries in Sub-Saharan Africa asked this question in round 7.[17] In round 8 (2019), which was not yet fully released at the time of writing, this proportion rose to 12.8 per cent, or more than one in every eight respondents (and higher than every tribal/ethnic group listed after the Kalanga). My goal here is thus to analyse the

---

[17] The only country which come anywhere close in the measure was the equally politically stable Mauritius (3.3 per cent), where ethnicity is defined in racial terms. The question yielded 99.9 per cent identifying as 'Swazi' only in Swaziland, while it was not asked at all in Cape Verde or the North Africa countries surveyed.

individual determinants of non-ethnicity using a multi-variate regression analysis. If my argument about the effects of industrialization is correct, then I should observe a negative correlation between not identifying an ethnic identity and being employed in agriculture. As control variables I included variables that took the value of 1 if respondents were female or had at least some secondary school education and controlled for the age of the respondent. Inasmuch as non-ethnic identification could vary according to the individual interviewer asking the question, I included interviewer-fixed effects alongside enumeration area-fixed effects (n = 150). Finally, I added a separate column on the determinants of national identification as an alternative way to examine the determinants of non-ethnic identification. In all cases I clustered the standard errors at the enumeration area.

The results, as indicated in Table 7.1, provide strong evidence that agricultural employment is negatively associated with both non-ethnicity and national identification, such that working in agriculture is associated with a 9 per cent decreased probability of not identifying with an ethnic group and an 11 per cent decreased probability of identifying more with the Botswanan nation than one's ethnicity. What is particularly striking is that none of the other variables are consistently associated with non-ethnicity and national identification, including education, which corresponds with evidence from Chapters 4 and 5 about the lack of a role for education in promoting homogenization and assimilation, and

TABLE 7.1. *Determinants of non-ethnicity and national identification in Botswana, Afrobarometer round 8 (2019)*

Dependent variable	Motswana only	National>ethnic identification
	(1)	(2)
Agricultural employment	−0.089**	−0.113*
	(0.038)	(0.032)
Age (logged)	−0.053*	0.042
	(0.028)	(0.046)
Female	0.027*	0.002
	(0.015)	(0.024)
Secondary schooling	−0.023	0.048
	(0.023)	(0.038)
Interviewer fixed effects	yes	yes
Enumeration area fixed effects	yes	yes
Clusters	150	150
Observations	1169	1002
R^2 (within)	0.259	0.231

* $p \leq 0.1$, ** $p \leq 0.05$, *** $p \leq 0.01$ (two-tailed test); robust standard errors clustered at the enumeration area. In column #2 the dependent variable takes the value of 1 when individuals answered the question on national vs ethnic identification that they either felt 'more Botswanan than [their ethnic identity]' or 'only Botswanan', and 0 otherwise.

also echoes previous work on how education can lead towards more ethnic conflict rather than less (Lange, 2012).[18]

Additional qualitative evidence for how industrialization has led to assimilation in Botswana comes from examining how changes in the relative value of land can affect ethnic salience. The capital city of Gaborone grew rapidly in size as Botswana urbanized and thus began to encroach upon Tlokweng, the tribal land of the Batlokwa clan which now comprises part of South-East district. As land prices in Gaborone rose and non-Batlokwa Botswanans began to buy up local property in Tlokweng instead, the area began to be known for its xenophobia. Indeed, it is most notably in Tlokweng that non-Batlokwa Botswanans have repeatedly suffered overt discrimination: as one Presidential Commission from 1991 noted, 'Tlokweng has an in-built jealousy and the society is intrinsically tribalistic. The non-Batlokwa who reside there are not happy because although they are Batswana, they are always referred to as *Batswakwa* [foreigners]' (Government of Botswana, 1991, p. 55). As pressures on Batlokwa land grew, the local land board froze land allocation in the area in 1992 and subsequently the national government prohibited people who already owned land in greater Gaborone from accessing land in Tlokweng, in order to ease tensions.

When I visited Botswana in 2012 the government had just completed allocating plots of land in Tlokweng to 285 citizens out of 10,256 eligible applicants via a lottery system (Moeng & Seretse, 2012), which caused a huge amount of controversy among Batlokwa locals inasmuch as only eight of the 285 recipients were Batlokwa (Keoregn, 2012). The distribution of the plots – which were originally advertised in 2009 – was delayed by a number of months due to protests from Batolokwa leaders like the deputy *Kgosi* Michael Gaborone, who claimed that 'we no longer have land to give away to other tribes ... we will fight to the bitter end for our tribal rights' (Gaotlhobogwe, 2013). Indeed, in an interview the then MP for Tlokweng, Olebile Gaborone, denied the charge that the Batlokwa were tribalistic, but nonetheless claimed that the small size of Tlokweng relative to other tribal areas gave him concern about the survival of the Batlokwa culture. 'We want to remain a cohesive group', he argued, claiming that the Bakwena and members of other tribes should be encouraged to settle in other areas to preserve Tlokweng land for Batlokwa.[19]

It is interesting in this respect to contrast Tlokweng with Kweneng, the tribal land of the Bakwena people to the north of Gaborone. Here too migration has led to increased pressures on land, especially in the city of Mogoditshane which is essentially a suburb of Gaborone and saw the highest population growth of

---

[18] These results are robust to dropping Gaborone from the analysis, date-of-interview fixed effects, and including additional variables capturing unemployment, peri-urban residence and speaking Setswana as the main language at home.

[19] Interview with MP Olebile Gaborone (Tlokweng), Gaborone; 10 July 2012.

any city in Botswana in the 1980s. However, as Kweneng is much bigger than Tlokweng land prices in the district have not risen as much, which has meant that the salience of tribal identity is lower than it is in Tlokweng. Thus, as the Presidential Commission put it, 'there is no tribalism in the outlook of Mogoditshane society. The Land Board is not tribalistic and it accepts non-Bakwena' (Government of Botswana, 1991, p. 55).

7.5 DEBATES AROUND ETHNIC IDENTITY AND INDIGENEITY IN BOTSWANA

If we turn towards Botswanan politics, it is clear that attempts to politicize ethnicity have largely failed, both within opposition parties like the Botswana National Front as well as the ruling BDP (Makgala & Botlhomilwe, 2017). Indeed, as with the case of Uganda in the previous chapter, it is useful here to examine official discourse on ethnicity from the parliament and the country's political elite. To begin with, the Balopi Commission Report explicitly warned about the problems associated with listing tribes in the constitution. It noted that:

As the experience of countries such as South Africa, Canada and the USA indicate, the identification of tribes is possible. This could be done with reference to such attributes as historical, linguistic, cultural and geographical identity, as well as population size. The Commission is also of the view that if there is to be an expanded list of tribes, the said list should not appear in the Constitution itself, but could rather be incorporated in separate legislation. This method would have the advantage of allowing for the modification of such a list due to changing circumstances ... [However], the very act of compiling an inventory could lead to a continuous process of disintegration of existing communities. This could prove divisive and thus compromise the ideal of building a united and proud nation. (Government of Botswana, 2000, pp. 116–17)

The commission recommended representation by territory rather than ethnic group in the House of Chiefs, arguing that:

Ethnic representation, as opposed to territorial representation, could bring about disintegration of communities. During the consultative meetings conducted by the Commission, it was evident that the mere prospect of a separate representation has resulted in divisions within some communities that previously existed as a single and cohesive unit. It is for this reason that some Batswana opined that ethnic representation would undermine nation-building. The Commission agrees with this view ...

Territoriality or land is a constant, while the concept of tribe or ethnic identity is immutable and ever changing. It is, therefore, futile to try to define 'tribe' in ethnic terms or characteristics. In Botswana, there is no single community that is made up of only one pure ethnic group because groups have co-assimilated due to factors such as intermarriage ... (Government of Botswana, 2000, pp. 118–19)

Again in contrast to Uganda, where Indians were denied a place in the list of indigenous communities as they originated in an immigrant community, the commission added that another argument against making the House of Chiefs based on ethnic identity was that immigration would result in an 'ever-growing number of representatives in the House [of Chiefs]' (Government of Botswana, 2000, p. 120).

When the debate over the Balopi Commission Report moved to the parliament, it continued to be guided by constructivist understandings of ethnicity rather than the primordialist nature of debates in Uganda. Indeed, when the debate on the composition of the House of Chiefs first arose in 1988, Patrick Balopi himself, then the MP from Francistown and Minister of Local Government and Lands, claimed that:

You go to Kgalagadi [in western Botswana], you will still find within the Bakgalagadi that there are Barolong, there are Bangwaketse for instance, there will be other tribes. Because that is really how the societal network has been structured. Even amongst us here, if you trace each one of us's [*sic*] ancestry, you will find that we originate from so many different tribes. Some of us, we call ourselves Bakalaka [=Kalanga] today when in fact we originated from South Africa ... Today Botswana is such a peaceful country, simply because the various tribes in Botswana have come to accept each other, we have integrated so well. You see a child from Makaleng working as a district commissioner in Ghanzi, you pick a boy from Ghanzi marrying a girl from Bobonong, she gets here, she does not feel a stranger, she feels at home and if at this day and age we still have political leaders for that matter who want to bring division within our nation on a tribal basis, I am afraid we are heading for a dangerous moment.[20]

In concluding the parliamentary debate after the Balopi Commission Report was published, many MPs expressed similarly constructivist views on ethnic identity, such as David Magang (Lentsweletau):

This country, Mr. Speaker, has done very well in so far as integration of our societies are concerned. When the government took over this country not only has the government encouraged integration, even in relation to work our people are employed anywhere in this country wherever their abilities could be recognized. They would be posted anywhere, as a result we are integrated, intermarrying among ourselves. I do not see any single ethnic group that can claim purity because we are so integrated ... There is nowhere that you can say that any particular group is pure. Nor can most of us claim that all of us originated from this country. At least I have seen only one tribe claiming to be the first people of this country ... We have all converged into this country. It does not matter where we came from. The fact that I am a Mokwena I cannot claim that everybody in Kweneng is a Mokwena ... Like all African countries, we are composed of a variety of ethnic groups, some within the same country, some coming from outside. In fact, we are still accepting immigrants. In fact, even after independence a lot of people in the Okavango area were admitted into this country from Angola and other countries. So, we are bound to have that and once they are admitted, whether they speak our language or not, once we accept them into our country, they become Batswana irrespective of their color.[21]

---

[20] Parliament of Botswana Hansard #95, 2 December 1988, pp. 495–6.
[21] Parliament of Botswana Hansard #138, 29 April 2002, pp. 11–12.

Nor were such constructivist statements limited to backbench MPs. The then Minister of Health, Joy Phumaphi (Francistown East) similarly noted that 'we must all accept that everybody came from somewhere else and that we were constantly moving and there is no tribal grouping here in Botswana today who cannot claim a particular piece of Botswana'.[22] Minister of Foreign Affairs Lt. General Mompati Merafhe (Mahalapye) also added:

When I talk to my children about these issues I cannot communicate with them because they grew up in Gaborone, one of them went to America and stayed there for eight years, another one went to Canada for five years and the other one Cape Town for five years so they do not know what I am talking about. When I try to reason with them, they look at me and say *hee*! What is wrong with dad, what is the subject of discussion in this family because they believe *gore* [that] they are all Batswana once and for all. They are Batswana first, nothing else and I only hope that this generation would be the last one which is going to attach importance to issues of this nature.[23]

Merafhe commented as well on the fact that he is a member of the Banyai or Batalaote group which originally migrated to Zimbabwe from south of the Limpopo River and then to Botswana only in the eighteenth century. In explaining his background he noted that:

We got to Shoshong, assimilated into [the] Bangwato to the point of losing our own language, the culture, we still have … We are Shonas, re Batalaote. We are the Moyos and quite honestly this is a totem that goes back to the early centuries … But strictly speaking these things do not really matter to us. They do not matter to us. Why should we dwell on the past? Tell me. Can anybody tell me why we should dwell on the past. You should only look at the past as a point of reference.[24]

Finally, the then Minister of Finance and Development Planning, Baledzi Gaolathe (specially elected), claimed that due to good infrastructure 'All parts of Botswana are accessible and there is a free movement and the right to work wherever you want to work. The deployment of Batswana irrespective of tribe or ethnicity to go and serve in Gumare or wherever, and there is no better medicine than people mixing as we are mixing now.'[25]

It is perhaps best to conclude here with an apt intervention from one MP who noted that, 'for my children, my great grand-children, I have confidence that this [discussion about which tribes will be listed in the constitution] will not be an issue. They will never have to go and check who is listed [in the constitution] and who is not listed simple because they want to be engineers, they want to be IT specialists.'[26]

[22] Parliament of Botswana Hansard #138, 30 April 2002, pp. 83–4.
[23] Parliament of Botswana Hansard #138, 30 April 2002, p. 124.
[24] Parliament of Botswana Hansard #138, 30 April 2002, p. 127.
[25] Parliament of Botswana Hansard #138, 30 April 2002, p. 167.
[26] Parliament of Botswana Hansard #138, Part 11: 30 April 2002, p. 134.

7.6 ALTERNATIVE EXPLANATIONS FOR ETHNIC CHANGE IN BOTSWANA

The evidence presented in this chapter suggests that the relative decline in the value of rural land and an increase in the importance of urban formal-sector employment has contributed to an ongoing process of assimilation in Botswana. However, there are several alternative explanations for ethnic homogenization which we should examine here. One such claim is that the Batswana have a long and unusually strong history of ethnic integration via state institutions that dates back to the pre-colonial period and survived colonial rule, and is thus unrelated to processes of industrialization (Hjort, 2010, p. 703; J. A. Robinson & Parsons, 2006, p. 134). Yet this explanation does not hold water: while Botswanan *merafe* historically did accept non-members, there remained a traditional hierarchy within each *merafe* with those of 'pure' descent at the top, followed by those of Tswana descent from other *merafe* and those of non-Tswana descent at the bottom (with those of Basarwa or San ancestry below everyone) (Smieja, 2003, p. 33). Moreover, this history of ethnic homogenization was by no means limited to Botswana: the pre-colonial state of Buganda, for instance, was able to acquire new territories in what is now southern Uganda and not only assimilate them into Bugandan culture but even erase former linguistic differences within the matter of three generations (Green, 2010a, pp. 13–14).

A similar argument exists about how the common threat of Afrikaner overrule in the colonial period encouraged co-operation between tribes and helped to promote a common Botswanan identity before independence (Acemoglu et al., 2003, p. 94; Hjort, 2010, p. 704; J. A. Robinson & Parsons, 2006). In Africa the prime example of national mobilization in defeat of a common non-African enemy was Ethiopia's defeat of Italy in the Battle of Adwa in 1896, the only African defeat of a European army during the colonial period. Yet, despite this impressive display of unity in the late nineteenth century, a century later Ethiopia would be wracked by dictatorship, famine, civil war and secession, thereby demonstrating the lack of importance of anti-colonial mobilization in the late twentieth century.

A third such explanation could be to claim that ethnic differences in Botswana were shallower to begin with than elsewhere, since the Tswana tribes share similar cultures while many ethnic groups in Uganda and other parts of Africa are from completely different language groups. Yet there are two problems with such an argument. First, it is incorrect to think that smaller ethnic differences are less troublesome than larger ones, as in the experience of Somalia in the previous chapter, not to mention the Rwandan genocide or the breakup of Yugoslavia in the 1990s. Indeed, the Canadian academic and politician Michael Ignatieff notably found Sigmund Freud's concept of the 'narcissism of minor differences' useful in understanding the way a Serbian soldier fighting in the Yugoslav wars told him that the main difference between

Serbs and Croats was in the types of cigarettes they smoked. Thus, culturally similar ethnic groups which previously lived alongside each other, whether in Somalia, Yugoslavia or Rwanda – or potentially in Botswana – can turn on each other and transform what were previously minor differences between them into ones large enough to inspire people to kill their neighbours (Ignatieff, 1998, pp. 35–53).

Another problem with ascribing assimilation in Botswana to the existence of relatively shallow ethnic differences is that, while the differences between tribes in Botswana are not huge, they are large enough that locals can place each other quite easily. For instance, there are notable linguistic differences between Tswana tribes, such that there are between three and six clearly recognized dialects spoken within Botswsana (Babito, 1999, p. 3; Jansen & Tsonope, 1991, pp. 46–8). (Moreover, while Setswana has been standardized to a certain extent, as noted above the teaching of Setswana in schools has remained unsystematic, certainly in comparison with the example of the Somali language mentioned in the previous chapter.) There are also cultural markers that continue to distinguish tribes from each other: during my time in the country multiple Botswanans mentioned to me differences in burial customs as an important distinction between tribes, whereby the Batlokwa bury their dead in their homesteads while members of other tribes bury their dead in cemeteries.[27]

Another alternative explanation is that ethnic minorities in Botswana have had lower population growth levels than the Batswana majority, and thus what appears to be assimilation is merely the outcome of differential population growth rates. Indeed, there is evidence that the fertility rate among the Basarwa was unusually low in the 1960s and 1970s considering their early marriage age and almost complete lack of access to modern contraception, such that one study found a Total Fertility Rate (TFR) of 4.7 in the 1970s (G. R. Bentley, 1985), or considerably lower than the overall Botswana TFR of 6.4–6.6 given by UN demographic statistics. However, by the 1980s Botswana had begun its fertility decline, such that it had reached an overall TFR of 4.3 by the early 1990s and 3.2 a decade later; while it is difficult to estimate Basarwa-specific fertility,[28] there is evidence that, as elsewhere, fertility in Botswana remains higher among uneducated and married rural-dwellers (Campbell & Campbell, 1997), all of which applies to the Basarwa. Similarly, while we do not have ethnic-specific data on mortality in Botswana, we do know that HIV/

---

[27] Cf. interview with Bishop Valentine Tsamma Seane, Gaborone, 12 July 2012; interview with MP Olebile Gaborone (Tlokweng), Gaborone; 10 July 2012. It is possible, albeit speculative, that this practice has persisted among the Batlokwa as it serves to prevent non-Batlokwa from purchasing land that contains the remains of ancestral graves and thus helps to deal with the land shortages in Tlokweng discussed above.

[28] DHS (Demographic and Health Survey) survey results for Botswana, which may or may not have ethnic-specific fertility level data, are not publicly available.

AIDS is again less common among rural dwellers like the Basarwa. Thus it is very unlikely that the differential population growth would account for the increase in the percentage of Batswana over the late twentieth century.

7.7 CONCLUSION

In this chapter I have presented a variety of evidence about how industrialization and the structural transformation of the Botswanan economy has led to ethnic homogenization and assimilation into the Batswana majority. The shift out of agriculture and into the modern urban, industrial sector has led to a decrease in the salience of rural tribal identities in favour of an overarching Botswanan identity, as well as a constructivist understanding of ethnicity that acknowledges the existence of ethnic change. The Botswanan case thus shows that processes of industrialization and assimilation are unusual but not impossible in the African context.

I would like to conclude this chapter with two further thoughts on Botswana as it relates to the other two African cases. First, far from being aided by the post-colonial Botswanan state, assimilation has been hindered by it, especially in the continued codification of ethnicity in the House of Chiefs and the general lack of pro-active nation-building policies. Indeed, efforts by the Botswanan government and BDP activists to promote a rural, agrarian sense of national identity based around farming and cattle ranching have failed to halt rural–urban migration and the transformation of Botswanan society. In an ironic twist, the supposed 'potentially damaging effects of urbanism on Tswana cultural values' (Molosiwa, 2013, p. 242) have instead promoted a new, common sense of Tswana identity that previously did not exist. As in Uganda and Somalia, there is no clear line to be drawn in Botswana from government efforts at nation-building to successful assimilation.

Second, all the evidence presented here should not be taken as a statement that ethnicity is no longer salient in Botswana, or that ethnic divisions are entirely smooth. Batswana–Kalanga relations, for instance, remain somewhat touchy, even as inter-marriage between the two groups remains high.[29] Many Kalanga are still regularly accused of being foreigners from Zimbabwe due to the fact that there are Kalanga in Zimbabwe as well. Due to Kalanga over-representation among the country's elite one former national newspaper editor claimed in 2001 that the 'it is the Kalanga who are marginalizing other ethnic groups not the other way round', while another claimed that the Kalanga 'were the kings and the Batswana have become servants' (Nyamnjoh, 2002, p. 765). On the Kalanga side, activists created the Society for the Preservation of the iKalanga Language in 1993 in response to the lack of government efforts to focus attention and resources on minority language preservation.

---

[29] Interview with Professor Zibani Maundeni, Gaborone; 9 July 2012.

My point here is simply that whatever inter-ethnic tension exists in Botswana is less consequential and less important to most citizens than in other African contexts, since these tensions do not revolve around access to resources like land. As elsewhere, the process of urbanization and industrialization in Botswana is ongoing, so we should not expect assimilation to be a finished product at this point. What is, however, clear is that ethnicity is clearly viewed in Botswana in a constructivist manner, whereby ethnic identity is changeable and something that will alter as the country transforms from an agrarian to an industrial economy. In this sense it is appropriate to close with a quote from Botswana's former President Festus Mogae, who warned the Basarwa living in the Kalahari about their potential survival as a community in the future: 'How can you have a Stone Age creature continuing to exist in the age of computers? If the Bushmen want to survive, they must change, or otherwise, like the dodo, they will perish' (Wilmsen, 2002, p. 840). While Mogae was rightly criticized for treating the Basarwa as 'creatures' rather than fellow Botswanan citizens, his statement clearly holds within it an assumption that ethnic change is necessary and normal in the modern age, which is typical of the Botswanan experience.[30]

---

[30] It is interesting to contrast Mogae's statement with one from the then South African President Thabo Mbeki, who when handing over a deed of 25,000 hectares to a San (Basarwa) community in South Africa, noted that 'this is a step towards the rebirth of a people that nearly perished because of oppression' (Wilmsen, 2002, p. 841). If Mogae likened the Basarwa to creatures, Mbeki instead treated them like an endangered species.

8

Ethnic Change among Native Americans in the United States

8.1 INTRODUCTION

In this chapter and the next I examine the process of ethnic change among native or indigenous peoples in the four former settler colonies of Australia, Canada, New Zealand and the United States. These communities are relevant and worthy of detailed analysis here for three important reasons. First, they urbanized much later than the majority immigrant communities in the same countries, such that indigenous communities did not become recorded as majority urban in censuses until 1961 in New Zealand, 1986 in Australia, 1990 in the USA and 2001 in Canada. This delay has meant that there is more data and research into the effects of industrialization and non-agricultural employment among indigenous communities than among other groups. I can thus draw upon detailed ethnographies, histories, autobiographies and other texts that are unavailable for groups that industrialized much earlier.

A second important point about the indigenous communities in these four countries is their high levels of pre-existing rural ethnic diversity, making it relatively easy to trace changes in identity over time. Over the next two chapters I show that industrialization has generated processes of assimilation among all four groups as land becomes less important economically and the de-isolating effects of industrialization has brought formerly diverse groups of people together. In large part I show that it is industrialization that is responsible for investing pan-ethnic indigenous identities with actual meaning and creating a sense of ethno-national identity within each country.

Third and finally, the two cases I focus on in particular, namely the Native Americans[1] in the USA in this chapter and the Māori in New Zealand in the

---

[1] In accordance with American terminology, I do not distinguish between Native Americans in the USA and American Indians here.

following chapter, are interesting because they present examples where there is a reversal in the independent variable, allowing me to test for in-case variation. More specifically, if it is the decreasing economic incentives associated with rural identities which lead people to emphasize a higher-level ethnic identity when they leave agricultural employment and move to a city, then we would expect to see this process reverse if these rural identities were re-invested with economic value. However, in most of the cases we have encountered so far in this book – with the partial exception of Tlokweng in Botswana in the previous chapter – the economic incentives associated to rural identities have not been re-vitalized after the onset of modern industrialization. Yet the Native Americans and Māori both pose clear examples of this process, in that tribal identities in the USA have become economically valuable due to the creation of Native American casinos on tribal land, while in New Zealand fishery rights have been granted to Māori *iwi* (tribes). In accordance with my theory these shifting economic incentives have led to re-tribalization in both cases, as both Native Americans and Māori re-identify with lower-level rural identities in order to reap the benefits accrued to members of select tribes. These two cases thus allow for a more robust causal identification of the relationship between industrialization and ethnic identity change.

In the rest of this chapter I focus on the effects of industrialization on assimilation among Native Americans. I begin below by tracing the history of Native Americans from the pre-colonial period through periods of population decline in the nineteenth century before population growth spurred urbanization and industrialization in the twentieth century, which in turn encouraged the formation and increased salience of pan-tribal identities. I focus on the life of urban Indians, who have drawn relatively little attention in the academic literature relative to reservation residents.[2] However, I show that the rise of Native American casinos from the 1980s onwards has revived the economic value of reservation land and the tribes which owned them, thereby leading to the revitalization of tribal identities.

8.2 PRE-INDUSTRIAL LIFE AMONG NATIVE AMERICANS, FROM THE PRE-COLONIAL PERIOD UP TO 1900

In northern North America,[3] as in Sub-Saharan Africa, pre-modern rural Native American society was remarkably diverse, featuring far more language

---

[2] One anthropologist wrote in 1976 that 'the urban Indian is one of America's forgotten people' (Fixico, 2000, p. 182). Arguably not much has changed in the intervening period: to take one example, a recent book by the noted scholar Mahmood Mamdani on the politics of settler and native identities has a whole chapter devoted to Native Americans yet never once mentions urban Indians (Mamdani, 2020).

[3] For the rest of this chapter I refer to North America as constituting northern North America, i.e., Canada and the United States.

stocks (the highest level of language groups, above that of language families) than any other continent (Nettle, 1999). Before the arrival of European explorers, the parts of North America that would later become Canada and the USA were among the least urbanized parts of the world, with estimates from Bairoch (1988) and others that there were no towns of 5,000 people or more in the fifteenth century. As in Africa the pre-colonial era was marked by large amounts of migration, a trend which continued after European settlers began to push Native Americans westward.

As is well known, upon arriving in the New World Europeans brought with them smallpox, measles and other diseases which ravaged the population of Native Americans in what would become the lower forty-eight states of the USA and reduced it from around 5 million in 1492 to a low of 250,000 in the 1890s (Thornton, 1990, p. 43). This long period of population decline and outright genocide was paralleled by political decline, whereby Native Americans continued to lose their land as white settlers broke free of British rule and then pursued territorial expansion to the Pacific coast in the nineteenth century. One important moment in this process was the passing of the Indian Removal Act by the US Congress in 1830, which authorized the president to grant federal land west of the Mississippi river to Native Americans then living on land east of the river. While the removal of Indians from the East Coast was only supposed to be voluntary, Native Americans were nonetheless pressured to emigrate in the so-called Trail of Tears, with the federal land upon which they settled turned into reservations upon the enactment of the Indian Appropriations Act in 1851. To manage Native American affairs the US government created the Office of Indian Affairs in 1824, which was initially housed within the War Department but was transferred to the Department of the Interior in 1849 and renamed the Bureau of Indian Affairs (BIA) in 1947. Native Americans were discouraged from migrating to cities, in part by revoking tribal membership to children born outside reservations.

As with African Americans, the high levels of exploitation and violence meted out by white Americans upon Native Americans led to incipient forms of pan-Indianism in the late nineteenth and early twentieth centuries, especially among the Plains Indians (Thomas, 1965, p. 77). Perhaps the most important pan-Indian organization to come out of this period was the Society of American Indians (SAI), founded in 1911 in Columbus, Ohio by six Native American professionals from a variety of tribal backgrounds. One of its key founding members was Charles Eastman, who was born on a Dakota reservation in rural Minnesota but educated at Dartmouth and Boston University, while another was Laura Cornelius Kellogg, who was born on an Oneida reservation in Wisconsin before studying at a variety of universities. But perhaps the most interesting founding member was Carlos Montezuma, whose poem 'Changing is not Vanishing' forms the epigraph to this book. Montezuma was born to Apache parents in rural Arizona but was captured by Pima raiders and sold for $30 to an Italian-American immigrant, who briefly enlisted Montezuma in the

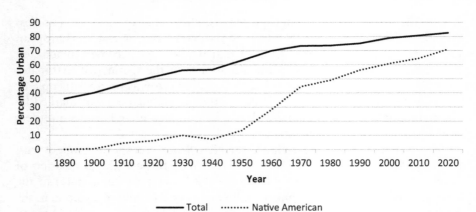

FIGURE 8.1. Urbanization in the United States, 1890–2020
(*Source:* US census reports)

theatrical troupe of Buffalo Bill before bringing him up in Chicago and New York. He studied medicine in Illinois and became first Native American man to ever receive a medical degree in the USA, and started the SAI's monthly magazine, named *Wassaja* after Montezuma's birth name, in 1916.

The SAI was explicitly super-tribal in that its focus was 'the preservation of a more or less abstract native identity and pride' (Cornell, 1988, p. 116), and advocated the abolishment of both the BIA and the reservation system. Yet despite its lofty beginnings the SAI descended into factionalism within a few years of its founding and disappeared by the mid-1920s. The major problem with the SAI was how removed it was from the rest of Native American society, which was almost entirely based on the reservations that the SAI wanted to abolish (Cornell, 1988, p. 117). Indeed, as seen in Figure 8.1 only 4.5 per cent of Native Americans lived in cities in 1910, or some 40 per cent lower than the national average at the time. This low level of urbanization meant that the SAI had few potential members and thus was destined to remain small in numbers even if it had not faced the factionalism that it did.[4]

The forced re-location of Native Americans onto reservations coincided with a continued decline in population through the late nineteenth century. While smallpox was the biggest killer, other diseases such as cholera, malaria, measles, mumps, scarlet fever, tuberculosis, typhoid and whooping cough led to high mortality rates (Thornton, 1990, pp. 91–104). This period of demographic and political decline led to a shift in US policy towards Native

---

[4] A similar story can be told for the American Indian Foundation, another super-tribal organization founded in 1934 with a goal of abolishing the BIA. A third organization, the National Congress of American Indians, was established in 1944 with more success due to the fact that it was organized as an organization of tribes rather than as a super-tribal organization (Cornell, 1988, pp. 118–19).

Americans in the Indian Appropriation Act of 1871, such that the tribes were no longer treated as sovereign entities but henceforth became wards of the state. An important outcome of this shift was the General Allotment Act, or Dawes Act, of 1887, which transferred communal lands to Native Americans as private property as a way to bring Indians into the capitalist economy. However, to enact this shift in property rights the US government had to first establish who was or was not a tribal member, which led to the creation of laws that defined tribal membership according to descent. This system of 'blood quantum' would later become very important, as I discuss below in more detail.

8.3 INDUSTRIALIZATION AND URBANIZATION AMONG NATIVE AMERICANS, FROM 1900 TO THE PRESENT

By the late nineteenth century Native Americans had reached a demographic and political nadir. However, by the beginning of the twentieth century populations began to stabilize and, after the Spanish Flu outbreak of the late 1910s, began to rise again. Thus between 1920 and 1970 the Native American population managed to triple in size from 271,000 to 827,000 (T. K. Young, 1994, p. 32).

As elsewhere, this turnaround was a consequence of declining mortality. Smallpox vaccination was increasingly implemented on a large scale in the late nineteenth century, while better access to modern healthcare reduced general levels of mortality (Thornton, 1990, p. 102). The BIA, which had previously largely delegated authority over Native American health to religious and charitable groups, began to focus on health education in reservations; it also started to require medical degrees for physicians serving on reservations in 1878 and began to hire nurses directly in the 1890s (Pfefferbaum, Strickland & Rhoades et al., 1995, pp. 369–70). A chief medical supervisor was appointed in 1908, and in the 1910s the BIA organized campaigns against 'tuberculosis, trachoma, infant mortality, house flies, alcoholism, and tooth decay' (Jones, 2006, p. 2128; Pfefferbaum et al., 1995, p. 375). Moreover, in 1911 the US Congress began to authorize specific annual funds to provide health services to Indians, which rose from an initial appropriation of $40,000 in 1911 to $350,000 in 1917 and $4.0 million in 1936, and which contributed to a decline in the Native American crude mortality rate from 35.6/1,000 to 15.1/1,000 over the same time period (Pfefferbaum et al., 1995, pp. 377, 379). After World War II new measures included the transfer of control over public health on reservations from the BIA to the US Department of Health, Education and Welfare in 1955 as well as the Sanitation Facilities Construction Act of 1959 and the Indian Health Care Improvement Act of 1976, all of which led to increased healthcare funding and great improvements in public health measures like vaccinations, sanitation infrastructure and neo-natal care.

The consequence of this sudden population growth was an increased amount of crowding on reservations which were designed to hold much smaller numbers. The obvious result was that Native Americans began to migrate from their reservations to cities, especially as the USA began to urbanize rapidly from the 1890s through the 1920s (see Figure 8.1). This trend was only accelerated during World War II when many Indians moved to work in the defence and related industries.[5] Not only did many of these new urban migrants fail to return home after the war, but many also provided beachheads for relatives and other migrants to migrate in larger numbers from the reservations to the cities in the 1950s and 1960s.

Interestingly, the improvement in Native American health coincided with a shift in US government Indian policy. Due largely to the leadership of John Collier, Commissioner of the BIA between 1933 and 1945, Washington halted the aforementioned nineteenth-century allotment policy that had created private land on reservations, returned millions of acres to tribal control, encouraged the formation of tribal governments and constitutions and expanded educational and employment opportunities on reservations. Indeed, as part of New Deal policies in the USA under President Roosevelt, the BIA obtained more than $100 million for road building and soil conservation projects on the reservations, and created reservation jobs for Indians in resource management, forestry and soil conservation. Yet, despite being progressive, these policies did not include any measures that would assist Indians outside the reservations. As such, the BIA drew criticism at the time from urban Indians like John St. Pierre (of the Yankton Sioux tribe), who argued that he and other urban Indians 'do not want to be segregated and kept off by ourselves because that leads to the development of Indians back to the blanket [i.e., returning to tribal manners and customs], and that will not be the solution of this Indian problem' (Rawls, 1996, p. 34).

The post-war era saw the involvement of the US government in encouraging Native American rural–urban migration for the first time. In 1945 one BIA officer noted that 'the overcrowded reservations, with no economic outlet available, if allowed to continue will quickly result in human misery [and] malnutrition on a tremendous scale' (Ulrich, 2010, p. 12). Predictions that the Native American population would grow by 120,000 over the next twenty-five years – which itself would be far below the actual increase of 439,285 recorded in the 1970 census – led the BIA to note that the reservations, even if they were expanded, could not hold future Native American populations (Ulrich, 2010, p. 111). Indeed, reservations had long had very poor employment prospects

---

[5] The volume of wartime migration was so large that it actually led to labour shortages on reservations as regards agricultural work, at least as regards Pueblo and Apache reservations (Rawls, 1996, p. 15). On one reservation in Oregon so many men left that, by the time they returned home, 'deer and elk were crossing the reservation roads in their plentifulness' (Rosenthal, 2012, p. 25).

outside of agriculture, not only due to their remote locations and poor infra-structure but also the general lack of formal education and wealth among reservation residents.

These concerns were echoed by long-standing concerns that agricultural employment would not be able to provide enough jobs for reservation resi-dents. For instance, in southern California a number of reservations suffered severe droughts in the 1920s, which led both to increased mortality numbers and out-migration (Rosenthal, 2012, pp. 14–15). Even more dramatic, how-ever, was a near-famine in the harsh winter of 1947–8 on Navajo and Hopi reservations, which led the US government to pass the $90-million Navajo–Hopi Act of 1950 in order to rehabilitate the two tribes and prevent future occurrences. An investigation into the Navajo–Hopi situation by the Department of the Interior concluded that their reservations could only sustain 35,000 of their 55,000 inhabitants, and that allowing Navajo, Hopi and other Native Americans to migrate to cities would be far cheaper and less compli-cated than passing more acts for other reservations (Burt, 1986, pp. 87–8). As a result, in 1948 the BIA began to operate job-placement services in Denver, Salt Lake City and Los Angeles for Navajo who wished to migrate out of their reservations (Neils, 1971, p. 47).

At the national level the federal government proposed the twin strategies of 're-location' and 'termination' as a means to move Native Americans off the reservations and end government commitment towards Native Americans by privatizing the reservations and handing out tribal assets to members in per-capita payments, respectively. For a brief period termination was an active policy of the BIA, who prepared a (never-enacted) plan to terminate pro-grammes for California Indians in 1948, while the US Congress authorized a budget of $50,000 for the BIA to begin terminating its relationship with tribes in 1952 (Ulrich, 2010, p. 14). In the end some 104 tribes, including the two large tribes of the Klemaths of Oregon and the Menominees of Wisconsin, were terminated between 1954 and 1962 before the Kennedy administration ended termination as a federal policy. However, numerous tribes were subsequently restored by the US Congress from 1973 onwards in order to make amends for its previous policies (Ulrich, 2010, pp. 247–8).

While termination was a short-lived policy that only directly affected some 13,000 Native Americans (Ulrich, 2010, p. 18), re-location policies led to the reservation–urban migration of more than 100,000 Native Americans to such cities as Chicago, Denver, Los Angeles and Detroit, among others (Edmunds, 2004, p. 402; Nagel, 1995, p. 954). The BIA assisted urbanization in Oregon, for instance, by offering funds to Native Americans to move to Portland for vocational courses (Rosenthal, 2002, p. 419). Many job-placement services put varied groups of Native Americans together in the same workplace: in the 1950s the Wells Manufacturing Corporation of Skokie, Illinois, for instance, employed nineteen Indians from ten different tribes such as the Choctaw (whose reservations lie in Oklahoma and Mississippi), Cherokee (Oklahoma),

Zuni (New Mexico), Navajo (Arizona and New Mexico) and Winnebago (Nebraska and Wisconsin) (Neils, 1971, p. 60). In San Francisco the BIA's Employment Assistance Program and Adult Vocational Training Program encouraged migration such that by the early 1960s about two-thirds of San Francisco's population of 10,000 Native Americans had urbanized through government re-location programmes (Ablon, 1965, p. 297). In Los Angeles re-located women were offered training to work as secretaries, stenographers, office clerks, beauticians, nurses and dental assistants, while men were trained to work in some of the same lines as women as well as airline and automobile mechanics, radio and television repairmen, truck drivers, welders, barbers, bookkeepers, cooks and upholsterers (Rosenthal, 2012, pp. 56, 58–9). The result was that by 1970 Los Angeles and San Francisco had the largest Native American populations in the USA, with over one hundred tribal groups represented in each city (Spicer, 1980, p. 171).

Many Native Americans who were re-located in urban areas returned home; in San Francisco, for instance, more than three-quarters of those re-located in the early years of the programme went back to their reservations. However, this number fell to 35 per cent by the early 1960s (Ablon, 1965, p. 297), and many others who returned home eventually re-located again at a later date (Neils, 1971, pp. 59, 127). Moreover, urbanization continued even after the BIA's re-location programmes were altered to a focus on employment assistance in 1961 and the official end of re-location policies with the Indian Self-Determination and Education Assistance Act of 1975 (Snipp, 1997, p. 66). Indeed, studies done in Chicago and Minneapolis in the late 1960s showed that only 14.8 per cent and 12.5 per cent of Indian migrants, respectively, had been re-located by the BIA (Woods & Harkins, 1968, p. 47). Due in part to continued high levels of unemployment on the reservations,[6] national Native American urbanization levels crossed 40 per cent by 1970 and 50 per cent by 1990 (Burt, 1986, p. 95), as seen in Figure 8.1. In New York City, for instance, the population of Native Americans increased by 30 per cent in the 1960s, in part due to immigration from far-flung parts of the USA (Wagner, 1976, p. 217). In contrast, the percentage of Indian males who worked as farmers and farm labourers dropped from 46.7 per cent and 21.7 per cent in 1940 to 2.3 per cent and 5.7 per cent, respectively, by 1970 (Littlefield, 1998, p. 340).

8.4 A 'NEW URBAN TRIBE IN A NEW URBAN HOMELAND': ETHNIC HOMOGENIZATION AMONG NATIVE AMERICANS

The BIA's goal throughout this period was summed up in its use of the word 'termination', which meant giving up the US government's responsibility over

---

[6] The agricultural basis for the reservations' economies can be seen in the seasonal variation in unemployment, with winter unemployment levels reaching 75–90 per cent among many reservations in Arizona, New Mexico and the Dakotas in the 1970s and 1980s (Rawls, 1996, p. 81).

Native Americans and encouraging integration 'into the mainstream melting pot' of American society (Fixico, 2013, p. 112).[7] As such it actively encouraged the re-location of Native Americans to cities furthest from their homes while also refusing to give out names of fellow Native Americans to newly urbanized migrants in order to encourage isolation and thus assimilation (Burt, 1986, p. 91). BIA officials even refused to grant time off from training courses for travel to reservations or inter-tribal events, and actively discouraged interaction between Indians in Portland as 'when Indian groups get together [there is] too much drinking and unacceptable behavior' (Rosenthal, 2012, p. 62). In Chicago the BIA even tried to scatter Indians across the city in an effort to 'facilitate a more normal and happy integration of persons into the life of the community' (Lagrand, 2002, p. 112). This drive towards integration – which included some degree of support for eliminating the BIA altogether – was, of course, part of a broader effort in post-war America towards breaking down special group statuses that instead emphasized individual rights and equality under the law for all US citizens, regardless of their origins (Lagrand, 2002, pp. 46–7, 49).

Yet despite these efforts, the unintended consequence of the BIA's policies was instead the creation of 'a new ethnic group, the American Indian' (Thomas, 1965, p. 75), or, as Neils (1971, p. 128) writes, 'a new urban tribe in a new urban homeland'.[8] Pan-Indian identity was not necessarily a new creation *ex nihilo*: as with the impact of slavery on African-American identity, the common experience of being on reservations and being treated as 'Indians' already promoted a common identity in the nineteenth century (Jarvenpa, 1985, p. 31). Yet it was rural–urban migration which 'caused a gradual shift away from tribal self-identification to a more general awareness of themselves as Indians who shared interests and needs with each other that differed from those of other city groups', as one scholar has put it (Nichols, 2014, p. 152).

The idea that urbanization imbued Native American identity with real meaning in the late twentieth century was not just held by non-Indian scholars but also among Native Americans themselves. Thus, according to one Native migrant to San Francisco, 'by bringing together in the cities Indians from all tribes, relocation has contributed to pan-Indianism, the movement to forsake individual tribal differences in favour of common goals' (Moisa, 1998, p. 157). Similarly, as Lanada Boyer, who was re-located from her Shoshone and Bannock reservation to San Francisco in 1965, remarked, 'on the reservations,

---

[7] In this light it is interesting to note that, while the population of Native Americans reached a nadir in 1900, their proportion of the total US population instead reached a nadir of 0.23 per cent in 1950, which may have contributed to the idea that they could easily assimilate into broader American society without affecting the composition of the latter in any significant way. The proportion of (non-multiple race) Native Americans increased to 1.12 per cent in the 2020 census.

[8] Furlan (2017, p. 16) documents the scholarly debate on what to call urban Indian identity, from 'neo-Indian' to 'ethnic Indian', 'pan-Indian' and 'supratribal', among other terms.

it was easy to divide Indians against Indians; but in a major city, we are so glad to see other Indians, we don't care what tribe they are. They are natives, and that's all that counts' (Boyer, 1998, p. 436). Ignatia Broker, who had migrated from the White Earth Indian Reservation in northern Minnesota to Minneapolis, noted too how urban Native children 'do not make any distinctions as to their tribes. They do not say, "I am Ojibway", or "I am Dakota", or "I am Arapaho", but they say, "I am an Indian"' (Broker, 1983, p. 7). Finally, the Native American historian Donald Fixico has written extensively on how urbanization created a new Indian identity that 'transformed from tribalism on reservations to Indianness in cities' (Fixico, 2013, p. 114). In particular, Fixico has focussed on the way urbanization broke down many of the barriers and conflicts that had previously existed between tribes:

For instance, the Navajo and the Hopi of the Southwest had long regarded each other as enemies because of land disputes between them. In the city, these arguments seemed less relevant. The shared experience of Navajo and Hopi urban dwellers as part of the Indian minority in a primarily non-Indian city population drew these people closer together than the disputes of their tribes tore them apart. (Fixico, 1991, p. 83)

Early writings on pan-Indianism were sceptical about its true nature and its future, with one anthropologist, for instance, writing of 'urban "Indian" communities' as potentially 'only temporary stopping places for individual Indians who will later become part of the more general middle class' (Thomas, 1965, p. 81). Of course, most Native American rural–urban migrants did not immediately assimilate into a broader pan-Indian identity upon moving from their reservations to the cities. Indeed, at least in early 1960s San Francisco most Native Americans appeared to self-segregate by tribe (Ablon, 1965, pp. 298–9). Yet there was already at this point evidence for a 'neo-Indian social identity which is pan-Indian in its orientation' (Ablon, 1965, p. 303), especially among those who had moved away from their reservations long before the newer migrants. These older migrants were the ones behind such organizations as the American Indian Council of the Bay Area, the American Indian Centre, the American Indian Youth Council of the Bay Area and American Indian Alcoholics Anonymous. Despite assumptions from the BIA and others that urbanization would promote assimilation into American society, these older migrants were 'the most vocal in expressing belligerency against whites, and in extolling a fierce pride in Indian identity' (Ablon, 1965, p. 300).[9]

As a result, many American cities began to see the creation of new pan-Indian organizations. In Phoenix, for example, urban Native Americans founded the Southwestern Indian Development (SID) in 1968; while originally only comprised of Navajo, members of other tribes soon joined as well

---

[9] As two historians have noted, 'being Native American in the city was an important ingredient to personal identity, often as important as membership in any particular tribe' (Olson & Wilson, 1984, p. 165).

(Amerman, 2003, p. 610). In Portland, Oregon, the Voice of the American Indian Association was established in 1959, with its initial mission to help Indians back on the reservations but eventually with the goal of providing a community space for urban Indians to meet each other. The Portland American Indian Center (PAIC) was also founded in 1959, followed by the Native American Rehabilitation Association for recovering alcoholics in 1970 and the overarching Urban Indian Council in 1971. The PAIC began to sponsor an annual summer powwow in 1969, which allowed urban Indians to express their tribal cultures through dress and dance while also featuring non-tribal Indian events like 'softball games, church services and a pageant to crown Miss Indian Northwest', as well as an 'Indian meal' with dishes from fifteen distinct tribes (Rosenthal, 2002, pp. 424–5). A sense of common Indian identity was clear among Portland Indians, with one resident claiming that, 'though we are all from different tribes, we have the same goals and the same interests, because we are all Indians' (Rosenthal, 2012, p. 112).

The experience of Indians in Los Angeles deserves special attention, since by 1980 it had the largest population of urban Indians in the country at 60,893 and clearly functioned as a 'melting pot of tribal people', with inter-tribal powwows that brought together Indians from all around the country (Rosenthal, 2012, p. 70). In the early 1970s the BIA helped to finance the creation of the Urban Indian Development Association (UIDA) in Los Angeles, which not only took charge of housing all new re-located Indians and but also introduced them to other Indians upon arrival and attend powwows.[10] The city had previously seen the birth of the American Indian Progressive Association (AIPA) in 1924, whose goal was generally integrationist inasmuch as its explicit goal was to 'obtain the proper social and political status of the American Indian as a citizen of the United States of America' (Rosenthal, 2012, p. 106). Nonetheless, membership in the AIPA was restricted to Indians, and one of its main goals, as with another Los Angeles association, the Wigwam Club, was to bring Indians together at social events such as dances and the annual Indian Day celebration from 1928 (Rosenthal, 2012, p. 108). In 1935 the Los Angeles Indian Center (LAIC) was founded by Mira Frye Bartlett, a Kickapoo Indian born in Oklahoma, with a purpose of producing a newsletter of events as well as providing a space for socializing. Indeed, the LAIC 'consciously cultivated a larger sense of Indianness that transcended tribal differences' (Rosenthal, 2012, p. 117), inasmuch as members and the newsletter repeatedly referred to 'Los Angeles Indians' and rejoiced in the numerous occasions when members of many different tribes came together.

Late twentieth-century pan-Indian nationalism was perhaps most prominent, however, in the two Midwestern cities of Chicago and Minneapolis.

---

[10] This shift in policy towards promoting interactions between urban Indians rather than discouraging it was part of the general shift in Native American policy that took place under Presidents Kennedy, Johnson and Nixon.

Indians moved to Chicago from a variety of locations and tribes, leading some to set up the Indian Center as a source of emergency assistance to migrants while also sponsoring various activities and cultural programmes which brought migrants together. In 1962 the city saw the establishment of the St. Augustine's Center for American Indians by the Episcopal Church, which provided pastoral support as well as financial aid and job assistance to recent immigrants (Neils, 1971, pp. 66–7). According to data collected by researchers from the University of Minnesota in 1968, more than sixty tribes were represented among the 1,250 people that St. Augustine's served, with a plurality identifying as Chippewa (29.7 per cent of the total), followed by the Menominee (17.6 per cent) and Sioux at 9.0 per cent. Many came from other Midwestern or Great Plains states such as Wisconsin (46.6 per cent of the total), Minnesota (8.5 per cent) and South Dakota (6.9 per cent), among others, and a majority (55.4 per cent) were born on a reservation. Only 1.2 per cent were born in Chicago, with 45 per cent having arrived within the past three years, with another 23.3 per cent arriving four to seven years earlier. A majority were men (53.7 per cent), and a majority (56.6 per cent) were between 20 and 34 years old, with another fifth (22.6 per cent) between 35 and 44 (Noeg, Woods & Harkins, 1970, pp. 6–11).

The size of the Chicago Native American community and its central location led the anthropologist Sol Tax to choose the city to house a pan-Indian congress that could address issues common to all Native Americans. This conference came together in June 1961 as the American Indian Chicago Conference and drew 450 delegates from ninety tribes from across the country in order to discuss current issues affecting all Native Americans (Neils, 1971, p. 128). Upon its conclusion the conference produced a 'Declaration of Indian Purpose', which, in language reminiscent of the US Constitution, used the phrase 'we, the Indian people', in its opening sentence. Indeed, merely by bringing a variety of Indians together the conference helped to spread the idea of pan-Indian nationalism, with one Indian attendee noting that, 'when I came here, I thought only of my people and our problems, and now I think of all the Indian people and all their problems' (Ablon, 1979, p. 452). Moreover, the conference helped not only to end the US government's termination policies but also spur greater inter-tribal co-operation through such organizations as the Great Lakes Intertribal Council and spawn the first-ever national Native American newspaper, *Indian Voices*, which was able to utilize the conference mailing list to great effect.

Interestingly, one of the more controversial topics of the conference was the degree to which individuals sent as tribal delegates should receive more votes than those representing unrecognized tribes and urban groups, which the attendees ended up resolving by weighting tribal votes against those of individuals on a 60/40 basis (Ablon, 1979, p. 451). Foreshadowing future clashes on who has the right to speak for Indian communities, one tribal leader at the conference, Robert Burnette of the Rosebud Sioux, wrote to Tax that 'we are oppressed in this because most of those people present will be city Indians and will clash with the official voice of the tribes' (Lagrand, 2002, p. 173). Tellingly, the anonymous questionnaires completed by all attendees afterwards showed a sharp divide in terms of attitudes towards pan-Indianism: while urban Indians answered the question on why they had attended with comments like 'in the hopes that the Indians would all agree as a race rather than tribes' or 'because I am Indian', tribal delegates instead tended to write that they attended 'for the welfare of my people on our reservation' (Lagrand, 2002, pp. 177–8).

The other great Midwest destination for Native American rural–urban migrants, namely Minneapolis, spawned the most prominent Native American political organization of the late twentieth century, the American Indian Movement (AIM). The city had long been the home of pan-Indian organizations, many of which like the Ojibway–Dakota Research Society were originally founded along tribal lines but which came to accept other Native Americans as members in due course (Shoemaker, 1988, p. 444). A 1967 study of 743 Indian job-seekers in Minneapolis by researchers at the University of Minnesota showed that most of the migrants tended to be Chippewa (82.6 per cent of the total), male (74.2 per cent), non-high school graduates (78 per cent) and were very recent migrants, having arrived in Minneapolis less than a year before the study (51.1 per cent of the total) (Harkins & Woods, 1969).

The AIM was established in 1968 in large part in response to the lack of strong politically active pan-Indian coalitions in Minneapolis, inasmuch as self-help groups such as the Upper Midwest American Indian Center (UMAIC; established in 1961) were more focussed on advice, counselling and social events. AIM's initial focus was on promoting the employment of Indians in city government programmes based on the 2:1 ratio of African Americans to Indians in the city. It also created an 'Indian Patrol' to prevent police harassment in south Minneapolis, and sued the *Minneapolis Tribune* for discrimination based on an allegedly discriminatory cartoon (Harkins & Woods, 1969, pp. 12–14). As with the SAI half a century earlier, many founding members of the AIM were rural–urban migrants, including Russell Means, who was born on the Pine Ridge Indian Reservation in South Dakota to Sioux parents who migrated to San Francisco when he was three, and Clyde and Vernon Bellecourt, born on the White Earth Indian Reservation before their family migrated to Minneapolis.[11] Other AIM leaders such as the late Anna Mae Aquash was born on the Indian Brook 14 reserve to Mi'kmaq parents in Nova Scotia, Canada, before moving to Boston as a teenager, while member Leonard Peltier (who was of Chippewa and Dakota Sioux descent) grew up on the Turtle Mountain Indian Reservation in North Dakota before settling in Seattle. In his autobiography Peltier described how leaving reservations allowed

---

[11] Ironically, another founding member, Dennis Banks, noted that 'urbanization was ... part of the destruction of the Indian community' despite AIM's urban origins (Shoemaker, 1988, p. 431).

Indians like him to realize a pan-Indian identity: 'instead of disappearing, dissolving as a people, as we were expected to do, we found a new social consciousness and a new sense of ourselves in the human cauldron of the cities' (Peltier, 1999, pp. 93–4).

What distinguished both AIM and another pan-Indian organization founded in the 1960s, the National Indian Youth Council, from previous organizations was their explicit attempt to promote a pan-Indian identity, as seen in the AIM's use of a set of symbols borrowed from Plains Indians such as the headdress/warbonnet as national symbols common to all Native Americans (J. R. Hanson, 1997, p. 202). The occupation of Alcatraz Island off the coast of San Francisco by Native American activists is also instructive in this sense. The island had famously been used as a prison up until 1963 but had been declared surplus federal property in 1964, which, according to one interpretation of the Treaty of Fort Laramie from 1868, meant that it should have reverted to Native American ownership. Several Sioux activists originally occupied the island for four hours in 1964 before yielding it back to state control. The island was re-occupied in November 1969, this time by a group entitled Indians of All Tribes under the leadership of Richard Oakes (Mohawk) and Adam Fortunate Eagle (Chippewa), John Whitefox (Choctaw), Millie Ketcheshawno (Muscogee), Ed Castillo (Cahuilla) and Shirley Guevara (Mono), among others.[12] The occupation was forcibly ended in June 1971 but inspired the AIM to submit a list of twenty grievances designed to improve the lives of all Native Americans to the BIA and occupied the BIA offices in Washington, DC, for one week in November 1972 before leaving in a non-violent fashion. The list of grievances called for a repeal of the 1871 federal statute that had prohibited further treaty-making between tribes and the US government, and instead called for a treaty relationship between the USA and the 'Indian Tribes and Nations' (Rawls, 1996, p. 126). The next year the AIM occupied the town of Wounded Knee in South Dakota for seventy-one days in protest against the corrupt leadership of the Pine Ridge Indian Reservation, which, as with related activism in the late 1960s and early 1970s, had a strong influence on President Nixon's relatively progressive policies towards Native Americans (Kotlowski, 2003).

Pan-Indian activism also took less dramatic but still important forms in the 1970s. For instance, the decade saw the founding of multiple pan-tribal newspapers such as *Wassaja* from San Francisco in 1973, which revived the title from the SAI's monthly magazine and self-styled itself 'a national newspaper of Indian America', while formerly tribe-specific newspapers like *Lakota Times* and *Akwesasne Notes* expanded their coverage and evolved into pan-Indian periodicals. Finally, Russell Means, Vernon Bellecourt and other activists were

---

[12] One activist at Alcatraz claims that the US federal government representative, Bob Robertson, tried to set tribal leaders against them by claiming that the activists were not just militants but were also '"urban Indians" … [who] were after a slice of the "federal economic pie"' (Boyer, 1998, p. 444).

instrumental in combating stereotypes about Native Americans, both in school textbooks and in the use of college and professional sports team mascots. In response to such activism, from the 1970s onwards various colleges and universities dropped indigenous-based mascots such as the 'Braves', 'Chiefs', 'Indians', 'Redmen', 'Redskins', 'Savages' and 'Warriors'.[13]

Back on the reservations tribal leaders were largely opposed to pan-Indian activities inasmuch as their collective leadership and authority was comprised by urban activists. Tribal leaders and organizations which represented tribal governments such as the National Congress of American Indians and the National Tribal Chairmen's Association vocally criticized the occupation of Wounded Knee. In particular leaders of more traditional tribes such as the Wisconsin Winnebagos, the Hopis or the Navajos refused to participate in pan-Indian activities and derogatorily branded pan-Indianism as 'the work of mixed-bloods and assimilated Native Americans who have surrendered much of their tribal identities' (Olson & Wilson, 1984, p. 191).

Indeed, just because pan-Indianism emerged through the process of industrialization and urbanization does not mean that tribal identities were forgotten. Instead, it would be more appropriate to think of pan-tribal and tribal identities as co-existing with each other in urban spaces, with individuals 'still conscious of tribal differences, even as they shared tribal culture and learned from one another' (Rosenthal, 2012, p. 118). The reason for this continued co-existence was that there were still strong economic incentives for individuals to retain their tribal identities, since BIA assistance could only be granted to individuals who lived on tribal reservations or who retained links with their reservations. Nonetheless it is still notable that in the 1970 census some 30 per cent of urban Native Americans failed to identify a tribal affiliation compared to only 10 per cent on reservations (Thornton, 2004, p. 80).

We can also observe the process of Native American language loss alongside the use of English as a lingua franca within the urban environment, which arguably contributed to the creation of pan-tribal identities (Howard, 1955, p. 219). Indeed, the 1970 US census showed that while only 31.9 per cent of all Native Americans spoke an Indian language as a mother tongue compared to 50.5 per cent who spoke English, on reservations the percentages were instead 58.2 per cent and 25.8 per cent, respectively. We can examine the statistical relationship between urbanization and Indian language retention due to the detailed collection of data at the tribal level in the 1980 US census, which is an ideal data source for two reasons. First, the 1980 census was unique in its collection of data at the tribal level in its special report on Native Americans (located in Volume II, Chapter PC80–2-1C): the 1970 census report on Native

---

[13] This issue has been more controversial at the level of American professional sports: it took the George Floyd protests of 2020 to finally push the Washington Redskins and the Cleveland Indians to change their names; however, other teams such as the Atlanta Braves, Chicago Blackhawks and Kansas City Chiefs have so far refused to change their names.

Americans, for instance, only collected data at the state level, and then only for states with 10,000 or more Native American inhabitants, while the 1960 and 1950 censuses did not contain separate reports for Native Americans.[14] The lack of comparable data from other censuses means that I am limited to a cross-sectional analysis and thus cannot trace the effects of urbanization across time as I have done in other chapters of this book.

A second reason why the 1980 census is useful in understanding the relationship between urbanization and language retention is the large variation across tribes. More specifically, the percentage of people over the age of five who spoke a Native American or Alaska Native language at home ranged from 0.0 per cent among the Heliwa and Shinnecock to 97.2 per cent among the San Felipe; levels of urbanization similarly varied from 2.2 per cent among the San Felipe to 94.5 per cent among the Shinnecock. While the census contains data on hundreds of tribes, I only include data here on the 123 tribes with populations greater than 1,000 people; when there are two levels of identification I use the lower tribal level rather than the national group – or the Seneca and Mohawk rather than the Iroquois – with similar results if I use the higher level instead. (The results also do not change substantially if I instead use larger population thresholds.)

In Figure 8.2 I plot the percentage of Native Americans over the age of five who speak a Native American or Alaska Native language on the y-axis against the percentage in each tribe who live in urban areas on the x-axis with 95 per cent confidence intervals. As expected, the relationship is negative and statistically significant, with a t-statistic of –2.91 and an R^2 of 0.117.

I next present the results of regressing native-language use at home on levels of urbanization by tribe in Table 8.1. To the analysis I add four basic controls. First, I control for the log of median household income to control for the possibility that urbanization is a mere proxy for general well-being. Second, I control for the log of total population to account for the possibility that larger groups are more likely to have their tribal language printed in books and newspapers and taught in schools. Third, I control for median age to control for different levels of fertility and life expectancy as additional measures of well-being. Perhaps most importantly I control for the percentage in each tribe with a high-school degree to account for the influence of education; however, as it is moderately correlated with the log of median household income ($r = 0.42$) I add it as a separate control in column 2. (The results are the same if I instead control for the percentage with university degrees.)

---

[14] Going forward in time, the 1990 census has data by tribe and contains data on urbanization and whether individuals speak a language other than English, but it does not specify whether or not the non-English language is an Indian language. (This a particularly important distinction for those tribes which live in the southern United States like the Spanish-speaking Yaqui of Arizona or the French-speaking Houma of Louisiana.) Finally, the 2000 and 2010 censuses do not list urbanization levels for Native Americans, either by tribe or by state.

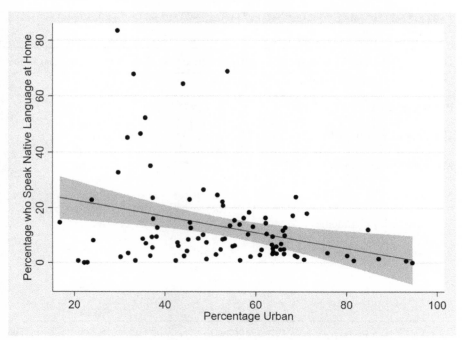

FIGURE 8.2. Urbanization and Indian language retention among Native American tribes with populations larger than 1,000 in 1980
(*Source:* 1980 US census)

As expected, the coefficient on the urbanization variable is negative and statistically significant at the 1 per cent level in both regressions; an increase of one standard deviation in the value of the urbanization variable decreases the proportion who speak a Native language by 8.8 per cent, or 37 per cent of the standard deviation. The log of median household income is also statistically significant in both columns, a result which suggests that native-language retention is better among tribes with lower incomes. However, there is no relationship between education and language retention, which corresponds with evidence presented in previous chapters.

8.5 THE REVITALIZATION OF LAND THROUGH NATIVE AMERICAN CASINOS

As noted above, Native American urbanization has been driven by demographic and economic factors. This pattern of rural–urban migration led many Native Americans to de-emphasize their tribal identities and instead focus their attention on the creation of a new Native American identity as their tribal

TABLE 8.1. *Urbanization and Indian language retention among Native Americans in 1980*

Dependent variable: % who speak a Native American/Alaska native language at home		
	(1)	(2)
Percentage urban	−0.447***	−0.441***
	(0.123)	(0.121)
Total population (log)	0.023	0.022
	(0.016)	(0.016)
Median household income (log)	−0.338***	−0.328***
	(0.111)	(0.114)
Median age	−0.0001	−0.0001
	(0.00005)	(0.0001)
Secondary school graduates (%)		−0.052
		(0.134)
Constant	3.409***	3.348***
	(1.054)	(1.069)
N	123	123
R²	0.324	0.324

* $p \leq 0.1$, ** $p \leq 0.05$, *** $p \leq 0.01$ (two-tailed test); robust standard errors in parentheses. The table only considers tribes with more than 1,000 members in 1980.

identities became less important to them economically. Of course throughout this period migrants were still concerned about losing touch with their tribal reservations such that the numbers of urban Native Americans were probably under-counts if evidence from the 1980 census is generalizable, with Native Americans in Chicago claiming beforehand that they were reluctant to be counted as urban since they were expected to be living on their reservations (Tax, 1978, p. 126).

Thus, Native American rural–urban migrants made a rational decision to emphasize a broader identity (Native American) above a narrower one (their tribe). However, if incentives were to alter and tribal membership were to yield greater access to resources than identifying more generally as a Native American, then according to my theory we would see a reversal in this process of ethnic change. So far in this book I have not been able to provide an example where the process of industrialization has been reversed and rural land has re-acquired value. However, in the case of Native Americans we can see a perfect example of this phenomenon via the rise of Native American casinos, which are allowed to be erected only on tribal land. If I am correct, the onset of gaming among tribes should alter the incentives for urban Native Americans to empha-size their identities as Native Americans over their tribal identities. Instead, among tribes which re-distribute casino revenues to tribal members either directly as per-capita payments or indirectly via social services, there should be a shift towards re-tribalization among Native Americans who wish to gain access to the new economic benefits of being a tribal member.

Before discussing casinos, it is important to review evidence on other new sources of tribal revenue that has led both to tightening of tribal rules on adoption as well as conflicts over genealogy. The Seminoles are an instructive case study here: originally a group of runaway Creeks in Florida that also attracted runaway slaves of African descent, the group gradually became recognized as a distinct tribe in the late eighteenth century. Upon being re-located to Oklahoma in the nineteenth century, both Native American and so-called Black Seminoles (of full or partial African American descent) were listed among the tribe's members despite the fact that the two groups lived separately and spoke different languages. Thus, when the US government awarded $56 million to the tribe in 2000 as compensation for displacement of the tribe in the 1820s, the tribal government decided to exclude Black Seminoles from tribal membership since it claimed that Black Seminoles joined the group after 1866 and were thus not eligible for compensation. Needless to say, these actions drew protests from Black Seminoles and the BIA (S. A. Miller, 2005), which withheld funds from the Seminole tribe for a time as a consequence.

In fact, restrictions on tribal membership have long been linked to economic incentives for joining tribes. For instance, up until 1953 there was no definition of what was required to be a member of the Navajo other than being born into the tribe. However, the discovery of uranium on Navajo land in 1951, the appropriation of $88 million due to the aforementioned Navajo–Hopi Rehabilitation Act of 1950 and the onset of several lawsuits against the US government caused the Tribal Council to worry that the tribe would be 'awash in claims for membership' (Spruhan, 2007, p. 4).[15] Rather than choosing to restrict identity along cultural lines such as knowledge of the Navajo language or membership of a Navajo clan, the council instead chose to restrict future Navajo applicants to those who could prove that their ancestry was at least one-quarter Navajo. Such individuals could then apply to the BIA for a coveted Certificate of Degree of Indian Blood, which would officially state their membership in the Navajo tribe.

The idea of giving per-capita payments to tribal members also goes back decades, with the Indian Claims Commission (ICC) established in 1946 for the purpose of handling claims by tribes that their land had been unjustly seized by the government in the past without market-price compensation. By the time the ICC had concluded in 1978, it was responsible for awarding more than $800 million to tribes. Since the ICC based its valuation on how much the land was worth at the time it was appropriated rather than contemporary values, the

---

[15] Tribal Council minutes from 1951 note that 'initiation of the Long-Range Rehabilitation Program and other developments have been accompanied by applications on the part of persons claiming Navajo blood, but whose names do not now appear on the Tribal rolls' (Spruhan, 2007, p. 4).

per-capita cheques sent to Indians were generally small, such as the one-off sum of $668.51 sent to California Indians in 1959. Nonetheless, the idea that tribal membership was economically valuable did have an effect, such that the Miami tribal roll expanded from 317 members to more than 3,000 after the ICC awarded them $8 million in 1960 (Rawls, 1996, p. 37).

However, it was the advent of casino revenues which greatly increased the incentives in tribal identification, with a concomitant increase in conflict over tribal membership. Native American casinos first came into existence after a Chippewa couple in Minnesota were given a tax bill by the local county despite living on the Leech Lake Indian Reservation. The couple appealed for legal assistance, and received help from both the reservation government and the Native American Rights Fund, which is a non-profit pan-tribal organization founded in 1970. The case worked its way up to the Supreme Court, which ruled in 1976 that states were prohibited from taxing residents on reservations or even from regulating economic activities on tribal land, which led soon thereafter to the first establishment of Native American lotteries, bingo halls and casinos. Particularly after the Indian Gaming Regulatory Act of 1988 opened up the scope for tribes to bypass state laws, numerous tribal governments began to open very profitable casinos on their tribal reservations, many of which have led to strong spillover effects via hotels and other forms of entertainment. The number of reservations that have casinos reached over 490 in 2017, with more than $32 billion in annual revenues (Frye, Mollica & Parker, 2020, p. 29). Tribal governments have used the revenues for improvements in education (via college scholarships), public health (clinics and water quality maintenance), public safety (police and fire fighters) and other types of public goods. The result has been a decline in the rate of urbanization among Native Americans, as well as evidence that, for tribes which opened a casino four or more years previously, their reservation populations increased by 12 per cent; that this increase is almost entirely among the population under the age of 65 suggests that many Native Americans are staying at home rather than migrating to cities for economic reasons (Evans & Topoleski, 2002).

Given the economic incentives associated with tribal identification in areas with Native American casinos, we would expect to find some positive correlation between tribal gaming and self-identification as Native American. Recent evidence from Antman and Dunan (2021) using censuses and annual American Community Survey (ACS) data suggests that there is indeed a positive correlation between state approval of tribal gaming in an individual's birth state and the subsequent likelihood of Native American identification, and that this association increases with the strength of the individual's self-reported Native American ancestry. (In other words, for those with no ancestral ties there is a negative correlation, but this correlation turns positive for those with any documented Native American ancestry.) These results hold for both children and adults and when using casino opening dates instead of tribe–state compact dates; moreover, the coefficients on the point estimates for those with some

Native American ancestry are higher for states with tribes who allocate casino revenues on a per capita basis, thereby providing further evidence for the role of economic incentives in generating higher levels of Native American self-identification.

While showing that the opening of casinos is positively correlated with the probability of Native American self-identification (at least for those with some Native American ancestry), Antman and Dunan (2021) cannot, however, identify whether gaming is generating incentives for individuals to identify as members of specific tribes due to a lack of information. Indeed, neither census nor ACS data contain consistent tribal categories over time, making it impossible to generate panel data that measures the association between gaming and tribal identification. However, it is still possible to examine qualitative data on how casinos have generated incentives for identity change among Native Americans. For instance, there are multiple examples of groups of people being dis-enrolled or suspended as members of tribes that have recently begun to receive revenue from casinos or other windfalls, such as among the Pala Band of Mission Indians in California, the Isleta Pueblo in New Mexico, the Paiute in Nevada or the Narrangasett in Rhode Island. In other cases, tribes have not dis-enrolled members but instead prevented those who did not live on the reservations from receiving per-capita payments. In the case of the Lower Sioux Indian Community of Minnesota for instance, a law which limited per-capita payments only to reservation residents or those who lived within ten miles of the reservation cut off payments to around two-thirds of enrolled tribal members (Rand & Light, 1996, pp. 419–20).

The rise of Native American casinos has also led to many cases where people suddenly become interested in joining tribes due to the benefits they might receive, which may or may not be followed by subsequent cases of tribal suspension. Thus, as one council member of the Tunica–Biloxi tribe of Louisiana and son of the tribal chairman, Earl Barbry Jr., which has per-capita casino payments, noted that 'what was [previously] considered improper and shunned – being a member of the tribe – is now coveted and frequently requested' (Goldsmith & Mueller, 2003, pp. 44–5). In some cases, such as the Eastern Band of Cherokee Indians in North Carolina, tribal leaders increased the minimum blood quantum required for membership – which currently ranges among tribes from a minimum of 1/32nd Native ancestry to a full 100 per cent – while in others foreign citizens applied for membership, as happened with the alleged long-lost Bahamian cousins of the Mashantucket Pequot Tribe of Connecticut once the latter group opened up their highly profitable casino (Rand & Light, 1996, pp. 422–3). In others, such as the Pechanga Band of Luiseño Mission Indians in Riverside County in southern California, and operators of the largest casino in the state, the tribe received 'hundreds' of applications for membership after they opened their first casino in 1995, many of which were from people of Native American descent but not of

Pechanga ancestry (Pechanga Tribal Council, 2007). With membership worth between $120,000 and $180,000 per year in 2006, the Tribal Council not only rejected many such applications but ousted some 133 members in 2004 on grounds that their Pechanga ancestor had left the reservation in the 1920s; the subsequent lawsuit worked its way up to the US Supreme Court, which refused to hear the case and thus by default allowed the Tribal Council's ruling to stand.

Similar controversies have plagued tribes whose per-capita payments are much less, such as the Picayune Rancheria of the Chukchansi Indians in California, who grant their members around $3,600 in annual casino stipends.[16] Here again there is some evidence that the casino revenues have brought in large number of applicants to the tribe, leading the tribal council to consider making a paternity test part of the requirement of becoming a tribal member (Geddes, 2011). Sometimes applicants apply to become a member of a tribe merely in anticipation that the tribe will eventually open a casino, as with the Lumbees of North Carolina, who for a while only accepted applications for a period of a few months every two or three years due to the large volume of applications they receive (Morello, 2001). Finally, in the case of the Shakopee Mdewakanton Sioux (Dakota) of Minnesota, after opening up its first casino in 1992 the tribes saw 'hundreds of enrolment applications' come in, with one such member claiming that 'these Mdewakanton that are coming back here, they have never lived here and never been enrolled here and yet they want to come here [to enjoy the more than $1 million in annual per capita casino payments]' (Diaz, 2007).

The economic advantages flowing to small tribes who can become rich through casinos or other types of revenue-generating activities have even spurred on new applications to the US government for tribal recognition, since only federally recognized tribes can set up a casino on tribal land. Many of the 291 groups whose application was under consideration at the BIA in 2004 had already signed on with casino investors before sending in their application, with eight of the twelve groups awaiting final decisions from the BIA at that point bankrolled by people in the gambling industry.[17] While federal recognition of tribes began in 1978, the vast majority of applications to date were submitted after reservation gambling was legalized in 1988, with the BIA rejecting thirty-four of the fifty-six decisions it had made through the end of 2021.[18] Many of

---

[16] Senior citizens receive around $10,000. As with other tribes these numbers are estimates due to financial confidentiality rules (Capriccioso, 2021).

[17] The application itself can cost millions of dollars in part due to the requirements to provide genealogical records that establish the tribe as continuously extant since 1900, descendent from a historical tribe and have political influence over its members, among other criteria (Peterson, 2004).

[18] <www.bia.gov/as-ia/ofa/decided-cases>

the tribes rejected could not establish links with a historical tribe or their continuous existence since 1900: for instance, the Juaneño Band of Mission Indians, Acjachemen Nation, claimed descent from an older band of Mission Indians in what is now Orange County, California, whose existence as a separate tribe ceased after a smallpox epidemic in 1862 before it re-grouped in 1997 to apply to the BIA (Bureau of Indian Affairs, 2011). Other rejected cases include tribes who could not demonstrate that their membership list was valid, such as the Sokoki Band of Abenakis of Vermont, whose application only provided proof of Abenaki ancestry for eight of its 1,171 members, or the Mobile-Washington County Band of Choctaw Indians of South Alabama, who could only demonstrate Native American ancestry for 1 per cent of its members (Bureau of Indian Affairs, 1997, 2007).[19]

Some of the cases for recognition have been incredibly weak, especially those received in the first decade after recognition began. For instance, in the case of the Southeastern Cherokee Confederacy (SECC) and two other groups the tribes' joint application in the 1980s provided no evidence whatsoever that they had historical links to the historic Cherokee nation, with the BIA commenting in one instance that 'current mail addressed to an individual who uses an Indian name is not historical evidence, nor does it necessarily show Indian ancestry or recognition as Indian' (Bureau of Indian Affairs, 1985, p. 39048). Indeed, although it called itself Cherokee, the SECC allowed membership to anyone who claimed Indian ancestry of any kind, and has held powwows and Indian dances that have no particular link to Cherokee traditions (G.s Roth, 1992, p. 201).

However, dubious applications for tribal recognition have continued: more recently the BIA noted that the membership of the proposed Nipmuc tribe of Massachusetts, whose leaders had already signed a contract with a casino operator, 'is to a considerable extent the result of a deliberate recruitment effort undertaken from 1989 to 1994 [or just after Native American casinos were fully legalized], and brought [into the tribe] many families that had no significant social ties prior to that time into the organization called the Nipmuc Nation' according to the BIA (Dignam, 2001). Finally, and perhaps most impressive of all, was an application by the Central Band of Cherokee of Tennessee, who not only failed to demonstrate that it had existed as a group prior to the year 2000 but whose ancestry records showed its members to be descendants of immigrants from the British Isles, France and Germany who settled in Tennessee from the early nineteenth century onwards (Bureau of Indian Affairs, 2010).

---

[19] While tribes do not have to demonstrate that 100 per cent of their proposed members are direct descendants of a historical tribe, the BIA has noted that no successful application has had less than 80 per cent of its members demonstrating valid historical descent (Bureau of Indian Affairs, 2012).

8.6 CONCLUSION

In this chapter I have shown that urbanization among Native Americans in the United States has led to pan-Indian movements and a shift in salience from rural tribal identities to a broader urban Native American identity. This shift was in large part due to the decreasing economic importance of rural land as emphasizing their common bonds across tribal lines in urban areas became more important to indigenous peoples. These migrants did not integrate into broader mainstream American society, as the US government had expected them to do, but instead managed to create a new urban Indian identity that drew from tribal identities but was explicitly pan-tribal in orientation. As one scholar has noted, this process has become so advanced that 'it may make sense at some future time to speak of Native Americans mainly as people of Native American ancestry or ethnicity' rather than members of their individual tribes (Thornton, 1997, p. 39).

Yet this process of assimilation from tribal identities into a broader Native American identity was halted by the advent of casino revenues, which did not flow to Native Americans as a group but instead accrued to individual tribes according to the gaming profits generated on their tribal land. The result has been the re-tribalization of Native Americans, such that tribal identities are again salient, so much so that many tribes have excluded current and potential members while the leaders of others apply for official tribal recognition from the US government. This shift in the relative value of land – such that the process of industrialization has been partially halted or even reversed among Native Americans – has thus led to the increased salience of tribal over Native American identities, just as my theory would suggest.

The result of this transformation is that, just as in Somalia and Uganda, the way ethnicity is conceptualized among Native Americans has become increasingly primordial in nature. In writings and discussions, individuals who claim to be Native American are essentially forced to list their tribe(s) after their name in parentheses to be acknowledged as 'genuine', while others (like Massachusetts senator Elizabeth Warren) attempt to 'prove' their Native American ancestry with DNA tests. This practice precludes both assimilation into and out of tribes, problematizes Native American identity for those who have lost their tribal documentation due to ancestors who hid their Native identities, and reduces the importance and salience of a singular, common pan-tribal Native American identity as such. It is thus not surprising to see Native American scholars like Kimberly TallBear and Ward Churchill despair at how Native American identity has become racialized and quantified to the point where tribal membership is only defined via DNA and not commitment to the tribe or individual action or agency (Kelly, 2011; TallBear, 2003).[20]

A similar consequence of the rise of Native American casinos has been the re-birth in inter-tribal conflict after a period where urbanization helped to ease

---

[20] The case of Churchill himself is instructive, inasmuch as his claims to Native American ancestry have been disputed by Creek and Cherokee leaders who have questioned whether his blood quantum is sufficient enough to allow him to be admitted to tribal membership (Kelly, 2011).

internal Native conflict. For instance, conflict erupted in 1997 in Wisconsin between leaders of the Menominee and the Oneida Nation in response to the latter's opposition to an off-reservation casino site then being considered by the Menonimees, despite the fact that the Oneida Nation already enjoyed the benefits of a tribal casino, with the former arguing that 'gaming has separated all tribes into Haves and Have Nots' (Iverson & Davies, 2015, p. 209). In Oregon similar tensions ensued between the Warm Springs and Grand Ronde tribes, whereby the former proposed a new casino on non-reservation tribal land that was also claimed by the latter, who also already had a casino in another location. As documented by the Native American scholar Brook Colley, these conflicts – which have also broken out in Arizona and California – appear to be on the rise since the late 1990s as tribal leaders have realized their ability to maintain economic advantages by blocking other tribes' access to casino revenue (B. Colley, 2018, p. 124).

An appropriate way to close this chapter might be to contrast, albeit briefly, the tribal basis of Native American identity today – where anything less than 100 per cent pure descent can cause controversy – with the much more inclusive understanding of African-American identity, which incorporates those with mixed heritage like Barack Obama and Tiger Woods.[21] Thus, when the long-anticipated National Museum of the American Indian (NMAI) opened in Washington, DC, in 2004, a decision was taken to allocate space largely on a tribal basis, whereby exhibits were designed to showcase individual tribal histories but whose narratives failed to cohere into a singular whole and tell the history of Native Americans as a group.[22] Despite criticism of the NMAI's New York City predecessor, the Museum of the American Indian, that it neglected the life of urban Indians in favour of a 'glorified (and constructed) primitive past' (Arieff, 1995, p. 84), urban Indians are still represented unequally at the NMAI: an exhibit entitled *Our Lives: Contemporary Life and Identities* features eight communities, of which only one is urban (in Chicago). It is easy to draw a sharp contrast between the NMAI and the National Museum of African American History and Culture (NMAAHC), which opened in 2016 only a mile away on the other side of the National Mall and which focussed on the whole African American experience, rather than segmented according to origin or location.[23] It is these two very different concepts of ethnic or racial identity – one primordial and descent-based, another based on individual agency and voluntary assimilation – which run through many of the chapters of this book.

---

[21] These two differing concepts of ethnic/racial identity came together in the case of Radmilla Cody, the half-black, half-Navajo woman who was crowned as Miss Navajo Nation for 1997–8 and later nominated for a Grammy nomination as a recording artist. Cody's attempts to navigate her bi-racial heritage are expertly documented by Jacobsen-Bia (2014).

[22] Remarkably, only in 2017 did the NMAI include an exhibition on the 'Trail of Tears' as part of its 'Americans' exhibit.

[23] It is thus not surprising, perhaps, to note that annual attendance numbers for the NMAI are relatively low and declining over time, compared to the high and steady figures for the NMAAHC (<www.si.edu/newsdesk/about/stats>).

9

Ethnic Change among the Māori in New Zealand

9.1 INTRODUCTION

In the previous chapter I examined ethnic change among Native Americans in the United States, first through an examination of how the shift from reservations to urban living led to a newly salient pan-Indian Native American identity, and then how an increased value attached to tribal land led to re-tribalization, such that Native American understandings of ethnicity have become increasingly primordial in recent decades. In this chapter I examine the case of the Māori in New Zealand, who currently constitute around 15 per cent of the population of New Zealand. Here again I show how both industrialization has led to assimilation into a pan-tribal identity, as well as how a shift in the economic incentives attached to lower-level tribal identities – namely the allocation of fishery profits to Māori tribes or *iwis* – has seen a reversal of this process in recent decades. As I show below, there are multiple similarities between the Native American and Māori experiences; my interest in the latter here is to show that the processes of urban-led assimilation and then economic-induced re-tribalization are not particular or unique to the US example, and that the same incentives drive ethnic change in both cases. In order to help clarify these processes even more, I also discuss the nature of ethnic change and industrialization among indigenous peoples in the other two notable 'neo-Europes' at the end of the chapter, namely the Aborigines of Australia and First Nations of Canada.

In the rest of this chapter I first provide some historical background before examining how urbanization among the Māori in the mid-twentieth century led to assimilation and the increased salience of a pan-tribal Māori identity. I then discuss how the allocation of fishery rights and profits to Māori *iwi* has led to the re-tribalization of Māori identity, just as it has among Native Americans.

Using New Zealand census data, I show that there is a positive relationship between fishery quota share values per capita and subsequent *iwi* identification. I then conclude the chapter by briefly examining the two contrasting cases of the First Nations in Canada and Aborigines in Australia, where urbanization has led to homogenization but where the lack of any increase in value attached to tribal land has meant that re-tribalization has not occurred.

9.2 THE MĀORI UP TO WORLD WAR II

The first Polynesians settled in New Zealand at some time in the tenth century, with subsequent social organization based around the seven *waka* (canoes) with which they first arrived from their mythical homeland of *Hawaiki* (possibly Tahiti or Ra'iatea in French Polynesia) (A. Hanson, 1989, p. 891). While many Māori still trace their origin to a particular *waka* group, by the nineteenth century numerous new social groups were created through population growth , migration, defeat in war and other reasons which left the *iwi* (tribe) as the largest operative social group, followed by *hapū* (clans) and then *whānau* (extended families). It was only European settlement that encouraged the Māori to even conceive of themselves as a single group of people, whereupon they adopted the word 'Māori' ('ordinary', as opposed to European settlers) as their group title (Hill, 2016, p. 145).

The first European to arrive in New Zealand, James Cook, came in 1769, and was soon followed by other British settlers. The Treaty of Waitangi was signed in 1840, thereby bringing New Zealand into the British Empire, and in 1852 the British Parliament passed the Constitution Act for New Zealand, which set up a functional government representing European settlers while also establishing the potential for Māori to live in 'native districts' not unlike Native American reserves in the USA. However, after Māori protests these districts were never established; instead the New Zealand government created a Department for Native Affairs in 1858 (known as the Department for Māori Affairs after 1947) to manage Māori concerns, one goal of which was to bring Māori eventually under the same set of laws as Europeans. Indeed, unlike with Native Americans the Māori were considered British subjects equal in legal status to whites, and thus the professed goal of the New Zealand government was to encourage integration into white society, albeit in a relatively passive way. Thus the Native Schools Act in 1867 established the practice of English-language schooling for all New Zealanders (Spolsky, 2003, p. 557), while an official ban on the use of Māori in schools in 1903 and decades of English-language education led to widespread bi-lingualism by the mid-twentieth century (Spolsky, 2003, p. 558). Similarly, the government granted universal male adult suffrage along with four seats in parliament in 1867 to Māoris on the assumption that they would integrate into European society and fully participate in the national government (Stokes, 1992, p. 179).[1] As such, there was very little need to have exact definitions of who was and who was not Māori, which led not only to fluid tribal identities within the Māori community but a more relaxed attitude to inter-racial marriage as well.

While legally Māori were encouraged to integrate, at the same time the government took their land away in a series of steps. The Treaty of Waitangi gave the government a monopoly on land acquisitions, which led to many government agents purchasing land from Māori at below-market rates, and in 1846 it declared that any Māori land that was deemed to be unused or surplus became Crown land. With a rapid increase in European settlement the government acquired vast tracts for farming and sheep grazing, and when the Māori offered armed resistance to these policies the government authorized the confiscation of rebel Māori land in 1864. One aspect of this armed resistance was the establishment of the King Movement in an attempt to unite all Māori under a single monarch. While various *iwis* from the North Island came together to crown a pan-*iwi* king in 1857, widespread infighting among Māori meant that King Pōtatau and his successors never commanded political support from much more than a quarter of all Māori.

The result of the so-called land wars was both the gradual military defeat of the Māori resistance as well as a sharp drop in land holdings from 66.4 million acres in 1840 to 11 million by 1891, much of which was marginal and had poor quality soil. (This was especially true on the South Island, where Māori held almost no land by the turn of the century, while they retained 40 per cent of the North Island.) Moreover, the government attempted to introduce private land ownership by limiting ownership to a maximum of ten owners per plot and thereby nullifying communal land ownership, which further limited Māori access to good land. Due to exposure to European diseases like measles and whooping cough the Māori also saw their numbers drop from around 86,000 in 1769 to a low of 42,000 in 1896 as they settled in 'isolated villages' with 'virtually nonexistent' contact between Māori and Europeans (Ausubel, 1961, pp. 220, 223; A. Coleman, Dixon & Maré, 2005, p. 11).

9.3 MĀORI URBANIZATION AND HOMOGENIZATION FROM WORLD WAR II TO THE PRESENT

In the early twentieth century New Zealand government policy was to encourage Māoris to practice commercial farming and stay in rural areas (Collette &

---

[1] Interestingly, the Māori enjoyed universal male adult suffrage a full eleven years before the same right was accorded to white New Zealanders in 1879. The four seats were allocated along geographic lines, namely Eastern, Western, Northern and Southern. These seats remained in the New Zealand Parliament until 1996, when they were replaced by five Māori electoral colleges (followed by six in 1999 and seven since 2002). Thus, all parts of New Zealand are covered by both a general and a Māori electorate, and Māori voters can choose in which electorate they wish to be registered.

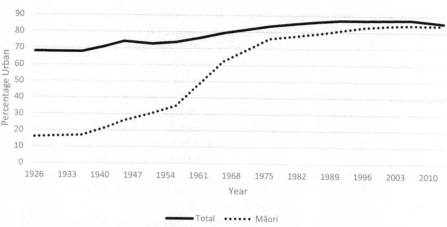

FIGURE 9.1. Urbanization in New Zealand, 1926–2013
(*Source:* A. Coleman et al., 2005; Gibson, 1973; Statistics New Zealand, 2014)

O'Malley, 1974, p. 149). However, at the same time the extension of medical care to rural Māori, which was especially important in the treatment of maternal mortality and tuberculosis (Pool, 1967, pp. 88–9), meant that Māori mortality rates rapidly declined in the early twentieth century. Subsequent high population growth rates thus led to increasing amounts of rural unemployment, which then led many to migrate to New Zealand's bustling cities (Ausubel, 1961, p. 222). Moreover, an urban labour shortage led the government to encourage up to 25 per cent of all Māori adults to migrate into urban areas during World War II. While most of these migrants returned back to rural areas once the war ended, enough of them stayed to create a beachhead for further rural–urban migrants (Collette & O'Malley, 1974, p. 150). The urbanization of the Māori can be seen in Figure 9.1, which uses census data to plot the percentage urban for both Māori and the overall population of New Zealand from 1926 to 2013.[2] (The 2018 census results have only partially been released at the time of writing.) As in Canada and the United States, the 1950s and 1960s were clearly a period of rapid urbanization, especially in the main destination city of Auckland where Māoris as a percentage of the total population increased from 1.8 per cent in 1945 to 6.2 per cent in 1966 (Rowland, 1971, p. 22).

---

[2] Data on Māori urbanization only begins in 1926; before this date New Zealand censuses counted Māori and Europeans in separate censuses and enumerated those Māori who did not live with their *hapū* in villages as European (A. Coleman et al., 2005, p. 3). The 2011 census was postponed until 2013 due to the 2011 earthquake in Christchurch.

During this period of rapid urbanization the New Zealand government began to encourage Māori integration into white New Zealand society, based on the idea that 'Māori and Europeans form one people', to quote one government document from the 1950s (Hill, 2012, p. 258). In 1960 Prime Minister Walter Nash commissioned an influential review of the Māori Affairs Department which came to the conclusion that 'evolution is clearly integrating Māori and *pakeha* [European New Zealanders]' and that the goal of the government was to encourage this process (D. V. Williams, 2019, p. 38). The result was that successive national governments promoted such policies as the 'pepper potting' housing policy that distributed Māori families within previously all-white neighbourhoods at a 1:10 ratio, abandoned employment schemes for Māori in rural areas and encouraged Māori to sell rural land (Hill, 2012, p. 263; D. V. Williams, 2019, p. 38).

However, as with Native Americans, urbanization among the Māori led many to shed their attachments to their *iwi* tribal identities and instead rely upon new multi-tribal urban associations for support (Barcham, 1998, pp. 304–5; Maaka, 1994, p. 314). Thus, according to the Māori academic Roger Maaka, the typical urban Māori would claim that 'in the city I operate as a Māori but at home [in the countryside] I am a tribal person' (Maaka, 1994, p. 329). While some scholars ascribed this new 'supra-tribal' sense of Māori nationalism to a reaction against white racism (Ausubel, 1961, p. 224), many others agreed on the direct causal link between urbanization and the formation of a new form of Māori ethnicity or nationhood. As the New Zealand political scientist Simon Chapple notes:

'Māori ethnicity' has been constructed through the process of post-war urbanization . . . Those descended from Māori people came to recognize certain areas of commonality and community of interests in the new urban environment and at some point after the second world war these links became sufficiently strong for one to speak with confidence of the existence of a Māori ethnic group. (Chapple, 2000, p. 103)

Thus, while all urban Māori studied by Metge (1964) in 1951 could identify their *iwi* when the urbanization level among the Māori was only 30 per cent (compared to 73 per cent for New Zealand as a whole), by 1991 27.9 per cent of all Māori declined to specify an *iwi* while urbanization levels among the Māori had reached 81 per cent, or only 6 per cent lower than for New Zealand as a whole (Statistics New Zealand, 2007).[3]

Urban Māori began to create new pan-tribal centres where they could interact. For instance, Auckland saw the establishment of pan-tribal organizations like the Waipareira Trust in 1984 in western Auckland and the Manukau Urban Māori Authority in 1985 in southern Auckland, both of which served first-generation rural–urban Māori migrants from diverse *iwi* (Keiha & Moon, 2008, p. 10). However, perhaps most striking has been the creation of pan-

---

[3] The 1991 census was the first census since 1901 to ask Māori about their *iwi* identities.

tribal *marae,* or meeting places. While each *hapū* has had its own *marae,* since the nineteenth century urban Māori have created their own *marae* as places to gather, dance and hold funerals. The first *marae* open to all Māori – Te Puea, in Auckland – opened in 1965, with the first purely pan-tribal *marae* established in 1973 (Gagné, 2013, p. 97). Today some two-dozen urban *marae* exist in Auckland, only a small minority of which are associated with a particular *hapū* or *iwi.* One such *marae* is Hoani Waititi, whose architecture features the legendary fleet of seven canoes symbolizing the Māori migration to New Zealand rather than the more traditional sculptures of actual individual ances-tors (Rosenblatt, 2011, pp. 415–17). In another case in west Auckland, a local Māori leader noted that the local *marae* 'was mean to be pan-tribal. [It] left no room for the tribal bit. You had to leave your tribalism at the door' (Tapsell, 2002, p. 155). Finally, in 1997 the National Museum of New Zealand Te Papa Tongarewa opened its own pan-tribal *marae,* Rongomaraeroa, which was designed by Māori artist Cliff Whiting using symbols from various Māori myths and legends. As one Māori scholar has noted, the creation of these multiple *marae* with a 'kinlike but nontribal structure' has been nothing short of revolutionary in its re-conceptualization of Māori identity that successfully reconciles modernity and indigeneity, leaving the maintenance of tribal identity to be considered as 'a backward step that belonged in the dark ages' (Tapsell, 2002, pp. 165–6).

The main consequence of this cross-tribal interaction in the new urban environment was to spur pan-Māori nationalism in the late twentieth century, known locally as the Māori Renaissance, *Māoritanga* (Māori-ness) or *Mana Māori* (Māori Power). Pan-Māori organizations created after World War II included the Māori Women's Welfare League in 1945, the Māori Council in 1962 and the National Māori Congress in 1990. Alongside these more conser-vative organizations, which focused on improving Māori health, scrutinizing legislation and attempting to influence government policy, radical Māori activ-ists called for 'brown power', 'Māori liberation' and 'Māori sovereignty'. The radical youth group *Nga Tamatoa* (Young Warriors) was formed at the University of Auckland in 1970 after gaining inspiration from the Black Power movement in the USA. Among its actions were protests at the annual Treaty of Waitangi celebrations, during which members wore black armbands (Hokowhitu, 2013, p. 360), as well as sponsoring a petition signed by 30,000 people to the government in 1973 asking for better Māori language teaching. Pressure by the petition led the government's Department of Māori Affairs to establish in 1982 the first set of *kohanga reo* ('language nests'), or pre-schools that taught Māori to children under the age of five, which expanded to a total of 444 schools by 1986 servicing 8,500 children, or roughly one out of five Māori children (Spoonley, 1989, p. 582).

The new Māori nationalists focussed on improving socio-economic condi-tions for the Māori as well as cultural issues. In one case activists successfully campaigned against the aforementioned pepper-potted housing policy, which was brought to an end in the 1970s (Hill, 2012, p. 269). In another case, continued pressure from Māori groups led the government to pass the Māori Language Act of 1987, which made the Māori language an official language of New Zealand for the first time and created a Māori Language Commission in order to promote the Māori language (Spolsky, 2003, p. 564). Māori intellectuals were behind the creation of the Waikato University Centre for Māori Studies and Research in 1972, which was followed by Māori studies departments at other universities.

Another major focus for Māori activists was land rights, which was a concern as land alienation had steadily continued from the late nineteenth century up to the enactment of a law in 1967 which allowed the government to acquire Māori land for developmental purposes. Activists organized a Māori Land March of 30,000 people to parliament in 1975 in order to protest land alienation, followed by the occupation of Bastion Point in an Auckland suburb for 506 days over 1977–8. Shortly thereafter, the Māori activist movement led to the creation of a new political party in 1979, the Mana Māori Motuhake, by a former Minister of Māori Affairs Matiu Rata, and, after merging with three other parties to form the Alliance party, saw three of its candidates elected as MPs in the 1990s. Two other Māori parties founded in the 1990s, namely the Mana Māori Movement and the Mana Wahine Te Ira Tangata, failed to win much support; however, in 2004 Tariana Turia and Pita Sharples – who was the director of the Hoani Waititi *marae* in Auckland noted above – created the Māori Party,[4] which won four seats in parliament in 2005 and five in 2008 before its support faded in the 2010s.

As with Native Americans, this process of Māori identity formation took place in a context of linguistic assimilation and native language loss. Here I can use official New Zealand census data to examine the relationship between Māori language retention and urbanization. I collected data from the 2001 New Zealand census as *iwi* identification in later censuses may have been influenced by fisheries legislation as explained below. Unlike in the United States the data on Māori language is listed according to ability rather than whether or not it is spoken at home; thus my dependent variable here is the percentage of each *iwi* who speak at least some Māori. As with Native Americans I only examine groups with 1,000 or more members (although my results are robust to smaller and larger sub-samples). Most *iwis* are listed individually in the census; however, in some cases like the Te Āti Awa or the Ngāti Kahungunu they are listed according to *rohe* (tribal territory) within a wider *iwi* grouping. As such I cluster my standard errors at the *iwi* grouping to account for similarities among members of the same group, with similar results when aggregating data by *iwi* grouping.

---

[4] Interestingly, both Turia and Sharples are of mixed descent: Turia is half-American while Sharples is half white New Zealander (of English ancestry).

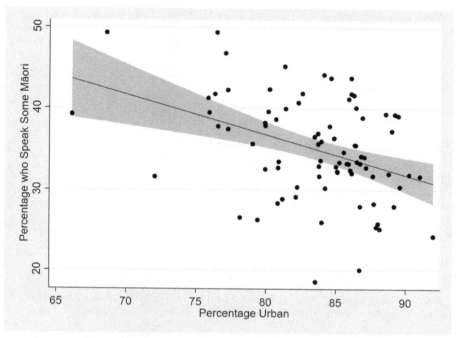

FIGURE 9.2. Urbanization and Māori language retention among *iwi* with populations larger than 1,000 in 2001
(*Source:* Stats NZ)

Due perhaps to a much smaller geographic spread and less linguistic diversity among Māori than among Native Americans, the variation in Māori language ability and urbanization is not as large. Nonetheless, the percentage of each *iwi* who spoke some Māori in 2001 ranged from Ngāti Tama (17.6 per cent) and the Ngāi Tahu (18.6 per cent), both of the South Island, to the Waitaha from the Rotorua area (51.9 per cent) and the Ngāi Tāmanuhiri (49.4 per cent) of the East Coast region. Urbanization similarly varied from the Ngāi Tāmanuhiri (63.4 per cent) and the Muaūpoko from the Wellington area (64.3 per cent) to the Te Atiawa ki Whakarongotai (92.1 per cent) and the Te Atiawa of Wellington (92.0 per cent).

In Figure 9.2 I plot the percentage of Māori who speak some Māori on the y-axis against the percentage in each *iwi* who live in urban areas on the x-axis with 95 per cent confidence intervals. As expected, the relationship is negative and statistically significant (with a t-statistic of –3.60 and R^2 of 0.155). Moreover, the statistical results, which can be found in Table 9.1, demonstrate a robust negative correlation between urbanization and Māori language use. As in the previous chapter I first regress language ability on urbanization with the

TABLE 9.1. *Urbanization and Māori language retention among Māori in 2001*

| | Dependent variable: % who speak some Māori | |
	(1)	(2)
Percentage urban	−0.428***	−0.436***
	(0.148)	(0.137)
Total population (log)	−0.010*	−0.008
	(0.005)	(0.005)
Median household income (log)	−0.371***	−0.533***
	(0.098)	(0.110)
Median age	−0.012***	−0.012***
	(0.003)	(0.003)
Secondary school graduates (%)		0.423***
		(0.159)
Constant	4.626***	6.050
	(0.859)	(0.975)
N	83	83
R^2	0.483	0.518

* $p \leq 0.1$, ** $p \leq 0.05$, *** $p \leq 0.01$ (two-tailed test); robust standard errors in parentheses. The table only considers *iwi* with more than 1,000 members in 1980 and is clustered at the *iwi* group level.

basic controls of log total population, log median household income and median age, with secondary-school graduates added in column #2. The urbanization coefficient is negative and statistically significant in both columns at the 1 per cent level, with an increase of one standard deviation in the value of the urbanization variable decreasing the proportion who speak some Māori by 2.5 per cent, or 31 per cent of the standard deviation. The coefficients on median age and log of median household income are also statistically significant with the right sign, while population size is not correlated with native language ability. Interestingly, education is positively correlated with Māori ability, which corresponds with my findings in earlier chapters on the mixed influence of education on assimilation and ethnic homogenization. These results show that urbanization has contributed to language loss among the Māori, and that the increased salience of *Māoritanga* has not been impeded by the decreased ability to speak Māori. Indeed, as I note below, there are multiple dialects of the Māori language that are often *iwi*-specific, and thus losing Māori language ability could also lead to a decrease in *iwi*-specific markers among those identifying as Māori.

9.4 FISHERIES AND 'NEOTRIBALISM' AMONG THE MĀORI

For the Māori, as for the other indigenous peoples examined here, urbanization helped to erase tribal differences and bring indigenous people together in a common setting. As tribal land became less important, urban Māori began to focus their attention on developing pan-Māori institutions and organizations, which eventually led to an increased sense of Māori ethnic or national identity. The Māori case thus provides another example that supports my argument about the role of industrialization and urbanization in promoting assimilation.

As with Native Americans, however, government policies designed to grant more economic resources to the Māori have had important consequences in reversing this trend. This process began with the creation of the Waitangi Tribunal in 1975, whose mandate was to make recommendations as regards the New Zealand government's violations of the Treaty of Waitangi. Initially the tribunal was to consider only breaches that occurred after its creation and was seen largely as symbolic in nature; the ruling National Party (which was not aligned with Māori interests) even refused to let the tribunal sit until 1977. However, after the Labour Party came back into power in 1984, the remit of the tribunal was extended back to 1840, and led to a vast and unanticipated increase in the scale and range of the tribunal's focus (Sherman, 2006, p. 520). The tribunal's recommendations have led to the successful settlement of twenty-three cases, which has led to monetary compensation as well as renewed control over specific natural resources (Walling, Small-Rodriguez & Kukutai, 2009, pp. 2–3). However, rather than allocate this compensation to the Māori as a whole or to specific *hapū* or individuals, the government instead decided to identify the claimants as *iwi* on the basis that it was the *iwis* themselves which first negotiated with European settlers in the nineteenth century. Thus the New Zealand justice minister in 1989 noted that the two sets of parties that would negotiate compensation and resource rights would be the government and the *iwi*, which in the former case would 'recognize the right of *iwi* to organize as *iwi* and, under law, to control the resources they own' (Stokes, 1992, p. 189).

Soon the tribunal began to focus on the allocation of fishery rights to *iwis*, especially after the government passed the Māori Fisheries Act and the Treaty of Waitangi (Fisheries Claims) Settlement Act in 1989 and 1992, respectively, which granted the Māori control over 23 per cent of New Zealand's offshore commercial fisheries.[5] In order to facilitate the transfer of rights to *iwi* in 1993 the government created the Treaty of Waitangi Fisheries Commission (Te Ohu Kaimoana, or TOK), which was allocated some cash, a 50 per cent share in Sealord Products, New Zealand's biggest fishing company, and a quota of 20 per cent of all new species of fish brought into New Zealand's quota management system; collectively these assets were worth NZ$400 million at the time of its creation, or over 33 per cent of the New Zealand fishery industry (Webster, 2002, p. 348). While the 1989 Act only stated that TOK would control the fisheries assets for 'all Māori', the 1992 Act instead clarified that

---

[5] New Zealand's offshore exclusive economic zone (EEZ) covers more than four million square kilometres, which is fifteen times the size of the country's land area and the sixth-largest EEZ in the world.

TOK should allocate its revenues to the correct *iwi* beneficiaries (Webster, 2002, pp. 349–50).

One key issue that arose immediately was how TOK should allocate fishery assets to inland *iwi*. Indeed, while leaders of *iwi* with *rohe* along the coast argued that the revenues should be given in proportion to the amount of each *iwi*'s coastline, inland *iwi* instead argued that the distribution should be in proportion to each *iwi*'s population. In response TOK commissioners voted seven to six in 1994 to allocate money from inshore fishing according to each *iwi*'s coastline while deepwater (below 300 metres) fishing would henceforth be distributed partially on the basis of coastline and partially along population lines (H. Anderson, 1997). However, urban Māori who did not claim member-ship in an *iwi* demanded a share of the revenue as well. Thus in 1995 two urban Māori organizations sued TOK in court to stop them from allocating fisheries assets exclusively to *iwi* based on the claim that most urban Māori have no active links with their *iwi* and are often unable to name their *iwi,* in part due to poor birth records; to prove their point various urban Māori groups recruited over 10,000 non-*iwi* affiliated members who wanted access to a share of the fisheries allocation. However, TOK countered that many unaffiliated Māori merely needed assistance in identifying their *iwi*, and thus set up an '*iwi* helpline' in 1996 to help Māori with genealogical queries, with 2,900 enquiries in its first six months (Webster, 2002, p. 360).[6]

This issue eventually reached the courts, with the New Zealand Court of Appeal taking up the case and ruling in favour of the urban Māori in 1996 because, the court argued, the '*iwis*' referred to in the 1992 Act should be thought of as a 'national people' rather than a 'tribe' (Webster, 2002, p. 357). However, the Privy Council in London overturned this ruling in 1997 and asked New Zealand courts to re-define the concept of *iwi* (Maaka & Fleras, 2000, pp. 105–6). As a result, TOK defined *iwi* in a 1998 document as tribes that have (1) shared descent from a single *tipuna* (ancestor), (2) *hapū*, (3) *marae*, (4) a historical connection with a *takiwā* (tribal district, an alterna-tive word for *rohe*) , and (5) 'an existence traditionally acknowledged by other *iwi*' (Webster, 2002, p. 350). After a final appeal from urban Māori organiza-tions, the Privy Council then subsequently ruled in 2001 that only *iwi* defined according to these criteria could claim access to the fishing quota (Gregory, 2001).

As a result, TOK ruled in 1997 that the deepwater allocation would be 60 per cent on the basis of coastline and 40 per cent along population lines, and also decided to create an NZ$20 million development fund, called the Te Putea

---

[6] Yet TOK also noted that some 26 per cent of Māori claimed membership in more than one *iwi* as a result of inter-*iwi* marriage (Webster, 2002, p. 361). As such, the New Zealand High Court claimed in 2003 that 'it is simplistic to assert urban Māori can and should locate their *iwi*. On the evidence, the real world presents real difficulties. *Iwi* benefits will not reach those whom *iwi* do not know' (McGechan, 2003).

Whakatupu Trust, for those Māori who either have no *iwi* membership or who do not receive any benefits from an *iwi* organization. Yet even this decision led to further dissatisfaction, in this case not only from urban Māori but even from within TOK, whose deputy commissioner complained in 2000 that the Ngāi Tahu, whose *rohe* consists of almost all of the South Island of New Zealand and thus has the largest coastline among all *iwis* by far, would receive NZ$86 million (or NZ$2195 per member listed in the 2001 census). In contrast, the Ngāpuhi – with a smaller coastline but three times the population of Ngāi Tahu at the time – would receive only NZ$22 million (Bidois, 2000). Part of this debate was about control over TOK, whose initial leader was Sir Tipene O'Regan, also chairman of the Ngāi Tahu Māori Trust Board, until he was replaced in 2000.

This issue continued to simmer after the government appointed new TOK members in 2000 that saw more representation given to urban Māori, while attempts by the new chairman, Shane Jones, to hold the TOK assets centrally rather than distribute them to individual *iwis* drew anger from leaders of *iwis* with large coastlines. After more discussion – and the re-election of Helen Clark's Labour government in 2002, which held large Māori support – the Māori Fisheries Act of 2004 gave a final deepshore quota allocation model of 25 per cent according to coastline and 75 per cent according to population (Kersey, 2003, p. 4). The act also set up Aotearoa Fisheries Ltd, which consolidated Sealord and other Māori-owned enterprises, with 80 per cent of income shares accruing to *iwi* by population and 20 per cent to TOK. Finally, the act ordered that *iwi* could only be allocated their quotas once they had set up individual organizations with capacity to manage their new resources in the form of Mandated *Iwi* Organizations (MIOs), which were to be constitutionally based organizations with elected or appointed leaders that maintained lists of current *iwi* members. These MIOs then subsequently established an *Iwi* Chairs Forum in 2005, which regularly hosts the *Iwi* Leadership Group, which itself mediates with the New Zealand government on behalf of Māori interests (Hill, 2016, p. 155).

9.5 EVIDENCE FOR RE-TRIBALIZATION IN NEW ZEALAND

As a result of this process *iwi* membership has arguably new-found economic importance in New Zealand, leading one noted scholar to call the *iwis* 'neo-tribes' (Rata, 2011).[7] In other words, we would thus expect not only the percentage of Māori who claim membership of an *iwi* to rise as membership creates new-found privileges, but we would also expect to observe a fracturing of *iwi* identity as claims to resources create the incentives to exclude others from an *iwi* identity in order to obtain more resources per capita. Finally, we would

---

[7] Barcham (1998, p. 305) similarly writes of 're-*iwi*-isation'.

TABLE 9.2. Iwi *in New Zealand censuses, 1991–2013*

Census year	% of Māori with 1+ *Iwi*	% of Māori with 2+ *Iwi*	% of Māori with 3+ *Iwi*
1991	72.1	–	–
1996	73.5	20.0	5.3
2001	75.2	26.8	9.0
2006	79.6	30.4	10.6
2013	80.1	30.4	10.6

Data on the percentage of people reporting two or more *iwi* is not available for the 1991 census.

expect to see a notable increase in people claiming membership in more than one *iwi* due to the potential for remunerative benefits from *iwi* membership.

To test these hypotheses I use data from New Zealand's quinquennial national censuses, which have asked questions about *iwi* membership since 1991 and, unlike in the USA, have not changed the way they categorize or ask about ethnic identification between censuses. In each census respondents are first asked if they are of Māori descent; if they answer yes, then they are asked if they know the name of their *iwi*. In the 1991 census respondents would then write in the 'main *iwi* (tribe) you belong to', followed by the option to list up to two other *iwis* that they have 'strong ties with'; from 1996 onwards respondents instead had the ability to list up to five *iwi*. Respondents are not asked to choose from a set list of *iwi* although a list has been provided in the Help Notes from 2001.[8] Each *iwi* also holds data on tribal registration, but that data is not publicly available; however, in one analysis of tribal vs census population data differences between the two were found to be very minor (Walling et al., 2009).

The evidence from this use of census data clearly supports all of my hypotheses. As seen in Table 9.2, the percentage of Māori who reported membership in at least one *iwi* rose from 72.1 per cent in the 1991 census to 80.1 per cent in 2013 (with data from the 2018 census not yet available). Moreover, the number of Māori who identified with at least two *iwi* rose from 20.0 per cent in 1996 to 30.4 per cent in 2006 and 2013, while the proportion of those who reported membership in three or more *iwi* doubled from 5.3 per cent in 1996 to 10.6 per cent in 2006 and 2013.

Of course, there could be other reasons besides the fisheries quotas that could be driving rising levels of *iwi* identification. I can thus also use the New Zealand census data to test for the relationship between each *iwi*'s coastline quota share value per capita and its population growth from 1991, on the assumption that individuals would be incentivized to identify with *iwis* with

---

[8] The Help Notes explicitly state that it is a guide only and that 'all *iwi* names are counted even if they are not listed below'.

larger quota share values per capita. However, two processes must be complete before any fisheries revenues can be shared with *iwi* members. First, as noted above, *iwis* must set up an MIO, whose constitution must be approved by TOK. Second, each MIO must reach agreements about the exact length of its coastline with MIOs representing neighbouring *iwis* as well as TOK. The first process was initiated in 2005 and, by the time of writing, had been completed for forty-four *iwis*, while the second process took an average of 2.5 years long after the creation of the MIO. Only forty-two of the forty-four MIOs have reached agreements on their coastlines, of whom five are located inland and thus have no coastline at all. The quota share values are publicly available in TOK's Decision Register,[9] which I have reproduced in Table 9.3 alongside each *iwi*'s regional grouping or *waka* and the value of coastline quota shares per capita using 2018 census data. The quota share values as well as the values per capita vary hugely from one *iwi* to another: the highest absolute quota share value is for Ngāi Tahu of the South Island, at NZ$61.5 million (US$41.6 million), compared to none for four *iwis*; similarly, the highest share value per capita is NZ$20,779 per capita, for the Moriori, who had only 592 members in the 2018 census but whose coastline quota share values came to NZ$12.3 million. All of the top six values per capita come from either the Chatham Islands, located some 840 miles east of Christchurch, or the South Island, which has a much lower population density than the North Island but a similarly sized coastline. Map 9.1 depicts the approximate *rohe* of all *iwi* which have completed coastline agreements.[10]

In Figure 9.3 I plot the change in population (logged) between 1996 and 2018 against the (logged) quota share value per capita for all *iwis* who reached an agreement on their quota share values before the 2018 census, with 95 per cent confidence intervals.[11] The relationship is clearly positive and statistically significant, with a t-statistic of 6.11 and an R^2 of 0.500, and suggests that variation in quota share values are driving *iwi* self-identification. I have labelled the obvious outlier of the Moriori, with lower population growth than would be expected given its large coastline quota share value. This anomaly can be explained by the distinct history of the Moriori, who originate in the Chatham Islands. Despite the islands being settled by fellow Māori around AD 1500, its isolation from the rest of New Zealand led to a distinct language and culture and the ethnogenesis of the Moriori (itself a cognate of the word 'Māori',

---

[9] <https://teohu.maori.nz/iwidecisionregister>

[10] The map does not include *iwi* whose *rohe* is located in the Chatham Islands. Note that Ngāti Tuwharetoa appears to be landlocked but still receives some fisheries revenue via an inter-tribal agreement with the Te Arawa *waka*. I thank Tony Sole from the Te Puni Kōkiri/Ministry of Māori Development for this information.

[11] I calculate the coastline quota share value per capita based on census population data from 1996 as that was the last census taken before the 1997 TOK ruling on how to allocate fisheries revenues. The results are almost identical using census data from 2001 instead.

TABLE 9.3. Iwi *coastline quota values*

Iwi	Regional grouping/waka	Coastline quota share value	Coastline quota share value per capita (2018)
Moriori	Te Wai Pounamu	NZ$12,300,993	NZ$20778.70
Ngāti Mutunga (Chathams)	Te Wai Pounamu	12,300,993	6755.08
Ngāti Tama (Te Tau Ihu)	Te Tau Ihu	1,606,498	4272.60
Ngāti Apa ki te Rā Tō	Te Tau Ihu	1,606,498	1744.30
Ngati Rarua	Te Tau Ihu	1,606,498	1598.51
Rangitāne (Te Tau Ihu)	Te Tau Ihu	1,606,498	1154.92
Ngāti Wai	Tai Tokerau	6,763,597	1084.43
Ngāi Tahu	Te Wai Pounamu	61,546,817	1045.95
Ngāti Koata	Te Tau Ihu	1,606,498	1043.18
Ngāti Kuia	Te Tau Ihu	1,606,498	815.48
Te Atiawa (Te Tau Ihu)	Te Tau Ihu	1,606,498	729.56
Rangitane (North Island)	Manawatū	3,061,818	708.75
Ngāpuhi / Ngāti Kahu ki Whaingaroa	Tai Tokerau	1,518,661	668.72
Ngāi Tamanuhiri	Takitimu	1,012,713	575.41
Ngāti Toa Rangatira	Te Upoko O Te Ika	2,498,125	483.29
Te Atiawa (Wellington)	Te Tau Ihu	317,576	396.97
Ngāti Kahungunu	Takitimu	16,933,500	266.07
Ngāti Whātua	Tai Tokerau	3,306,541	223.01
Ngāti Kahu	Tai Tokerau	1,859,069	211.96
Iwi of Hauraki	Tainui	9,758,721	137.44
Ngāti Apa (North Island)	Manawatū	456,027	134.60
Taranaki	Taranaki	855,697	129.42
Ngā Rauru	Hauāuru	542,812	127.03
Ngāiterangi	Tauranga Moana	1,401,643	104.29
Ngāti Pukenga	Tauranga Moana	243,764	99.33
Ngāti Ranginui	Tauranga Moana	792,233	79.94
Ngāti Mutunga (Taranaki)	Taranaki	211,921	75.31
Ngā Ruahine	Hauāuru	391,865	70.33
Ngāti Ruanui	Hauāuru	407,193	54.87
Waikato	Tainui	1,888,987	42.13
Whakatōhea	Mātaatua	473,053	38.61
Ngāti Awa	Mātaatua	473,053	28.09
Ngāti Maniapoto	Tainui	928,978	25.38
Te Atiawa (Taranaki)	Taranaki	398,591	23.44
Ngāpuhi	Tai Tokerau	2,439,760	19.06
Te Arawa	Te Arawa	907,229	18.41
Te Atihaunui a Paparangi	Hauāuru	154,854	12.30
Ngāti Tuwharetoa	Te Arawa	256,640	6.99
Tuhoe	Mātaatua	137,309	3.76

Iwi	Regional grouping/waka	Coastline quota share value	Coastline quota share value per capita (2018)
Ngāti Hauiti	Hauāuru	o	o
Ngāti Manawa	Mātaatua	o	o
Ngāti Maru (Taranaki)	Taranaki	o	o
Ngāti Raukawa	Tainui	o	o
Ngāti Whare	Mātaatua	o	o

(*Source:* Stats NZ, TOK)

MAP 9.1. *Iwi* recognized in the Māori Fisheries Act of 2004

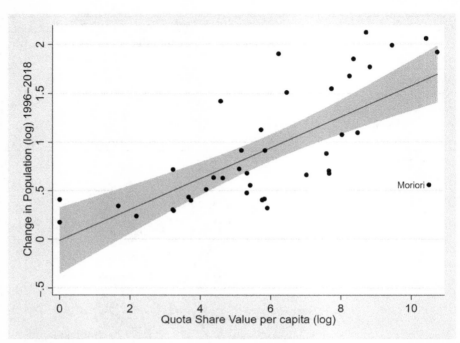

FIGURE 9.3. Māori population growth and coastline quota share value per capita, 1996–2018
(*Source:* Stats NZ; TOK)

meaning 'ordinary people'). In the 1830s the islands were invaded by Māori settlers from Wellington, who massacred or enslaved the vast majority of the population as part of the ongoing civil wars between Māori which took place in the early nineteenth century, in what many scholars now call a genocide (Brett, 2015). This cultural and historical distinctiveness is thus plausibly responsible for why the Moriori have not seen large-scale population growth despite the high value of their coastline quota.

If Figure 9.3 suggests that economic incentives over access to fishery rights quotas are correlated with trends in *iwi* identification, qualitative evidence also suggests that New Zealand fisheries policies have led to a fracturing of Māori identity as membership in individual *iwis* has arguably become more important than being Māori per se. It is not difficult to find example of Māori leaders emphasizing their *iwi* identities over their Māori identities, particularly for members of *iwis* that stand to benefit from their coastline quota share values. For instance, the former TOK chairman Sir Tipene O'Regan claimed that 'it is only *pakeha* and the Crown identifying us all as Māori which makes us Māori', while his successor as chairman of the Ngāi Tahu Māori Trust Board, Mark

Solomon, noted that 'there is no such thing as a Māori, but only a member of an *iwi*; one cannot be a Māori without being part of an *iwi*' (Gover & Baird, 2002, pp. 45–6). Finally, another notable Ngāi Tahu member, Charles Crofts, notably dismissed the entire concept of Māori living in cities outside their *rohe* as non-existent: 'there is no such thing as urban Māori, never has been, never will be' (Barcham, 1998, p. 308). Thus, as Rata (2011, p. 335) notes, the focus on *iwi* identity has reconceptualized Māori identity as 'pre-national', or one not based on any voluntarist social contract but instead on the traditionalist, pre-industrial hierarchies of *iwi* leadership.

There is also evidence that many Māori *iwi* leaders have focussed more on the development of *iwi*-specific dialects than the Māori language itself, which, remarkably, remains unstandardized. Thus the Ngāi Tahu Board created a language manager to promote the local Ngāi Tahu dialect with a goal to have 1,000 households speaking the dialect by 2025 (Spolsky, 2003, p. 568), alongside other efforts by organizations representing the Taranaki and Ngāpuhi (Keegan, 2017, pp. 135–6). In addition, there exists thirty-odd *iwi*-based radio stations around New Zealand such as Turanga FM in Gisborne and Radio Kahungunu in Hawke's Bay that promote the use of *iwi*-based dialects.

While the lexical, idiomatic, grammatical and phonological differences between dialects are noticeable enough to locate people's origins by their speech, these differences are considered relatively minor by linguists (Keegan, 2017): thus North Island dialects share between 73 and 85 per cent of their basic vocabulary, while the South Island dialect shares between 65 and 76 per cent of its basic vocabulary with North Island dialects (Harlow, 2012, p. 59). In other words, these differences are thus roughly comparable to the difference between Setswana dialects as discussed in Chapter 8. However, instead of seeing Māori activists promoting linguistic homogenization as a means towards facilitating a common identity, a recent trend has been for Māori 'to preserve at least those features of their dialect which serve to mark their tribal connections', which even includes actively attempting to learn their *iwi*-specific 'phonological forms and lexical items' in order to distinguish themselves from other Māori (Harlow, 2012, pp. 43–4; Keegan, 2017, p. 135). As such, there is an arguably growing tension between urban Māori promoting a pan-Māori language acquisition via *Kura Kaupapa Māori* (immersion schools) and *Kōhanga Reo* ('language nest', or cross-generational transmission), and rural *iwi* organizations who oppose the promotion of a single standardized Māori language (Spolsky, 2005, p. 79).

Finally, as among Native Americans, there exists ongoing conflict between urban Māori groups and tribal leaders that demonstrates a lack of unity in Māori affairs. An obvious example here is the existence of pan-tribal *marae* in Auckland, much of which is land traditionally owned by the Ngāti Whatua. In the 1960s and 1970s the existence of such *marae* was largely unproblematic in the face of weakened tribal leadership, but more recently at least some members of the Ngāti Whatua *iwi* have objected to the establishment of these *marae* without the explicit permission of all relevant tribal organizations on the basis that pan-tribal *marae* might 'trample the *mana* (authority) of the local people' (Rosenblatt, 2011, p. 416; Tapsell, 2002). Similarly, an attempt by Māori residents of the poor neighbourhood of Otara in south Auckland to get the government to clean up a local polluting power station almost adjacent to their pan-*iwi marae* were stymied by the fact that the Māori residents were predominantly migrants and thus could not claim to be *tangata whenua* (people of the land) on land that technically belongs to the territory of the Ngāi Tai (Coombes, 2013).

9.6 THE OTHER TWO NEO-EUROPES: INDIGENOUS COMMUNITIES IN CANADA AND ABORIGINES IN AUSTRALIA

9.6.1 Canada

Turning now back to North America, Canada's aboriginal or indigenous peoples constitute roughly 5 per cent of the country's population and are usually divided into three categories, namely First Nations (aka North American Indians, who numbered 977,230 in the most recent 2016 census), Métis (of mixed Native and European settler descent, most of whom live in western Canada, numbering 587,545) and the Inuit of northern Canada (65,025).[12] The Indian Act of 1876 both initiated the process of creating native reserves and created lists of Indians and the bands or tribes to which they belonged, which were eventually consolidated into an 'Indian Register' in 1951. The affairs of such groups – known as 'Status Indians', which confusingly do not include Métis or Inuit – were overseen by the Department of Indian Affairs (later Aboriginal Affairs and Northern Development Canada), which to the present manages reserved lands in trust. Up until 1960, when all indigenous people obtained the right to vote, being a Status Indian and a Canadian citizen were seen as mutually exclusive.

High mortality rates and government policies that confined indigenous communities to reserves which they could not leave without permission of the relevant Indian agent meant that urbanization among indigenous communities remained below 10 per cent until the 1950s (Wilson & Peters, 2005, p. 399). (The consequence of leaving without permission could be to lose their 'status' and place on the Indian Register, which happened to numerous Indian soldiers who had fought in World War II.) However, as elsewhere the late twentieth century saw large-scale urbanization among indigenous communities due to high population growth, over-crowding on reserves and loss of habitat such that a majority lived in urban areas by 2001 (T. K. Young, 1994, p. 32). The

---

[12] The three communities are collectively referred to as either Aboriginal or indigenous communities; I use the latter term here to avoid confusion with the Aboriginals/Aborigines of Australia.

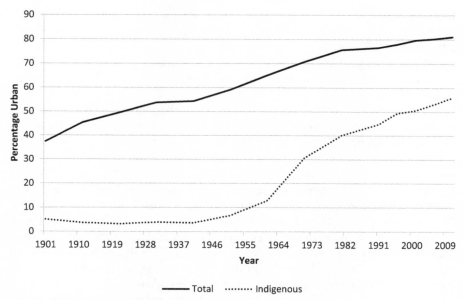

FIGURE 9.4. Urbanization in Canada, 1901–2011
(*Source:* Norris & Clatworthy, 2011; Peters, 2002b)

trend for urbanization among indigenous communities and the overall Canadian population from 1901 to 2011 can be seen in Figure 9.4,[13] with the 1950s, 1960s and 1970s clearly a period of major urbanization for indigenous communities. Indeed, by 2011 the gap in urbanization levels between indigenous communities and the overall Canadian population had closed to 25.1 per cent, or the lowest point since records began in 1901.

Successive Canadian governments welcomed the advent of an urbanized indigenous community, inasmuch as they saw urbanization as contributing to its long-term goal of integration into white Canadian society (Desbiens, Levesque & Comat, 2016, p. 79). Yet, as in New Zealand and the USA, indigenous urban dwellers instead began to 'form strategic alliances and develop intertribal bonds with other First Nations peoples from across Canada' (Wilson & Peters, 2005, p. 407). The desire of rural–urban migrants to ally with other indigenous citizens from other tribes led indigenous urbanites to emphasize their cultural similarities, such as a pan-Indian belief in the Creator and Mother Earth or a myth that North America was formed on the back of a turtle. In their interviews with Odawa and Ojibway citizens in urban Ontario, Wilson and Peters (2005) encountered several interviewees who emphasized their need to form new larger forms of identity with citizens from

---

[13] The most recent 2016 census did not break down urbanization figures according to ethnicity.

other indigenous communities. For instance, one resident in the city of Sudbury noted that 'Native people are getting together despite their differences. In the city we have to look beyond those differences and come together as Native people ... some people call it pan-Indianism or something like that but it is sort of inevitable when you move to the urban centre' (Wilson & Peters, 2005, p. 408).[14]

As in the USA and New Zealand, urban members of Canadian indigenous communities formed numerous pan-tribal self-help groups, known locally as Native Friendship Centres, in order to alleviate the lack of services and resources available to indigenous communities inasmuch as band councils' remit only includes Indians living on reserves (Desbiens et al., 2016, p. 82); examples of such centres include the Native Canadian Centre and Native Women's Resource Centre in Toronto and the Council of First Nations and Indian Family Centre (Peters, 2002a; A. M. Williams, 1997). Urban indigenous Canadians in the Northwest Territories also created the first-ever television station for aboriginal people in North America in 1987, namely Television Northern Canada, which was re-branded the Aboriginal Peoples Television Network (APTN) after receiving a national broadcast licence. Similarly, a group of aboriginal Canadians started the Aboriginal Voices Radio Network in 1998 across four cities in southern Canada; while its licence was revoked in 2015, its frequencies in Ottawa and Toronto were nonetheless taken over by a subsidiary of APTN, First Peoples Radio.

This period also saw the creation of National Indian Brotherhood (NIB) in 1970, which was an umbrella organization for provincial and territorial organizations (PTOs) and which was succeeded by the Assembly of First Nations (AFN) in 1982. However, the shift from the NIB to the AFN only led to greater representation for chiefs, rather than for urban Indians, who are instead represented alongside rural non-reserve-dwelling Indians by the Congress of Aboriginal Peoples (formerly the Native Council of Canada). Indeed, continued fragmentation of the Canadian indigenous community into First Nations, Métis and Inuit, alongside the divide between 'Status Indians' and non-Status Indians and division between provinces, has arguably stymied independent collective action,[15] and it is interesting to note in this context the lack of radical left-wing indigenous organizations in Canada relative to those in the USA, Australia and New Zealand. Nonetheless, indigenous Canadians have been successful at reaching high political office: the first Méti MPs were elected in 1871, followed

---

[14] Unfortunately, the Statistics Bureaus of Australia or Canada do not keep information on language use by tribe, which prevents me from employing the same statistical analysis as I employed above.

[15] The predecessor to the NIB, the National Indian Council, was established in 1961 but collapsed by 1967 precisely due to infighting between Status Indians, non-Status Indians and Métis. The Métis and Inuit continue to be represented by separate organizations, namely the Méti National Council and Inuit Tapiriit Kanatami, respectively.

by the first First Nation MP in 1968, and indigenous representation in the House of Commons reached a high in 2015 with ten MPs, or 3 per cent of the total.

While there is thus evidence of the influence of urbanization on the development of pan-Indianism in Canada, we cannot, however, observe a process of re-tribalization as occurred in the USA or New Zealand. Tribal casinos do exist in Canada but operate according to provincial rather than federal law, which has meant that some provinces have allocated percentage shares of casino revenues to members of indigenous communities while others have been allowed to operate casinos on tribal land, which in some cases return part of their revenue back to the province. Moreover, unlike the USA all First Nations in the relevant province share in casino revenues rather than specific tribes only (Campell & Smith, 1998, pp. 26–7). In any case, Native American casinos in Canada do not have the same sort of monopoly on gambling that they do in large parts of the USA and are thus not as profitable.

9.6.2 Australia

As in North America, the native inhabitants of Australia, or Aboriginals, were historically spread across hundreds of different tribes or ethnic groups, speaking languages which belong to some twenty-seven separate language families.[16] European settlement in the late eighteenth and nineteenth centuries led to a wave of epidemics of chickenpox, smallpox, influenza and measles as well as the appropriation of Aboriginal land, such that the total numbers of Aborigines declined from an estimated 314,500 in 1788 to a nadir of 67,314 in 1933 (M. J. Lewis, 2003, p. 22). Those that survived lived mostly in rural areas and turned to rural farm/ranch employment as a major livelihood due to the loss of their land. In an effort to cut down on white/Aboriginal conflict and stem the decline in Aboriginal populations, Australian state governments began to issue protective legislation from 1850 onwards that set aside reserve territory for Aborigines. Unlike in the USA or Canada, however, these reserves were not designed to yield land to Aborigines that they had used in the pre-colonial era but were instead intended in large part to separate Aborigines from white contact. Indeed, both entrance to and exit from the reserves were strictly controlled by the various state-level Aboriginal Protection Boards, and the government restricted rural–urban migration through laws which only allowed Aborigines to reside in cities legally if they had already secured employment. However, it is estimated that only 33 per cent of Aborigines in New South Wales lived in the state's reserves in 1936 (Doukakis, 2006, p. 52). Due to these failures many reserves were closed from the 1920s onwards to push Aborigines

---

[16] The largest of these families by far is the Pama-Nyungan family, which encompasses most of Australia except for the northern parts of Western Australia and the Northern Territory.

into fewer but larger reserves,[17] many of which were on the outskirts of towns for the purposes of employment.

After reaching its nadir in the 1930s the Aboriginal population began to rise again due to public health improvements, with populations rising from 67,314 in 1933 to 75,567 in 1954 and 101,978 in 1966. The growth in population led to an increase in rural–urban migration, as did service in the military in World War II, the search for jobs and government assistance to Aborigines interested in migration through the Aboriginal Family Voluntary Resettlement Scheme (A. Gray, 1989; J. Taylor, 1997, p. 101). Some of this migration was involuntary as Aboriginal children were forcibly re-located to urban areas in the infamous example of the 'stolen generations', one of whose explicit goals was to encourage the integration of mixed-race Aboriginals into white Australian society. In addition, a small degree of Aboriginal urbanization was due to health-based migration, whereby the Australian government began to discourage the provision of free rural healthcare to Aboriginals in the 1950s while simultaneously offering free healthcare for all Australians in select urban hospitals (Gale, 1972, p. 193). Finally, in 1962 the government allowed Aborigines to freely choose their place of residence (and vote in national elections) (J. Taylor, 1989, p. 49), which opened up migration flows even more.

Multiple changes in the definitions of urbanization and Aboriginal identity in Australia make it impossible to compare the differences between Aboriginals and Non-Aboriginals across time. Nonetheless, it is clear urbanization rose among Aboriginals in the late twentieth century, with urbanization rising from 20 per cent in 1961 to 39 per cent in 1981 according to one earlier definition (Armitage, 1995, p. 32). Moreover, evidence suggests that the gap between the two groups has closed across time: while census data from 1986 shows urbanization levels of 65.8 per cent among Aboriginals compared to 85.5 per cent among the general population, or a gap of 19.7 per cent, by 1996 Aboriginal urbanization had risen to 72.6 per cent compared to a general urbanization level of 86 per cent, for a gap of 13.4 per cent.

As with Native Americans, some incipient pan-Aboriginal organizations were established in the early twentieth century such as the Australian Aborigines' League of the 1930s, but with the aim of achieving Australian citizenship and assimilation (Merlan, 2005, pp. 480–1).[18] It was in Sydney where Aboriginal immigrants first began to establish pan-Aboriginal organizations. Various rural–urban migrants like Charles Perkins, who was raised in Adelaide in the 1950s before becoming the first Aborigine to graduate from

---

[17] One such reserve, Arnhem Land Reserve in Northern Territory, is larger than Azerbaijan, Hungary or the United Arab Emirates.

[18] Other organizations which did promote Aboriginal self-determination such as the Australian Aboriginal Progressive Association (AAPA) did not last long; the AAPA, for instance, was established in Sydney in 1924 but never extended its influence outside New South Wales and fell apart after 1927 (Maynard, 1997).

university in Sydney, established the Foundation for Aboriginal Affairs in 1959 (Foley, 2001, p. 7). In part these new activists were inspired by other countries, including African-American soldiers on leave from the war in Vietnam who exposed Aboriginals in Sydney to American identity politics (Foley, 2001, p. 9). Indeed, the practice of Aboriginals referring to themselves as 'black' appears to date back to this period, with an Australian Black Panther party established in Brisbane in 1972 (Martinez, 1997, p. 139).

However, Aboriginal activists were also determined to forge a pan-Aboriginal national identity rather than merely a 'black' one. As such, activists established a 'Tent Embassy' on the lawns of the Parliament House in Canberra in 1972, with a 'High Commissioner', and promoted an Aboriginal flag of a yellow disc imposed on a red and black background (Martinez, 1997, p. 140). (The flag had been created the year before by Aboriginal artist Harold Thomas; the colours represent the land [red], the people [black] and the sun [yellow].) As earlier the main activists behind the Tent Embassy included rural–urban migrants such as Roberta 'Bobbi' Sykes, who grew up in Queensland before moving to Brisbane and Sydney, as well as Paul Coe and Pearl Gibbs, both of whom were originally from rural New South Wales (Foley, 2001, p. 19). Other notable events at the time were the establishment of the Aboriginal Legal Service in Redfern, a suburb of Sydney, in 1970 (Merlan, 2005, p. 484), the establishment of the National Black Theatre Company in 1972 and the first-ever election of an Aboriginal to the Australian Parliament in 1972.[19] As with Native Americans in the USA, older traditions previously associated with a particular region such as the 'dot' painting of central Australia were appropriated as national pan-Aboriginal symbols (G. Morgan, 2003, p. 441). The result has thus been a 'growing sense of Aboriginal identity which the urban environment seems to force upon their members' (Gale, 1972, p. 259).

The process of re-tribalization did not, however, occur in Australia as it did in the USA or New Zealand. As with Canada, the relationship between the Aborigines and the government exists largely at the state rather than the federal level, which has meant differing relationships with land ownership. The Northern Territory has gone the furthest in restoring land to Aboriginal control, with the Aboriginal Land Rights (Northern Territory) Act of 1976 granting land to Aborigines if they could provide evidence of their traditional association with the land. The act has led to the creation of various land councils in the Northern Territory, including Central Land Council, which covers a territory larger than the size of Afghanistan, Chile or Zambia. Some of these councils govern land which is rich in mineral resources whose exploitation has yielded large amounts of revenue to local Aborigines. However, unlike among the Māori or American Indians, in Australia the government

---

[19] The senator in question was named Neville Bonner; he was initially appointed to fill a vacancy in 1971 by the Liberal party but was re-elected to the post numerous times until he was dropped by the party for the 1983 election.

has often withdrawn public funds from stations or reserves which benefit from mining revenues such that some mining areas are at risk of ending up poorer than those without mines (O'Faircheallaigh, 2004). Thus, as with Native American casinos in Canada, the economic incentives of Aboriginal identity are not as straightforward as in the USA or New Zealand and it is not surprising that there is no clear evidence for re-tribalization.

9.7 CONCLUSION

In this chapter I have shown that industrialization and urbanization among the Māori of New Zealand has led to pan-indigenous movements and a shift in salience from rural tribes to broader urban ethnic identification. These shifts were in large part due to the decreasing economic importance of rural land as Māori citizens began to emphasize their common bonds across tribal or *iwi* lines in urban areas. However, as in the USA, government actions re-invested rural tribal lands with economic importance via fishery rights and thus led to re-tribalization along *iwi* lines. As such, I used New Zealand census data to demonstrate a positive correlation between fishery quota share values per capita and subsequent *iwi* self-identification. Finally, I showed how urbanization has led to greater pan-native identity formation in both Canada and Australia, very much along the same lines as it has in the United States and New Zealand, but without the incentives for re-tribalization.

As with Native Americans, there is great irony in the fact that government actions in New Zealand have not once, but twice, contributed to unanticipated ethnic change among the Māori: first, via a process of urbanization that was originally promoted by the government as a means of integrating indigenous people into white society but which led instead to new forms of pan-tribal identification, and second, via government policies that provided *iwi* with renewed economic resources, thereby leading to re-tribalization. Moreover, this process has led to increased internal conflicts and growing inequality within the Māori community due to unequal access to fisheries revenues both within and across *iwis*. Indeed, as one Māori academic has written, a political movement that began among 'poor urban Māori women and men' was only two decades later led by 'male and wealthy' Māori, many of whom had been knighted by Queen Elizabeth (leading one critic to call them the 'Knights of the Brown Table') (Hokowhitu, 2013, p. 367).

In concluding, it is perhaps interesting to reflect on one pan-tribal Māori organization, namely the aforementioned Waipareira Trust of western Auckland (*Te Whanau o Waipareira*). The Trust – whose name literally means 'the family of Waipareira [west Auckland]' – applied in 1993 to become an *iwi* authority, which would make it eligible for government funding. After years of consultation, the Waitangi Tribunal granted it recognition in 1998. The tribunal's reasoning is clearly based on a constructivist understanding of Māori identity, and is worth quoting extensively:

It is clear that far from being static, Māori communities have changed over time. No doubt they will continue to do so ... The concept of *iwi* authorities has grown, exercising corporate functions previously unheard of, and so too national bodies, each valid if they serve the needs of Māori in a new age. In addition new urban communities have grown as well, and these for many may now represent the communities of their choice ...

The Treaty no more invalidates those things that happened after it than it did those things that happened before. It did not freeze Māori in time. It accommodates change for it is the customary values and the principles that remain the same ...

We can find no fundamental tenet of custom law that says that Māori can be serviced only through tribes. On the contrary, there is evidence that Māori were creative in adopting a range of institutions to meet their needs that were not based on kinship, but were Māori none the less. This creativity was consistent with a freedom of choice, and there is historical evidence that Māori valued their freedom. (Waitangi Tribunal, 1998, pp. 218–19)

As expected, the recognition of the trust was controversial among more traditional Māori groups, but drew praise from others as 'a witness to the resilience of the Māori spirit' (Keiha & Moon, 2008, p. 12). What is perhaps most interesting in the context of this book is the way in which the tribunal clearly focussed on how change and flexibility are inherent to identity, and how this conception contrasts with a more primordial understanding of Māori identity based on *iwi* membership which is 'locked into a shape that bears little relevance to contemporary society, and which is not allowed to develop in the way that all societies are naturally inclined to do' (Keiha & Moon, 2008, p. 15). Here, as elsewhere, both industrialization and government policies that reinstate rural land with economic value thus continue to generate competing concepts of ethnicity and ethnic change.

10

Conclusion

10.1 INTRODUCTION

In a 2007 public lecture the noted American political scientist Robert Putnam commented that 'the most certain prediction that we can make about almost any modern society is that it will be more diverse a generation from now than it is today' (Putnam, 2007, p. 137). Putnam was referring to how rising levels of immigration have increased levels of ethnic diversity around the world, which he showed was correlated with lower levels of inter-personal trust. He suggested that the solution to this problem was to create a 'new, broader sense of "we"' by promoting public policies that create more spaces for meaningful interaction across ethnic groups and thereby bypass the negative effects of ethnic diversity (Putnam, 2007, p. 139).

In this book I have tried to show that industrialization has successfully created this 'broader sense of "we"' across a wide variety of contexts. Based upon a long tradition of social theory and history reaching back in particular to Gellner and Marx, among others, I used a variety of qualitative and quantitative evidence to show that industrialization causes a decline in both ethnic fractionalization and the salience of rural, tribal identities, while leading to an increase in the salience of broader urban-based ethnic identities. Moreover, in contrast to Putnam's (2007) argument, I showed that public policies aimed at promoting assimilation have, in numerous cases, failed to achieve their goals when not accompanied by the homogenizing incentives created by industrialization.

My goal in this final chapter is two-fold: first, I examine four broader conclusions that follow from this book about how to study ethnicity and ethnic change, and then I speculate on the future of the relationship between ethnicity and industrialization.

10.2 FOUR LESSONS ON HOW TO STUDY ETHNICITY AND ETHNIC CHANGE

My first conclusion is that, on an empirical level, future research into ethnicity and ethnic identification cannot continue to assume that ethnicity is exogenous, especially in regression models that include measures of industrialization as independent variables. This problem is especially pernicious in quantitative studies which use ELF as an instrumental variable for various types of political institutions and phenomena, such that ELF is assumed to be an exogenous variable that can help identify causality in a given relationship. Indeed, one recent paper documented that ethnicity/ELF was the most popular among six widely used instruments (including elevation, immigrant enclaves, religion, sibling structure and weather) across 960 papers from top-ranked journals in economics from 1995 to 2013, and remained in the top three through 2019 (Gallen & Raymond, 2020).[1] Beyond the multiple econometric pitfalls identified by Gallen and Raymond (2020), the evidence presented in this book suggests that there is no theoretical justification for the use of ELF or any measure of ethnicity as an instrument in any serious piece of research.

One concrete suggestion for scholars who wish to use measures of ethnicity as an independent variable when employing panel data at the country or subnational level should make more of an effort to capture the dynamics of ethnic identity, either through surveys, censuses or other measures. I have made my new country-census year dataset on ethnic identification from Chapter 4 available to all researchers upon publication of this book, which may help in this regard. Another data source which is useful in this regard include Demographic and Health Surveys (DHS) data, which, alongside the comparable Multiple Indicator Cluster Surveys (MICS), have already been used in scholarship that examines the dynamics of ethnic identity in Africa (Green, 2021). Other data sources that capture change in ethnic identity over time include the various cross-national 'Barometer' surveys like the Afrobarometer, Asiabarometer, Eurobarometer and Latinobarometer surveys, although in many cases the lack of a stable list of ethnic categories makes comparing these surveys over time more difficult. As difficult as this task might appear, refusing to engage with this material would be the scholarly equivalent to having one's head stuck in the sand, which would only lead to further unproductive and flawed work.

A second conclusion from this study is about normative understandings of ethnic change. As noted at the beginning of the book, there is a lot of evidence for a 'folk' primordial theory of ethnicity, whereby non-academics understand ethnicity to be primordial and never changing. The result is that many people misunderstand and even oppose the idea of ethnic identity change in multiple

---

[1] For some recent examples of this phenomenon see Freille, Haque and Kneller (2007), Méon and Sekkat (2008), Michaelides, Milidonis and Nishiotis (2019) and Wang (2013), who use ELF as an instrument for such phenomena as corruption, institutional quality and press freedom.

contexts, with those who alter their sense of ethnic identity often stigmatized as strange, self-interested or even greedy. To take one example, a Native American staff member at an Indian Education Program in the USA complained to the anthropologist Deborah Jackson about:

The number of people that will turn up and want to enroll their kids in the program simply because they think they can join a tribe and get casino profits. But they don't care *one thing* about Indian education, Indian issues, Indian people, Indian culture ... They just say, 'Gimme, gimme, gimme!' (Jackson, 2002, p. 45; emphasis in original)

Yet, in the same interview, the staff member also admitted that many people in her programme had difficulties documenting their Native American ancestry due to decisions made by their parents or grandparents to hide their ancestors to survive in a racist environment. Indeed, Jackson's study of urban Indians in an Upper Midwest US town documents numerous cases of Indians who have no obvious Native American phenotypes and who could thus easily 'pass' as white (or black, in some cases), but who wanted to reconnect with their Indian heritage via participation in Indian cultural and educational activities (Jackson, 2002, pp. 46–7).

It is thus vitally important to sympathize with, rather than stigmatize, individuals who choose to self-identify ethnically in ways different to those identities assigned to them at birth. In most of the examples of this book the subjects who are engaged in such processes are either poor or come from poor backgrounds, and thus their identity shifts are part of their strategies of survival rather than examples of greed. In this sense the ways in which economic incentives generates shifts in ethnic identities should be viewed no differently from their effect on caste or religious identities, about which there is now a substantial literature from economics and economic history (Cassan, 2015; Michalopoulos, Naghavi & Prarolo, 2018; Platteau, 2019; Saleh, 2018). As such it would be useful to encourage further research into the degree to which incentives drive identity formation and change across a variety of contexts.[2]

Of course, we can go even further and discuss the incentives that may drive individuals to re-identify not just in terms of caste, ethnicity or religion, but also race. An instructive example here is the famous case of Rachel Dolezal, an American woman who was born to white parents but who chose to identify as African American as an adult and who successfully 'passed' as black until she was 'outed' in the media in 2015. Dolezal was portrayed in the media as someone identified as African American for personal financial gain, since she was elected president of her local chapter of the NAACP, taught African studies part-time at her local college and served as a police ombudsman before her 'outing'. She not only subsequently lost all of these jobs, but became

---

[2] It is encouraging to see recent work from economics beginning to tackle this issue as regards food consumption (Atkin et al., 2021) and mixed marriages (Jia & Persson, 2021; Rademakers & van Hoorn, 2021).

immediately infamous in the USA and was labelled a liar, cheat and fantasist by Americans from multiple racial backgrounds.

Yet Dolezal's story was more complicated than a simple motive of greed would suggest: during her childhood her parents adopted three African American children (over one of whom she later obtained legal guardianship after he sought emancipation from their parents), she attended Howard University – a historically black university – for her master's degree, she married an African American man (with whom she had a son) and later changed her legal name to the West-African sounding Nkechi Amare Diallo. In other words, it is plausible that her identification as African American was driven by her desire to separate herself from her parents, whom she claims beat her as a child and with whom she has long severed all contact, alongside growing attachment to her adopted siblings, husband and son, and that this decision was not taken lightly or quickly. And indeed many scholars of ethnicity and race have been sympathetic to Dolezal, the British theatre director Anthony Ekundayo Lennon (whom I discuss more below) and others who have attempted to identify along racial lines different from those they were assigned at birth (cf. Brubaker, 2016, pp. 28–30).

However, it would be just as derelict to dismiss concerns from members of historically disadvantaged groups like African Americans, Native Americans, Māori or others, who are concerned about completing lifting all barriers to anyone who wished to identify as members of such groups, whether for psychological reasons or for personal financial benefits (like receiving a job or scholarship). For those without any ancestral relationship to those communities, identification can thus merely constitute ticking a box on a survey or census rather than living as a member of such group on a day-to-day basis, and other notorious examples of 'reverse passing' in the USA such as Jessica Krug or Andrea Smith are arguably more difficult to defend than Dolezal. As I discussed in Chapter 2, these and other similar controversies are perhaps inevitable in cases of attempted horizontal ethnic change, as opposed to the vertical ethnic change which I have focussed on in this book.

I would not want to suggest that either a simplistic emic – or self-defined – approach to ethnic or racial identification is any more legitimate than an etic (other-defined) approach, as both can be taken to extremes. But one lesson that emerges from this study is the need to acknowledge that ethnic change is not only possible but common and even inevitable in some contexts, and that individuals who are living through periods of structural transformation often have a dynamic understanding of their identities which we should seek to comprehend rather than condemn. We still live in a world dominated by 'everyday primordialism' (Fearon & Laitin, 2000, p. 848), as seen in the strong, often violent reactions to attempts by people to change their ethnic identity, and there remains much more work to be done in allowing more space for people to have multiple identities that can help them navigate modern society.

A third conclusion from my study relates to the role of the state in promoting identity change. I have shown repeatedly in this book that attempts by states to impose assimilation on their citizens have failed and backfired and led both to resistance and alternative forms of ethnic change that were un-anticipated and un-intended by lawmakers. In Chapter 5, for instance, I showed how often violent Turkish state attempts to force Kurds to re-identify as Turks failed, especially relative to the non-violent incentives provided to other ethnic minorities in mid-twentieth century Turkey like the Circassians and Laz who ended up assimilating into the Turkish nation. Subsequent attempts by Turkish ethnographers to eliminate a question on ethnicity from the census have had little effect in promoting assimilation among the Kurds, many of whom continue to support some form of autonomy from the Turkish state. The case study of Native Americans in Chapter 8 also showed how attempts to 'terminate' tribes in the 1950s led not to the intended outcome of integration into broader American society but the creation of a new pan-tribal Native American identity, alongside similar processes in New Zealand in Chapter 9. Indeed, the two cases of Native Americans and the Māori showed how efforts by lawmakers to grant revenue to indigenous groups – but according to individual tribes rather than the broader community – had the unintended effects of promoting the fragmentation of pan-tribal identities in more recent decades.

In this regard, one key lesson from this book is that the power of states to shape identity formation is often overstated, even among those scholars who are attuned to the power of people to resist state policies. A notable and recent example here is the anthropologist and political scientist James Scott, whose work on the geographic basis of ethnic identity I discussed in Chapter 1. In his 2012 book *Two Cheers for Anarchism* Scott discusses multiple examples of how individuals act collectively against state power and often act illegally for the purposes of positive social change, as with the American civil rights movement or resistance to Nazi rule in occupied France. Yet at the same time he describes the power of the modern state to homogenize populations as nearly unbounded as, 'nearly everywhere [in the modern world], the state proceeded to fabricate a nation: France set about creating Frenchmen, Italy set about creating Italians' (Scott, 2012, p. 54). While he admits that the homogenizing efforts of the state were never as complete as policymakers' goals, Scott nonetheless claims that modern states have destroyed vernacular languages and cultures and replaced them with standardized national systems and practices, all without any agency imparted to individual citizens. What is clear from this book is how individuals have responded to the economic incentives generated by industrialization by adopting new, broader forms of ethnic identity, often in direct contradiction to the expectations of lawmakers. In this sense Scott's mistake is, as one scholar of Polish immigrants in Imperial Germany's Ruhr Valley put it, to have a 'touching confidence in the effectiveness of authoritarian government' by assuming that assimilation is always the result of top-down policies rather than bottom-up processes of identity change (Murphy, 1983, p. 6).

Another aspect of state influence on ethnic identity which I explored in this book was the focus on state education as a mechanism for nation-building, as proposed by Gellner in his 'top-down' mechanism that I discussed in Chapter 1 (and by Scott as well as a key mechanism of linguistic homogenization; Scott, 2012, p. 54). What was clear from multiple quantitative analyses of the relationship between education and assimilation – whether at the cross-national level in Chapter 4, or in Turkey in Chapter 5, Native Americans in Chapter 8 or the Māori in Chapter 9 – is that education has little to no effect on promoting assimilation in a variety of contexts, and even seems to be negatively associated with the propensity to not identify ethnically in Botswana and positively associated with continued indigenous language use in New Zealand, or the opposite of what would be expected. While initially surprising, these results echo the findings of Lange (2012), who finds that levels of education increase the amount of ethnic conflict, particularly in lower-income countries and those with high levels of ethnic fractionalization.

However, I do not wish to claim here that states have no influence on ethnic identification, particularly as regards state policies towards industrialization. Indeed, as seen in Chapters 6 and 7, the Botswanan government not only pursued good economic policies that contributed towards structural transformation but also allocated diamond revenues to the central government, which then created incentives for individuals to assimilation as Batswana, while in Somalia the regime was more focussed on military spending than industrial development, leading instead to ethnic fractionalization and conflict. The Turkish government's industrialization drive in the mid-twentieth century also had a clear effect on incentivizing assimilation among its Muslim ethnic minorities. Finally, better state health policies for Native Americans and Māori encouraged population growth and subsequent rural–urban migration, as did government efforts that directly promoted urbanization in both cases.

It is also true that state policies can have a major impact on the relative economic value of land, and thereby alter the incentives that drive ethnic identity choice. Re-tribalization among indigenous communities in both the USA and New Zealand are clear examples of this phenomenon from this book, but they are by no means not the only ones. Indeed, governments continue to politicize land rights for the purposes of staying in office, particularly in the developing world (Albertus, 2021; Boone, 2014). In many cases, especially in Africa, the politicization of property rights has encouraged individuals to retain or adopt rural ethnic identities that they might otherwise have dropped. Of course, these policies are most effective in poorer, unindustrialized countries where access to rural land remains paramount for large parts of the population.

Lastly, it is important to recognize that the homogenizing effect of industrialization can have negative consequences as regards minority languages, and that states thus have a role to play in promoting minority languages whose survival is at stake. As we saw in Chapter 7, the fact that the Botswanan state has been relatively passive in promoting Setswana language use has not meant that language homogenization has not happened and that indigenous languages like iKalanga or Shiyei are not at risk as individuals from minority groups shift their language use for instrumental reasons. In such cases – as in all of the country case studies discussed in this book – state efforts to promote minority language rights and subsidize the use of minority languages in print, radio and TV would not necessarily inhibit individuals from identifying ethnically as they see fit. It is thus in in this light that Botswanan efforts to promote an annual Languages Day since 2010 that celebrates the country's linguistic diversity are an important step forward, although the fact that minority language use in schools is still prohibited – as it is in Turkey and numerous countries around the world – remains a problem.

A fourth and final lesson from my book is about the policy implications of my analysis. More specifically, if industrialization contributes to assimilation then governments should encourage more industrialization if they want to bypass the negative effects of ethnic diversity on economic and political development. This is a markedly different policy prescription than previous attempts to manage the negative effects of ethnic diversity: as noted, Putnam (2007) has called for more public policies that encourage inter-ethnic interaction, while Laitin (2007) has argued that governments should instead create sub-national ethnically distinct or homogenous jurisdictions. He also argues that 'whatever the costs of cultural heterogeneity, the costs of eliminating heterogeneity (at least in the short term) are surely higher', a conclusion that according to my results only holds if the costs of industrialization are higher than the costs of ethnic diversity.

Promoting industrialization as a way to reduce ethnic diversity may not, however, sit well with a broader shift away from industrialization as a policy focus across the world. As multiple heterodox economists have noted, industrialization and the structural transformation which it promotes has fallen out of favour with policymakers since the advent of neo-liberalism in the 1970s (Chang, 2013; Hauge & Chang, 2019; Reinert, 2006). The focus within the development community on promoting micro-finance, the provision of basic services, fair trade, the services industry and poverty reduction more broadly, such that the ultimate goal is for individuals to accumulate more capital rather than promote structural change, is thus 'development without development' in Ha-Joon Chang's apt words.

A similar problem can be found within attitudes towards rural–urban migration and urbanization more generally, which continues to be viewed in negative terms. To take one example, the New Zealand anthropologist Joan Metge wrote about how rapid urbanization in the late twentieth century has meant that 'Māori rural communities have suffered generations of emigration, some more than others, losing both their more troublesome and their more able members' (Metge, 1995, p. 75).[3] This emphasis on 'suffering' and 'loss' in rural areas, rather than on what rural–urban migrants might gain by moving to the city, has parallels in the development literature, which shifted in the 1960s from a pro-urbanization stance to one that has tried to restrict and reduce urbanization up to the present day (Ferguson, 2007; Fox, 2014, p. 199). This 'anti-urban bias' arguably has roots in the nineteenth-century Romantic movement that arose in response to European industrialization, persisting within the social science community in sharp contrast to a continued interest in rural–urban migration outside academia (Couclelis, 1990, p. 42). However, there is plenty of evidence of an anti-urban and anti-industrialization tradition outside the West as well, most famously in Mahatma Gandhi's idea of a village-based form of economic development in twentieth-century India. Indeed, within Africa in particular, governments have sought to discourage rural–urban migration, particularly by making services more widely available in rural areas, as we saw in the case of Botswana in Chapter 7.

One prominent non-academic example of the degree to which industrialization has become something of a dirty word comes from Darren Aronofsky's popular film *Noah* (2014), which sets up conflict between the biblical protagonist and the descendants of Cain who built up a 'great industrial civilization'. Indeed, in the film the main antagonist is represented by the character of Tubal-Cain, the first bronze- and iron-worker mentioned in the Old Testament,[4] and the great flood is thus a chance to restore balance in the world by washing away this evil, industrial society and starting afresh. One contribution of this book could thus be to help restore industrialization as a potential force for good in the modern world, rather than something that only contributes to environmental destruction.

10.3 PROSPECTS FOR INDUSTRIALIZATION AND ASSIMILATION IN THE FUTURE

I would like to close my study by shifting attention away from the historical evidence of the homogenizing effect of industrialization, and towards speculation about how the relationship between industrialization and ethnicity may evolve in the future. One way to discuss this topic is to return to my analysis of

---

[3] Metge followed up this negative characterization of rural–urban migration with a statement that this period of rapid urbanization 'was marked by a significant rise in Māori consciousness of identity, expressed in an efflorescence in traditional and contemporary Māori arts and Māori initiatives in education, health welfare and justice' (Metge, 1995, p. 75), with no attempt to square these contradictory statements.

[4] While the film represents Tubal-Cain and his kin as bad because they disrespect nature and the environment, with obvious parallels to contemporary debates around climate change, the use of the word 'industrial' is nonetheless clearly used in Aronofsky's script as a synonym for corrupt, wasteful and polluting.

cross-country census data that I used in Chapter 4 and include a variable that interacts my various measures of industrialization with the time trend in order to see if there is any evidence of increasing or decreasing effects of industrialization on ethnicity over time. As such, in Table 10.1 I present the results from regressing ELF on my main measure of carbon emissions alongside my alternative measures of cement production, urbanization, electricity consumption and shares of agricultural and industrial employment, along with the interaction term, time trend and country fixed effects.

What is striking about the results in Table 10.1 is that, while the main variable capturing industrialization remains statistically significant with the right sign for five of the six specifications, the interaction term in all but one case is also statistically significant but with the opposite sign, suggesting that the effect of industrialization on ELF is diminishing over time. (It does not hold for industrial employment share in column #6, although the direction of the sign remains correct.)[5] As the interaction effect is small in size and thus difficult to interpret I also plot the results in Figure 10.1, with carbon emissions on the x-axis and the linear prediction of ELF on the vertical axis; I then added separate slopes of the relationship at given years to show how the effect of industrialization on ethnic diversity diminishes over time to the point where the effect is predicted to disappear entirely by the year 2040. (The same result holds when using other measures of industrialization.)

The obvious next step is to investigate why industrialization is having a diminishing effect on ethnic fractionalization over time. I examined multiple variables as alternative interaction terms, namely GDP per capita, education (as measured by years of schooling and primary completion rate) population size, democracy and health (as measured by infant mortality), with no effect, which suggests that some other unmeasured factor is altering the relationship between industrialization and ethnicity. There are two potential explanations for this finding, namely that the nature of industrialization is changing over time, or that ethnic fractionalization is becoming harder to change. The former is unlikely given the multiple measures of industrialization that I employed in Table 10.1 that all yielded the same result. In other words, if I had obtained very mixed results with the same alternative measures I employed in Chapter 5, then these results would indicate that the relationship between these measures was breaking down; instead, however, the results are consistent across all six columns.

The other potential reason for the results in Table 10.1 is that ethnic identity is becoming more resistant to change over time. Here there is abundant

---

[5] One possible reason for the declining effect of industrialization on ethnic fractionalization is that there is a natural limit to industrialization measures like urbanization and sectoral employment as they approach 0 or 100 per cent, which would suggest that these interaction effects are proxying for the existence of a quadratic relationship. Yet I find no evidence of a quadratic relationship with any of my measures of industrialization.

TABLE 10.1. *Industrialization and ethnic change with year-interaction effects*

	Dependent variable: ELF					
	(1)	(2)	(3)	(4)	(5)	(6)
CO_2 emissions per capita (log)	-0.041*** (0.015)					
Cement production per capita (log)		-0.028*** (0.009)				
Urbanization			-0.307*** (0.101)			
Electricity consumption per capita (log)				-0.037*** (0.011)		
Agricultural employment (as a % of total)					0.268*** (0.074)	
Industrial employment (as a % of total)						-0.540*** (0.161)
Industrialization measure * Time trend	0.0005** (0.0002)	0.0005** (0.0002)	0.004*** (0.001)	0.0006*** (0.0002)	-0.004*** (0.001)	0.005 (0.004)
Constant	0.399*** (0.026)	0.307*** (0.043)	0.544*** (0.045)	0.579*** (0.079)	0.240*** (0.051)	0.478*** (0.044)
Country fixed effects	yes	yes	yes	yes	yes	yes
Time trend	yes	yes	yes	yes	yes	yes
Countries	92	75	100	83	81	81
N	263	183	285	213	189	189
R^2 (within)	0.190	0.171	0.139	0.220	0.266	0.299

* $p \leq 0.1$, ** $p \leq 0.05$, *** $p \leq 0.01$ (two-tailed test); robust standard errors clustered at the country level in parentheses. Immigrants as a percentage of the population is included as a control variable in all regressions but is not shown here.

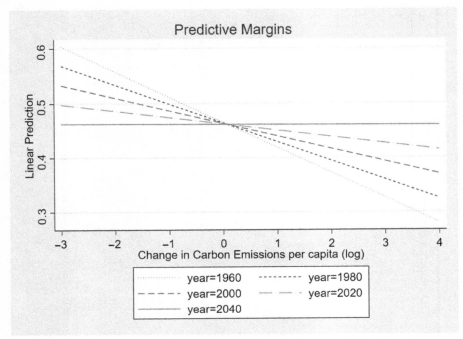

FIGURE 10.1. Interaction effects for carbon emissions and year on ELF using census data

evidence that there is increasing resistance to assimilation, and a concomitant rise in movements which promote interest and pride in multi-culturalism and ethnic minority identities. In this sense, one can view the increasing number of officially recognized ethnic groups in Uganda in Chapter 6, the creation of the Odoki Commission in Botswana in Chapter 7 and the rise in Native American tribal and Māori *iwi* identities in Chapters 8 and 9, respectively, all as cases of a broader trend towards ethnic minority identity recognition. This process has been well documented and discussed by a wide variety of scholars from the Canadian philosopher Charles Taylor, who has attempted to delineate the modern origins of what he calls 'the politics of recognition' (C. Taylor, 1992), to a more recent attempt by the American political scientist Francis Fukuyama to understand the rise of identity politics in the United States and other western societies (Fukuyama, 2018).

One form of evidence in favour of this explanation is the increasing number of country censuses that ask questions about ethnic or racial identity in countries that had previously omitted such questions in the name of forming more national unity, which can have the effect of increasing the number of salient ethnic groups in society (Lieberman & Singh, 2017). Country censuses that have introduced such questions include Canada (in its 1996 census), Ireland

(2006), New Zealand (1991), Poland (2002), Puerto Rico (2000)[6] and the United Kingdom (1991), while in Australia an ethnic origin question was introduced in 1986 but only appeared again regularly from 2001 onwards. Nor is this phenomenon limited to the Global North: while some former colonies such as Angola, the Dominican Republic, Lesotho, Rwanda and Tanzania have not asked questions about race or ethnicity on their censuses for decades, there has been no general increase in the number of censuses which omit a question on ethnic or racial origin. In fact, the general trend has been the other way around, such that in many countries like Costa Rica (2000), Ecuador (2001), Indonesia (2000), Malawi (2018), Mexico (2000),[7] Peru (2017) and Uganda (1991) census questions on ethnicity have been introduced or re-introduced for the first time since the colonial period. In other cases like Thailand there has been a moderate shift towards the census recognition of ethnic minorities via a question on home language use from 2000, but without a similar question on ethnic identification (Draper & Selway, 2019).

However, perhaps most notable of all in this respect is the way one can observe an increase in the number of ethnic categories for censuses which already ask questions on ethnicity, as a means to encompass additional ethnic or racial identities as well as a move towards recognized multi-ethnic or multi-racial identities. This phenomenon has been particularly notable in – and largely limited to – the Western Hemisphere, arguably since the concept of multi-racial identity is more salient and acceptable to many than multi-ethnic identities. Thus, as noted in Chapter 4, the United States moved towards allowing individuals to check more than one box in the 2000 census question on race, thereby allowing for multi-racial identification, although inhabitants of US-held island territories like American Samoa, Guam and the Northern Mariana Islands had been able to do so since 1980. Similar multi-racial options were also introduced for the 1996 Canadian and 2001 UK censuses (Thompson, 2012), while multiple Caribbean island states like Anguilla (2011), Antigua and Barbuda (2011), Montserrat (2011) and the US Virgin Islands (2010) have added a Hispanic category to their census racial categories. Other states in the Americas have added multi-racial categories to their census, such as in Belize (a Creole option, in 1991), Ecuador (*Montubio* [mestizos from the Pacific coast], 2010) and Suriname (Mixed, in 2004). Finally, in Argentina (2010), Mexico (2020) and Venezuela (2011) census enumerators included categories for those of African descent, after decades of struggle for recognition.

This increasing trend of ethnic minority recognition has been paralleled by a similar trend in other types of social identities. One striking social change in the

[6] The US-administered decennial census omitted questions on race in Puerto Rico between 1960 and 1990.

[7] Prior to 2000 and 2001 the Mexican and Ecuadorian censuses, respectively, asked questions about fluency in indigenous (non-Spanish) languages, but thereafter added self-defined questions about ethnicity (Novo, 2014; Villarreal, 2014).

2010s was the increasing recognition of transgender identities, such that individuals who previously would have identified as either male or female – or, to use the language of this book, assimilated into one or another of the two basic gender identities – are increasingly comfortable identifying with neither and instead choosing to call themselves transgender. This trend was arguably spearheaded by the American former Olympic Gold Medal winner Caitlyn Jenner and her decision to re-identify as a transwoman in 2015, but has also found parallels in India, where the transgender *hijra* were recognized by the Indian Supreme Court as a third gender in 2014, as well as other countries like Denmark and Germany which either allow individuals to legally change their gender and/or recognize a third gender.

In his recent book *Trans* (2016) the sociologist Rogers Brubaker has cleverly contrasted this trend towards the greater acceptance of transgender identities with the resistance in recognizing transracial identity as a phenomenon, as personified in the aforementioned case of Rachel Dolezal (Brubaker, 2016). He shows, correctly in my view, that supporting individuals' rights to self-define themselves as transgender but not supporting a similar right to self-define as transracial is hypocritical and fails to match our understanding of race as a social construct (as compared to the partially biological basis of gender or sex identities). Brubaker also helpfully spells out two reasons why there is increased space for racial and ethnic 'choice and change' in recent years (Brubaker, 2016, p. 141), namely due to a rise in multi-racial marriage and its recognition and celebration on the one hand, as well as a broader shift from essentialist, primordial understandings of race and ethnicity towards a more performative understanding of identity on the other hand, such that 'race and ethnicity are increasingly understood as something we *do,* not something we *have'* (Brubaker, 2016, p. 143; emphasis in original).

What is striking in Brubaker's account, however, is that his discussion is entirely limited to a discussion of trans identities in the United States, despite his own history of research into ethnicity and nationalism in Europe and elsewhere (Brubaker, 1996). One explanation for this narrow focus could be interest in quickly publishing a book that can insert itself into a topical national dialogue before the conversation shifts elsewhere, but another could be that the transgender and transracial debate was and still is very specific to the USA and the Western Hemisphere more generally. Indeed, to take one example, the furore which surrounded the Dolezal affair in the USA was not even close to replicated in the UK when the theatre director Anthony Ekundayo Lennon was 'outed' as white in 2018 despite being accused of passing as black to apply for funding available to members of ethnic minority groups. The unusual circumstances of Lennon's story – including his mixed complexion and curly hair despite his white Irish parents, which in turn led to his inability to 'pass' as white throughout his youth, multiple efforts to change his name, and a DNA test that suggested he had 32 per cent West African ancestry (Hattenstone,

2019) – has yet to generate a single academic article in response, let alone the multiple articles and books that have covered the Dolezal debate.

It is thus not surprising that debates around multi-culturalism and the politics of recognition – as seen in the aforementioned texts by Brubaker, Fukuyama and Taylor, among many others – have largely taken place in North America, while similar evidence documents the rise of identity politics in Latin America (De Micheli, 2021; C. R. Hale, 1997). What countries in North and South America have in common, of course, is a history of European immigration and racialized ethnic categories largely based on black, white and indigenous identities, which, as noted in Chapter 2, are the broadest of all ethnic categories and are thus internally diverse enough to allow for shifting definitions and boundaries over time. With rare exceptions – most obviously South Africa, but also Australia and New Zealand to a certain degree – these broad racial divisions are limited to the Western Hemisphere.[8]

In contrast, there is relatively little evidence for a broader trend of changing norms in the fragmentation and recognition of ethnic identity in other major parts of the world where ethnic identities have historically been defined more narrowly. Thus, for instance, in the study of African politics contemporary scholars have placed more emphasis on the role of institutions as an explanation for the nature of ethnic politics than on any significant societal changes since the mid-twentieth century (Posner, 2005), even as inter-ethnic marriages have increased over time, with a similar emphasis on the role of changing borders and institutions in explaining ethnic politics in Eastern Europe and the former Soviet Union (Henry E. Hale, 2008; Kelley, 2004). As elsewhere in the post-colonial world, India's identity cleavages remain rooted in colonial-era divisions and definitions, with little evidence of change in categorization in recent decades (Lieberman & Singh, 2017).

The geographically specific nature of this trend towards the increased recognition and prominence of ethnic, racial and even gender identities can be seen in Table 10.2, where I use the same specification from column #1 of Table 10.1 and drop each major region of the world one at a time to see if the interaction effect still holds. It is clear from columns #1–4 that the coefficients remain statistically significant and similar in size when excluding Africa, Asia, Europe and Oceania. Yet it is the result in column #5 which is most interesting here, which demonstrates that there is no evidence for a declining effect of industrialization once one removes countries in the Western Hemisphere. Indeed, when restricting the sample entirely to countries in the Western Hemisphere in column #6 (with only twenty-two countries and seventy observations), the coefficients on both the carbon emission variable and interaction terms rise remarkably high, with a concomitant increase in the goodness of fit (R^2).

---

[8] It is thus not coincidental that Davenport's (2020) discussion of racial fluidity is limited to a focus on the USA and Latin America.

TABLE 10.2. *Industrialization and ethnic change with year-interaction effects, sub-samples*

Sub-sample	Dependent variable: ELF					
	Excluding Africa	Excluding Asia	Excluding Europe	Excluding Oceania	Excluding Americas	Only Americas
	(1)	(2)	(3)	(4)	(5)	(6)
CO_2 emissions per capita (logged)	−0.064***	−0.053***	−0.028*	−0.040**	−0.025**	−0.068**
	(0.017)	(0.020)	(0.015)	(0.015)	(0.010)	(0.027)
CO_2 emissions * Time Trend	0.001***	0.0005**	0.0004*	0.0005**	0.0002	0.002***
	(0.0003)	(0.0002)	(0.0002)	(0.0002)	(0.0002)	(0.0003)
Constant	0.378***	0.386***	0.470***	0.405***	0.368***	0.435***
	(0.032)	(0.026)	(0.024)	(0.027)	(0.031)	(0.027)
Country-fixed effects	yes	yes	yes	yes	yes	yes
Time trend	yes	yes	yes	yes	yes	yes
Number of countries	74	72	68	84	70	22
Observations	215	207	205	232	193	70
R^2 (within)	0.304	0.222	0.146	0.179	0.230	0.520

* $p \leq 0.1$, ** $p \leq 0.05$, *** $p \leq 0.01$ (two-tailed test); robust standard errors clustered at the country level in parentheses. Immigrants as a percentage of the population is included as a control variable in all regressions but is not shown here.

So what is one to conclude from these results? At the very least, we can posit that there is a clear declining effect of industrialization on ethnic fractionalization in the Western Hemisphere, which is arguably driven by shifting norms of minority identity recognition, for both race and ethnicity but also for gender and other formerly neglected social identities. In contrast to the Americas, there is no obviously identifiable trend for the rest of the world, although this lack of a relationship could be driven by a lack of data. It is plausible that, in future years, this trend may be more easily identified globally as this debate spreads wider across the world. In any case, I can conclude by suggesting that both this trend as well as the relationship between industrialization and assimilation more broadly remains a topic for future research.

Appendix

Country-Level Data Used in Chapter 4

TABLE A.1. *Descriptive statistics*

	Number	*Mean*	*St. dev*	*Minimum*	*Maximum*
Panel A: ANM data					
ELF, 1961	131	0.440	0.281	0.003	0.909
Δ ELF, 1961–85	131	−0.002	0.061	−0.147	0.269
Carbon emissions per capita, 1961 (log)	131	−0.669	1.820	−4.761	3.595
Δ Carbon emissions, 1961–85	131	0.830	0.678	−1.106	2.611
Δ Immigrants (% of the population, 1960–85)	131	0.001	0.047	−0.190	0.249
Δ Largest ethnic group 1960–85	131	−0.003	0.051	−0.179	0.172
Panel B: census data					
Year	262	1996	14.970	1960	2018
ELF	262	0.449	0.269	0.013	0.935
Carbon emissions per capita (log)	262	0.700	1.541	−3.204	4.015
Immigrants (% of population)	262	0.086	0.110	0.0004	0.624
Largest ethnic group	262	0.670	0.242	0.158	0.993

TABLE A.2. *Industrialization and ethnic change, sub-samples*

	Excluding Sub-Sahar. Africa	Only Sub-Saharan Africa	Excluding Americas	Excluding Asia	Excluding Europe	Excluding ex-British colonies	Excluding mono-ethnic countries	Excluding small states
	(1)	(2)	(3)	(4)	(5)	(6)	(7)	(8)
Δ CO_2 emissions per capita, 1960–85 (log)	−0.035*** (0.012)	−0.021*** (0.007)	−0.28*** (0.010)	−0.044*** (0.009)	−0.025*** (0.008)	−0.036*** (0.010)	−0.034*** (0.009)	−0.022*** (0.008)
Δ Immigrants as a % of the population, 1960–85	0.542** (0.235)	0.028 (0.217)	0.429* (0.223)	0.782*** (0.221)	0.360*** (0.217)	0.638** (0.276)	0.532** (0.227)	0.365 (0.242)
Constant	0.031*** (0.012)	0.002 (0.006)	0.018* (0.010)	0.032*** (0.008)	0.016* (0.009)	0.027*** (0.010)	0.022** (0.009)	0.016** (0.006)
N	93	38	104	102	108	94	113	109
R^2	0.252	0.156	0.224	0.394	0.138	0.311	0.266	0.159

* $p \leq$ 0.1, ** $p \leq$ 0.05, *** $p \leq$ 0.01 (two-tailed test); robust standard errors in parentheses. Small states are defined here as states with a population lower than 500,000 in 1960.

TABLE A.3. *Countries included in statistical analysis (years only with urbanization data are in bold)*

Country	ANM data	Census years
Afghanistan	x	
Albania	x	1960, 1979, 1989
Algeria	x	
American Samoa		2000, 2010
Angola	x	
Antigua & Barbuda		1991, 2001
Argentina	x	
Armenia		2001, 2011
Aruba		1991, 2000, 2010
Australia	x	2001, 2006, 2011, 2016
Austria	x	1971, 1981, 2001
Azerbaijan		1999, 2009
Bahamas	x	
Bahrain	x	
Barbados		1960, 1980, 2010
Belarus		1999, 2009, 2019
Belgium	x	
Belize	x	1991, 2000, 2010
Benin	x	1992, 2013
Bermuda		1970, 1980, 2016
Bolivia	x	1976, 1992, 2001
Bosnia & Herzegovina		1991, 2013
Botswana		2001, 2012
Brazil	x	1980, 1990, 2000, 2010
Brunei	x	1971, 1981, 1991, 2011
Bulgaria		1992, 2001, 2011
Burkina Faso	x	1985, 2006
Burundi	x	
Cambodia	x	1998, 2008
Cameroon	x	
Canada	x	1996, 2001, 2006
Cape Verde	x	
Chad	x	
Chile	x	1992, 2002
China	x	2000, 2010
Colombia	x	2005, 2018
Comoros	x	
Congo, Dem. Rep. of	x	
Congo, Republic of	x	
Costa Rica	x	
Croatia		2001, 2011
Cuba	x	1980, 2002, 2012

TABLE A.3. (*continued*)

Country	ANM data	Census years
Cyprus	x	2001, 2011
Denmark	x	
Djibouti	x	
Dominica		1960, 1991, 2001, 2011
Dominican Republic	x	
Ecuador	x	
Egypt	x	
El Salvador	x	
Equatorial Guinea	x	
Estonia		2000, 2011
Ethiopia	x	1994, 2007
Fiji	x	1966, 1976, 1986, 1996, 2007
Finland	x	1970, 1985, 2000, 2010
France	x	
French Polynesia	x	
Gambia	x	1973, 1983, 1993, 2003, 2013
Georgia		2002, 2014
Ghana	x	1960, 2000, 2010
Greece	x	
Grenada		1960, 1981, 2001, 2011
Guam		1980, 2000, 2010
Guinea	x	
Guinea-Bissau	x	
Guyana	x	1980, 1991, 2002, 2012
Haiti	x	
Honduras	x	
Hong Kong	x	2001, 2006, 2011, 2016
Hungary	x	1960, 1980, 2001, 2011
Iceland	x	
India	x	1981, 1991, 2001, 2011
Indonesia	x	2000, 2010
Iran	x	2011, 2016
Iraq	x	
Ireland	x	2006, 2011, 2016
Israel	x	
Italy	x	
Ivory Coast	x	1975, 1998
Jamaica	x	1960, 1982, 2001, 2011
Japan	x	
Jordan	x	
Kazakhstan		1999, 2009
Kenya	x	1962, 1969, 1979, 2009, 2019
Kiribati		1995, 2000
Korea, South	x	
Kyrgyzstan		1999, 2009

TABLE A.3. – *(continued)* - *Part A*

Country	ANM data	Census years
Laos	x	1995, 2005
Latvia		2000, 2011
Lebanon	x	
Liberia	x	1984, 2008
Libya	x	
Lithuania		2001, 2011
Luxembourg	x	
Macao	x	2001, 2011, 2016
Madagascar	x	
Malaysia		2000, 2010
Mali	x	
Malta	x	
Mauritania	x	
Mauritius	x	1983, 1990, 2000
Mexico	x	
Micronesia, F. S. of		1994, 2000
Moldova		2004, 2014
Mongolia	x	1963, 2000, 2010
Montenegro		2003, 2011
Morocco	x	
Mozambique	x	
Myanmar	x	
Namibia		2001, 2011
Nepal	x	2001, 2011
Netherlands	x	
New Caledonia	x	1976, 1983, 1989, 1996, 2009, 2014, 2019
New Zealand	x	1996, 2001, 2006, 2013, 2018
Nicaragua	x	
Niger	x	1988, 2001
Nigeria	x	
North Macedonia		1991, 2002
Northern Mariana Isl.		2000, 2010
Norway	x	
Panama	x	
Paraguay	x	
Peru	x	1972, 2007
Philippines	x	1975, 1990, 2000
Poland	x	2002, 2011
Portugal	x	
Puerto Rico		2000, 2010, 2020
Romania	x	1977, 1992, 2002, 2011
Rwanda	x	1978, 1991
Samoa	x	
Sao Tome & Principe	x	

TABLE A.3. – *(continued)* - *Part A*

Country	ANM data	Census years
Saudi Arabia	x	
Senegal	x	
Serbia		2002, 2011
Seychelles		1971, 2002
Sierra Leone	x	
Singapore	x	1970, 1980, 1990, 2000, 2010, 2020
Slovakia		2001, 2011
Slovenia		1991, 2002
Solomon Islands	x	1970, 1976, 2009
Somalia	x	
South Africa	x	1960, 1970, 1996, 2001, 2011
Spain	x	
Sri Lanka	x	1971, 1981, 2001, 2012
St Lucia		1970, 1980, 1991, 2001, 2010
St Vincent		1991, 2001
Sudan	x	
Suriname		2004, 2012
Swaziland	x	
Sweden	x	
Switzerland	x	1970, 2000
Syria	x	
Tajikistan		2000, 2010
Tanzania	x	
Thailand	x	2000, 2010
Togo	x	1960, 1981
Tonga	x	1986, 1996, 2006, 2016
Trinidad & Tobago	x	1970, 1980, 2011
Tunisia	x	
Turkey	x	
Uganda	x	1991, 2002
United Kingdom	x	2001, 2011
Uruguay	x	
USA	x	1960, 1970, 1980, 1990
US Virgin Islands		1980, 1990
Venezuela	x	
Vietnam	x	1979, 1999, 2009, 2019
Yemen	x	
Zambia		1990, 2000, 2010

TABLE A.4. *Data sources for Tables 4.1–4.4*

Dependent variables

ELF: Change in ELF between 1961 and 1985 as measured by the ANM (Tables 4.1–4.2) or ELF as measured by census data (Tables 4.3–4.4).

Largest ethnic group: Change in the size of the largest ethnic group between 1961 and 1985 as measured by the ANM (Tables 4.1–4.2) or size of the largest ethnic group as measured by census data (Tables 4.3–4.4).

Independent variables

*Agricultural employment (as a % of the total):*percentage of labour force in agriculture. Source: World Development Reports 1979–81, 1984 and 1985; World Bank World Development Indicators.

CO_2 emissions: Log of CO_2 emissions in metric tons per capita. Source: World Bank World Development Indicators, with data originally taken from the Carbon Dioxide Information Analysis Center at Oak Ridge National Laboratory (run by the US Department of Energy).

Cement production per capita: log of cement production in metric tons per capita. Source: Cross-national Times Series Data Archive (through 1998) and US Geological Survey (from 1999 through 2018). For countries recorded as having no cement production for the initial date but some production at a later date I assigned a value of 0.001 tons per capita for the initial date in order to avoid taking the log of zero.

Electricity consumption per capita: log of electric power consumption per capita in kWh. Source: US Energy Information Administration.

GDP/capita: Gross Domestic Product per country. Source: World Bank World Development Indicators.

Immigrants (% of the population): ratio of total migrants to the total population per country. Source: United Nations Population Division, World Population Prospects.

Industrial employment (as a % of the total): percentage of labour force in industry. Source: World Development Reports 1979–81, 1984 and 1985; World Bank World Development Indicators.

Infant mortality: Log of infant mortality rate. Source: United Nations Population Division, World Population Prospects.

Mean years of schooling: Mean years of primary and secondary schooling per country. Source: Barro and Lee (2010).

Newspaper circulation per capita: Daily newspaper circulation per capita per country. Source: Cross-national Times Series Data Archive.

Taxation as a % of GDP: taxation as a percentage of GDP per country. Source: Cross-national Times Series Data Archive.

Urbanization: Percentage of a country's population living in urban areas. Source: United Nations, World Urbanization Prospects, Department of Economic and Social Affairs/Population Division.

V-Dem polyarchy index: Country-year democracy rating. Source: Varieties of Democracy.

TABLE A.5. *Data alterations from the ANM*

The following countries were left out of the ANM analysis for the following reasons:

- **Anguilla, Antigua and Barbuda, Barbados, Dominica, Grenada, Montserrat, Saint Kitts and Nevis, and Saint Lucia, Saint Vincent and the Grenadines.** Listed together as one unit in the 1961 but separately in the 1985 Atlas.
- **Bangladesh** and **Pakistan.** Listed together under Pakistan in the 1961 Atlas but separately in the 1985 Atlas due to the partition of Pakistan in 1971.
- **Cape Verde.** The 1961 Atlas lists groups according to language (where all Portuguese-speakers are listed as one group) while the 1985 Atlas lists group according to nationality (with native Cape Verdeans and Portuguese listed separately).
- **Central African Republic.** The 1985 Atlas lists several indigenous ethnic groups not included in the 1961 Atlas, including the Ngbandi (10.6% of the population), Sara (6.9%) and Mbum (4.0%), among others.
- **Gabon.** The 1985 Atlas lists several indigenous ethnic groups not included in the 1961 Atlas, including the Mbete (14.2% of the population) and the Ngundi (5.3%).
- **Kiribati** and **Tuvalu.** Listed together under the Gilbert and Ellice Islands in the 1961 Atlas but separately in the 1985 Atlas due to their separate independence in 1976.
- **Papua New Guinea.** Listed separately as New Guinea and Papua in the first volume as the two constituent units of what was then the Territory of Papua and New Guinea.
- **Réunion.** The 1961 Atlas lists groups according to language (where all French-speakers are listed as one group) while the 1985 Atlas lists group according to race (with Creoles and French listed separately).
- **Suriname.** The 1961 Atlas lists groups according to language (where all Dutch-speakers are listed as one group) while the 1985 Atlas lists group according to race (with Creoles, 'Bush Negros' and Dutch listed separately).

In the following cases I coded ELF differently from Roeder (2001):

- **Algeria, Iraq, Lebanon, Libya, Morocco, Sudan, Syria** and **Tunisia.** I coded Arabs as one ethnic group rather than coding them by nationality.
- **Brunei.** I coded the Malays and Kedayan as one group in 1985 inasmuch as they were coded as one group in 1961 (and in every census in Brunei since 1960).
- **Liberia.** I coded the Grebo, Kran and Kru as one group in 1985 inasmuch as they were recorded as one group in 1961.
- **Mali.** I coded the Bambara, Duala and Mandinka as one group in 1985 inasmuch as they were recorded as one group in 1961.
- **Netherlands.** I coded the Flemish as Dutch in 1985 to match the fact that both were recorded as one group in 1961.
- **Switzerland.** I coded the French speakers, German speakers and Italian speakers as single ethnic groups in 1985 to match the fact that they were recorded as such in 1961.
- **Vietnam.** I added data for 1961 to the dataset inasmuch as it was listed as a single unit in 1961 despite the fact that it was partitioned between 1954 and 1975.

Finally, I added the following countries which were listed in both Atlases but were not included in (Roeder, 2001)'s original dataset: Belize, Bermuda, French Polynesia, Guam, Hong Kong, Macao, Solomon Islands, São Tomé and Príncipe, Seychelles, Timor-Leste, Tonga and the US Virgin Islands.

Bibliography

Ablon, Joan. (1965). Relocated American Indians in the San Francisco Bay Area: Social Interaction and Indian Identity. *Human Organization*, 23(4), 296–304.

(1979). The American Indian Chicago Conference. In R. Hinshaw (Ed.), *Currents in Anthropology* (pp. 445–56). The Hague: Mouton.

Abouharb, M. Rodwan, and Anessa L. Kimball. (2007). A New Dataset on Infant Morality Rates, 1816–2002. *Journal of Peace Research*, 44(6), 743–54.

Acemoglu, Daron, and Pierre Yared. (2010). Political Limits to Globalization. *American Economic Review*, 100(2), 83–8.

Acemoglu, Daron, and Simon Johnson. (2007). Disease and Development: The Effect of Life Expectancy on Economic Growth. *Journal of Political Economy*, 115(6), 925–85.

Acemoglu, Daron, Simon Johnson, and James A. Robinson. (2003). An African Success Story: Botswana. In Dani Rodrik (Ed.), *In Search of Prosperity: Analytical Narratives on Economic Growth* (pp. 80–119). Princeton: Princeton University Press.

Acton, Peter. (2014). *Poiesis: Manufacturing in Classical Athens.* New York: Oxford University Press.

Ahlerup, Pelle, and Ola Olsson. (2012). The Roots of Ethnic Diversity. *Journal of Economic Growth*, 17(2), 71–102.

Ahmad, Feroz. (1977). *The Turkish Experiment in Democracy, 1950–1975.* London: C. Hurst.

(1993). *The Making of Modern Turkey.* London: Routledge.

Ahn, Elise S. (2011). *Seeing Turkish State Formation Processes: Mapping Language and Education Census Data.* (PhD Dissertation.) College of Education, University of Illinois at Urbana-Champaign.

Alba, Richard. (2009). *Remaking the American Mainstream: Assimilation and Contemporary Immigration.* Cambridge, MA: Harvard University Press.

Albertus, Michael. (2021). *Property without Rights: Origins and Consequences of the Property Rights Gap.* Cambridge: Cambridge University Press.

Alesina, Alberto, Arnaud Devleeshauwer, William Easterly, Sergio Kurlat, and Romain Wacziarg. (2003). Fractionalization. *Journal of Economic Growth*, 8(2), 155–94.

Alesina, Alberto, Bryony Reich, and Alessandro Riboni. (2020). Nation-building, Nationalism, and Wars. *Journal of Economic Growth*, 25(4), 381–430.

Alesina, Alberto, Caterina Gennaioli, and Stefania Lovo. (2019). Public Goods and Ethnic Diversity: Evidence from Deforestation in Indonesia. *Economica*, 86(341), 32–66.

Allen, Robert C. (2003). Progress and Poverty in Early Modern Europe. *Economic History Review*, 56(3), 403–43.

Allport, Gordon W. (1954). *The Nature of Prejudice*. Reading, MA: Addison-Wesley.

Alvarez, Jose H. (1966). A Demographic Profile of the Mexican Immigration to the United States, 1910–1950. *Journal of Inter-American Studies*, 8(3), 471–96.

Amerman, Stephen K. (2003). 'Let's Get In and Fight!' American Indian Political Activism in an Urban Public School. *American Indian Quarterly*, 27(3/4), 607–38.

Amory, Patrick. (1994). Names, Ethnic Identity, and Community in Fifth- and Sixth-Century Burgundy. *Viator: Medieval and Renaissance Studies*, 25, 1–30.

Anderson, Benedict. (1991). *Imagined Communities: Reflections on the Origins and Spread of Nationalism*. London: Verso.

Anderson, Helene. (1997, February 9). Settlement Net's Almighty Tangle. [Auckland] *Sunday Star-Times*.

Andrews, Peter A. (1989). Introduction. In Peter A. Andrews (Ed.), *Ethnic Groups in the Republic of Turkey* (pp. 17–52). Wiesbaden: Dr. Ludwig Reichert Verlag.

Angrist, Joshua D., and Jörn-Steffen Pischke. (2009). *Mostly Harmless Econometrics: An Empiricist's Companion*. Princeton: Princeton University Press.

Antman, Francisca, and Brian Dunan. (2021). *American Indian Casinos and Native American Self-Identification*. Mimeo, Department of Economics, University of Colorado Boulder.

Arieff, Allison. (1995). A Different Sort of (P)Reservation: Some Thoughts on the National Museum of the American Indian. *Museum Anthropology*, 19(2), 78–90.

Armitage, Andrew. (1995). *Comparing the Policy of Aboriginal Assimilation: Australia, Canada and New Zealand*. Vancouver: UBC Press.

Arnold, Caroline E. (2012). In the Service of Industrialization: Etatism, Social Services and the Construction of Industrial Labour Forces in Turkey (1930–50). *Middle Eastern Studies*, 48(3), 363–85.

Aronson, Dan R. (1980). Kinsmen and Comrades: Towards a Class Analysis of the Somali Pastoral Sector. *Nomadic Peoples*, 7, 14–23.

Ashforth, Adam. (1997). Lineaments of the Political Geography of State Formation in Twentieth-Century South Africa. *Journal of Historical Sociology*, 10(2), 101–26.

Aslan, Senem. (2011). Everyday Forms of State Power and the Kurds in the Early Turkish Republic. *International Journal of Middle East Studies*, 43(1), 75–93.

Atkin, David, Eve Colson-Sihra, and Moses Shayo. (2021). How Do We Choose Our Identity? A Revealed Preference Approach Using Food Consumption. *Journal of Political Economy*, 129(4), 1193–251.

Ausubel, David P. (1961). The Maori: A Study in Resistive Acculturation. *Social Forces*, 39(3), 218–27.

Ayata, Bilgin, and Serra Hakyemez. (2013). The AKP's Engagement with Turkey's Past Crimes: An Analysis of PM Erdoğan's 'Dersim Apology.' *Dialectical Anthropology*, 37(1), 131–43.

Babito, H. M. (1999). A Lexicostatistical Survey of the Setswana Dialects Spoken in Botswana. *South African Journal of African Languages*, 19(1), 2–11.

Bairoch, Paul. (1988). *Cities and Economic Development: From the Dawn of History to the Present*. Chicago: University of Chicago Press.

Bakonyi, Jutta. (2015). Ideoscapes in the World Society: Framing Violence in Somalia. *Civil Wars*, 17(2), 242–65.

Balthasar, Dominik. (2012). *State-Making in Somalia and Somaliland: Understanding War, Nationalism and State Trajectories as Processes of Institutional and Socio-Cognitive Standardization*. (PhD Dissertation). London School of Economics.

Bandyopadhyay, Sanghamitra, and Elliott D. Green. (2013). Nation-Building and Conflict in Modern Africa. *World Development*, 45, 108–18.

Banti, Giorgio. (2000). Notes on Somali Camel Terminology. In Rainer Voßen, Angelika Mietzner, and Antje Meißner (Eds.), *'Mehr als nur Worte ...': Afrikanistische Beiträge zum 65. Geburtstag von Franz Rottland* (pp. 45–62). Cologne: Rüdiger Köppe.

Barcham, Manuhuia. (1998). The Challenge of Urban Maori: Reconciling Conceptions of Indigeneity and Social Change. *Asia Pacific Viewpoint*, 39(3), 303–14.

Barkley, Andrew P. (1990). The Determinants of the Migration of Labor Out of Agriculture in the United States, 1940–85. *American Journal of Agricultural Economics*, 72(3), 567–73.

Barro, Robert, and Jong-Wha Lee. (2010). *A New Data Set on Educational Attainment in the World, 1950–2010*. NBER Working Paper #15902, National Bureau of Economic Research.

Bartlett, Robert. (2001). Medieval and Modern Concepts of Race and Ethnicity. *Journal of Medieval and Early Modern Studies*, 31(1), 39–56.

Bates, Robert H. (1974). Ethnic Competition and Modernization in Contemporary Africa. *Comparative Political Studies*, 6(4), 457–84.

Bayar, Yeşim. (2011). The Trajectory of Nation-building Through Language Policies: The Case of Turkey During the Early Republic (1920–38). *Nations and Nationalism*, 17(1), 108–28.

Baycroft, Timothy. (2004). *Culture, Identity and Nationalism: French Flanders in the Nineteenth and Twentieth Century*. Woodbridge: Boydell Press & Royal Historical Society.

Beach, Brian, and Daniel B. Jones. (2017). Gridlock: Ethnic Diversity in Government and the Provision of Public Goods. *American Economic Journal: Economic Policy*, 9(1), 112–36.

Bell, David A. (2001). *The Cult of the Nation in France: Inventing Nationalism, 1680–1800*. Cambridge, MA: Harvard University Press.

Belsley, David A., Edwin Kuh, and Roy E. Welsch. (1980). *Regression Diagnostics: Identifying Influential Data and Sources of Collinearity*. New York: John Wiley.

Benninghaus, Rüdiger . (1989). The Laz: An Example of Multiple Identification. In Peter A. Andrews (Ed.), *Ethnic Groups in the Republic of Turkey* (pp. 497–502). Wiesbaden: Dr. Ludwig Reichert Verlag.

Bentley, G. Carter. (1987). Ethnicity and Practice. *Comparative Studies in Society and History*, 29(1), 24–55.

Bentley, Gillian R. (1985). Hunter-Gatherer Energetics and Fertility: A Reassessment of the !kung San. *Human Ecology*, 13(1), 79–109.

Bergen, Doris L. (1994). The Nazi Concept of 'Volksdeutsche' and the Exacerbation of Anti-Semitism in Eastern Europe, 1939–1945. *Journal of Contemporary History*, 29(4), 569–82.

Berghahn, Volker. (1999). Germans and Poles, 1871–1945. In Keith Bullivant, Geoffrey Giles, and Walter Pape (Eds.), *Germany and Eastern Europe: Cultural Identities and Cultural Differences* (pp. 15–36). Amsterdam: Rodopi.

Berkes, Niyazi. (Ed.) (1959). *Turkish Nationalism and Western Civilization: Selected Essays of Ziya Gökalp*. London: George Allen & Unwin.

Berreman, Gerald D. (1972). Social Categories and Social Interaction in Urban India. *American Anthropologist*, 74(3), 567–86.

Besteman, Catherine. (1996). Violent Politics and the Politics of Violence: The Dissolution of the Somali Nation-State. *American Ethnologist*, 23(3), 579–96.

Bezuidenhout, Andries, and Sakhela Buhlungu. (2010). From Compounded to Fragmented Labour: Mineworkers and the Demise of Compounds in South Africa. *Antipode*, 43(2), 237–63.

Bichachi, Odoobo C. (9 August 2014). Let's Remove Tribes from Uganda's Constitution: Commentary. [Kampala] *Daily Monitor*.

Bidois, Vanessa. (29 March 2000). Māori Fish Deal Leader Rejects Share-out Plan. *New Zealand Herald*.

Bigsten, Arne, and Steve Kayizzi-Mugerwa. (1992). Adaptation and Distress in the Urban Economy: A Study of Kampala Households. *World Development*, 20(10), 1423–41.

Blanksten, George I. (1960). The Politics of Latin America. In Gabriel A. Almond and James S. Coleman (Eds.), *The Politics of the Developing Areas* (pp. 455–531). Princeton: Princeton University Press.

Bleaney, Michael, and Arcangelo Dimico. (2011). How Different are the Correlates of Onset and Continuation of Civil Wars? *Journal of Peace Research*, 48(2), 145–55.

Blecking, Diethelm. (2015). Integration through Sports? Polish Migrants in the Ruhr, Germany. *International Review of Social History*, 60(S1), 275–93.

Bloom, David E., David Canning, and Günther Fink. (2014). Disease and Development Revisited. *Journal of Political Economy*, 122(6), 1355–66.

Boone, Catherine. (2003). *Political Topographies of the African State: Territorial Authority and Institutional Choice*. Cambridge: Cambridge University Press.

    (2014). *Property and Political Order: Land Rights and the Structure of Politics*. Cambridge: Cambridge University Press.

Boserup, Ester. (1965). *The Conditions of Agricultural Growth: The Economics of Agrarian Change under Population Pressure*. London: Allen & Unwin.

Boustan, Leah P., Devin Bunten, and Owen Hearey. (2013). *Urbanization in the United States, 1800–2000*. NBER Working Paper #19041, National Bureau of Economic Research.

Boyer, Lanada. (1998). Reflections of Alcatraz. In Susan Lobo and Steve Talbot (Eds.), *Native American Voices: A Reader* (pp. 436–46). New York: Longman.

Bradbury, Mark. (2008). *Becoming Somaliland*. Oxford: James Currey.

Brandfon, Robert L. (1991). The End of Immigration to the Cotton Fields. In George E. Pozzetta (Ed.), *Immigrants on the Land: Agriculture, Rural Life and Small Towns* (pp. 1–21). New York: Garland.

Brett, André. (2015). The Miserable Remnant of this Ill-used People': Colonial Genocide and the Moriori of New Zealand's Chatham Islands. *Journal of Genocide Research*, 17(2), 133–52.

Breuilly, John. (1993). *Nationalism and the State*. Manchester: Manchester University Press.

Broker, Ignatia. (1983). *Night Flying Woman*. St. Paul, MN: Minnesota Historical Society Press.

Brubaker, Rogers. (1996). *Nationalism Reframed: Nationhood and the National Question in the New Europe*. Cambridge: Cambridge University Press.

(2009). Ethnicity, Race and Nationalism. *Annual Review of Sociology, 35*, 21–42.

(2016). *Trans: Gender and Race in an Age of Unsettled Identities*. Princeton: Princeton University Press.

Bruk, Solomon I. (1986). *Naselenie Mira Etnodemograficheskii Spravochnik*. Moscow: Izd-vo 'Nauka'.

Bruk, Solomon I., and V. S. Apenchenko. (1964). *Atlas Narodov Mira*. Moscow: Glavnoe upravlenie geodezii I Kartografii Gosudarstvennogo geologicheskogo komiteta SSSR, Institut etnografii im. N. H. Miklukho-Maklaia Akademii nauk SSSR.

Bruner, Edward M. (1961). Urbanization and Ethnic Identity in North Sumatra. *American Anthropologist, 63*(3), 508–21.

Bulutay, Tuncer. (1995). *Employment, Unemployment and Wages in Turkey*. Ankara: State Institute of Statistics Printing Division.

Bureau of Indian Affairs (1985). Final Determination That the Southeastern Cherokee Confederacy, Inc., the Northwest Cherokee Wolf Band, and the Red Clay Inter-Tribal Indian Band Do Not Exist as Indian TrIbes. *Federal Register, 50*(187), 39047–8.

(1997). Final Determination against Federal Acknowledgment of the Mobile–Washington County Band of Choctaw Indians of South Alabama (MOWA). *Federal Register, 62*(247), 67398–400.

(2007). Final Determination against Federal Acknowledgment of the St. Francis/Sokoki Band of Abenakis of Vermont. *Federal Register, 72*(126), 36022–5.

(2010). Proposed Finding against Federal Acknowledgment of the Central Band of Cherokee. *Federal Register, 75*(159), 51105–07.

(2011). Final Determination against Acknowledgment of the Juaneño Band of Mission Indians, Acjachemen Nation. *Federal Register, 76*(54), 15337–8.

(2012). Final Determination against Federal Acknowledgment of the Central Band of Cherokee. *Federal Register, 77*(62), 19315–17.

Burgess, Robin, Remi Jedwab, Edward Miguel, Ameet Morjaria, and Gerard Padró i Miquel. (2015). The Value of Democracy: Evidence from Road Building in Kenya. *American Economic Review, 105*(6), 1817–51.

Burt, Larry W. (1986). Roots of the Native American Urban Experience: Relocation Policy in the 1950s. *American Indian Quarterly, 10*(2), 85–99.

Çağaptay, Soner. (2002). Reconfiguring the Turkish Nation in the 1930s. *Nationalism and Ethnic Politics, 8*(2), 67–82.

(2004). Race, Assimilation and Kemalism: Turkish Nationalism and the Minorities in the 1930s. *Middle Eastern Studies*, 40(3), 86–101.

(2006). *Islam, Secularism and Nationalism in Modern Turkey: Who Is a Turk?* New York: Routledge.

Campbell, Eugene K., and Puni G. Campbell. (1997). Family Size and Sex Preferences and Eventual Fertility in Botswana. *Journal of Biosocial Science*, 29(2), 191–204.

Campell, Colin S., and Garry J. Smith. (1998). Canadian Gambling: Trends and Public Policy Issues. *Annals of the American Academy of Political and Social Science*, 556, 22–35.

Campos, Nauro F., and Vitaly S. Kuzeyev. (2007). On the Dynamics of Ethnic Fractionalization. *American Journal of Political Science*, 51(3), 620–39.

Caney, John C. (1982). *The Modernisation of Somali Vocabulary, With Particular Reference to the Period from 1972 to the Present* (PhD Dissertation). SOAS University of London.

Capriccioso, Rob. (14 June 2021). Comeback Watch: Picayune Chukchansi Tribe Erases Mountain of Debt, Shares Leadership Lessons. [Grand Rapids, MI] *Tribal Business News*.

Carter, Ian. (1974). The Highlands of Scotland as an Underdeveloped Region. In Emanuel De Kadt and Gavin Williams (Eds.), *Sociology and Development* (pp. 279–314). London: Tavistock.

Caselli, Franceso, and Wilbur J. Coleman II. (2013). On the Theory of Ethnic Conflict. *Journal of the European Economic Association*, 11(s1), 161–92.

Cashdan, Elizabeth. (1986). Competition between Foragers and Food-Producers on the Botletli River, Botswana. *Africa: Journal of the International African Institute*, 56 (3), 299–318.

(2001). Ethnic Diversity and its Environmental Determinants: Effects of Climate, Pathogens and Habitat Diversity. *American Anthropologist*, 103(4), 968–91.

Cassan, Guilhem. (2015). Identity Based Policies and Identity Manipulation: Evidence from Colonial Punjab. *American Economic Journal: Economic Policy*, 7(4), 103–31.

Cawkwell, G. L. (1983). The Decline of Sparta. *The Classical Quarterly*, 33(2), 385–400.

Cederman, Lars-Erik, and Luc Girardin. (2007). Beyond Fractionalization: Mapping Ethnicity onto Nationalist Insurgencies. *American Political Science Review*, 101(1), 173–86.

Chai, Sun-Ki. (1996). A Theory of Ethnic Group Boundaries. *Nations and Nationalism*, 2(2), 281–307.

(2005). Predicting Ethnic Boundaries. *European Sociological Review*, 21(4), 375–91.

Chandra, Kanchan. (2006). What Is Ethnic Identity and Does It Matter? *Annual Review of Political Science*, 9, 397–424.

(2008). Ethnic Invention: A New Principle for Institutional Design in Ethnically Divided Democracies. In Margaret Levi, James Johnston, Jack Knight, and Susan Stokes (Eds.), *Designing Democratic Government: Making Institutions Work* (pp. 89–116). New York: Russell Sage.

Chandra, Kanchan, and Cilanne Boulet. (2012). A Baseline Model of Change in an Activated Ethnic Demography. In Kanchan Chandra (Ed.), *Constructivist Theories of Ethnic Politics* (pp. 229–76). Oxford: Oxford University Press.

Chandra, Kanchan, and Steven I. Wilkinson. (2008). Measuring the Effect of 'Ethnicity'. *Comparative Political Studies*, 41(4–5), 515–63.

Chang, Ha-Joon. (2013). Hamlet Without the Prince of Denmark: How Development has Disappeared from Today's 'Development' Discourse. In David Held and Charles Roger (Eds.), *Global Governance at Risk* (pp. 129–48). Cambridge: Polity.

Chapple, Simon. (2000). Maori Socio-Economic Diversity. *Political Science*, 52(2), 101–15.

Chirot, Daniel. (1978). Social Change in Communist Romania. *Social Forces*, 57(2), 457–99.

Chochiev, Georgi. (2007). On the History of the North Caucasian Diaspora in Turkey. *Iran and the Caucasus*, 11(2), 213–26.

Churchill, Sefa A., Janet E. Ocloo, and Diana Siawor-Robertson. (2017). Ethnic Diversity and Health Outcomes. *Social Indicators Research*, 134(3), 1077–112.

Churchill, Sefa A., and Russell Smyth. (2017). Ethnic Diversity and Poverty. *World Development*, 95, 285–302.

Cicero (1853). On the Laws (C. D. Yonge, Trans.). In C. D. Yonge (Ed.), *The Treatises of M. T. Cicero* (pp. 389–485). London: Henry G. Bohn.

Cinnirella, Francesco, and Ruth Schueler. (2018). Nation Building: The Role of Central Spending in Education. *Explorations in Economic History*, 67, 18–39.

Clark, Gregory. (2001). *The Secret History of the Industrial Revolution*. Department of Economics, University of California, Davis.

Clark, William R., and Matt Golder. (2006). Rehabilitating Duverger's Theory: Testing the Mechanical and Strategic Modifying Effects of Electoral Laws. *Comparative Political Studies*, 36(6), 679–708.

Cohen, Abner. (1969). *Custom and Politics in Urban Africa: A Study of Hausa Migrants in Yoruba Towns*. London: Routledge.

  (1974). Introduction: The Lesson of Ethnicity. In Abner Cohen (Ed.), *Urban Ethnicity* (pp. ix–xxiv). London: Routledge.

Cohen, Edward E. (2000). *The Athenian Nation*. Princeton: Princeton University Press.

Cohen, Ronald. (1978). Ethnicity: Problem and Focus in Anthropology. *Annual Review of Anthropology*, 7, 379–403.

Coleman, Andrew, Sylvia Dixon, and David C. Maré. (2005). *Māori Economic Development: Glimpses from Statistical Sources*. Motu Working Paper 05-13, Motu Economic and Public Policy Research, Wellington.

Coleman, James S. (1954). Nationalism in Tropical Africa. *American Political Science Review*, 48(2), 404–26.

Collard, Ian F., and Robert A. Foley. (2002). Latitudinal Patterns and Environmental Determinants of Recent Human Cultural Diversity: Do Humans Follow Biogeographic Rules? *Evolutionary Ecology Research*, 4(3), 371–83.

Collette, John, and Pat O'Malley. (1974). Urban Migration and Selective Acculturation: The Case of the Maori. *Human Organization*, 33(2), 147–54.

Colley, Brook. (2018). *Power in the Telling: Grand Ronde, Warm Springs, and Intertribal Relations in the Casino Era*. Seattle: University of Washington Press.

Colley, Linda. (1992). *Britons: Forging the Nation, 1707–1837*. New Haven, CT: Yale University Press.

Collier, Paul, and Anke Hoeffler. (2004). Greed and Grievance in Civil War. *Oxford Economic Papers*, 56(4), 563–95.

Condor, Susan, Stephen Gibson, and Jackie Abell. (2006). English Identity and Ethnic Diversity in the Context of UK Constitutional Change. *Ethnicities*, 6(2), 123–58.

Connor, Walker. (1994). *Ethnonationalism: The Quest for Understanding*. Princeton: Princeton University Press.

Constantinescu, Ilinca P., Dragoș Dascălu, and Cristina Sucală. (2017). An Activist Perspective on Industrial Heritage in Petrila, a Romanian Mining City. *The Public Historian*, 39(4), 114–41.

Coombes, Brad. (2013). Maori and Environmental Justice: The Case of 'Lake' Otara. In Evelyn Peters and Chris Andersen (Eds.), *Indigenous in the City: Contemporary Identities and Cultural Innovation* (pp. 334–53). Vancouver, Canada: UBC Press.

Cornell, Stephen. (1988). *The Return of the Native: American Indian Political Resurgence*. Oxford: Oxford University Press.

Costalli, Stefano, Luigi Moretti, and Costantino Pischedda. (2017). The Economic Costs of Civil War: Synthetic Counterfactual Evidence and the Effects of Ethnic Fractionalization. *Journal of Peace Research*, 54(1), 80–98.

Couclelis, Helen. (1990). Urban Liveability: A Commentary. *Urban Geography*, 11(1), 42–7.

Crush, Jonathan. (1994). Scripting the Compound: Power and Space in the South African Mining Industry. *Environment and Planning D: Society and Space*, 12(3), 301–24.

Currey, Robert L., Jr. (1987). Poverty and Mass Unemployment in Mineral-Rich Botswana. *American Journal of Economics and Sociology*, 46(1), 71–87.

Da Silva, Milton M. (1975). Modernization and Ethnic Conflict: The Case of the Basques. *Comparative Politics*, 7(2), 227–51.

Danskikh, Siarhei. (2008). Regional Modes of Urbanization and National Identity Development (Case Study of Belarus). *LIMES*, 1(1), 88–98.

Darden, Keith, and Harris Mylonas. (2016). Threats to Territorial Integrity, National Mass Schooling, and Linguistic Commonality. *Comparative Political Studies*, 49 (11), 1446–79.

Dark, Ken. (2001). Proto-industrialization and the Economy of the Roman Empire. In Michel Polfer (Ed.), *L'artisanat romain : évolutions, continuités et ruptures (Italie et provinces occidentales)* (pp. 19–29). Montagnac, France: Mergoil.

Davenport, Lauren. (2020). The Fluidity of Racial Classifications. *Annual Review of Political Science*, 23, 221–40.

Davidson, Neil. (2000). *The Origins of Scottish Nationhood*. London: Pluto Press.

Davies, I. R. L., C. Macdermid, G. G. Corbett, et al. (1992). Color Terms in Setswana: A Linguistic and Perceptual Approach. *Linguistics*, 30(6), 1065–103.

Davies, P. A. (2017). Articulating Status in Ancient Greece: Status (In)Consistency as a New Approach. *Cambridge Classical Journal*, 63, 29–52.

Davis, Natalie Z. (1983). *The Return of Martin Guerre*. Cambridge, MA: Harvard University Press.

De Micheli, David. (2021). Racial Reclassification and Political Identity Formation. *World Politics*, 73(1), 1–51.

Deane, Phyllis, and W. A. Cole. (1969). *British Economic Growth 1688–1959*. Cambridge: Cambridge University Press.

Declich, Francesca. (2000). Fostering Ethnic Reinvention: Gender Impact of Forced Migration on Bantu Somali Refugees in Kenya. *Cahiers d'Études Africaines*, 40 (157), 25–53.

Degn, Inge, Lisbeth V. Hansen, Anne Magnussen, and Jens R. Rasmussen. (2004). The Construction and Deconstruction of Nation and Identity in Modern Belgium. In Hans L. Hansen (Ed.), *Disciplines and Interdisciplinarity in Foreign Language Studies* (pp. 131–50). Copenhagen: Museum Tusculanum.

Depetris-Chauvin, Emilio, Ruben Durante, and Filipe Campante. (2020). Building Nations through Shared Experiences: Evidence from African Football. *American Economic Review*, 110(5), 1572–602.

Derks, Ton. (2009). Ethnic Identity in the Roman Frontier: The Epigraphy of Batavi and Other Lower Rhine Tribes. In Ton Derks and Nico Roymans (Eds.), *Ethnic Constructs in Antiquity: The Role of Power and Tradition* (pp. 239–82). Amsterdam: Amsterdam University Press.

Desbiens, Caroline, Carole Lévesque, and Iona Comat. (2016). 'Inventing New Places': Urban Aboriginal Visibility and the Co-Construction of Citizenship in Val-d'Or (Quebec). *City and Society*, 28(1), 74–98.

Deutsch, Karl W. (1953). The Growth of Nations: Some Recurrent Patterns of Political and Social Integration. *World Politics*, 5(2), 168–95.

Diaz, Kevin. (22 April 2007). Whose Riches? The Fight Over Mystic Lake. [Minneapolis] *Star Tribune*.

Dignam, John. (28 September 2001). Feds Rule Against Nipmucs' Recognition Bid; Band's Casino Plans are Dashed. [Worcester, MA] *Telegram & Gazette*, p. A1.

Doak, Kevin M. (1996). Ethnic Nationalism and Romanticism in Early Twentieth-Century Japan. *Journal of Japanese Studies*, 22(1), 77–103.

Doukakis, Anna. (2006). *Aboriginal People, Parliament and 'Protection' in New South Wales, 1856–1916*. Sydney: Federation Press.

Draper, John, and Joel S. Selway. (2019). A New Dataset on Horizontal Structural Ethnic Inequalities in Thailand in Order to Address Sustainable Development Goal 10. *Social Indicators Research*, 141(1), 275–97.

Dundar, Fuat. (2014). Measuring Assimilation: 'Mother Tongue' Question in Turkish Censuses and Nationalist Policy. *British Journal of Middle Eastern Studies*, 41(4), 385–405.

Easterly, William R., and Ross Levine. (1997). Africa's Growth Tragedy: Policies and Ethnic Divisions. *Quarterly Journal of Economics*, 112(4), 1203–50.

Eckert, Andreas. (1999). African Rural Entrepreneurs and Labor in the Cameroon Littoral. *Journal of African History*, 40(1), 109–26.

Edel, May. (1965). African Tribalism: Some Reflections on Uganda. *Political Science Quarterly*, 80(3), 357–72.

Edmunds, R. David. (2004). Native Americans and the United States, Canada and Mexico. In Philip Deloria and Neal Salisbury (Eds.), *A Companion to Native American History* (pp. 397–421). Indianapolis, IN: Wiley.

Eisenstadt, Shmuel N., and A. Shacher. (1987). *Society, Culture and Urbanization*. Newbury Park, CA: Sage.

Emberling, Geoff. (1997). Ethnicity in Complex Societies: Archaeological Perspectives. *Journal of Archaeological Research*, 5(4), 295–344.

Epstein, A. L. (1967). Urbanization and Social Change in Africa. *Current Anthropology*, 8(4), 275–95.

Ergil, Dogu. (2000). The Kurdish Question in Turkey. *Journal of Democracy*, 11(3), 122–35.

Eriksen, Thomas H. (1993). *Ethnicity and Nationalism: Anthropological Perspectives*. London: Pluto Press.

Erk, Jan. (2005). Sub-State Nationalism and the Left–Right Divide: Critical Junctures in the Formation of Nationalist Labour movements in Belgium. *Nations and Nationalism*, 11(4), 551–70.

Evans, Williams N., and Julie H. Topoleski. (2002). *The Social and Economic Impact of Native American Casinos*. NBER Working Paper #9198, National Bureau of Economic Research.

Farooq, Ghazi M., and Baran Tuncer. (1974). Fertility and Economic and Social Development in Turkey: A Cross-Sectional and Time Series Study. *Population Studies*, 28(2), 263–76.

Fearon, James D. (1999). *Why Ethnic Politics and 'Pork' Tend to Go Together*. Department of Political Science, Stanford University.

 (2003). Ethnic and Cultural Diversity by Country. *Journal of Economic Growth*, 8(2), 195–222.

Fearon, James D., and David D. Laitin. (2000). Violence and the Construction of Ethnic Identity. *International Organization*, 54(4), 845–77.

 (2003). Ethnicity, Insurgency, and Civil War. *American Political Science Review*, 97 (1), 75–90.

Feldmann, Horst. (2012). Ethnic Fractionalization and Unemployment. *Economics Letters*, 117(1), 192–5.

Ferguson, James. (2007). Formalities of Poverty: Thinking about Social Assistance in Neoliberal South Africa. *African Studies Review*, 50(2), 71–86.

Feyrer, James. (2009). *Trade and Income: Exploiting Time Series in Geography*. NBER Working Paper #14910, National Bureau of Economic Research.

Findley, Carter V. (2010). *Turkey, Islam and Modernity: A History, 1789–2007*. New Haven, CT: Yale University Press.

Fixico, Donald. (1991). *Urban Indians*. New York: Chelsea House.

 (2000). *The Urban Indian Experience in America*. Albuquerque: University of New Mexico Press.

 (2013). *Indian Resilience and Rebuilding*. Tucson: University of Arizona Press.

Foley, Gary. (2001). *Black Power in Redfern: 1968–1972*. Mimeo, accessed at <www.kooriweb.org/foley/resources/pdfs/228.pdf>

Foot, Sarah. (1996). The Making of Angelcynn: English Identity before the Norman Conquest. *Transactions of the Royal Historical Society*, 6, 25–49.

Fox, Sean. (2014). The Political Economy of Slums: Theory and Evidence from Sub-Saharan Africa. *World Development*, 54, 191–203.

Freille, Sebastian, M. Emranul Haque, and Richard Kneller. (2007). A Contribution to the Empirics of Press Freedom and Corruption. *European Journal of Political Economy*, 23, 838–62.

Frye, Dustin, Andrew Mollica, and Dominic P. Parker. (2020). *Ethnicity, Nationalism, and Inclusive Growth: Evidence from Tribal Nations*. Department of Economics, Vassar College.

Fukuyama, Francis. (2018). *Identity: The Demand for Dignity and the Politics of Resentment*. New York: Profile Books.

Fuller, Harcourt. (2008). *Civitatis Ghaniensis Conditor*: Kwame Nkrumah, Symbolic Nationalism and the Iconography of Ghanaian Money 1957 – The Golden Jubilee. *Nations and Nationalism*, 14(3), 520–41.

Furlan, Laura M. (2017). *Indigenous Cities: Urban Indian Fiction and the Histories of Relocation*. Lincoln: University of Nebraska Press.

Gagné, Natacha. (2013). *Being Maori in the City: Indigenous Everyday Life in Auckland*. Toronto: University of Toronto Press.

Galaty, John. (1982). Being 'Maasai'; Being 'People-of-Cattle': Ethnic Shifters in East Africa. *American Ethnologist*, 9(1), 1–20.

Gale, Fay. (1972). *Urban Aborigines*. Canberra: Australian National University Press.

Gallen, Trevor, and Ben Raymond. (2020). *Broken Instruments*. Unpublished paper, Department of Economics, Purdue University.

Gaotlhobogwe, M. (25 February 2013). Tlokweng Land War. [Gaborone] *Mmegi*.

Gapa, Angela. (2017). Identity Management: The Creation of Resource Allocative Criteria in Botswana. *African Studies Quarterly*, 17(1), 1–22.

Geary, Patrick J. (2002). *The Myth of Nations: The Medieval Origins of Europe*. Princeton: Princeton University Press.

Geddes, Linda. (18 June 2011). Tribal Wars. *New Scientist*, 818.

Gellner, Ernest. (1964). *Thought and Change*. London: Weidenfeld & Nicolson.

(1994). *Encounters with Nationalism*. Oxford: Blackwell.

(2006 [1983]). *Nations and Nationalism*. Oxford: Blackwell.

Gerring, John. (2007). *Case Study Research: Principles and Practices*. Cambridge: Cambridge University Press.

Gibson, Campbell. (1973). Urbanization in New Zealand: A Comparative Analysis. *Demography*, 10(1), 71–84.

Gil-White, Francisco J. (1999). How Thick Is Blood? The Plot thickens …: If Ethnic Actors are Primordialists, What Remains of the Circumstantialist/Primordialist Controversy? *Ethnic and Racial Studies*, 22(5), 789–820.

Giliomee, Hermann. (1989). The Beginnings of Afrikaner Ethnic Consciousness, 1850–1915. In Leroy Vail (Ed.), *The Creation of Tribalism in Southern Africa* (pp. 21–54). Berkeley: University of California Press.

Gillingham, John. (1992). The Beginnings of English Imperialism. *Journal of Historical Sociology*, 5(4), 392–409.

Giordano, Benito. (2000). Italian Regionalism or 'Padanian' Nationalism: the Political Project of the Lega Nord in Italian politics. *Political Geography*, 19(4), 445–71.

Glazer, Nathan, and Daniel P. Moynihan. (1963). *Beyond the Melting Pot: The Negroes, Puerto Ricans, Jews, Italians and Irish of New York City*. Cambridge, MA: Harvard University Press.

Gluckman, Max. (1960). Tribalism in Modern British Central Africa. *Cahiers d'Études Africaines*, 1(1), 55–70.

Gökay, Bülent. (Ed.) (1997a). *British Documents on Foreign Affairs: Reports and Papers from the Foreign Office Confidential Print. Part II: From the First to the Second World War. Series B: Turkey, Iran and the Middle East, 1918–1939*. (Vol. 32: Turkey, January 1930–December 1932). Frederick, MD: University Publications of America.

(Ed.) (1997b). *British Documents on Foreign Affairs: Reports and Papers from the Foreign Office Confidential Print. Part II: From the First to the Second World War. Series B: Turkey, Iran and the Middle East, 1918–1939*. (Vol. 34: Turkey, January 1936–December 1937). Frederick, MD: University Publications of America.

(Ed.) (2008). *British Documents on Foreign Affairs: Reports and Papers from the Foreign Office Confidential Print. Part V: From 1951 through 1956. Series B: Near and Middle East* (Vol. 7: Afghanistan, Turkey, Persia, Iraq and Levant (General), 1954). Frederick, MD: University Publications of America.

Goldsmith, Sarah S., and Risa Mueller. (2003). *Nations Within: The Four Sovereign Tribes of Louisiana.* Baton Rouge: Louisiana State University.

Gollin, Douglas, Remi Jedwab, and Dietrich Vollrath. (2016). Urbanization With and Without Industrialization. *Journal of Economic Growth,* 21(1), 35–70.

Gollin, Douglas, Stephen Parente, and Richard Rogerson. (2002). The Role of Agriculture in Development. *American Economic Review,* 92(2), 160–4.

Gören, Erkan. (2014). How Ethnic Diversity Affects Economic Growth. *World Development,* 59, 275–97.

Gourevitch, Peter A. (1979). The Reemergence of 'Peripheral Nationalisms': Some Comparative Speculations on the Spatial Distribution of Political Leadership and Economic Growth. *Comparative Studies in Society and History,* 21(3), 303–22.

Gover, Kirsty, and Natalie Baird. (2002). Identifying the Māori Treaty Partner. *University of Toronto Law Journal,* 52(1), 39–68.

Government of Botswana (1979). *National Development Plan 1979–1985.* Ministry of Finance and Development Planning. Gaborone.

  (1991). *Presidential Commission of Inquiry into Land Problems in Mogoditshane and other Peri-Urban Villages.* Gaborone.

  (2000). *Report of the Presidential Commission of Inquiry into Sections 77, 78 and 79 of the Constitution of Botswana.* Gaborone.

Government of Turkey (1936). *Genel nüfus sayimi, 20 ilktesrin 1935 [Population Census of October 20, 1935].* Ankara: Office of the Census.

Government of Uganda (1987). *Report of the Commission of Inquiry into the Local Government System.* Kampala.

  (2003). *The Report of the Commission of Inquiry (Constitutional Review): Findings and Recommendations.* Kampala.

Grabolle-Çeliker, Anna. (2013). *Kurdish Life in Contemporary Turkey: Migration, Gender and Ethnic Identity.* London: I.B. Tauris.

Gray, Alan. (1989). Aboriginal Migration to the Cities. *Journal of the Australian Population Association,* 6(2), 122–44.

Gray, Albert L., Jr. (1989). The Economy of the Somali Democratic Republic in the 1980s. *Ufahamu: A Journal of African Studies,* 17(2), 118–37.

Green, Elliott D. (2006). Ethnicity and the Politics of Land Tenure Reform in Uganda. *Commonwealth and Comparative Politics,* 44(3), 370–88.

  (2007). Demography, Diversity and Nativism in Contemporary Uganda: Evidence from Uganda. *Nations and Nationalism,* 13(4), 717–36.

  (2008a). Decentralization and Conflict in Uganda. *Conflict, Security and Development,* 8(4), 427–50.

  (2008b). Understanding the Limits to Ethnic Change: Evidence from Uganda's Lost Counties. *Perspectives on Politics,* 6(3), 473–85.

  (2010a). Ethnicity and Nationhood in Precolonial Africa: The Case of Buganda. *Nationalism and Ethnic Politics,* 16(1), 1–21.

  (2010b). Patronage, District Creation and Reform in Uganda. *Studies in Comparative International Development,* 45(1), 83–103.

  (2013). Explaining African Ethnic Diversity. *International Political Science Review,* 34(3), 235–53.

(2018). Ethnicity, National Identity and the State: Evidence from Sub-Saharan Africa. *British Journal of Political Science*, 50(2), 757–9.

(2021). The Politics of Ethnic Identity in Sub-Saharan Africa. *Comparative Political Studies*, 54(7), 1197–226.

Greenfeld, Liah. (1992). *Nationalism: Five Roads to Modernity*. Cambridge, MA: Harvard University Press.

Gregory, Angela. (18 July 2001). Urban Māori Victims of History. *New Zealand Herald*.

Griffin, John H. (2004 [1961]). *Black Like Me*. San Antonio, TX: Wings Press.

Griffiths, Anne M. O. (2019). *Transformations on the Ground: Space and the Power of Land in Botswana*. Bloomington: Indiana University Press.

Grigoriadis, Ioannis N. (2006). Political Participation of Turkey's Kurds and Alevis: A Challenge for Turkey's Democratic Consolidation. *Southeast European and Black Sea Studies*, 6(4), 445–61.

Gruen, Erich S. (2013). Did Romans Have an Ethnic Identity? *Antichthon*, 47, 1–17.

Grusky, David. (1983). Industrialization and the Status Attainment Process: The Thesis of Industrialism Reconsidered. *American Sociological Review*, 48(4), 494–506.

Gulliver, P. H. (1969). Introduction. In P. H. Gulliver (Ed.), *Tradition and Transition in East Africa: Studies of the Tribal Element in the Modern Era* (pp. 5–38). London: Routledge.

Gundel, Joakim. (2003). The Migration–Development Nexus: Somalia Case Study. *International Migration*, 40(5), 255–81.

Gündüz-Hoşgör, Ayşe., and Jeroen Smits. (2002). Intermarriage between Turks and Kurds in Contemporary Turkey: Inter-Ethnic Relations in an Urbanizing Environment. *European Sociological Review*, 18(4), 417–32.

Gürel, Burak. (2011). Agrarian Change and Labour Supply in Turkey, 1950–1980. *Journal of Agrarian Change*, 11(2), 195–219.

Guy, Kolleen M. (2003). *When Champagne Became French: Wine and the Making of a National Identity*. Baltimore: Johns Hopkins University Press.

Gwebu, Thando D. (2006a). Contemporary Patterns, Trends and Development Implications of International Migration from Botswana. In Aderanti Adepoju, Ton Van Naerssen, and Annelies Zoomers (Eds.), *International Migration and National Development in Sub-Saharan Africa: Viewpoints and Policy Initiatives in the Countries of Origin* (pp. 117–40). Leiden: Africa-Studiecentrum.

(2006b). Towards a Theoretical Exploration of the Differential Urbanization Model in Sub-Saharan Africa: The Botswana Case. *Tijdschrift voor Economische en Sociale Geografie*, 97(4), 418–33.

Habtu, Alem (2004). Ethnic Pluralism as an Organizing Principle of the Ethiopian Federation. *Dialectical Anthropology*, 28(2), 91–123.

Habyarimana, James, Macartan Humphreys, Daniel N. Posner, and Jeremy M. Weinstein. (2007). Why Does Ethnic Diversity Undermine Public Goods Provision? *American Political Science Review*, 101(4), 709–26.

Hale, Charles R. (1997). Cultural Politics of Identity in Latin America. *Annual Review of Anthropology*, 26, 567–90.

Hale, Henry E. (2004). Explaining Ethnicity. *Comparative Political Studies*, 37(4), 458–85.

(2008). *The Foundations of Ethnic Politics: Separatism of States and Nations in Eurasia and the World.* Cambridge: Cambridge University Press.

Hall, Jonathan M. (1997). *Ethnic Identity in Greek Antiquity.* Cambridge: Cambridge University Press.

(2002). *Hellenicity: Between Ethnicity and Culture.* Chicago: University of Chicago Press.

Hammett, Daniel. (2012). Envisaging the Nation: The Philatelic Iconography of Transforming South African National Narratives. *Geopolitics, 17*(3), 526–52.

Hann, Chris. (1997). Ethnicity, Language and Politics in North-East Turkey. In Cora Govers and Hans Vermeulen (Eds.), *The Politics of Ethnic Consciousness* (pp. 121–56). New York: St. Martin's.

Hann, Chris, and Idikó Béller-Hann. (1998). Markets, Morality and Modernity in North-East Turkey. In T. M. Wilson & H. Donnan (Eds.), *Border Identities: Nation and State at International Frontiers* (pp. 237–62). Cambridge: Cambridge University Press.

Hansen, Gary D., and Edward C. Prescott. (2002). Malthus to Solow. *American Economic Review, 92*(4), 1205–17.

Hanson, Allan. (1989). The Making of the Maori: Culture Invention and Its Logic. *American Anthropologist, 91*(4), 890–902.

Hanson, Jeffrey R. (1997). Ethnicity and the Looking Glass: The Dialectics of National Indian Identity. *American Indian Quarterly, 21*(2), 195–208.

Harbers, Imke. (2010). Decentralization and the Development of Nationalized Party Systems in New Democracies: Evidence from Latin America. *Comparative Political Studies, 43*(5), 606–27.

Harkins, Arthur M., and Richard G. Woods. (1969). *The Social Programs and Political Styles of Minneapolis Indians: An Interim Report.* Minneapolis: University of Minnesota.

Harlow, Ray. (2012). *Maori: A Linguistic Introduction.* Cambridge: Cambridge University Press.

Harries, Patrick. (1989). Exclusion, Classification and Internal Colonialism: The Emergence of Ethnicity Among the Tsonga-Speakers of South Africa. In Leroy Vail (Ed.), *The Creation of Tribalism in Southern Africa* (pp. 82–117). Berkeley: University of California Press.

Harvey, Charles. (1992). Botswana: Is the Economic Miracle Over? *Journal of African Economies, 1*(3), 335–68.

Hattenstone, Simon. (7 September 2019). Anthony Ekundayo Lennon on Being Accused of 'Passing' as a Black Man: 'It Felt like an Assassination'. *Guardian.*

Hauge, Jostein, and Ha-Joon Chang. (2019). The Role of Manufacturing Versus Services in Economic Development. In Patrizio Bianchi, Clemente R. Duran, and Sandrine Labory (Eds.), *Transforming Industrial Policy for the Digital Age: Production, Territories and Structural Change* (pp. 12–36). Cheltenham: Edward Elgar.

Hausmann, Ricardo, Brad Cunningham, John Matovu, Rosie Osire, and Kelly Wyett. (2014). *How Should Uganda Grow?* ESID Working Paper #30, Effective States and Inclusive Development Research Centre, School of Environment and Development, University of Manchester.

Hawkins, Cameron. (2011). Spartans and Perioikoi: The Organization and Ideology of the Lakedaimonian Army in the Fourth Century B.C.E. *Greek, Roman and Byzantine Studies, 51*, 401–34.

Hayes, Bernadette C., and Ian McAllister. (2001). Sowing Dragon's Teeth: Public Support for Political Violence and Paramilitarism in Northern Ireland. *Political Studies, 49*(5), 901–22.

Haynes, Kyle. (2016). Diversity and Diversion: How Ethnic Composition Affects Diversionary Conflict. *International Studies Quarterly, 60*(2), 258–71.

Hechter, Michael. (1975). *Internal Colonialism: The Celtic Fringe in British National Development, 1536–1966*. London: Routledge.

Hegre, Håvard, and Nicholas Sambanis. (2006). Sensitivity Analysis of Empirical Results on Civil War Onset. *Journal of Conflict Resolution, 50*(4), 508–35.

Heiberg, Marianne. (1975). Insiders/Outsiders: Basque Nationalism. *European Journal of Sociology, 16*(2), 169–93.

Helander, Bernhard. (1996). The Hubeer in the Land of Plenty: Land, Labor and Vulnerability among a Southern Somali Clan. In Catherine Besteman and Lee V. Cassanelli (Eds.), *The Struggle for Land in Southern Somalia: The War Behind the War*. Boulder, CO: Westview Press.

Heper, Metin. (2007). *The State and Kurds in Turkey: The Question of Assimilation*. Basingstoke: Palgrave Macmillan.

Hill, Richard S. (2012). Maori Urban Migration and the Assertion of Indigeneity in Aotearoa/New Zealand, 1945–1975. *Interventions, 14*(2), 256–78.

(2016). New Zealand Maori: The Quest for Indigenous Autonomy. *Ethnopolitics, 15* (1), 144–65.

Hitchcock, Robert K., and Hassan Hussein. (1987). Agricultural and Non-agricultural Settlements for Drought-afflicted Pastoralists in Somalia. *Disasters, 11*(1), 30–9.

Hjort, Jonas. (2010). Pre-colonial Culture, Post-colonial Economic Success? The Tswana and the African Economic Miracle. *Economic History Review, 63*(3), 688–709.

(2014). Ethnic Divisions and Production in Firms. *Quarterly Journal of Economics, 129*(4), 1899–946.

Hobsbawm, Eric J. (1992). *Nations and Nationalism since 1780: Programme, Myth, Reality* (2nd ed.). Cambridge: Cambridge University Press.

(1999). *Industry and Empire: From 1750 to the Present Day*. New York: Free Press.

Hokowhitu, Brendan. (2013). Producing Indigeneity. In Evelyn Peters and Chris Andersen (Eds.), *Indigenous in the City: Contemporary Identities and Cultural Innovation* (pp. 354–76). Vancouver: UBC Press.

Holleran, Claire. (2012). *Shopping in Ancient Rome: The Retail Trade in the Late Republic and the Principate*. Oxford: Oxford University Press.

Holm, John D., and Emmanuel Botlhale. (2008). Persistence and Decline of Traditional Authority in Modern Botswana Politics. *Botswana Notes and Records, 40*, 74–87.

Horowitz, Donald L. (2000). *Ethnic Groups in Conflict*. Berkeley: University of California Press.

Hotham, David. (1972). *The Turks*. London: John Murray.

Howard, James H. (1955). Pan-Indian Culture of Oklahoma. *Scientific Monthly, 81*(5), 215–20.

Huang, Shu-Min, and Shao-Hua Liu. (2016). Discrimination and Incorporation of Taiwanese Indigenous Austronesian Peoples. *Asian Ethnicity*, 17(2), 294–312.

Ignatieff, Michael. (1998). *The Warrior's Honor: Ethnic War and the Modern Conscience*. London: Vintage.

Independent, The. (7 February 2020). MP Lutanywa Granted Leave to Introduce Constitutional Amendment Bill. *The Independent*.

Ingiriis, Mohamed H. (2016). *The Suicidal State in Somalia: The Rise and Fall of the Siad Barre Regime, 1969–1991*. Lanham, MD: University Press of America.

International Labour Organization (1989). *Generating Employment and Incomes in Somalia: Report of an ILO/JASPA Inter-Disciplinary Employment and Project-Identification Mission to Somalia*. Geneva: International Labour Organization.

Iverson, Peter, and Wade Davies. (2015). *'We Are Still Here': American Indians since 1890* (2nd ed.). Oxford: Wiley Blackwell.

Jackson, Deborah D. (2002). *Our Elders Lived It: American Indian Identity in the City*. Dekalb: Northern Illinois University Press.

Jacobsen-Bia, Kristina. (2014). Radmilla's Voice: Music Genre, Blood Quantum, and Belonging on the Navajo Nation. *Cultural Anthropology*, 29(2), 385–410.

Jamal, Vali, and John Weeks. (1993). *Africa Misunderstood or Whatever Happened to the Rural–Urban Gap?* London: Macmillan.

Jansen, Tore, and Joseph Tsonope. (1991). *Birth of a National Language: The History of Setswana*. Gaborone: Heinemann Botswana.

Jarvenpa, Robert. (1985). The Political Economy and Political Ethnicity of American Indian Adaptations and Identities. *Ethnic and Racial Studies*, 8(1), 29–48.

Jia, Ruixue, and Torsten Perrsson. (2021). Choosing Ethnicity: The Interplay between Individual and Social Motives. *Journal of the European Economic Association*, 19(2), 1203–48.

Johnson, Corey, and Amanda Coleman. (2012). The Internal Other: Exploring the Dialectical Relationship Between Regional Exclusion and the Construction of National Identity. *Annals of the Association of American Geographers*, 102(4), 863–80.

Jones, David S. (2006). The Persistence of American Indian Health Disparities. *American Journal of Public Health*, 96(12), 2122–34.

Kalaycıoğlu, Ersin. (2005). *Turkish Dynamics: Bridge Across Troubled Lands*. New York: Palgrave Macmillan.

Kallen, Horace M. (1996 [1915]). Democracy Versus the Melting-Pot: A Study of American Nationality. In Serner Sollors (Ed.), *Theories of Ethnicity: A Classical Reader* (pp. 67–92). New York: New York University Press.

Kamusella, Tomasz. (2004). The Szlonzokian Ethnolect in the Context of German and Polish Nationalisms. *Studies in Ethnicity and Nationalism*, 4(1), 19–39.

(2005). Upper Silesia 1870–1920: Between Region, Religion, Nation and Ethnicity. *East European Quarterly*, 38(4), 443–62.

Kanovsky, Martin. (2007). Essentialism and Folksociology: Ethnicity Again. *Journal of Cognition and Culture*, 7(3–4), 241–81.

Karaömerlioğlu, M. Asim. (1998). The People's Houses and the Cult of the Peasant in Turkey. *Middle Eastern Studies*, 34(4), 67–91.

Karpat, Kemal H. (1963). The People's Houses in Turkey: Establishment and Growth. *Middle East Journal*, 17(1/2), 55–67.

Kasfir, Nelson. (1979). Explaining Ethnic Political Participation. *World Politics, 31*(3), 365–88.

Kasimis, Demetra. (2018). *The Perpetual Immigrant and the Limits of Athenian Democracy.* Cambridge: Cambridge University Press.

Kaya, Ayhan. (2005). Cultural Reification in Circassian Diaspora: Stereotypes, Prejudices and Ethnic Relations. *Journal of Ethnic and Migration Studies, 31*(1), 129–49.

Kedourie, Elie. (1960). *Nationalism.* London: Hutchinson.

Keegan, Peter J. (2017). Māori Dialect Issues and Māori Language Ideologies in the Revitalisation Era. *MAI Journal, 6*(2), 129–42.

Keiha, Pare, and Paul Moon. (2008). The Emergence and Evolution of Urban Maori Authorities: A Response to Maori Urbanisation. *Te Kaharoa, 1,* 1–17.

Kelley, Judith G. (2004). *Ethnic Politics in Europe: The Power of Norms and Incentives.* Princeton: Princeton University Press.

Kelly, Casey R. (2011). Blood-Speak: Ward Churchill and the Racialization of American Indian Identity. *Communication and Critical/Cultural Studies, 8*(3), 240–65.

Kennedy, Rebecca F. (2014). *Immigrant Women in Athens: Gender, Ethnicity, and Citizenship in the Classical City* New York: Routledge.

Keoregn, Ephraim. (15 June 2012). Tlokweng: A Maelstrom of Politics, Poverty and Tribalism in the land Question. [Gaborone] *Mmegi.*

Kersey, Harry A. (2003). The Maori Fisheries Allocation Model of 2003: Distributive Justice or a Violation of Treaty Rights? *Maritime Studies, 128,* 1–8.

Kertzer, David, and Dominique Arel. (Eds.). (2002). *Census and Identity: The Politics of Race, Ethnicity and Language in National Censuses* Cambridge: Cambridge University Press.

Keyes, Charles (1966). Ethnic Identity and Loyalty of Villagers in Northeastern Thailand. *Asian Survey, 6*(7), 362–9.

  (2002). Presidential Address: 'The Peoples of Asia' – Science and Politics in the Classification of Ethnic Groups in Thailand, China, and Vietnam. *Journal of Asian Studies, 61*(4), 1163–204.

Kibre, Pearl. (1948). *The Nations in the Mediaeval Universities.* Cambridge, MA: Mediaeval Academy of America.

Kiliç, H. Ayla. (1998). Democratization, Human Rights and Ethnic Policies in Turkey. *Journal of Muslim Minority Affairs, 18*(1), 91–110.

King, Gary, and Langche Zeng. (2001). Improving Forecasts of State Failure. *World Politics, 53*(4), 623–58.

Kohn, Hans. (1945). *The Idea of Nationalism: A Study in its Origins and Background.* New York: Macmillan.

Koo, Hagen. (2001). *Korean Workers: The Culture and Politics of Class Formation.* Ithaca, NY: Cornell University Press.

Kotlowski, Dean J. (2003). Alcatraz, Wounded Knee, and Beyond: The Nixon and Ford Administrations Respond to Native American Protest. *Pacific Historical Review, 72* (2), 201–27.

Kramon, Eric, and Daniel N. Posner. (2016). Ethnic Favoritism in Education in Kenya. *Quarterly Journal of Political Science, 11*(1), 1–58.

Krawchenko, Bohdan. (1980). The Impact of Industrialization on the Social Structure of Ukraine. *Canadian Slavonic Papers / Revue Canadienne des Slavistes, 22*(3), 338–57.

Kudamatsu, Masayuki. (2012). Has Democratization Reduced Infant Mortality in Sub-Saharan Africa? Evidence from Micro Data. *Journal of the European Economic Association*, 10(6), 1294–317.

Kumar, Krishan. (2003). *The Making of English National Identity*. Cambridge: Cambridge University Press.

(2010). Negotiating English Identity: Englishness, Britishness and the Future of the United Kingdom. *Nations and Nationalism*, 16(3), 469–87.

Kuyucu, Ali T. (2005). Ethno-religious 'Unmixing' of 'Turkey': 6–7 September Riots as a Case in Turkish Nationalism. *Nations and Nationalism*, 11(3), 361–80.

Kwesiga, Pascal. (9 November 2019). Why Indians Want to be a Tribe in Uganda. [Kampala] *New Vision*.

LaGrand, James B. (2002). *Indian Metropolis: Native Americans in Chicago, 1945–75*. Urbana: University of Illinois Press.

Laitin, David D. (1976). The Political Economy of Military Rule in Somalia. *Journal of Modern African Studies*, 14(3), 449–68.

(1979). The War in the Ogaden: Implications for Siyaad's Role in Somali History. *Journal of Modern African Studies*, 17(1), 95–115.

(1998). *Identity in Formation: The Russian-Speaking Populations in the Near Abroad*. Ithaca, NY: Cornell University Press.

(2007). *Nations, States and Violence*. Oxford: Oxford University Press.

Laitin, David D., and Daniel N. Posner. (2001). The Implications of Constructivism for Constructing Ethnic Fractionalization Indices. *APSA-CP*, 12, 13–17.

Laitin, David D., and Said S. Samatar. (1984). Somalia and the World Economy. *Review of African Political Economy*, 11(30), 58–72.

Lamprou, Alexandros. (2015). *Nation-Building in Modern Turkey: The 'People's Houses', the State and the Citizen*. London: I.B. Tauris.

Lange, Matthew. (2012). *Educations in Ethnic Violence: Identity, Educational Bubbles and Resource Mobilization*. Cambridge: Cambridge University Press.

Lape, Susan. (2010). *Race and Citizen Identity in the Classical Athenian Democracy*. Cambridge: Cambridge University Press.

Laws, Glynis, Ian Davies, Greville Corbett, Tiny Jerrett, and David Jerrett. (1995). Colour Terms in Setswana: The Effects of Age and Urbanization. *Language Sciences*, 17(1), 49–64.

Lerner, Daniel. (1958). *The Passing of Traditional Society: Modernizing the Middle East*. New York: Free Press.

Levine, Hal B. (1999). Reconstructing Ethnicity. *Journal of the Royal Anthropological Institute*, 5(2), 165–80.

Lewis, Geoffrey. (1974). *Modern Turkey* (Vol. 4). London: Ernest Benn.

Lewis, I. M. (2002). *A Modern History of the Somali* (4th ed.). Oxford: James Currey.

Lewis, Milton J. (2003). *The People's Health: Public Health in Australia, 1788–1950*. Westport, CT: Praeger.

Lewis, W. Arthur. (1954). Economic Development with Unlimited Supplies of Labour. *Manchester School*, 22(2), 139–91.

Lieberman, Evan S. (2007). Ethnic Politics, Risk, and Policy-Making: A Cross-National Statistical Analysis of Government Responses to HIV/AIDS. *Comparative Political Studies*, 40(12), 1407–32.

Lieberman Evan S. and Prerna Singh. (2012). The Institutional Origins of Ethnic Violence. *Comparative Politics, 45*(1), 1–24.

(2017). Census Enumeration and Group Conflict: A Global Analysis of the Consequences of Counting. *World Politics, 69*(1), 1–53.

Lipset, Seymour M. (1959). Some Social Requisites of Democracy: Economic Development and Political Legitimacy. *American Political Science Review, 53*(1), 69–105.

Littlefield, Alice. (1998). Native American Labor and Public Policy in the United States. In Susan Lobo and Steve Talbot (Eds.), *Native American Voices: A Reader* (pp. 333–40). New York: Longman.

Lomas, Kathryn. (1996). Greeks, Romans and Others: Problems of Colonialism and Ethnicity in Southern Italy. In Jane Webster and Nicholas J. Cooper (Eds.), *Roman Imperialism: Post-Colonial Perspectives* (Vol. 3, pp. 135–44). Leicester: Leicester Archaeological Monographs.

(1998). Roman Imperialism and the City in Italy. In Ray Laurence and Joanne Berry (Eds.), *Cultural Identity in the Roman Empire* (pp. 64–78). London: Routledge.

Lonsdale, John. (2012). Ethnic Patriotism and Markets in African History. In Hiroyki Hino, John Lonsdale, Gustav Ranis, and Frances Stewart (Eds.), *Ethnic Diversity and Economic Instability in Africa: Interdisciplinary Perspectives* (pp. 19–55). Cambridge: Cambridge University Press.

Luebke, Frederick C. (1977). Ethnic Group Settlement on the Great Plains. *Western Historical Quarterly, 8*(4), 405–30.

Luraghi, Nino. (2008). *The Ancient Messenians: Constructions of Ethnicity and Memory*. Cambridge: Cambridge University Press.

Maaka, Roger C. A. (1994). The New Tribe: Conflicts and Continuities in the Social Organization of Urban Maori. *The Contemporary Pacific, 6*(2), 311–36.

Maaka, Roger C. A. and Augie Fleras. (2000). Engaging with Indigeneity: Tino Rangatiratanga in Aotearoa. In Duncan Ivison, Paul Patton, and Will Sanders (Eds.), *Political Theory and the Rights of Indigenous Peoples* (pp. 89–112). Cambridge: Cambridge University Press.

Mahasenan, Natesan, Steve Smith, and Kenneth Humphreys. (2002). *The Cement Industry and Global Climate Change: Current and Potential Future Cement Industry CO_2 Emissions*. Richland, WA: Pacific Northwest National Laboratory.

Makgala, Christian J., and Mokganedi Z. Botlhomilwe. (2017). Elite Interests and Political Participation in Botswana, 1966–2014. *Journal of Contemporary African Studies, 35*(1), 54–72.

Malešević, Sinisa. (2013). *Nation-States and Nationalisms*. Cambridge: Polity Press.

Mamdani, Mahmood. (1996). *Citizen and Subject: Contemporary Africa and the Legacy of Late Colonialism*. Princeton: Princeton University Press.

(2020). *Neither Settler nor Native: The Making and Unmaking of Permanent Minorities*. Cambridge, MA: Harvard University Press.

Manby, Bronwen. (2018). *Statelessness and Citizenship in the East African Community*. Nairobi, Kenya: NHCR Regional Service Centre.

Mango, Andrew. (1994). Turks and Kurds. *Middle Eastern Studies, 30*(4), 975–97.

Manotas–Hidalgo, Beatriz, Fidel Pérez-Sebastián, and Miguel A. Campo-Bescós. (2021). The Role of Ethnic Characteristics in the Effect of Income Shocks on African Conflict. *World Development, 137*, 105153.

Marcson, Simon. (1950). A Theory of Intermarriage and Assimilation. *Social Forces, 29* (1), 75–8.

Martinez, Julia. (1997). Problematising Aboriginal Nationalism. *Aboriginal History, 21,* 133–47.

Marx, Karl. (1964 [1857–8]). *Pre-Capitalist Economic Foundations.* New York: International Publishers.

(1978 [1852]). The Eighteenth Brumaire of Louis Bonaparte. In Robert C. Tucker (Ed.), *The Marx–Engels Reader* (2nd ed., pp. 594–617). New York: W.W. Norton.

(1978 [1853]). The British Rule in India. In Robert C. Tucker (Ed.), *The Marx–Engels Reader* (2nd ed., pp. 653–8). New York: W.W. Norton.

Marx, Karl, and Friedrich Engels. (1947 [1846]). *The German Ideology.* New York: International Publishers.

(1978 [1848]). Manifesto of the Communist Party. In Robert C. Tucker (Ed.), *The Marx–Engels Reader* (2nd ed., pp. 469–500). New York: W.W. Norton.

Matemba, Yonah H. (2003). The Pre-colonial Political History of BaKgatla ba ga Mmanaana of Botswana, c.1600–1881. *Botswana Notes and Records, 35,* 53–67.

Mathisen, Ralph. (2009). *Provinciales, Gentiles,* and Marriages between Romans and Barbarians in the Late Roman Empire. *Journal of Roman Studies, 99,* 140–55.

Mauro, Paulo. (1995). Corruption and Growth. *Quarterly Journal of Economics, 110* (3), 681–712.

Maynard, John. (1997). Fred Maynard and the Australian Aboriginal Progressive Association (AAPA): One God, One Aim, One Destiny. *Aboriginal History, 21,* 1–13.

McCrone, David. (2002). Who Do You Say You Are? Making Sense of National Identities in Modern Britain. *Ethnicities,* 2(3), 301–20.

McGechan, J. (2003). High Court–Fisheries Settlement, Urban Maori Challenge. *Maori Law Review,* 2003–2004, 7–10.

Meeker, Michael E. (1971). The Black Sea Turks: Some Aspects of Their Ethnic and Cultural Background. *International Journal of Middle East Studies,* 2(4), 318–45.

Menkhaus, Ken. (2003). Bantu Ethnic Identities in Somalia. *Annales d'Ethiopie, 19,* 323–39.

Méon, Pierre-Guillaume, and Khalid Sekkat. (2008). Institutional Quality and Trade: Which Institutions? Which Trade? *Economic Inquiry,* 46(2), 227–40.

Meredith, Martin. (2007). *Diamonds, Gold and War: The Making of South Africa.* London: Pocket Books.

Merlan, Francesca. (2005). Indigenous Movements in Australia. *Annual Review of Anthropology,* 34(1), 473–94.

Metge, Joan. (1964). *A New Maori Migration: Rural and Urban Relations in Northern New Zealand.* London: Athlone Press.

(1995). *New Growth from Old: The Whanau in the Modern World.* Wellington, NZ: Victoria University Press.

Metz, Bert, Ogunlade Davidson, Heleen De Coninck, Manuela Loos, and Leo Meyer. (Eds.). (2005). *IPCC Special Report on Carbon Dioxide Capture and Storage.* Cambridge: Cambridge University Press.

Michaelides, Alexander, Andreas Milidonis, and George P. Nishiotis. (2019). Private Information in Currency Markets. *Journal of Financial Economics*, *131*(3), 643–65.

Michalopoulos, Stelios. (2012). The Origins of Ethnolinguistic Diversity: Theory and Evidence. *American Economic Review*, *102*(4), 1508–39.

Michalopoulos, Stelios, Andreas Naghavi, and Giovanni Prarolo. (2018). Trade and Geography in the Spread of Islam. *Economic Journal*, *128*(616), 3210–41.

Miguel, Edward, and Mary K. Gugerty. (2005). Ethnic Diversity, Social Sanctions, and Public Goods in Kenya. *Journal of Public Economics*, *89*(11–12), 2325–68.

Miguel, Edward, Shanker Satyanath, and Ernest Sergenti. (2004). Economic Shocks and Civil Conflict: An Instrumental Variables Approach. *Journal of Political Economy*, *112*(4), 725–53.

Miller, Alexei. (2015). The Romanov Empire and the Russian Nation. In Stefan Berger and Alexei Miller (Eds.), *Nationalizing Empires* (pp. 309–68). Budapest: Central European University Press.

Miller, Susan A. (2005). Seminoles and Africans under Seminole Law: Sources and Discourses of Tribal Sovereignty and 'Black Indian' Entitlement. *Wicazo Sa Review*, *20*(1), 23–47.

Min, Brian. (2015). *Power and the Vote: Elections and Electricity in the Developing World*. Cambridge: Cambridge University Press.

Minns, Chris, Clare H. Crowston, Raoul De Kerf, et al. (2019). The Extent of Citizenship in Pre-industrial England, Germany, and the Low Countries. *European Review of Economic History*, *24*(3), 601–25.

Moeng, Gothataone, and Lawrence Seretse. (15 June 2012). More Land Lottery in the Offing. [Gaborone] *Mmegi*.

Moerman, Michael. (1965). Ethnic Identification in a Complex Civilization: Who are the Lue? *American Anthropologist*, *67*(5), 1215–30.

Mogalakwe, Monageng. (1997). *The State and Organized Labour in Botswana: 'Liberal Democracy' in Emergent Capitalism*. Aldershot: Ashgate.

Moisa, Ray. (1998). The BIA Relocation Program. In Susan Lobo and Steve Talbot (Eds.), *Native American Voices: A Reader* (pp. 154–8). New York: Longman.

Molosiwa, Phuthego P. (2013). *'The Tragedy of the Ababirwas': Cattle Herding, Power and the Socio-Environmental History of the Ethnic Identity of the Babirwa in Botswana, 1920 to the Present* (PhD Dissertation). University of Minnesota.

Monitor, The (13 June 2008). Uganda: Ethnic Minority Groups Demand Review of the Constitution. *The [Kampala] Monitor*.

(11 June 2013). Bunyoro King Warns Bagungu Against Secession. *The [Kampala] Monitor*.

Montalvo, José G., and Marta Reynal-Querol. (2005a). Ethnic Diversity and Economic Development. *Journal of Development Economics*, *76*(2), 293–323.

(2005b). Ethnic Polarization, Potential Conflict, and Civil Wars. *American Economic Review*, *95*(3), 796–816.

Moore, Robert. (1972). Race Relations in the Six Counties: Colonialism, Industrialization, and Stratification in Ireland. *Race*, *14*(1), 21–42.

Morello, Carol. (7 April 2001). Native American Roots, Once Hidden, Now Embraced. *Washington Post*.

Morgan, George. (2003). Autochthonous Australian Syncretism. *Current Sociology, 51* (3–4), 433–51.

Morgan, Kenneth O. (1971). Welsh Nationalism: The Historical Background. *Journal of Contemporary History,* 6(1), 153–72.

Morning, Ann. (2008). Ethnic Classification in Global Perspective: A Cross-National Survey of the 2000 Census Round. *Population Research and Policy Review,* 27(2), 239–72.

Motzafi–Haller, Pnina. (2002). *Fragmented Worlds, Coherent Lives: The Politics of Difference in Botswana.* Westport, CT: Bergin & Garvey.

Mubarak, Jamil A. (1997). The 'Hidden Hand' Behind the Resilience of the Stateless Economy of Somalia. *World Development,* 25(12), 2027–41.

Muhereza, Frank E. (2015). *The December 2010 'Balaalo' Evictions from Buliisa District and the Challenges of Agrarian Transformation in Uganda.* MISR Working Paper No. 17, Makerere Institute for Social Research, Makerere University, Kampala.

Munro, John M. (1974). Migration in Turkey. *Economic Development and Cultural Change,* 22(4), 634–53.

Murphy, Richard C. (1983). *Guestworkers in the German Reich: A Polish Community in Wilhelmian Germany.* Boulder, CO: East European Monographs.

Mustafa Kemal, Bicerli, and Gundogan Naci. (2009). *Female Labor Force Participation in Urbanization Process: The Case of Turkey.* Mimeo, Anadolu University, Eskişehir, Turkey.

Mutlu, Servet. (1996). Ethnic Kurds in Turkey: A Demographic Survey. *International Journal of Middle East Studies,* 28(4), 517–41.

Mwenda, Andrew M. (2007). Personalizing Power in Uganda. *Journal of Democracy,* 18(3), 23–37.

Mwenda, Andrew M. and Joseph Mugisa. (23 June 1999). 'War' Looms Over Break-Up of Toro. *The Monitor.*

Nagel, Joane. (1994). Constructing Ethnicity: Creating and Recreating Ethnic Identity and Culture. *Social Problems,* 41(1), 152–76.

(1995). American Indian Ethnic Renewal: Politics and the Resurgence of Identity. *American Sociological Review,* 60(6), 947–65.

Nagel, Joane, and Susan Olzak. (1982). Ethnic Mobilization in New and Old States: An Extension of the Competition Model. *Social Problems,* 30(2), 127–43.

Nairn, Tom. (1977). *The Break-Up of Britain: Crisis and Neo-Nationalism.* London: New Left Books.

Neils, Elaine M. (1971). *Reservation to City: Indian Migration and Federal Relocation.* Department of Geography Research Paper #131, University of Chicago.

Nettle, Daniel. (1996). Language Diversity in West Africa: An Ecological Approach. *Journal of Anthropological Archaeology,* 15(4), 403–38.

(1999). Linguistic Diversity of the Americas Can be Reconciled with a Recent Colonization. *Proceedings of the National Academy of Sciences of the United States of America,* 96, 3325–9.

Nfila, Bokang. I. (2002). *Standard in Setswana in Botswana.* (Master of Arts Dissertation). University of Pretoria.

Ng'ong'ola, Clement. (1997). Land Rights for Marginalized Ethnic Groups in Botswana, with Special Reference to the *Basarwa. Journal of African Law,* 41(1), 1–26.

Nichols, Roger L. (2014). *American Indians in U.S. History* (2nd ed.). Norman: University of Oklahoma Press.

Nix, Emily, and Nancy Qian. (2015). *The Fluidity of Race: Racial Passing in the United States, 1880–1940*. NBER Working Paper #20828.

Noeg, Prafulla, Richard G. Woods, and Arthur M. Harkins. (1970). *Chicago Indians: The Effects of Urban Migration*. Minneapolis: University of Minnesota.

Norris, Mary J., and Stewart Clatworthy. (2011). Urbanization and Migration Patterns of Aboriginal Populations in Canada: A Half Century in Review (1951 to 2006). *Aboriginal Policy Studies*, *1*(1), 13–77.

Novo, Carmen M. (2014). The Minimization of Indigenous Numbers and the Fragmentation of Civil Society in the 2010 Census in Ecuador. *Journal of Iberian and Latin American Research*, 20(3), 399–422.

NTV Uganda (2017). [Television series episode]. In NTV Uganda (Executive producer), *Tororo Ethnic Row: One Killed as Iteso-Japadhola Row Continues*. Kampala.

Nugent, Paul. (2008). Putting the History Back in Ethnicity: Enslavement, Religion and Cultural Brokerage in the Construction of Mandika/Jola and Ewe/Agotime Identities in West Africa, c. 1650–1930. *Comparative Studies in Society and History*, *50*(4), 920–48.

Nur, Hibaq. (2017). *Bibliocaust of Somali Libraries: Retelling the Somali Civil War*. Paper presented at the International Federation of Library Associations and Institutions World Library and Information Congress 2017, Wroclaw, Poland.

Nyamnjoh, Francis B. (2002). Local Attitudes towards Citizenship and Foreigners in Botswana: An Appraisal of Recent Press Stories. *Journal of Southern African Studies*, *28*(4), 755–75.

Nyati–Ramahobo, Lydia. (2009). *Minority Tribes in Botswana: The Politics of Recognition*. Briefing, Minority Rights Group International.

O'Brien, Patrick K. (1996). Path Dependency, or Why Britain Became an Industrialized and Urbanized Economy Long before France. *Economic History Review*, 49(2), 213–49.

O'Faircheallaigh, Ciaran. (2004). Denying Citizens their Rights? Indigenous People, Mining Payments and Service Provision. *Australian Journal of Public Administration*, 63(2), 42–50.

Obwona, Marios, Isaac Shinyekwa, Julius Kiiza, and Eria Hisali. (2014). *The Evolution of Industry in Uganda*. WIDER Working Paper No. 2014/021, World Institute for Development Economics Research.

Ogilvie, Sheilagh. (2011). *Institutions and European Trade: Merchant Guilds, 1000–1800*. Cambridge: Cambridge University Press.

Okamura, Jonathan. (1981). Situational Ethnicity. *Ethnic and Racial Studies*, 4(4), 452–65.

Olson, James S., and Raymond Wilson. (1984). *Native Americans in the Twentieth Century*. Urbana: University of Illinois Press.

Olsson, Ola. (2006). Diamonds Are a Rebel's Best Friend. *World Economy*, 29(8), 1133–50.

Olzak, Susan. (1983). Contemporary Ethnic Mobilization. *Annual Review of Sociology*, 9, 355–74.

Omolesky, Matthew. (3 September 2017). Somalia: Sweeping the Tombs. *Quadrant Online*. Retrieved from <https://quadrant.org.au/magazine/2017/06/somalia-sweeping-tombs>

Onoma, Ato. (2009). *The Politics of Property Rights Institutions in Africa*. Cambridge: Cambridge University Press.

Oran, Baskin. (2014). Exploring Turkishness: 'Turkish' and *Türkiyeli*. In Shane Brennan and Marc Herzog (Eds.), *Turkey and the Politics of National Identity: Social, Economic and Cultural Transformation* (pp. 23–37). London: I.B. Tauris.

Ordeshook, Peter C., and Olga V. Shvetsova. (1994). Ethnic Heterogeneity, District Magnitude and the Number of Parties. *American Journal of Political Science*, 38(1), 100–23.

Ostergren, Robert C. (1991). European Settlement and Ethnicity Patterns on the Agricultural Frontiers of South Dakota. In George E. Pozzetta (Ed.), *Immigrants on the Land: Agriculture, Rural Life and Small Towns* (pp. 197–230). New York: Garland.

Özdoğan, Günay G. (2010). Turkish Nationalism Reconsidered: The 'Heaviness' of Statist Patriotism in Nation-Building. In Ayhan Aktar, Niyazi Kızılyürek, and Umut Özkırımlı (Eds.), *Nationalism in the Troubled Triangle: Cyprus, Greece and Turkey* (pp. 47–60). Basingstoke: Palgrave Macmillan.

Padhola Elders' Forum (2019). *Letter To Speaker of Parliament*. Tororo.

Papa, Pius O. (9 January 2014). Tororo Rat Eater Angry at Museveni. *The [Kampala] Observer*.

Payne, Stanley. (1971). Catalan and Basque Nationalism. *Journal of Contemporary History*, 6(1), 15–51.

Pechanga Tribal Council (2007). Press Release: A Message from the Pechanga Tribal Council. Retrieved from <www.pechanga–nsn.gov/page?pageId=444>

Peltier, Leonard. (1999). *Prison Writings: My Life Is My Sun Dance* (H. Arden Ed.). New York: St. Martin's Press.

Peters, Evelyn J. (2002a). Aboriginal People in Urban Areas. In Caroline Andrew, Katherine A. Graham, and Susan D. Phillips (Eds.), *Urban Affairs: Back on the Policy Agenda* (pp. 45–70). Kingston, ON: McGill-Queen's University Press.

   (2002b). 'Our City Indians': Negotiating the Meaning of First Nations Urbanization in Canada, 1945–1975. *Historical Geography*, 30, 75–92.

Peterson, Iver. (29 March 2004). Would-Be Tribes Entice Investors. *New York Times*.

Petrescu, Dragos. (2009). Building the Nation, Instrumentalizing Nationalism: Revisiting Romanian National–Communism, 1956–1989. *Nationalities Papers*, 37(4), 523–44.

Pfefferbaum, Betty, Rennard Strickland, Everett R. Rhoades, and Rose L. Pfefferbaum. (1995). Learning How to Heal: An Analysis of the History, Policy, and Framework of Indian Health Care. *American Indian Law Review*, 20(2), 365–98.

Pirie, Paul S. (1997). *History, Politics and National Identity in Southern and Eastern Ukraine* (PhD Dissertation). University of London.

Pizzorno, Alessandro. (1973 [1962]). Three Types of Urban Social Structure and the Development of Industrial Society. In Gino Germani (Ed.), *Modernization, Urbanization and the Urban Crisis* (pp. 121–38). Boston: Little, Brown.

Platteau, Jean-Philippe. (2019). The Economics of Religious Conversion in Sub-Saharan Africa. In Emmanuel Nnadozie and Afeikhena Jerome (Eds.), *African Economic Development* (2nd ed., pp. 215–29). Bingley: Emerald.

Pool, D. I. (1967). Post-War Trends in Maori Population Growth. *Population Studies*, 21(2), 87–98.

Posner, Daniel N. (2004). The Political Salience of Cultural Difference: Why Chewas and Tumbukas Are Allies in Zambia and Adversaries in Malawi. *American Political Science Review*, 98(4), 529–46.

(2005). *Institutions and Ethnic Politics in Africa*. New York: Cambridge University Press.

Poteete, Amy R. (2013). The Absence of Intergroup Violence in Botswana: An Assessment of the Role of Development Strategies. In William Ascher and Natalia Mirovitskaya (Eds.), *The Economic Roots of Conflict and Cooperation in Africa* (pp. 183–220). New York: Palgrave Macmillan.

Przeworski, Adam, Michael E. Alvarez, Jose A. Cheibub, and Fernando Limongi. (2000). *Democracy and Development: Political Institutions and Well-Being in the World, 1950–1990*. Cambridge: Cambridge University Press.

Putnam, Robert D. (2007). E *Pluribus Unum*: Diversity and Community in the Twenty-First Century. The 2006 Johan Skytte Prize Lecture. *Scandinavian Political Studies*, 30(2), 137–74.

Rademakers, Robbert, and André van Hoorn. (2021). Ethnic Switching: Longitudinal Evidence on Prevalence, Correlates, and Implications for Measuring Ethnic Segregation. *Journal of Development Economics*, 152, 102694.

Rand, Kathryn R. L., and Steven A. Light. (1996). Virtue or Vice: How IGRA Shapes the Politics of Native American Gaming, Sovereignty, and Identity. *Virginia Journal of Social Policy and the Law*, 4, 381–438.

Ranger, Terence. (1989). Missionaries, Migrants and the Manyika: The Invention of Ethnicity in Zimbabwe. In Leroy Vail (Ed.), *The Creation of Tribalism in Southern Africa* (pp. 118–50). Berkeley: University of California Press.

Rata, Elizabeth. (2011). Encircling the Commons: Neotribal Capitalism in New Zealand since 2000. *Anthropological Theory*, 11(3), 327–53.

Rawls, James J. (1996). *Chief Red Fox Is Dead: A History of Native Americans Since 1945*. Forth Worth, TX: Harcourt Brace College.

Redfield, Robert. (1947). The Folk Society. *American Journal of Sociology*, 52(4), 293–308.

Reilly, Benjamin. (2001). Democracy, Ethnic Fragmentation and Internal Conflict: Confused Theories, Faulty Data and the 'Crucial Case' of Papua New Guinea. *International Security*, 25(3), 162–85.

Reinert, Erik. (2006). *Development and Social Goals: Balancing Aid and Development to Prevent 'Welfare Colonialism'*. UN Department of Economic and Social Affairs Working Paper #14. New York.

Richards, Audrey I. (Ed.) (1954). *Economic Development and Tribal Change: A Study of Immigrant Labour in Buganda*. Cambridge: Heffer.

Riga, Liliana. (2012). *The Bolsheviks and the Russian Empire*. Cambridge: Cambridge University Press.

Riker, William. (1962). *The Theory of Political Coalitions*. New Haven, CT: Yale University Press.

Robinson, Amanda L. (2014). National versus Ethnic Identification in Africa: Modernization, Colonial Legacy, and the Origins of Territorial Nationalism. *World Politics*, 66(4), 709–46.

Robinson, James A., and Q. Neil Parsons. (2006). State Formation and Governance in Botswana. *Journal of African Economies*, 15(AERC Supplement 1), 100–40.

Robinson, Richard D. (1963). *The First Turkish Republic: A Case Study in National Development*. Cambridge, MA: Harvard University Press.

(1965). Letter Number 34, 1 July 1949: Village Institutions. In *Letters from Turkey*: Reprinted for the Peace Corps by Permission of The Institute for Current World Affairs, Robert College.

Rodrik, Dani. (2016). Premature Deindustrialization. *Journal of Economic Growth*, 21(1), 1–33.

Roeder, Philip. (2001). Ethnolinguistic Fractionalization (ELF) Indices, 1961 and 1985. <http://weber.ucsd.edu/~proeder/elf.htm>

Rolston, Bill. (1980). Reformism and Class Politics in North Ireland: The Case of the Trade Unions. *The Insurgent Sociologist*, 10(2), 73–83.

Romeo, Ilaria. (2002). The Panhellenion and Ethnic Identity in Hadrianic Greece. *Classical Philology*, 97(1), 21–40.

Rosenblatt, Daniel. (2011). Indigenizing the City and the Future of Maori Culture: The Construction of Community in Auckland as Representation, Experience, and Self-Making. *American Ethnologist*, 38(3), 411–29.

Rosenthal, Nicolas. (2002). Repositioning Indianness: Native American Organizations in Portland, Oregon, 1959–1975. *Pacific Historical Review*, 71(3), 415–38.

(2012). *Reimagining Indian Country: Native American Migration and Identity in Twentieth-Century Los Angeles*. Chapel Hill: University of North Caroline Press.

Roshwald, Aviel. (2001). *Ethnic Nationalism and the Fall of Empires: Central Europe, Russia and the Middle East, 1914–1923*. London: Routledge.

Rostow, Walt W. (1960). *The Stages of Economic Growth: A Non-Communist Manifesto*. Cambridge: Cambridge University Press.

Roth, George. (1992). Overview of Southeastern Indian Tribes Today. In J. Anthony Paredes (Ed.), *Indians of the Southeastern United States in the Late 20th Century* (pp. 183–202). Tuscaloosa: University of Alabama Press.

Roth, Michael. (1988). *Somalia Land Policies and Tenure Impacts: The Case of the Lower Shabelle*. Mimeo, Land Tenure Center, University of Wisconsin.

Rouch, J. (1956). Migrations au Ghana. *Journal de la Société des Africanistes*, 26(19), 33–196.

Rousseau, Jerome. (1975). Ethnic Identity and Social Relations in Central Borneo. In Judith. Nagata (Ed.), *Contributions to Asian Studies* (Vol. 7, pp. 32–49). Leiden: EJ Brill.

Rowland, D. T. (1971). Maori Migration to Auckland. *New Zealand Geographer*, 27 (1), 21–37.

Saleh, Mohamed. (2018). On the Road to Heaven: Taxation, Conversions, and the Coptic–Muslim Socioeconomic Gap in Medieval Egypt. *Journal of Economic History*, 78(2), 394–434.

Samatar, Abdi I. (1997). Leadership and Ethnicity in the Making of African State Models: Botswana Versus Somalia. *Third World Quarterly*, 18(4), 687–707.

Samatar, Ahmed I. (1985). Underdevelopment in Somalia: Dictatorship without Hegemony. *Africa Today*, 32(3), 23–40.

(1987). Somalia Impasse: State Power and Dissent Politics. *Third World Quarterly*, 9 (3), 871–90.

Sambanis, Nicholas, and Moses Shayo. (2013). Social Identification and Ethnic Conflict. *American Political Science Review*, 107(2), 294–325.

Sambanis, Nicholas, Stergios Skaperdas, and William C. Wohlforth. (2015). Nation-Building Through War. *American Political Science Review*, 109(2), 279–96.

Saran, Nephan. (1974). Squatter Settlement (Gecekondu) Problems in Istanbul. In Peter Benedict, Erol Tümertekin, and Fatma Mansur (Eds.), *Turkey Geographic and Social Perspectives* (pp. 327–61). Leiden: Brill.

Sarigil, Zeki. (2009). *Comparative Ethnonationalism: The Laz vs. Kurds*. Paper presented to the Annual Meeting of the American Political Science Association, Toronto.

Satterthwaite, David, Gordon McGranahan, and Cecilia Tacoli. (2010). Urbanization and its Implications for Food and Farming. *Philosophical Transactions of the Royal Society B*, 365(1554), 2809–20.

Scarritt, James R., and Shaheen Mozaffar. (1999). The Specification of Ethnic Cleavages and Ethnopolitical Groups for the Analysis of Democratic Competition in Contemporary Africa. *Nationalism and Ethnic Politics*, 5(1), 82–117.

Schapera, Isaac. (1938). *A Handbook of Tswana Law and Custom*. Oxford: Oxford University Press.

Schneider, Friedrich. (2002). *Size and Measurement of the Informal Economy in 110 Countries Around the World*. Department of Economics, Johannes Kepler University of Linz.

Schroyens, Maarten. (2019). *Making Citizens 'National': Analysing the Impact of Ghana's National Service Scheme (NSS) and Nigeria's National Youth Service Corps (NYSC)*. (PhD Dissertation). Katholieke Universiteit Leuven.

Schultz, Emily. (1984). From Pagan to Pullo: Ethnic Identity Change in Northern Cameroon. *Africa: Journal of the International African Institute*, 54(1), 46–64.

Schultz, Theodore W. (1951). The Declining Economic Importance of Agricultural Land. *Economic Journal*, 61(244), 725–40.

Scott, James. (1998). *Seeing Like a State: How Certain Schemes to Improve the Human Condition Have Failed*. New Haven, CT: Yale University Press.

(2009). *The Art of Not Being Governed: An Anarchist History of Upland Southeast Asia*. New Haven, CT: Yale University Press.

(2012). *Two Cheers for Anarchism: Six Easy Pieces on Autonomy, Dignity and Meaningful Work and Play*. Princeton: Princeton University Press.

Selolwane, Onalenna D. (2004). *Ethnic Structure, Inequality and Governance of the Public Sector in Botswana*. UNRISD Project on Ethnic Structure, Inequality and Governance of the Public Sector, United Nations Research Institute for Social Development.

Serdar, Ayşe. (2019). Strategies of Making and Unmaking Ethnic Boundaries: Evidence on the Laz of Turkey. *Ethnicities*, 19(2), 335–69.

Shepherd, Gill. (1989). The Reality of the Commons: Answering Hardin From Somalia. *Development Policy Review*, 7(1), 51–63.

Sherman, Daniel J. (2006). Seizing the Cultural and Political Moment and Catching Fish: Political Development of Māori in New Zealand, the Sealord Fisheries Settlement, and Social Movement Theory. *Social Science Journal*, 43(4), 513–27.

Shoemaker, Nancy. (1988). Urban Indians and Ethnic Choices: American Indian Organizations in Minneapolis, 1920–1950. *Western Historical Quarterly*, 19(4), 431–47.

Silitshena, Robson M. K. (1984). Urbanization in Botswana. *Norsk Geografisk Tidsskrift – Norwegian Journal of Geography*, 38(2), 109–28.

Simson, Rebecca, and Elliott D. Green. (2020). Ethnic Favouritism in Kenyan Education Reconsidered: When a Picture Is Worth More Than a Thousand Regressions. *Journal of Modern African Studies*, 58(3), 425–60.

Siphambe, Happy K. (2007). *Growth and Employment Dynamics in Botswana: A Case Study of Policy Coherence*. Working Paper #82, Policy Integration and Statistics Department, International Labour Office, Geneva.

Skinner, Elliott P. (1963). Strangers in West Africa Societies. *Africa: Journal of the International African Institute*, 33(4), 307–20.

Smieja, Birgit. (2003). *Language Pluralism in Botswana: Hope or Hurdle?* Frankfurt am Main: Peter Lang.

Smith, Anthony D. (1991). *National Identity*. London: Penguin.

 (1998). *Nationalism and Modernism: A Critical Survey of Recent Theories of Nations and Nationalism*. New York: Routledge.

Smith, Stephen A. (2017). *Russia in Revolution: An Empire in Crisis, 1890 to 1928*. Oxford: Oxford University Press.

Snipp, C. Matthew. (1997). The Size and Distribution of the American Indian Population: Fertility, Mortality, Migration, and Residence. *Population Research and Policy Review*, 16(1/2), 61–93.

Solway, Jacqueline. (1994). From Shame to Pride: Politicized Ethnicity in the Kalahari, Botswana. *Canadian Journal of African Studies–Revue Canadienne Des Etudes Africaines*, 28(2), 254–74.

 (2004). Reaching the Limits of Universal Citizenship: 'Minority' Struggles in Botswana. In Bruce Berman, Dickson Eyoh, and Will Kymlicka (Eds.), *Ethnicity and Democracy in Africa* (pp. 128–47). Oxford: James Currey.

Southall, Aidan. (1970). The Illusion of Tribe. In Peter C. W. Gutkind (Ed.), *The Passing of Tribal Man* (pp. 28–50). Leiden: Brill.

Spicer, Edward H. (1980). *The American Indians*. Cambridge, MA: Harvard University Press.

Spolaore, Enrico, and Romain Wacziarg. (2009). The Diffusion of Development. *Quarterly Journal of Economics*, 124(2), 469–529.

Spolsky, Bernard. (2003). Reassessing Maori Regeneration. *Language in Society*, 32(4), 553–78.

 (2005). Maori Lost and Regained. In Allan Bell, Ray Harlow, and Donna Starks (Eds.), *Languages of New Zealand* (pp. 67–85). Wellington, New Zealand: Victoria University Press.

Spoonley, Paul. (1989). The Renegotiation of Ethnic Relations in New Zealand. *Journal of Ethnic and Migration Studies*, 15(4), 577–89.

Spruhan, Paul. (2007). The Origins, Current Status, and Future Prospects of Blood Quantum as the Definition of Membership in the Navajo Nation. *Tribal Law Journal*, 8(1), 1–17.

Statistics New Zealand (2007). *2006 Census of Population and Dwellings*. Wellington: Statistics New Zealand.

 (2014). *2013 Census of Population and Dwellings*. Wellington: Statistics New Zealand.

Stephen Parente, and Richard Rogerson. (2002). The Role of Agriculture in Development. *American Economic Review*, 92(2), 160–4.

Stevenson, Betsey, and Justin Wolfers. (2008). *Economic Growth and Subjective Well-Being: Reassessing the Easterlin Paradox*. NBER Working Paper #14282, National Bureau of Economic Research.

Stokes, Evelyn. (1992). The Treaty of Waitangi and the Waitangi Tribunal: Maori Claims in New Zealand. *Applied Geography*, *12*(2), 176–91.

Subotic, Jelena. (2010). No Escape from Ethnicity? Confessions of an Accidental CNN Pundit. PS: *Political Science and Politics*, *43*(1), 115–20.

Sutherland, William J. (2003). Parallel Extinction Risk and Global Distribution of Languages and Species. *Nature*, *423*(6937), 276–9.

Szabó, László, Ignacio Hidalgo, Juan C. Ciscar, and Antonio Soria. (2006). CO_2 Emission Trading Within the European Union and Annex B Countries: The Cement Industry Case. *Energy Policy*, *34*(1), 72–87.

Szyliowicz, Joseph S. (1966). Political Participation and Modernization in Turkey. *Western Political Quarterly*, *19*(2), 266–84.

TallBear, Kimberly. (2003). DNA, Blood, and Racializing the Tribe. *Wicazo Sa Review*, *18*(1), 81–107.

Tampke, Jürgen. (1978). *The Ruhr and Revolution: The Revolutionary Movement in the Rhenish-Westphalian Industrial Region, 1912–1919*. Canberra: Australian National University Press.

Tangri, Roger, and Andrew M. Mwenda. (2008). Elite Corruption and Politics in Uganda. *Commonwealth and Comparative Politics*, *46*(2), 177–94.

Tapsell, Paul. (2002). *Marae* and Tribal Identity in Urban Aotearoa/New Zealand. *Pacific Studies*, *25*(1/2), 141–71.

Taras, Ray. (1993). From Matrioshka Nationalism to National Interests. In Ian Bremmer and Ray Taras (Eds.), *New States, New Politics: Building the Post-Soviet Nations* (pp. 685–707). Cambridge: Cambridge University Press.

Tax, Sol. (1978). The Impact of Urbanization on American Indians. *Annals of the American Academy of Political and Social Science*, *436*, 121–36.

Taylor, Charles. (1992). *Multiculturalism and the Politics of Recognition*. Princeton: Princeton University Press.

Taylor, Charles L., and Michael C. Hudson. (1972). *World Handbook of Political and Social Indicators*. Ann Arbor, MI: ICSPR.

Taylor, Ian. (2012). Botswana as A 'Development-Oriented Gate-Keeping State': A Response. *African Affairs*, *111*(444), 466–76.

Taylor, John. (1989). Public Policy and Aboriginal Population Mobility: Insights from the Katherine Region Northern Territory. *Australian Geographer*, *20*(1), 47–53.

(1997). The Contemporary Demography of Indigenous Australians. *Journal of the Australian Population Association*, *14*(1), 77–114.

The Independent (5 November 2019). Museveni Directs Against Tabling Tororo, West Budama 'Boundary Report'. *The [Kampala] Independent*.

Themnér, Lotta, and Peter Wallensteen. (2012). Armed Conflicts, 1946–2011. *Journal of Peace Research*, *49*(4), 565–75.

Thies, Cameron G. (2009). National Design and State Building in Sub-Saharan Africa. *World Politics*, *61*(4), 623–69.

Thomas, Robert K. (1965). Pan-Indianism. *Midcontinent American Studies Journal*, *6*(2), 75–83.

Thompson, Debra. (2012). Making (Mixed-)Race: Census Politics and the Emergence of Multiracial Multiculturalism in the United States, Great Britain and Canada. *Ethnic and Racial Studies*, *35*(8), 1409–26.

Thornton, Russell. (1990). *American Indian Holocaust and Survival: A Population History Since 1492*. Norman: University of Oklahoma Press.

(1997). Tribal Membership Requirements and the Demography of 'Old' and 'New' Native Americans. *Population Research and Policy Review*, 16(1/2), 33–42.

(2004). Health, Disease and Demography. In Philip Deloria and Neal Salisbury (Eds.), *A Companion to American Indian History* (pp. 68–84). Indianapolis, IN: Wiley.

Tilly, Charles. (1994). States and Nationalism in Europe 1492–1992. *Theory and Society*, 23(1), 131–46.

Todaro, Michael P. (1969). A Model of Labor Migration and Urban Unemployment in Less Developed Countries. *American Economic Review*, 59(1), 138–48.

Toktas, Sule. (2005). Citizenship and Minorities: A Historical Overview of Turkey's Jewish Minority. *Journal of Historical Sociology*, 18(4), 394–429.

Tolz, Vera. (1998). Forging the Nation: National Identity and Nation Building in Post-Communist Russia. *Europe-Asia Studies*, 50(6), 993–1022.

Trigger, Bruce. (1980 [1972]). Determinants of Urban Growth in Pre-Industrial Societies. In Ivan Press and M. Estellie Smith (Eds.), *Urban Place and Process: Readings in the Anthropology of Cities* (pp. 143–66). New York: Macmillan.

Turok, Ivan. (2012). *Urbanisation and Development in South Africa: Economic Imperatives, Spatial Distortions and Strategic Responses*. Urbanization and Emerging Population Issues Working Paper #8, International Institute for Environment and Development, United Nations Population Fund.

Turville-Petre, Thorlac. (1996). *England the Nation: Language, Literature and National Identity, 1290–1340*. Oxford: Oxford University Press.

Ulrich, Roberta. (2010). *American Indian Nations from Termination to Restoration, 1953–2006*. Lincoln: University of Nebraska Press.

UNDP (2001). *Human Development Report 2001: Somalia*. New York: UNDP.

Üngör, Uğur Ü. (2008). Seeing Like a Nation-State: Young Turk Social Engineering in Eastern Turkey, 1913–50. *Journal of Genocide Research*, 10(1), 15–39.

United Nations (2019). *World Urbanization Prospects: The 2019 Revision*. Department of Economic and Social Affairs/Population Division.

Van den Berghe, Pierre L. (1967). *South Africa: A Study in Conflict*. Berkeley: University of California Press.

(1968). Ethnic Membership and Cultural Change in Guatemala. *Social Forces*, 46(4), 514–22.

Van der Veen, A. Maurits, and David D. Laitin. (2012). Modeling the Evolution of Ethnic Demography. In Kanchan Chandra (Ed.), *Constructivist Theories of Ethnic Politics* (pp. 277–311). Oxford: Oxford University Press.

Vanly, Ismet C. (1971). *Survey of the National Question of Turkish Kurdistan with Historical Background*. Rome: Organization of the Revolutionary Kurds of Turkey in Europe.

Villarreal, Andres. (2014). Ethnic Identification and its Consequences for Measuring Inequality in Mexico. *American Sociological Review*, 79(4), 775–806.

Wagner, Jean K. (1976). The Role of Intermarriage in the Acculturation of Selected Urban American Indian Women. *Anthropologica*, 18(2), 215–29.

Waitangi Tribunal (1998). *Te Whanau O Waipareira Report (Wai 414)*. Wellington: Ministry of Justice, Government of New Zealand.

Wallerstein, Immanuel. (1960). Ethnicity and National Integration in West Africa. *Cahiers d'Études Africaines*, 1(3), 129–39.

Walling, Julie, Desi Small-Rodriguez, and Tahu Kukutai. (2009). Tallying Tribes: Waikato-Tainui in the Census and Iwi Register. *Social Policy Journal of New Zealand*, (36), 2–15.

Wallman, Sandra. (1978). The Boundaries of 'Race': Processes of Ethnicity in England. *Man*, 13(2), 200–17.

Walter, Barbara F. (2006). Information, Uncertainty and the Decision to Secede. *International Organization*, 60(1), 105–35.

Wang, Cong. (2013). Can Institutions Explain Cross Country Differences in Innovative Activity? *Journal of Macroeconomics*, 37, 128–45.

Ward, Robert E., and Dankwart Rustow. (Eds.). (1964). *Political Modernization in Japan and Turkey*. Princeton: Princeton University Press.

Warsame, Ali A. (2001). How a Strong Government Backed an African Language: The Lessons of Somalia. *International Review of Education*, 47(3/4), 341–60.

Weber, Eugen J. (1976). *Peasants into Frenchmen: The Modernization of Rural France, 1870–1914*. Stanford, CA: Stanford University Press.

Weber, Max. (1978 [1922]). *Economy and Society: An Outline of Interpretive Sociology* (Vol. 2). Berkeley: University of California Press.

Webersik, Christian. (2004). Differences that Matter: The Struggle of the Marginalized in Somalia. *Africa: Journal of the International African Institute*, 74(4), 516–33.

Webster, Steven. (2002). Maori Retribalization and Treaty Rights to the New Zealand Fisheries. *The Contemporary Pacific*, 14(2), 341–76.

Wegenast, Tim C., and Matthias Basedau. (2014). Ethnic Fractionalization, Natural Resources and Armed Conflict. *Conflict Management and Peace Science*, 31(4), 432–57.

Werbner, Pnina. (2014). *The Making of an African Working Class: Politics, Law and Cultural Protest in the Manual Workers' Union of Botswana*. London: Pluto Press.

Werbner, Richard. (2002). Challenging Minorities, Difference and Tribal Citizenship in Botswana. *Journal of Southern African Studies*, 28(4), 671–84.

White, Jenny B. (2010). Tin Town to Fanatics: Turkey's Rural to Urban Migration from 1923 to the Present. In Celia Kerslake, Kerem Öktem, and Philip Robins (Eds.), *Turkey's Engagement with Modernity: Conflict and Change in the Twentieth Century* (pp. 425–42). Basingstoke: Palgrave Macmillan.

Whittacker, Dick. (1994). The Politics of Power: The Cities of Italy. In *L'Italie d'Auguste à Dioclétien. Actes du colloque international de Rome (25–28 mars 1992)* (pp. 127–43). Rome: École Française de Rome.

Williams, Allison M. (1997). Canadian Urban Aboriginals: A Focus on Aboriginal Women in Toronto. *Canadian Journal of Native Studies*, 17(1), 75–101.

Williams, David V. (2019). The Continuing Impact of Amalgamation, Assimilation and Integration Policies. *Journal of the Royal Society of New Zealand*, 49(S1), 34–47.

Willis, Justin. (1993). *Mombasa, the Swahili and the Making of the Mijikenda*. Oxford: Clarendon.

Wilmsen, Edwin N. (2002). Mutable Identities: Moving beyond Ethnicity in Botswana. *Journal of Southern African Studies*, 28(4), 825–41.

Wilson, Kathi, and Evelyn J. Peters. (2005). 'You Can Make a Place for It': Remapping Urban First Nations Spaces of Identity. *Environment and Planning D: Society and Space*, 23(3), 395–413.

Wimmer, Andreas. (2008). The Making and Unmaking of Ethnic Boundaries: A Multilevel Process Theory. *American Journal of Sociology, 113*(4), 970–1022.

(2013). *Waves of War: Nationalism, State Formation and Ethnic Exclusion in the Modern World*. Cambridge: Cambridge University Press.

(2015). Nation Building: A Long-Term Perspective and Global Analaysis. *European Sociological Review, 31*(1), 30–47.

(2018). *Nation Building: Why Some Countries Come Together While Others Fall Apart*. Princeton: Princeton University Press.

Wimmer, Andreas, Lars-Erik Cederman, and Brian Min. (2009). Ethnic Politics and Armed Conflict: A Configurational Analysis of a New Global Dataset. *American Sociological Review, 74*(2), 316–37.

Wirth, Louis. (1938). Urbanism as a Way of Life. *American Journal of Sociology, 44*(1), 1–24.

Withers, Charles W. J. (1998). *Urban Highlanders: Highland–Lowland Migration and Urban Gaelic Culture, 1700–1900*. East Linton: Tuckwell Press.

(2001). *Geography, Science and National Identity: Scotland Since 1520*. Cambridge: Cambridge University Press.

Wódz, Kazimiera, and Jacek Wódz. (2006). *Dimensions of Silesian Identity*. Katowice: Wydawnictwo Uniwersytetu Śląskiego.

Woods, Richard G., and Arthur M. Harkins. (1968). *Indian Americans in Chicago*. Minneapolis: University of Minnesota.

Woolf, Stuart. (2005). Nation, Nations and Power in Italy, c. 1700–1915. In Len Scales and Oliver Zimmer (Eds.), *Power and the Nation in European History* (pp. 295–314). Cambridge: Cambridge University Press.

World Bank (1987). *Somalia: Industrial Policies and Public Enterprise Reform*. Report No. 6639–SO, Industrial and Energy Operations Division, Eastern Africa Department.

(1991). *World Development Report 1991: The Challenge of Development*. Oxford: Oxford University Press.

Wrigley, E. Anthony. (1985). Urban Growth and Agricultural Change: England and the Continent in the Early Modern Period. *Journal of Interdisciplinary History, 15*(4), 683–728.

Yeğen, Mesut. (2009). 'Prospective-Turks' or 'Pseudo-Citizens:' Kurds in Turkey. *Middle East Journal, 63*(4), 597–615.

Young, M. Crawford. (1976). *The Politics of Cultural Pluralism*. Madison: University of Wisconsin Press.

Young, T. Kue. (1994). *The Health of Native Americans: Towards a Biocultural Epidemiology*. Oxford: Oxford University Press.

Yücel, Clémence S. (2016). Common Ground or Battlefield? Deconstructing the Politics of Recognition in Turkey. *Nationalism and Ethnic Politics, 22*(1), 71–93.

Zimmer, Kerstin. (2007). Trapped in Past Glory: Self-Identification and Self-Symbolisation in the Donbas. In Adam. Swain (Ed.), *Re-Constructing the Post-Soviet Industrial Region: The Donbas in Transition* (pp. 97–121). London: Routledge.

Index